Elements of Literature

Fifth Course

Essentials of American Literature

Holt Assessment: Literature, Reading, and Vocabulary

- Entry-Level Test and End-of-Year Test
- Collection Diagnostic Tests
- Selection Tests
- Collection Summative Tests
- Answer Key

HOLT, RINEHART AND WINSTON

A Harcourt Education Company

Orlando • **Austin** • New York • San Diego • Toronto • London

STAFF CREDITS

EDITORIAL

Project Director
Laura Wood

Managing Editor
Marie Price

Associate Managing Editor
Elizabeth LaManna

Writers and Editors
e2 Publishing Services, llc

Editorial Staff
Text Editor, Shelley Mack Hoyt; *Copyeditors,* Emily Force, Julia Thomas Hu, Nancy Shore; *Senior Copyeditors,* Christine Altgelt, Elizabeth Dickson, Leora Harris, Anne Heausler, Kathleen Scheiner; *Copyediting Supervisor,* Mary Malone; *Copyediting Manager,* Michael Neibergall; *Editorial Coordinator,* Erik Netcher; *Editorial Support,* Danielle Greer

ART, DESIGN, and PHOTO

Design Jeff Robinson

PRODUCTION/ MANUFACTURING

Senior Production Coordinators, Belinda Barbosa Lopez, Michael Roche; *Production Manager,* Carol Trammel; *Senior Production Manager,* Beth Prevelige

Printed in the United States of America

ISBN 0-03-068523-0

3 4 5 6 018 05 04

Table of Contents

Table of Contents

Collection 2 American Romanticism: 1800–1860

Collection 3 American Masters: Whitman and Dickinson

Table of Contents

Table of Contents

Collection 5 The Moderns: 1914–1939

Table of Contents

Collection 6 Contemporary Literature: 1939 to Present

Table of Contents

Table of Contents

Overview of ELEMENTS OF LITERATURE Assessment Program

Two assessment booklets have been developed for **ELEMENTS OF LITERATURE**.

(1) Assessment of student mastery of selections and specific literary, reading, and vocabulary skills in the **Student Edition:**

- ***Holt Assessment: Literature, Reading, and Vocabulary***

(2) Assessment of student mastery of workshops and specific writing, listening, and speaking skills in the **Student Edition:**

- ***Holt Assessment: Writing, Listening, and Speaking***

Diagnostic Assessment

Holt Assessment: Literature, Reading, and Vocabulary contains two types of diagnostic tests:

- The Entry-Level Test is a diagnostic tool that helps you determine (1) how well students have mastered essential prerequisite skills needed for the year and (2) to what degree students understand the concepts that will be taught during the current year. This test uses multiple tasks to assess mastery of literary, reading, and vocabulary skills.
- The Collection Diagnostic Tests help you determine the extent of students' prior knowledge of literary, reading, and vocabulary skills taught in each collection. These tests provide vital information that will assist you in helping students master collection skills.

Holt Online Essay Scoring can be used as a diagnostic tool to evaluate students' writing proficiency:

- For each essay, the online scoring system delivers a holistic score and analytic feedback related to five writing traits. These two scoring methods will enable you to pinpoint the strengths of your students' writing as well as skills that need improvement.

Ongoing, Informal Assessment

The **Student Edition** offers systematic opportunities for ongoing, informal assessment and immediate instructional follow-up. Students' responses to their reading; their writing, listening, and speaking projects; and their work with vocabulary skills all serve as both instructional and ongoing assessment tasks.

Overview of ELEMENTS OF LITERATURE Assessment Program *(continued)*

- Throughout the **Student Edition,** practice and assessment are immediate and occur at the point where skills are taught.
- In order for assessment to inform instruction on an ongoing basis, related material repeats instruction and then offers new opportunities for informal assessment.
- Skills Reviews at the end of each collection offer a quick evaluation of how well students have mastered the collection skills.

Progress Assessment

Students' mastery of the content of the **Student Edition** is systematically assessed in two test booklets:

- ***Holt Assessment: Literature, Reading, and Vocabulary*** offers a test for every selection. Multiple-choice questions focus on comprehension, the selected skills, and vocabulary development. In addition, students write answers to constructed-response prompts that test their understanding of the skills.
- ***Holt Assessment: Writing, Listening, and Speaking*** provides both multiple-choice questions for writing and analytical scales and rubrics for writing, listening, and speaking. These instruments assess proficiency in all the writing applications appropriate for each grade level.

Summative Assessment

Holt Assessment: Literature, Reading, and Vocabulary contains two types of summative tests:

- The Collection Summative Tests, which appear at the end of every collection, ask students to apply their recently acquired skills to a new literary selection. These tests contain both multiple-choice questions and constructed-response prompts.
- The End-of-Year Test helps you determine how well students have mastered the skills and concepts taught during the year. This test mirrors the Entry-Level Test and uses multiple tasks to assess mastery of literary, reading, and vocabulary skills.

Holt Online Essay Scoring can be used as an end-of-year assessment tool:

- You can use ***Holt Online Essay Scoring*** to evaluate how well students have mastered the writing skills taught during the year. You will be able to assess student

Overview of ELEMENTS OF LITERATURE Assessment Program *(continued)*

mastery using a holistic score as well as analytic feedback based on five writing traits.

Monitoring Student Progress

Both ***Holt Assessment: Literature, Reading, and Vocabulary*** and ***Holt Assessment: Writing, Listening, and Speaking*** include skills profiles that record progress toward the mastery of skills. Students and teachers can use the profiles to monitor student progress.

***One-Stop Planner*® CD-ROM with ExamView® Test Generator**

All of the questions in this booklet are available on the ***One-Stop Planner*® CD-ROM with ExamView® Test Generator.** You can use the ExamView Test Generator to customize any of the tests in this booklet. You can then print a test unique to your classroom situation.

Holt Online Assessment

You can use ***Holt Online Assessment*** to administer and score the diagnostic and summative tests online. You can then generate and print reports to document student growth and class results. For your students, this online resource provides individual assessment of strengths and weaknesses and immediate feedback.

FOR THE TEACHER

About This Book

Holt Assessment: Literature, Reading, and Vocabulary accompanies ELEMENTS OF LITERATURE. The booklet includes copying masters for diagnostic tests, selection tests, and summative tests to assess students' knowledge of prerequisite skills, their comprehension of the readings in the **Student Edition,** and their mastery of the skills covered in each collection.

Entry-Level Test

The **Entry-Level Test** is a diagnostic tool that enables you to evaluate your students' mastery of essential skills at the start of the year. This objective, multiple-choice test contains several reading selections followed by questions assessing students' comprehension of their reading and their knowledge of select literary skills. Other sections of the test evaluate students' command of vocabulary skills.

Collection Tests

The copying masters in ***Holt Assessment: Literature, Reading, and Vocabulary*** are organized by collection. There are three types of tests for each collection:

- A **Collection Diagnostic Test** is included for every collection. These multiple-choice tests cover literary terms and devices as well as reading and vocabulary skills. These tests will enable you to assess students' prior knowledge of the skills taught in each collection.
- A **Selection Test** accompanies every major selection in the **Student Edition.** Each Selection Test includes objective questions that assess students' comprehension of the selection, mastery of literary skills as they apply to the selection, and acquisition of vocabulary words. In addition, students write a brief essay in response to a constructed-response prompt that asks them to formulate answers independently using their newly acquired skills.
- A **Collection Summative Test** follows the selection tests for each collection. This test asks students to apply their new skills to a selection that does not appear in the **Student Edition.** Students are asked to read a brief selection and then respond to multiple-choice questions and constructed-response prompts that assess their comprehension of the selection and vocabulary, reading, and literary skills.

End-of-Year Test

The **End-of-Year Test** is a summative tool that assesses students' mastery of the skills and concepts taught during the year. Like the Entry-Level Test, this test uses a multiple-choice format to assess students' comprehension of several reading selections and their mastery of literary and vocabulary skills.

About This Book *(continued)*

Answer Sheets and Answer Key

Answer Sheets are provided for the Entry-Level Test and the End-of-Year Test. If you prefer, students may mark their answers on the tests themselves. For all collection tests, students should write their answers on the tests. The **Answer Key** provides answers to objective questions. It also provides model responses to constructed-response prompts.

Skills Profile

The **Skills Profile** lists the skills assessed by the tests in this booklet. You can use the Skills Profile to create a developmental record of your students' progress as they master each skill.

Administering the Tests

The format of the Entry-Level Test and the End-of-Year Test, with their accompanying answer sheets, replicates that of most standardized tests. You can use these tests to help familiarize your students with the types of standardized tests they will take in the future.

To administer these tests, prepare a copy of the appropriate test and answer sheet for each student. Some sections of the tests have sample items. Before students begin these sections, you may want to select the correct answer for the sample items with the class. Then, answer any questions students have about the samples. When students demonstrate that they understand how to do the items, have them begin these sections. Students may record their answers on the answer sheets or on the tests.

To administer the collection tests, prepare a copy of each test for your students. Students should mark their answers on the tests themselves. When administering Selection Tests that cover poetry, you may want to allow students to use the textbook, since these tests often require a response to the precise wording, rhythm, or meter of a particular poem. You also have the option of making any Selection Test an open-book test.

***One-Stop Planner*® CD-ROM with ExamView® Test Generator**

The tests in this booklet are included on the ***One-Stop Planner*® CD-ROM with ExamView® Test Generator.** Use the ExamView Test Generator to customize and print a test tailored to the needs of your students.

Holt Online Assessment

With ***Holt Online Assessment*** you can administer and score the diagnostic and summative tests online. Use this online tool to generate and print reports to record student mastery and class performance.

Entry-Level Test

Reading and Literary Analysis

DIRECTIONS Read the following narrative about Eric's experience on the Appalachian Trail. Then, answer questions 1 through 12.

Crossing Paths

Eric was weary after three weeks on the Appalachian Trail. For several summers since graduation, he and his childhood friend Brian had reunited for an invigorating, challenging hike along a different segment of the trail. This year, they had walked one of the highest parts of the trail along the border of Tennessee and North Carolina.

Despite the plan that neither would leave the other, Eric was camping alone this last evening. That morning Brian had left the trail to hike to Gatlinburg, Tennessee, to meet his family; and the next morning Eric would meet his father at the point where the trail crossed Junction Parkway at U.S. 441.

Although the boys often made new friends on the trail, Eric was startled by two figures edging out of the dusky woods. They wore crude leather shirts that hung to their knees over leather leggings, and one wore a colorful turban over long black hair. One young man knelt gracefully to take a tin of beans that Eric offered and examined it carefully. A beautiful silver chain laced with brightly colored beads and small orange-and-black feathers dangled from his neck.

The other youth bent toward Eric, who prepared to give him a high-five, but the reddish-haired boy jumped backward as if he thought Eric meant to strike him. "Name's Jesse," he said warily. "That's Dancing in the Rain. He's Cherokee."

Eric had only two cans of beans. He pulled the tabbed lid on Dancing in the Rain's can. In the closing darkness, he could barely see the boy's face as he scooped the food out with his fingers. Eric opened the other tin for Jesse.

The two guests stretched out on blankets. Sensing Eric's curiosity, Jesse began to tell about himself. In Vermont, he had been forced into apprenticeship with a tanner, who made him work from sunup to sundown. "Hated it," Jesse said, "so I headed down to Virginia. But the Tories tried to force me to fight for King George, so I lit out again; I met up with Dancing in the Rain, and he and I have been traveling together ever since. I'm looking to find some Whigs and fight against the Tories."

"Tories?" Eric asked.

ENTRY-LEVEL TEST

GO ON

"British loyalists!" Jesse spat out impatiently. "You know, those that are against the revolution." Jesse continued, "Dancing in the Rain is looking to join up with Dragging Canoe. Settlers swindled the Cherokee people out of thousands of acres of their hunting grounds. Dragging Canoe is a Cherokee leader who is fighting to get the land back."

Groggy and very confused, Eric began to nod off, vaguely agreeing to set off with his new friends in the morning. But the thought of fighting Jesse's or Dancing in the Rain's battle troubled his dreams, and he awoke to see Jesse out under the starlight, his blanket folded over his shoulder. "I worry that Dancing in the Rain and I could end up enemies," Jesse whispered, "so tell him to take care." He slipped into the forest, whose purple shadows welcomed him.

Eric awakened, alone, at daybreak. He sighed deeply. His mysterious companions had, obviously, turned out to be the inhabitants of a rather peculiar dream. He gathered his gear and an hour later was sliding onto the soft seat of his father's car.

At home, Eric unloaded his backpack. He pulled out two unopened cans of beans. Then, as he reached into a side pocket, his fingers touched something sleek and soft. His heart leapt as he pulled out an orange-and-black feather!

1 In this story, the term *Whigs* refers to colonists who—

- A were persecuted for their religious beliefs
- B were loyal to the British crown
- C began to settle America's interior
- D wanted independence from Britain

2 What is one effect of having a third-person narrator tell this story?

- A It gives the reader a wider, more revealing perspective.
- B It allows the reader to discount what the narrator says.
- C It tells us what Dancing in the Rain thinks.
- D It robs Brian of an important role he might have played.

3 Which of the following quotations from the story is the BEST example of sensory details?

- A "Eric was weary after three weeks. . . ."
- B "silver chain laced with brightly colored beads"
- C "The two guests stretched out on blankets."
- D "made him work from sunup to sundown"

GO ON

4 Which words from the story BEST create a mysterious tone or mood?

A Eric was camping alone.

B figures edging out of the dusky woods

C The other youth bent toward Eric.

D Sensing Eric's curiosity, Jesse began to tell about himself.

5 The author holds the reader's attention at the end of the story by—

A resolving whether Eric's guests were real or imaginary

B suggesting that Eric will see Jesse and Dancing in the Rain again

C giving mixed evidence about whether Eric was dreaming

D revealing that Eric is living back in the late 1700s

6 Which of the following BEST describes the relationship between Jesse and Dancing in the Rain?

A They met by accident but have become friends.

B They are on opposite sides of the American Revolution.

C They are united in their alienation from their families.

D They share a mutual distrust of authority.

7 The author uses Jesse's statements in paragraphs six and eight to—

A create a sense of foreboding and alarm

B help develop the characters

C add irony to the writing

D give hints about what will happen later in the plot

8 Which of the following is a theme expressed in Jesse's statements?

A the need for solitude

B personal responsibility

C people's conflict with nature

D a desire to be free

9 What literary device does the author use in the words "the forest, whose purple shadows welcomed him"?

A simile

B irony

C archetype

D personification

10 Which of the following is MOST responsible for engaging the reader's interest?

A a remote setting on a famous hiking trail

B the author's use of Colonial and other historical references

C the descriptions of the characters' appearances and actions

D the discussion of political parties and potential battles

11 To find a map to go with this story, the BEST term to use in searching the Internet would be—

A American Indians

B Colonial history

C Vermont

D Appalachian Trail

12 What characteristic of this narrative is typical of many American short stories?

A a surprise ending

B a realistic plot

C the absence of dialogue

D the lack of description

GO ON

Reading and Literary Analysis *(continued)*

DIRECTIONS Read this article about one man's memorable contribution during World War II. Then, answer questions 13 through 22.

Joe Rosenthal's Famous Photograph

It was February 23, 1945, on the South Pacific Island of Iwo Jima. With an instinctive click of his camera's shutter—in 1/400 of a second—a photographer captured the image of five United States Marines and one Navy hospital corpsman raising the Stars and Stripes during a long battle with entrenched Japanese troops. As a result, Joe Rosenthal became known as the man whose photograph has been one of the most reproduced in history.

Rosenthal has said that it was more a matter of luck than skill that he was there and was able to capture the event. The marine closest to the ground had his shoulder against the pipe they were using as a makeshift flagpole. Four other military men were perfectly staggered in posture and height, with arms up, raising the pole toward a perpendicular position. A sixth man's hands were extended upward, having just released the rising pole. A brisk wind blew the large flag to the right, over the heads of the soldiers; this lucky circumstance balanced the composition of the photo perfectly.

By the time Rosenthal returned to the United States, the U.S. military had taken Iwo Jima and the photo had boosted the nation's patriotic spirit. Rosenthal would win the coveted Pulitzer Prize in photography, and eventually the scene would be sculpted and cast into many tons of bronze for the U.S. Marine Corps War Memorial in Washington, D.C.

The story of how Rosenthal was able to capture this memorable image has an ironic twist. An experienced news photographer in San Francisco, he wanted to serve in the U.S. armed forces. He tried to enlist in the army and then the navy but was rejected because his vision was so poor. Still wanting to help the war effort, he accompanied the U.S. forces in the Pacific as an Associated Press photographer. Rosenthal had been on Iwo Jima for five days when the "poor" eyes that had kept him out of the military looked through a camera lens, capturing an image that allowed him to serve his country beyond his wildest dreams.

After the war, rumors persisted that Rosenthal had staged the picture. He readily admitted that the flag he photographed was not the first to be raised on that hill that day. Several hours before, a smaller American flag

GO ON

had been driven into the ground there; however, a U.S. officer insisted on replacing it with a bigger flag that could be seen across the small island. Soldiers found a larger flag, and Rosenthal was there to take the picture when it was being raised.

After the second flag raising, he posed eighteen members of a marine company around the base of the flag and photographed them waving their helmets and rifles. It is possible that this action led to the charge that the famous flag-raising photograph had been posed as well. It is unfortunate that Rosenthal had to defend his extraordinary, prize-winning image against such charges.

13 What is the primary purpose of this article?

A to inform

B to persuade

C to amuse

D to examine

14 The main purpose of the first paragraph is to—

A tell how a camera's shutter works

B provide background information

C describe an important battle

D identify important landmarks in the South Pacific

15 In the second paragraph, the author acquaints readers with the famous image by—

A giving a physical description of the island

B using Rosenthal's own words to recall the event

C giving other photographers' opinions of the picture

D describing each aspect of the scene in detail

16 Rosenthal's photograph became a symbol of—

A U.S. economic importance

B the futility of war

C patriotism and commitment

D the ironic nature of war

GO ON

17 **The author calls Joe Rosenthal's story *ironic* because the—**

A photograph won the Pulitzer Prize

B military had rejected Rosenthal, but his photograph promoted war efforts

C flag that Rosenthal photographed being raised was the second raised that day

D picture would later be used as a model for a statue to honor U.S. Marines

18 **Based on this article, it is reasonable to conclude that—**

A photographers usually get in the way during battles

B all photographic reporting of battles has to be staged

C a striking image can affect the attitude of a nation

D the picture's use by the military was accidental

19 **The last two paragraphs of the article show that the author was—**

A aware that Rosenthal's accomplishment was challenged

B uncertain whether the famous picture Rosenthal took was genuine

C eager to challenge the decision to give Rosenthal the Pulitzer Prize

D more interested in Rosenthal's career before he landed on Iwo Jima

20 **The author has stressed the ironic aspect of this story in order to—**

A criticize the U.S. armed forces

B praise the role of photojournalists

C give the article greater depth and interest

D honor the soldiers who died in World War II

21 **Which question would lead to the MOST relevant additional information about the subject of this article?**

A How are huge bronze statues made?

B Where was the photograph first published?

C What became of Iwo Jima after the war?

D What kinds of cameras do photographers use?

22 **The final statement of the passage is an example of—**

A a fact

B an opinion

C a contradiction

D an exaggeration

GO ON

Reading and Literary Analysis *(continued)*

DIRECTIONS Poet Jimmy Santiago Baca writes about the relationship between autumn and a life in the poem "Fall." Read the poem and answer questions 23 through 30.

Fall

Somber hue diffused on everything.
    Each creature, each emptied corn stalk,
    is richly bundled in mellow light.
In that open unharvested field of my own life,
I have fathered small joys and memories.
My heart was once a lover's swing that creaked in wind
of these calm fall days.
Autumn chants my visions to sleep,
and travels me back into a night
when I could touch stars and believe in myself . . .

Along the way, grief broke me,
    my faith became hardened dirt
    walked over by too many people.
My heart now, as I walk down this dirt road,
on this calm fall day,
    is a dented
    tin bucket
    filled with fruits
    picked long ago.
    It's getting harder
    to lug the heavy bucket.
    I spill a memory on the ground,
    it gleams,
    rain on hot embers
    of yellow grass.

—Jimmy Santiago Baca

23 **What might the speaker in "Fall" say that he has lost?**

A his ability to write
B his hope and confidence
C his unpleasant memories
D his fear of facing life

24 **"My heart now . . . / is a dented / tin bucket . . . " is an example of which poetic technique?**

A metaphor
B personification
C simile
D alliteration

25 **Touching stars represents a time of—**

A fear
B fantasy
C optimism
D regret

26 **Which of the following is an example of imagery that depicts the speaker's disappointment at this stage of his life?**

A "I have fathered small joys and memories."
B "when I could touch stars and believe in myself"
C "it gleams, / rain on hot embers / of yellow grass."
D "My heart was once a lover's swing. . . . "

27 **Baca uses a description of a field in order to comment about—**

A his reputation as a poet
B dangers to the environment
C the sadness of the seasons
D the experiences of the speaker's life

28 **The poem suggests that the speaker is unhappy because he—**

A has no pleasant memories
B planted crops that failed
C has been hurt by people
D is sad that summer is ending

29 **Which word from the poem suggests that the speaker feels that his life has not turned out as he once hoped it would?**

A creaked
B bundled
C gleams
D unharvested

30 **What is personified in this poem?**

A corn
B autumn
C wind
D dirt

NAME _______________ CLASS _______________ DATE _______________

Entry-Level Test

Vocabulary

DIRECTIONS Choose the word or group of words that means the same, or about the same, as the underlined word. Then, mark the space for the answer you have chosen.

SAMPLE A

Something tedious is—

A small
B intense
C boring
D necessary

31 Malice means—

A firm resolve
B ill will
C moral conduct
D sudden fear

32 Something that is lamentable is—

A distressing
B charming
C forceful
D passionate

33 Someone who is vigilant is—

A cruel
B sneaky
C corrupt
D watchful

34 To plunder a place is to—

A totally control it
B govern it badly
C rob it by force
D sell it for a profit

35 Singular means—

A inspired
B serious
C unstable
D remarkable

36 A quadruped has four—

A feet
B angles
C words
D stomachs

GO ON

ENTRY-LEVEL TEST

NAME ______________________ CLASS ____________ DATE ____________

Entry-Level Test

Vocabulary *(continued)*

DIRECTIONS Read each sentence in the box. Then, choose the answer in which the underlined word is used in the same way. Mark the space for the answer you have chosen.

SAMPLE B

The workers pitched the hay over the fence.

A The salesman pitched his product to the crowd.
B The campers pitched their tents near a river.
C I pitched some coins into an empty jar.
D Rosa pitched during today's baseball game.

37 Grandmother used plain language in her speaking and writing.

A His plain talk made his meaning clear.
B We looked out over the vast plain before us.
C Some people thought the famous model was plain.
D Was the missing object in plain view the whole time?

38 We picked fresh mint and delighted in the sharp, fresh smell.

A He has a very sharp temper.
B Please arrive at five o'clock sharp.
C Did her voice sound a little sharp to you?
D That food has a sharp taste of garlic.

39 Did you stay home in your little flat all afternoon?

A We carried groceries up to our flat on the third floor.
B He pressed his back flat against the wall.
C Did you put air into the flat tire on your car?
D This soda tastes flat.

40 Was he left in the charge of his elderly relative?

A The soldiers will charge the hill at dawn.
B She has charge of two young children.
C The tailor will charge you for alterations.
D I will charge my purchase rather than pay with cash.

GO ON

ENTRY-LEVEL TEST

NAME ____________ CLASS ____________ DATE ____________ SCORE ____________

LITERATURE
INFORMATIONAL TEXT
VOCABULARY

Encounters and Foundations to 1800

On the line provided, write the letter of the *best* answer to each of the following items. *(100 points; 10 points each)*

_____ **1.** The character of a wise old man who appears in literature throughout the ages is an example of a(n) —

A metaphor
B archetype
C allegory
D foil

_____ **2.** All of the following elements are characteristic of a **sonnet** *except* —

F rhyme scheme
G fourteen lines
H free verse
J iambic pentameter

_____ **3.** What is an **allusion**?

A The suggestion of two conflicting meanings in a work
B A word that sounds like what it means
C The associations evoked by a word
D A reference to something well known from literature, history, or religion

_____ **4.** **Autobiographies** are almost always written in the first person because —

F the authors are writing about their own lives
G most nonfiction writing uses first-person narration
H many readers prefer the immediacy of first-person narration
J the first-person point of view makes fiction more believable

_____ **5.** A writer's **style** is largely determined by all of the following elements *except* —

A sentence structure
B conflict
C word choice
D imagery

______ **6.** What is **parallelism,** or **parallel structure**?

F A series of stanzas that have a similar form in a poem

G Situations in a story in which different characters face identical problems

H Themes that appear in several stories

J The repetition of phrases or sentences that have the same grammatical structure

______ **7.** In **persuasive writing** an author may appeal to the audience's reason through the use of —

A loaded words

B figurative language

C statistics

D personal experiences

______ **8.** What are **counterclaims**?

F A comparison of ideas

G False evidence

H Questions that are asked for effect

J Opposing arguments

______ **9.** Which of the following strategies is the *best* way to determine the meaning of an unfamiliar word?

A Evaluate the author's purpose for writing

B Sound out the word

C Look for context clues

D Change the word's part of speech

______ **10.** Knowing a word's **etymology** is *most* useful in helping you to —

F understand an author's attitude

G recognize related words

H spell the word

J interpret a symbol

NAME ______ CLASS ______ DATE ______ SCORE ______

LITERARY PERIOD INTRODUCTION TEST **Student Edition page 6**

Encounters and Foundations to 1800

COMPREHENSION *(100 points; 10 points each)*

On the line provided, write the letter of the *best* answer to each of the following items.

______ **1.** The first Europeans to come to North America were —

- **A** explorers from Spain
- **B** Africans restrained in the holds of slave ships
- **C** Ice Age peoples who traveled across a land bridge from Asia
- **D** English Puritans who traveled across the Atlantic Ocean

______ **2.** When historian Francis Jennings says, "The so-called settlement of America was a resettlement . . . ," he means that —

- **F** European settlers took over land that American Indians had already settled
- **G** there were two distinct waves of European settlement
- **H** American Indians sold their property to Europeans
- **J** Europeans came to America, left, and then returned many years later

______ **3.** The Spanish explorer Álvar Núñez Cabeza de Vaca —

- **A** reached the shores of the New World before Columbus
- **B** was shipwrecked off the west coast of Florida
- **C** wrote a firsthand account about some southwestern American Indian tribes
- **D** told about tribes he lived with in Mexico

______ **4.** Which of the following statements about the English Puritans is *not* true?

- **F** They were Protestants who sought to purify the Church of England and return to a simpler form of worship.
- **G** They believed that the clergy and government should act as intermediaries between the individual and God.
- **H** Some of them thought the Church of England was too corrupt to reform and called for complete separation from it.
- **J** They wanted to establish a new society that would be a profitable colony modeled on God's word.

______ **5.** Because Puritans believed that the arrival of God's grace was demonstrated by saintly behavior, they —

- **A** thought it was easy to differentiate between the saved and the damned
- **B** could try to earn salvation by giving money to the church
- **C** tried to behave in as exemplary a way as possible
- **D** thought there was no need for rigorous self-examination

NAME ______ CLASS ______ DATE ______ SCORE ______

______ **6.** The Mayflower Compact paved the way for —

F a national church

G a constitutional democracy

H the Salem witch trials

J war against the American Indians

______ **7.** Rationalists believed that all people —

A were sinners in the eyes of God, with no hope of redemption

B were either saved or damned, according to God's will

C could change the course of human events through prayer

D could think in an ordered manner, thereby improving their lives

______ **8.** Cotton Mather is *best* remembered in the annals of science as the —

F experimenter who began a public campaign for inoculation against smallpox

G smallpox patient who believed himself to be one of the "elect" and refused treatment

H minister who said that inoculation against smallpox was unnecessary, since God's will would prevail

J devout Puritan who refused to support any smallpox treatment developed by Muslim doctors

______ **9.** According to the deists, the *best* form of worship was —

A deep introspection

B creating greater business profits

C regular prayer in church

D doing good for others

______ **10.** Benjamin Franklin's *The Autobiography* —

F tells in detail what Puritans believed

G describes Franklin's devout religious practices

H provides the model for the classic American rags-to-riches story

J shows that the notion of a self-made person is an unrealistic myth

NAME ______________________ CLASS ______________ DATE ____________ SCORE ________

The Sun Still Rises in the Same Sky: Native American Literature Joseph Bruchac

The Sky Tree *retold by* Joseph Bruchac

The Earth Only *composed by* Used-as-a-Shield

Coyote Finishes His Work *retold by* Barry Lopez

COMPREHENSION *(40 points; 4 points each)*

On the line provided, write the letter of the *best* answer to each of the following items.

______ **1.** Joseph Bruchac says the Longfellow's epic poem *Song of Hiawatha* is misnamed because —

A the title tells nothing of the struggles faced by Native Americans

B the poet attributes his story to the wrong native group

C there was never an Iroquois named Hiawatha

D Hiawatha was a Chippewa, not an Iroquois

______ **2.** What does Joseph Bruchac cite as part "of the problem" in the West's misrepresentation of Native American literature?

F The first European settlers feared American Indians.

G Until just recently, no one in the West knew American Indians had literature.

H The hundreds of different native languages posed a translation problem.

J Native speakers have never done translations of Indian literature.

______ **3.** In Bruchac's view, writers like M. Scott Momaday and Leslie Marmon Silko helped revitalize Native American literature because they —

A placed age-old stories in modern settings

B combined contemporary English with a native understanding of Indian story-telling traditions

C helped non-Native Americans see that Indians are no different than anyone else

D brought increased attention to Native American literature

______ **4.** In the Abenaki story of Gluskabe, Gluskabe's grandmother tells him to return the animals he has caught because —

F she is angry with him about something else

G it is both greedy and environmentally unsound to capture all the available game

H American Indians belong to matriarchal societies in which the women hold all the power

J the animals have spirits, just like humans

______ **5.** According to this essay, metaphors are especially powerful in the Native American literary tradition because —

A words themselves can be endowed with special powers

B Native American writers are inherently poetic

C American Indian writers use nature as inspiration

D oral tradition has, over time, improved the quality of the original work

______ **6.** Bruchac's description of the Lakota Sun Dance is an example of the Native American worldview that —

F how you get somewhere is just as important as what you do once you're there

G in nature, things happen cyclically, rather than in a straight line

H traditions are a basic part of human existence

J natural resources, like sunlight, should be celebrated

______ **7.** How does the author's description of the different ways Indians traveled to the Sun Dance support his contention that Indian traditions are "tenacious"?

A Despite the fact that they have been affected in profound ways by other cultures, Indians have persisted in honoring their own customs.

B The Lakota would walk miles to participate in this ceremony.

C Indians are adaptable and practical enough to use new forms of transport.

D No details of the Sun Dance have changed in hundreds of years.

______ **8.** In "The Sky Tree," Aataentsic *most* likely throws herself down the hole after the tree because —

F wood is precious in Sky Land

G without the tree, there can be no life

H the old chief commanded her to do so

J she wanted to taste the fruit at the top of the tree

______ **9.** In "The Earth Only," what might it be said does *not* endure?

A The sea and sky

B Living things

C Outmoded ideas

D The wind and the sun

______ **10.** In "Coyote Finishes His Work," Coyote helps the people when he —

F rids the world of evil spirits and teaches important skills

G amuses the people with tricks

H creates the mountains and the forests

J protects people from vicious predators

READING SKILLS: UNDERSTANDING CULTURAL CHARACTERISTICS *(30 points, 5 points each)*
On the line provided, write the letter of the *best* answer to each of the following items.

______ **11.** An important characteristic of American Indian literature is that it —

A is written in an ornate style

B is written in short sentences

C was originally not written but handed down orally

D was told to an eager audience

______ **12.** Bruchac makes the point that Western literature has its roots in stories told by word of mouth. Which of the following statements would that point support?

F Native American literature is no less valid than that found in the West.

G This sort of story is superior to work that began its life as written text.

H Western literature is flawed.

J All literature has come from foreign sources of some kind.

______ **13.** Which of the following statements is *not* a generalization that Bruchac makes about Native American literature?

A It provides an accurate historical record of events in Indian history.

B It teaches moral lessons about the natural world.

C It includes epic narratives, songs, and chants.

D It provides practical information.

______ **14.** What work does the author give as an example of Western literature finding inspiration in Native American tradition?

F *Beowulf*

G *The Song of Hiawatha*

H *The Odyssey*

J The story of Gluskabe

______ **15.** Different worldviews underlie the Native American literary tradition and the Western tradition. Which of the following phrases *best* describes that difference?

A Nature versus nurture

B Modern versus ancient

C Cycles versus linear progression

D Moral lessons versus narrative

______ **16.** "Coyote Finishes His Work" and "The Sky Tree" come from different cultures. What themes do they have in common?

- **F** Life on earth begins with an act of sacrifice.
- **G** Animals aid humans.
- **H** Everything is controlled by women.
- **J** Only the earth endures.

LITERARY FOCUS: ARCHETYPES *(20 points; 5 points each)*

On the line provided, write the letter of the *best* answer to each of the following items.

______ **17.** An **archetype** is a —

- **A** king or other leader in ancient myths
- **B** pattern that occurs over and over again in literature
- **C** way of telling an old story in a new way
- **D** written version of an oral story

______ **18.** In the Greek tale the *Odyssey*, the hero often gets his way by lying. Which character in the stories you just read does the hero most resemble?

- **F** Turtle
- **G** Old Man Above
- **H** Coyote
- **J** Aataentsic

______ **19.** In "Coyote Finishes His Work," the Old Man Above is an archetype of a —

- **A** mean old villain
- **B** wily trickster
- **C** valiant warrior
- **D** creator god

______ **20.** Many myths and legends deal with the "Other Side Camp" that Old Man Above talks about in "Coyote Finishes His Work." What do you think this "Camp" is?

- **F** An actual area on the far side of the continent.
- **G** A place where Earthwoman lives.
- **H** A place where human beings go after they die.
- **J** A place where Coyote can be found.

CONSTRUCTED RESPONSE *(10 points)*

21. In the last line of his essay, Joseph Bruchac writes, "The sun still rises in the same sky." On a separate sheet of paper, explain the meaning of this phrase. Then, use this notion to explain how Western and Native American literature differ.

Here Follow Some Verses upon the Burning of Our House, July 10, 1666 Anne Bradstreet

COMPREHENSION *(50 points; 5 points each)*

On the line provided, write the letter of the *best* answer to each of the following items.

______ **1.** In her poem, Bradstreet *mostly* criticizes herself for —

- A losing her faith in God's goodness
- B failing to react quickly in an emergency
- C not taking proper precautions against fire hazards
- D valuing material possessions too much

______ **2.** Bradstreet emphasizes both the things she has lost and —

- F the people who escaped the fire
- G the new home that neighbors are building for her
- H her memories of happy occasions in the house
- J the items she has rescued from the flames

______ **3.** When Bradstreet writes, "I blest His name that gave and took . . ." she implies that —

- A she is being punished for the sin of vanity
- B material objects are ultimately God's and not hers
- C she secretly wants all her possessions to vanish
- D God will be appeased if she says a prayer to Him

______ **4.** When Bradstreet writes, "Thou hast an house on high erect . . ." she means that —

- F whatever is destroyed can soon be rebuilt
- G God has prepared an eternal dwelling place for all believers
- H she is bitter about those people who still have homes
- J one should dwell upon the good things in life

______ **5.** Bradstreet's views might be described as spiritual because she —

- A repeatedly refers to God and His will
- B emphasizes that real value cannot be found in earthly things
- C writes movingly of the things she lost
- D clearly explains how a person feels after a disaster

______ **6.** What was the "thund'ring noise" that woke Bradstreet?

- F A clap of lightning
- G The drums of English soldiers
- H The burning of her home
- J A raging river

_____ **7.** Why, specifically, does Bradstreet say in line 18 that she should not "repine" the loss of her home and belongings?

A It is no time for accusations.

B She owned very few things.

C She has insurance.

D Everything ultimately belongs to God.

_____ **8.** In this poem, who is the "mighty Architect"?

F Bradstreet's uncle

G A kindly Puritan

H God

J The man who built Bradstreet's house

_____ **9.** In the last five lines, what does Bradstreet wish to no longer love?

A Possessions

B Human beings

C Those who set the fire

D Glory

_____ **10.** In the line "Nor at thy table eat a bit." the word *thy* refers to —

F her parents

G the owner of the house

H the house

J God

READING SKILLS: ANALYZING TEXT STRUCTURES—INVERSION *(10 points; 5 points each)*
On the line provided, write the letter of the *best* answer to each of the following items.

_____ **11.** Which of the following excerpts is the *best* example of inversion?

A "My hope and treasure lies above."

B "And them behold no more shall I."

C "Thou hast an house on high erect . . ."

D "No candle e'er shall shine in thee . . ."

_____ **12.** Which of the following word groups is *not* an example of inversion?

F "In silent night when rest I took . . ."

G "For sorrow near I did not look . . ."

H "I wakened was with thund'ring noise . . ."

J "And piteous shrieks of dreadful voice."

Literary Focus: The Plain Style *(15 points; 5 points each)*

On the line provided, write the letter of the *best* answer to each of the following items.

______ **13.** Plain style can be distinguished from high style because **plain style** —

A uses specific terminology commonly employed in farming

B emphasizes uncomplicated sentences and uses words from common speech

C was originally employed in the flat, treeless regions of the Great Plains

D employs a profound spiritual or religious tone

______ **14.** When Bradstreet writes "Then straight I 'gin my heart to chide . . ." she signals that her next words will be addressed to —

F God

G herself

H her neighbors

J the reader

______ **15.** In the last part of this poem, Bradstreet uses *house* as a metaphor for —

A the afterlife

B the things she has lost

C God

D friends and family

Constructed Response *(25 points)*

16. By using plain style, Anne Bradstreet makes the lessons in her poem accessible to as many readers as possible. On a separate sheet of paper, cite at least three lessons that the author tries to communicate to her readers. Quote specific lines from the poem to back up your answers.

NAME ______ CLASS ______ DATE ______ SCORE ______

SELECTION TEST **Student Edition page 33** LITERARY RESPONSE AND ANALYSIS

World, in hounding me . . .

Sor Juana Inés de la Cruz *translated by* Alan S. Trueblood

COMPREHENSION *(40 points; 8 points each)*

On the line provided, write the letter of the *best* answer to each of the following items.

______ **1.** What major theme is addressed by both de la Cruz and Anne Bradstreet?

A All destruction is final.

B The world is against us.

C The spiritual is more important than the worldly.

D Everything moves in cycles.

______ **2.** In this poem what is the difference between the "treasure" mentioned in the seventh line and the "treasure" mentioned in the eighth?

F The first treasure is spiritual, the second is worldly.

G The first treasure is not as valuable as the second.

H The first treasure is easier to achieve than the second.

J The first treasure is worldly, the second is spiritual.

______ **3.** De la Cruz refers to time as "the victor" over "All fair things" because she wants —

A us to see that all physical beauty passes away

B to make it clear that we should live for the moment

C to show how time is merely imaginary

D us to favor ugliness over beauty

______ **4.** To whom or what is the poet speaking in this work?

F A fellow nun

G The world

H Sinners

J God

______ **5.** Both de la Cruz and Bradstreet refer to vanity. Which of the following concerns might *not* be considered an example of such vanity?

A Concern for physical appearance

B Desire for material possessions

C Delight in a blooming rose

D Awareness of mortality

NAME ______________________ CLASS ______________ DATE __________ SCORE ________

LITERARY FOCUS: SONNET *(40 points; 10 points each)*

On the line provided, write the letter of the *best* answer to each of the following items.

______ **6.** The sonnet form was *first* popularized by —

- **F** Shakespeare
- **G** the Spanish
- **H** Native Americans
- **J** the Italian poet Petrarch

______ **7.** Unlike other poem forms, a **sonnet** must —

- **A** be divided into two parts
- **B** have an abba rhyme scheme
- **C** address the theme of love
- **D** have fourteen lines

______ **8.** In a **Petrarchan sonnet**, the sonnet is divided into —

- **F** two parts—the first eight lines and the second six lines
- **G** two parts—the first six lines and the second eight lines
- **H** eight parts consisting of two lines each
- **J** six parts—the first four lines and the second two lines

______ **9.** In this sonnet, the poet personifies time as —

- **A** the victor
- **B** a hound
- **C** a practiced eye
- **D** a nun

CONSTRUCTED RESPONSE *(20 points)*

10. By now you have read works from very different cultures. Both the Sioux chant "The Earth Only" and de la Cruz's "World, in hounding me . . ." have something to say about the material world as opposed to the spiritual world. On a separate sheet of paper, explain how these two works differ on this issue. What might they have in common? Cite elements from each work as you respond to this question.

from A Narrative of the Captivity . . . Mary Rowlandson

COMPREHENSION *(40 points; 4 points each)*

On the line provided, write the letter of the *best* answer to each of the following items.

______ **1.** At the beginning of this selection, Mary Rowlandson is —

A very ill

B wounded

C full of energy

D frightened

______ **2.** When Mary sits with her baby, her captors —

F tell her that her master will hit the child in the head

G give her comfort

H show her herbal remedies to take care of the child

J sing chants to her

______ **3.** In this selection, Mary Rowlandson's *main* intention is to —

A write a bestseller

B analyze another culture

C arouse hatred toward the Wampanoag

D show how her experience revealed God's purpose

______ **4.** The group that captures Rowlandson is forced to keep moving because of its —

F Colonial pursuers

G need for food

H treaty with the colonists

J religious practices

______ **5.** The *best* description of Rowlandson's attitude toward her children might be that she —

A misses them but believes that it builds character to live separately

B treats them as if they were adults capable of taking care of themselves

C cares passionately about them and grieves about being apart from them

D sternly disapproves of their weeping when she sees them

______ **6.** Rowlandson *primarily* draws strength from —

F her desire to return and tell her story to the Puritans

G her belief in God's ultimate purpose

H the medicine that a sympathetic woman gives her

J her desire to avenge the death of her child

______ **7.** Rowlandson receives food from several members of the tribe in exchange for —

A cooking

B washing clothes

C sewing

D gathering firewood

______ **8.** Mary Rowlandson writes "There was a squaw who spoke to me to make a shirt for her *sannup*." Her use of this Indian word for husband tells us that she —

F has absorbed some aspects of American Indian culture

G is being ironic about her captors' habits

H is not yet comfortable with her captor's ways

J must be an expert in foreign languages

______ **9.** When Mary Rowlandson writes, "the Lord would gather us together, and turn all those curses upon our enemies," the style of her language is most likely inspired by —

A the Bible

B an almanac

C Indian dialect

D novels

______ **10.** From his plunder, an Indian gives Mary Rowlandson an item that she sees as evidence of "God's mercy." That item is a —

F sewing machine

G Bible

H book of poetry

J small knife

READING SKILLS: ANALYZING TEXT STRUCTURES—CHRONOLOGICAL ORDER *(10 points; 5 points each)*
On the line provided, write the letter of the *best* answer to each of the following items.

______ **11.** Which of the following events occurs *last* in this excerpt from the narrative?

A Mary Rowlandson's master leads her to her son.

B Mary Rowlandson's child dies.

C Mary Rowlandson eats bear meat and ground nuts with a kind Indian.

D Mary Rowlandson helps carry an American Indian on a bier.

______ **12.** Which of the following events occurs *first*?

F Mary Rowlandson is reunited with her daughter.

G Mary Rowlandson learns to eat bear meat.

H Mary Rowlandson cares for her sick baby.

J One of the American Indians gives Mary Rowlandson a Bible.

NAME ______________________ CLASS ______________________ DATE ______________ SCORE ______________

LITERARY FOCUS: ALLUSIONS *(20 points; 5 points each)*

On the line provided, write the letter of the *best* answer to each of the following items.

_____ **13.** Which of these passages from Mary Rowlandson's narrative is *not* an allusion?

A "and through the Rivers they shall not overthrow thee"

B "like Jehu, they marched on furiously"

C "miserable comforters are ye all, as he said"

D "I earnestly entreated the Lord"

_____ **14.** Mary Rowlandson writes "I was fain to go and look after something to satisfy my hunger . . ." A more modern way of writing this line would be, I —

F was fainting and looked for food to satisfy my hunger

G was eager to find food to satisfy my hunger

H was asked to find food to satisfy my hunger

J faked them into believing I was looking for food

_____ **15.** Rowlandson uses an allusion to the biblical story of Jacob to describe —

A her disgust at cooking bear meat

B the trip along the river

C her captors' march from the English army

D the grief she feels after her daughter dies and the frustration at not being allowed to visit her other daughter

_____ **16.** Which of the following excerpts is an allusion that Rowlandson uses in the narrative?

F "Whereupon I earnestly entreated the Lord, that He would consider my low estate . . ."

G "Being very faint I asked my mistress to give me one spoonful of the meal . . ."

H "When thou passeth through the waters I will be with thee . . ."

J "it was the night after the Sabbath before all the company was got over."

Vocabulary Development *(10 points; 2 points each)*

Match the definition on the left with the Vocabulary word on the right. On the line provided, write the letter of the Vocabulary word.

______ **17.** regrettable; distressing

______ **18.** pains; hardships

______ **19.** tiring; dreary

______ **20.** asked sincerely; prayed to

______ **21.** goods seized, especially during wartime

a. tedious

b. lamentable

c. entreated

d. afflictions

e. plunder

Constructed Response *(20 points)*

22. On a separate sheet of paper, describe the link that Mary Rowlandson sees between her captivity and the suffering endured by people in the Bible. Support your ideas with at least two examples from the selection.

NAME ______ CLASS ______ DATE ______ SCORE ______

SELECTION TEST **Student Edition page 46** LITERARY RESPONSE AND ANALYSIS

from Sinners in the Hands of an Angry God

Jonathan Edwards

COMPREHENSION *(40 points; 4 points each)*

On the line provided, write the letter of the *best* answer to each of the following items.

______ **1.** When Edwards says that "men are held in the hand of God," he means that —

A all human being can fit into the palm of God's hand

B God is a kind father

C the fate of human beings is determined by God

D God will save everyone

______ **2.** According to Edwards, —

F human beings have done nothing to appease God

G God is determined to save human beings

H human beings have promised to obey God

J the Devil does not want to take them

______ **3.** In his sermon, Edwards *mainly* taps into his audience's fear of —

A their minister's wrath

B burning forever in a fiery pit

C associating with sinners

D floods and other natural disasters

______ **4.** When Edwards refers to the "unconverted persons in this congregation," he *chiefly* addresses the —

F men and women who do not believe in themselves

G church visitors who are followers of other religions

H parishioners who don't want Edwards as their leader

J members who do not accept Christ as their savior

______ **5.** Edwards presents God as a being who —

A wants humans to suffer

B continually redefines the universe

C is often angry and vengeful

D easily forgives repentant sinners

______ **6.** Edwards builds a sense of urgency and peril by suggesting that —

F death and damnation may occur at any moment

G the church is being persecuted by unholy forces

H ministers alone can determine who is to be saved

J the end of the world is coming soon

NAME ______ CLASS ______ DATE ______ SCORE ______

______ **7.** Edwards contends that the *only* way people can escape from God's anger is to —

A obey the Ten Commandments

B attend church regularly

C experience a "change of heart" and accept Christ

D reform all aspects of their life

______ **8.** Edwards's purpose in delivering this sermon is to —

F frighten his listeners so much that they never return to church

G jolt his congregation into mending their ways and seeking salvation

H give such a memorable speech that his congregation will never forget him

J dominate his congregation and maintain his position in the church

______ **9.** According to Edwards, the *only* thing that has saved his listeners from hell is God's —

A hand

B wrath

C compassion

D love

______ **10.** What does Edwards mean when he says, "The bow of God's wrath is bent, and the arrow made ready on the string"?

F God is violent.

G God's wrath is misdirected.

H God is prepared to demonstrate his anger.

J God's anger will cause much pain.

LITERARY FOCUS: FIGURES OF SPEECH *(30 points; 5 points each)*

On the line provided, write the letter of the *best* answer to each of the following items.

______ **11.** Which of the following quotations is the *best* example of a figure of speech?

A "However you may have reformed your life . . ."

B "your guilt in the meantime is constantly increasing . . ."

C "the mere arbitrary will, and uncovenanted, unobliged forbearance of an incensed God"

D "the floods of God's vengeance have been withheld . . ."

______ **12.** Edwards makes all of the following comparisons *except* that of —

F wickedness to the weight of lead

G forgiveness to a lightened load

H the wrath of God to dammed waters

J unsaved people to spiders

______ **13.** Jonathan Edwards *probably* uses the device of comparing God's fury to natural forces in order to —

A put abstract things into physical terms people can understand

B achieve a poetic effect

C suggest that it is nature, not God, that people should fear

D make God seem less terrifying

______ **14.** Which of the following word groups is *not* a figure of speech?

F The bow of God's wrath

G That world of misery

H Burns you like fire

J The floods of God's vengeance

______ **15.** Which of the following statements is more implicit than explicit in Edwards's speech?

A God is furious with those who will not accept his salvation.

B Eternal damnation is the lot of all who will not be saved.

C Salvation is possible for anyone who accepts Christ as his savior.

D Doom is at hand for those who do not repent of their sins.

______ **16.** Jonathan Edwards's *primary* intent in using such strong, graphic language is to —

F terrorize his audience

G make real the concept of sin and its punishment

H parade his own rhetorical gifts

J shock the staid Puritans

VOCABULARY DEVELOPMENT *(10 points; 2 points each)*

Match the definition on the left with the Vocabulary word on the right. On the line provided, write the letter of the Vocabulary word.

______ **17.** attributed to a certain cause	**a.** abhors
______ **18.** scorns; hates	**b.** abominable
______ **19.** physical condition	**c.** ascribed
______ **20.** disgusting; loathsome	**d.** appease
______ **21.** calm; satisfy	**e.** constitution

Constructed Response *(20 points)*

22. Examine Jonathan Edwards's speech again with the following questions in mind. Then, answer each question on a separate sheet of paper, using words from the speech to back up your assertion.

a. According to Edwards, is it enough to lead a good and decent life?

b. Is it enough to believe in God?

c. What role does having a good physical constitution play in salvation?

d. What is the one thing that one must do to avoid eternal damnation?

NAME ______ CLASS ______ DATE ______ SCORE ______

SELECTION TEST **Student Edition pages 52, 61, 62** **LITERARY RESPONSE AND ANALYSIS**

from The Interesting Narrative of the Life of Olaudah Equiano Olaudah Equiano
from To the Right Honorable William, Earl of Dartmouth . . . Phillis Wheatley
Honoring African Heritage Halimah Abdullah

COMPREHENSION *(40 points; 4 points each)*

On the line provided, write the letter of the *best* answer to each of the following items.

______ **1.** Equiano is permanently separated from his sister —

A immediately after they are abducted from their home

B on the morning of their third day in captivity

C after a brief reunion at the seacoast

D moments before Equiano is taken aboard the ship

______ **2.** Which of the following statements about the selection is *false*?

F Equiano's father had many slaves and a large family.

G Equiano seems to be adopted into the family of a wealthy widow.

H Equiano meets Ben Franklin upon arriving in America.

J Many captives on slave ships die during the voyage across the Atlantic Ocean.

______ **3.** The conditions of the enslaved people in the ship's hold are —

A cramped but sanitary, with plenty of food

B dangerous, because of frequent storms

C suffocating and stinking, with minimal food

D deadly, because of a tuberculosis epidemic

______ **4.** The destination of the slave ship is —

F Barbados

G Massachusetts

H Cuba

J Virginia

______ **5.** The *best* evidence that many of the crew members are motivated by cruelty as well as profit is that they —

A refuse to let captives eat fish, which the crew has in abundance

B refuse to let sick people come up onto the deck

C keep the enslaved people from knowing their destination

D force Equiano to look through a quadrant

_____ **6.** Upon arrival in Barbados, Equiano and his fellow passengers are —

F herded up like cattle and sold at auction

G released from confinement and given small farms

H reunited with their family members

J given food and new clothes

_____ **7.** While he is in the merchant's custody, Equiano is astonished to see —

A people in fine uniforms

B men riding horses

C familiar landmarks from his homeland

D flying fishes

_____ **8.** When Equiano first encounters ships, he and his fellow captives believe that ships are stopped by —

F wind

G engines

H magic

J slaves

_____ **9.** Phillis Wheatley writes, "What sorrows labor in my parent's breast?" Her parent's heart is filled with sorrow because Phillis has —

A been captured and taken into slavery

B run away from home

C married a British lord

D returned to Africa

_____ **10.** In "Honoring African Heritage" for Mr. Adae the ocean view represents —

F an escape to freedom

G a connection to his African ancestors' voyage here

H a memory of a family vacation

J the Jewish holocaust

READING SKILLS: MAKING INFERENCES ABOUT AN AUTHOR'S BELIEFS *(10 points; 5 points each)*
On the line provided, write the letter of the *best* answer to each of the following items.

_____ **11.** Equiano calls slave dealers "nominal" Christians because they —

A do not follow Christ's teachings

B actually practice other, non-Christian religions

C belong to a special sect of Christianity

D seek to convert slaves to Christianity

NAME ______ CLASS ______ DATE ______ SCORE ______

______ **12.** What can you tell from reading Equiano's narrative about his later life that is *not* explicitly mentioned in it?

F In time, he would be reunited with his sister.

G At some point, he must have gotten an education.

H Eventually, he would be sold to a slaveowner in America.

J He would never again return to Africa.

LITERARY FOCUS: AUTOBIOGRAPHY *(10 points; 5 points each)*

______ **13.** In Equiano's autobiographical account of his childhood before his capture, he writes that he —

A was unbearably unhappy

B was training to become a warrior

C had no brothers or sisters

D spent little time with his mother

______ **14.** In the selection from Equiano's autobiography, Equiano does *not* —

F recall his early years and family life

G express his feelings concerning the immorality of slavery

H write vividly of his horrific trip on the slave ship

J explain in detail his sister's experience as a slave

VOCABULARY DEVELOPMENT *(20 points; 4 points each)*

Match the definition on the left with the Vocabulary word on the right. On the line provided, write the letter of the Vocabulary word.

______ **15.** spacious — **a.** assailant

______ **16.** placed at intervals — **b.** distraction

______ **17.** attacker — **c.** alleviate

______ **18.** mental disturbance or distress — **d.** interspersed

______ **19.** relieve — **e.** commodious

CONSTRUCTED RESPONSE *(20 points)*

20. On a separate sheet of paper, compare the treatment Equiano receives during his enslavement in Africa with the treatment he receives on the slave ship. Make at least two references to details in the selection to support your comparison.

NAME ______ CLASS ______ DATE ______ SCORE ______

from The Autobiography Benjamin Franklin
from All I Really Need to Know I Learned in Kindergarten Robert Fulghum
from Poor Richard's Almanack Benjamin Franklin

COMPREHENSION *(40 points; 4 points each)*

On the line provided, write the letter of the *best* answer to each of the following items.

______ **1.** Franklin arrives in Philadelphia in his working dress because —

A he intends to find a job immediately

B his best clothes are coming around by sea

C he sympathizes with the plight of workers

D no one has ever told him how to dress in the city

______ **2.** In this selection from his autobiography, Franklin seems *most* eager to portray his —

F ability to work steadfastly toward his goals

G willingness to break away from convention

H deep resentment of people who have wronged him

J frugality in financial matters

______ **3.** Franklin considers moral perfection to be a(n) —

A illusion promoted by ministers and religion

B annoying claim made by hypocrites

C state attainable through study and practice

D pathway to heaven and God's grace

______ **4.** In developing a method for examining virtues, Franklin reveals his —

F doubt that real goodness can be attained

G logical and orderly mind

H scorn for traditional philosophy

J deeply emotional side

______ **5.** Franklin ranks the virtues according to —

A how the clergymen of his day ranked them

B the popularity of individual virtues among his friends

C the idea that the mastery of one virtue facilitates the mastery of the next virtue

D the belief that the most difficult virtues must be developed first

______ **6.** In *All I Really Need to Know I Learned in Kindergarten*, the "Credo" Robert Fulghum describes writing from an early age was essentially a —

- **F** list of things he wanted to accomplish
- **G** set of New Year's resolutions
- **H** personal statement of belief
- **J** short story

______ **7.** Fulghum compares the kindergarten rule "Clean up your own mess" to —

- **A** government policy
- **B** the need to keep a neat bedroom
- **C** apologizing for harm done to others
- **D** being honest

______ **8.** One saying from *Poor Richard's Almanack* suggests that successfully ordering your own affairs is a greater accomplishment than ordering things on paper. That saying is —

- **F** "'Tis hard for an empty bag to stand upright."
- **G** "Keep your eyes wide open before marriage, half shut afterward."
- **H** "One today is worth two tomorrows."
- **J** "He that composes himself is wiser than he that composes books."

______ **9.** The saying "If a man could have half his wishes, he would double his troubles" suggests that —

- **A** one needs to attain all one's wishes to deal with all of one's troubles
- **B** people usually wish for things that are not ultimately good for them
- **C** it is wrong to wish for more than what we have
- **D** there is a scientific, mathematical relationship between wishes and troubles

______ **10.** "Love your neighbors; yet don't pull down your hedge" is closest in meaning to which of these lines by the poet Robert Frost?

- **F** "I took the one [road] less traveled by"
- **G** "Good fences make good neighbors"
- **H** "But I have promises to keep, / And miles to go before I sleep"
- **J** "Two roads diverged in a wood"

READING SKILLS: MAKING INFERENCES *(15 points; 5 points each)*

On the line provided, write the letter of the *best* answer to each of the following items.

______ **11.** What probable reason does Franklin suggest for his giving the boatmen his only shilling, even though Franklin did the rowing?

A One must be scrupulously honest in all things.

B It is better for one's karma to overpay than to underpay.

C The poorer one is, the more generous, for fear of looking poor.

D Franklin hadn't actually done much rowing.

______ **12.** Why does Franklin place the attainment of virtues in a numerical order?

F He believes some virtues are more important than others.

G He believes some virtues are easier to acquire than others.

H The order is random.

J He believes that some virtues help pave the way for others.

______ **13.** Robert Fulghum's assertion that one can derive life lessons from kindergarten lessons suggests that —

A adults today are extremely immature

B the things that matter most in life are simple

C his own kindergarten experience was superior to that of others

D we learn more easily when we are young

LITERARY FOCUS: APHORISMS *(5 points)*

______ **14.** The aphorisms in *Poor Richard's Almanack* support the basic belief that —

F prudence in all things is best

G risks are an essential part of learning

H people cannot get along and shouldn't try

J knowledge is better than experience

VOCABULARY DEVELOPMENT *(20 points; 4 points each)*

Match the definition on the left with the Vocabulary word on the right. On the line provided, write the letter of the Vocabulary word.

______ **15.** correctness	**a.** arduous
______ **16.** following	**b.** rectitude
______ **17.** difficult	**c.** facilitate
______ **18.** eliminate	**d.** subsequent
______ **19.** make easier	**e.** eradicate

CONSTRUCTED RESPONSE *(20 points)*

20. Based on what Franklin reveals about his habits and experiences, which of the thirteen virtues do you imagine would be the most difficult for him to master? On a separate sheet of paper, name and discuss that virtue. Then, explain your opinion on this subject. Support your ideas with at least two details from the selection.

NAME ______ CLASS ______ DATE ______ SCORE ______

SELECTION TEST **Student Edition page 80** LITERARY RESPONSE AND ANALYSIS

Speech to the Virginia Convention Patrick Henry

COMPREHENSION *(40 points; 4 points each)*

On the line provided, write the letter of the *best* answer to each of the following items.

______ **1.** Henry points out a contradiction between British —

A claims of peaceful intent and their growing military presence in America
B settlement of America and maintenance of their government in Britain
C interest in the Colonies and neglect of the colonists' needs
D democratic tradition and the institution of royalty

______ **2.** Henry recounts several instances in which the colonists sought agreement and acceptable terms with the British. He reviews these incidents in order to persuade the delegates that —

F it is treason to seek peace with the British
G the colonists have behaved in a cowardly way
H the British army is weak and can be easily defeated
J all peaceful options have been tried and have failed

______ **3.** Henry states that the colonists have the advantage over the British because the colonists have —

A a more rigorously trained army
B a greater number of people
C moral correctness and conviction
D knowledge of the terrain

______ **4.** Henry advocates immediate action by the colonists because the —

F British army is preparing to march into Virginia
G king is too far away to order a quick response
H conflict has already begun and the colonists have no choice but to fight
J colonists will become apathetic or unconcerned if they don't act

______ **5.** The *main* purpose of Patrick Henry's speech is to —

A convince the delegates that he should be chosen to lead the revolution
B describe the history of British colonization in America
C seek revenge for personal injuries committed by the British king
D persuade his fellow delegates to fight against the British

______ **6.** One point that that Henry does *not* cite as a reason for immediate military action is the —

F buildup of British armed forces in the Colonies

G uselessness of further argument with the Crown

H past deeds of the British ministry

J boost that war would give the economy

______ **7.** With the words "God . . . will raise up friends to fight our battles for us," Henry is suggesting —

A other nations might come to the aid of the colonists

B the colonists need not fight; others will do it for them

C the colonists are dependent on an act of God for victory

D aid will appear mysteriously out of nowhere

______ **8.** Henry seeks to dissuade the delegates from resorting to argument because —

F the British might take recourse to military action

G after ten years all attempts at argument have been exhausted

H more can be achieved through reason than through hotheaded exchanges

J words can never settle anything

______ **9.** To whom is Henry addressing when he uses the word "sir"?

A The king of England

B The president of the convention

C An imaginary listener

D President Thomas Jefferson

______ **10.** When Henry uses the words "chains and slavery" near the end of his speech, he is referring to the —

F situation of African Americans in the Colonies

G price he does not want people to pay for peace

H possibility of enslaving captured British troops

J fact that the English seek to literally enslave the colonists

READING SKILLS: RECOGNIZING MODES OF PERSUASION *(10 points; 5 points each)*
On the line provided, write the letter of the *best* answer to each of the following items.

______ **11.** One mode of persuasion that Henry uses at the start of his speech is —

A fiction

B flattery

C oxymoron

D emotional appeal

______ **12.** Henry declares, "I know of no way of judging of the future but by the past. And judging by the past, I wish to know what there has been in the conduct of the British ministry for the last ten years, to justify those hopes with which gentlemen have been pleased to solace themselves . . ." In this passage, Henry is using —

F dramatic imagery to appeal to the emotions

G allusions to God

H figurative language

J logic to engage his listeners' attention

LITERARY FOCUS: PERSUASION *(10 points; 5 points each)*

On the line provided, write the letter of the *best* answer to each of the following items.

______ **13.** Which of the following excerpts is the *best* example of persuasion through an emotional appeal?

A "There is no retreat, but in submission and slavery! Our chains are forged!"

B "Sir, we have done everything that could be done . . ."

C "I ask gentlemen, sir, what means this martial array, if its purpose be not to force us to submission?"

D "it is natural to man to indulge in the illusions of hope."

______ **14.** Which of the following excerpts is the *best* example of persuasion through an appeal to reason?

F "Has Great Britain any enemy, in this quarter of the world, to call for all this accumulation of navies and armies?"

G "They are sent over to bind and rivet upon us those chains which the British ministry have been so long forging."

H "An appeal to arms and to the God of Hosts is all that is left us!"

J "The war is actually begun! The next gale that sweeps from the north will bring to our ears the clash of resounding arms!"

NAME ______ CLASS ______ DATE ______ SCORE ______

Vocabulary Development *(20 points; 4 points each)*

Match the definition on the left with the Vocabulary word on the right. On the line provided, write the letter of the Vocabulary word.

______ **15.** opponent	**a.** adversary
______ **16.** warlike	**b.** avert
______ **17.** to prevent; turn away	**c.** inevitable
______ **18.** sly; sneaky	**d.** insidious
______ **19.** not avoidable	**e.** martial

Constructed Response *(20 points)*

20. Imagine that you are a newspaper reporter covering Patrick Henry's speech. On a separate sheet of paper, write a lead paragraph for a news story about the speech. Describe the main point Henry makes, two ideas he uses to support it, and the delegates' different reactions to the speech.

NAME ______ CLASS ______ DATE ______ SCORE ______

SELECTION TEST **Student Edition page 87** LITERARY RESPONSE AND ANALYSIS

from The Crisis, No. 1 Thomas Paine

COMPREHENSION *(40 points; 4 points each)*

On the line provided, write the letter of the *best* answer to each of the following items.

______ **1.** Paine argues that the *best* way to defeat the British is for —

A each state to fight independently as the British approach

B the states to train their militias in guerrilla tactics

C the troops of all the states to join together in the fight

D the states to persuade the American Indians to join the revolution

______ **2.** Paine suggests that a state that surrenders its arms to the British would have to —

F face destruction by the British troops

G send its own ambassadors to Britain

H suffer the hostility of the other states

J create its own government

______ **3.** Paine contends that the Tories are —

A preparing to leave America to return to Britain

B committing treason by spying on their neighbors

C enjoying greater wealth than the average American

D possibly aiding and encouraging the British army

______ **4.** By comparing the British king to a thief and a housebreaker, Paine suggests that —

F British soldiers are launching sneak attacks against the colonists

G the king is in dire need of money for his treasury

H the British are trying to take what is not theirs

J Britain has robbed America of its natural resources

______ **5.** In his conclusion, Paine intends to inspire readers by —

A explaining why General Howe will succeed

B describing in detail the battle of Princeton

C recounting all of the wrongs the colonists have suffered

D pointing out the strengths of the Colonial army

______ **6.** Which of the following anecdotes does Paine use in the selection?

F General Gage's attack on Quebec

G The innkeeper who reads *Pilgrim's Progress*

H The Tory tavern keeper who makes a thoughtless statement in front of a child

J Washington's crossing of the Delaware River

_____ **7.** When Paine says, "though the flame of liberty may sometimes cease to shine, the coal can never expire," he is using analogy to suggest —

A liberty is a persistent, core virtue

B even if England vanquished the Colonies, liberty would live on

C coal is an essential Colonial resource

D the colonists' children cannot carry on the struggle

_____ **8.** Which of the following points is *not* a defense that Paine offers for the retreat of colonial troops in New Jersey?

F In time of war there is nothing ignoble in fear.

G They saved all their guns, ammunition, and stores.

H They retreated slowly to give more time for troops to be raised.

J They used two fierce actions to protect the retreat.

_____ **9.** Whom does Paine label a "sottish, stupid, stubborn, worthless, brutish man"?

A General Howe

B The king of England

C General Gage

D George Washington

_____ **10.** What kind of war does Paine describe as "murder"?

F Defensive war

G Offensive war

H Sneak attacks

J Revolution

READING SKILLS: RECOGNIZING MODES OF PERSUASION *(10 points; 5 points each)*
On the line provided, write the letter of the *best* answer to each of the following items.

_____ **11.** Which mode of persuasion is used in Paine's line "Tyranny, like hell, is not easily conquered"?

A Logic

B Personification

C Anecdote

D Analogy

____ **12.** Which of the following excerpts contains loaded words designed to create a negative impression?

F "I thank God that I fear not. I see no real cause for fear."

G "My own line of reasoning is to myself as straight and clear as a ray of light."

H "The summer soldier and the sunshine patriot will, in this crisis, shrink from the service of his country . . ."

J "A single successful battle next year will settle the whole."

LITERARY FOCUS: STYLE *(10 points; 5 points each)*

On the line provided, write the letter of the *best* answer to each of the following items.

____ **13.** When Paine writes, "The heart that feels not now, is dead: The blood of his children will curse his cowardice, who shrinks back at a time when a little might have saved the whole . . . ," he is using which of these elements of style?

A Dramatic imagery

B A family-based theme

C Allusions to emphasize his points

D Plain, ordinary language to present his thoughts

____ **14.** When Paine begins his speech with the phrase "These are the times that try men's souls," he is suggesting that —

F men, not women, will bear the brunt of the action to come

G colonists are living in a period that will force them to show their true characters

H it is likely that a period of boredom and inertia awaits the colonists

J those who fight in the revolution will be saved; others will be damned

VOCABULARY DEVELOPMENT *(20 points; 4 points each)*

Match the definition on the left with the Vocabulary word on the right. On the line provided, write the letter of the Vocabulary word.

____ **15.** well-articulated, persuasive speech — **a.** consolation

____ **16.** given up — **b.** eloquence

____ **17.** persistence — **c.** perseverance

____ **18.** comfort — **d.** relinquished

____ **19.** oppression — **e.** tyranny

CONSTRUCTED RESPONSE *(20 points)*

20. Read the following lines from Paine's essay.

> I call not upon a few, but upon all; not on *this* state or *that* state, but on *every* state; up and help us; lay your shoulders to the wheel; better have too much force than too little, when so great an object is at stake.

On a separate sheet of paper, describe how the quotation reflects one of Paine's themes. Explain what he means by "lay your shoulders to the wheel" and what the "object" is. Then, explain why his language is or is not effective.

NAME ______ CLASS ______ DATE ______ SCORE ______

SELECTION TEST **Student Edition page 97**

from The Autobiography: The Declaration of Independence

Thomas Jefferson

COMPREHENSION *(40 points; 4 points each)*

On the line provided, write the letter of the *best* answer to each of the following items.

______ **1.** Jefferson states that the king has established tyranny over the Colonies. To back up this statement, Jefferson —

A cites lies that are self-evident

B portrays the king as a pawn of greedy British nobles

C describes Britain's colonization of other nations

D lists several specific actions of the king

______ **2.** Jefferson emphasizes that the colonists —

F desire a form of self-government

G expect guidance from the British Parliament

H want to rebel against all formal rules and regulations

J need an army to restore law and order

______ **3.** The passage condemning Britain's involvement in the African slave trade was struck out of the original Declaration of Independence because —

A Jefferson disliked the way the passage was worded

B not all the states were involved in the slave trade

C two states wanted to continue importing slaves

D the passage would have been especially offensive to the British

______ **4.** Jefferson seems especially angered by the —

F outcome of the French and Indian War

G presence and actions of the British military in the Colonies

H king's ambassadors to the Colonies

J way in which the British handled the Boston Tea Party

______ **5.** Jefferson believes it is important to show how the original version of the Declaration of Independence was amended because —

A he wants people to know the framers' intentions—both what they included and what they did not

B he much preferred the earlier version

C he does not feel the document is complete without his notes

D at the time it was uncertain which version would be adopted

______ **6.** In the opening paragraphs, whom does Thomas Jefferson refer to as "pusillanimous"?

F George Washington

G People who seek to remain friends with England

H Anyone who will not sign the Declaration

J Slave owners

______ **7.** In the Declaration of Independence, the words "governments long established should not be changed for light and transient causes" and their supporting passages suggest that —

A a little revolution now and then is a good thing

B people have no right to overthrow a government

C the overthrow of a government is only justified by serious causes

D people are inherently fickle

______ **8.** According to the Declaration of Independence, colonists are at odds with their current government because —

F its laws are English, but they feel they are Americans

G they do not have the rights they would have in England

H the whole notion of a king is upsetting to them

J it is too liberal for their taste

______ **9.** According to the way Jefferson has edited this draft of the Declaration of Independence, the phrase "with a firm reliance on the protection of divine providence" in the second to last paragraph was —

A added in the final version

B written in the margin in the final version

C cut from the final version

D added to the final version on a separate sheet

______ **10.** What authority does the United States of America in General Congress cite in its Declaration of Independence?

F God alone

G The people under God

H President George Washington

J The House of Burgesses

READING SKILLS: ANALYZING MAIN IDEAS *(10 points; 5 points each)*
On the line provided, write the letter of the *best* answer to each of the following items.

______ **11.** Which of the following statements *best* summarizes Jefferson's main idea?

- **A** Responsibility should be avoided.
- **B** Freedom is right.
- **C** Chaos is always caused by liberty.
- **D** Everyone deserves a free press and freedom of religion.

______ **12.** Jefferson supports one of his main themes by —

- **F** urging the colonists to take up arms against the British army
- **G** making a case against slavery
- **H** explaining the reasons for taking action
- **J** listing everything that the Colonies have done to provoke the British

LITERARY FOCUS: PARALLELISM *(10 points; 5 points each)*
On the line provided, write the letter of the *best* answer to each of the following items.

______ **13.** Which of the following lines is the *best* example of **parallelism**?

- **A** "A prince whose character is thus marked by every act which may define a tyrant is unfit to be the ruler of a free people."
- **B** ". . . we mutually pledge to each other our lives, our fortunes, and our sacred honor."
- **C** "Prudence, indeed, will dictate that governments long established should not be changed for light and transient causes. . . ."
- **D** "We hold these truths to be self-evident: that all men are created equal. . . ."

______ **14.** Which of the following statements is *not* true of the parallel structures used by Jefferson?

- **F** Similar grammatical structures are used to introduce clauses.
- **G** Identical words or phrases are repeated at the beginning of several paragraphs.
- **H** The clauses, phrases, or sentences often have similar rhythms.
- **J** Clauses and phrases are always linked by conjunctions.

VOCABULARY DEVELOPMENT *(20 points; 4 points each)*

Match the definition on the left with the Vocabulary word on the right. On the line provided, write the letter of the Vocabulary word.

______ **15.** gave up power

______ **16.** seizure of property by authority

______ **17.** temporary; passing

______ **18.** forces

______ **19.** nobility of spirit

a. abdicated

b. confiscation

c. constrains

d. magnanimity

e. transient

CONSTRUCTED RESPONSE *(20 points)*

20. The Continental Congress first approached John Adams to write the Declaration of Independence. Adams declined and recommended Thomas Jefferson because Jefferson was the best writer among all the delegates. On a separate sheet of paper, explain what you think Adams admired in Jefferson's style. Describe at least two ways in which the Declaration displays the hallmarks of good writing.

NAME ______________________ CLASS ______________ DATE __________ SCORE __________

SELECTION TEST **Student Edition pages 107, 109, 110** LITERARY RESPONSE AND ANALYSIS

from The Iroquois Constitution Dekanawida
Letter to John Adams Abigail Adams
from Declaration of Sentiments Elizabeth Cady Stanton

COMPREHENSION *(60 points; 6 points each)*

On the line provided, write the letter of the *best* answer to each of the following items.

______ **1.** In Dekanawida's statement, the Tree of Great Peace is —

A just an actual tree

B only a symbol

C both an actual tree and a symbol for other things

D neither actual nor symbolic

______ **2.** In the Iroquois constitution, who has the ability to impeach chiefs?

F Dekanawida alone

G the Union Lords only

H The Onondaga Nation as a whole

J The women of the Confederacy

______ **3.** When Dekanawida says, "The Lords of the Confederacy of the Five Nations shall be mentors of the people for all time," he is declaring that the Lords will —

A guide the people of the Five Nations, whom they serve

B rule like kings over the people of the Five Nations

C settle disputes between people

D have eternal life

______ **4.** Which of the following seems to be the *most* important issue to Dekanawida?

F Ensuring economic stability

G Achieving and maintaining peace

H Securing absolute power for the Confederate Council

J Entertaining a wide audience

______ **5.** Abigail Adams suggests that the inclination of all men is to —

A build new laws

B be generous and favorable

C become tyrants

D remember the rights of ladies

NAME ____________ CLASS ____________ DATE ____________ SCORE ____________

______ **6.** Adams suggests that the key to success and happiness for a man is to —

F trade the title of Master for the title of Friend

G treat women with cruelty and indignity

H follow every word of her advice

J give up possessions

______ **7.** Which of the following statements *best* summarizes the main idea of Adams's letter?

A Women deserve the rights that are outlined in the Bible.

B Her husband should do as she says, or she will be furious.

C Women will not be bound by laws they did not make.

D Women should be favored by the law because they are the weaker sex.

______ **8.** What does Stanton ultimately cite as a support of the equal rights of women?

F The Bible

G Nature and God

H The natural superiority of women

J The Declaration of Independence

______ **9.** For what reason does Stanton suggest women are taxed unfairly?

A They pay money to the state like men do but do not get the same rights.

B Men are not taxed as heavily as women.

C Women earn less and should thus pay less tax on their income.

D Women must raise children and run the home, and thus, should not be taxed.

______ **10.** Stanton points out that two "degraded" groups of men have more rights than women. Which groups are these?

F Criminals and saloon keepers

G Soldiers and sailors

H Actors and comics

J Foreigners and natives

LITERARY FOCUS: POLITICAL POINTS OF VIEW *(20 points; 4 points each)*

On the line provided, write the letter of the *best* answer to each of the following items.

______ **11.** Which element of the Iroquois Constitution is *least* like the Constitution of the United States?

A A system of checks and balances

B Political and religious freedom

C Political power for women

D The goal of protecting life, property, and liberty

______ **12.** Jefferson's argument against the king of England parallels Stanton's against men. However, Stanton makes one complaint that Jefferson does not. She argues that —

F women have no voice in elected government

G women are taxed unfairly

H men do not allow women into the ministry

J men have deprived women of their natural rights

______ **13.** What does Stanton's parallel construction to the Declaration of Independence *primarily* imply about women's rights?

A They are equal to those of men and are already guaranteed by United States' law.

B Jefferson should have included a passage dealing with the rights of women.

C Women, not men, should hold executive power.

D The Declaration of Independence is a document condemning women, not tyranny.

______ **14.** What does Stanton say constitutes the "history of mankind"?

F A series of bloody military contests

G The building and dismantling of governments

H Repeated wrongs towards women

J Slow but steady progress towards rights for all

______ **15.** What do both Stanton and Abigail Adams resent most about current laws?

A Women had no voice in their creation.

B The laws overtax women.

C The laws were made by men.

D The laws are not enforced.

CONSTRUCTED RESPONSE *(20 points)*

16. Ask yourself: Have things changed in America since Stanton penned her document? Which of Stanton's grievances do you think have been addressed? which have not? Does inequality still exist between the sexes in this country? On a separate sheet of paper, write your response, listing any specific issues Stanton cited that are still a problem today.

Encounters and Foundations to 1800

This test asks you to use the skills and strategies you have learned in this collection. Read this passage from "What Is an American?," and answer the questions that follow.

FROM "What Is an American?" Letters from an American Farmer
by Michel-Guillaume Jean de Crèvecoeur

I wish I could be acquainted with the feelings and thoughts which must agitate the heart and present themselves to the mind of an enlightened Englishman when he first lands on this continent. He must greatly rejoice that he lived at a time to see this fair country discovered and settled; he must necessarily feel a share of national pride when he views the chain of settlements which embellishes these extended shores. When he says to himself, this is the work of my countrymen, who, when convulsed by factions, afflicted by a variety of miseries and wants, restless and impatient, took refuge here. They brought along with them their national genius, to which they principally owe what liberty they enjoy and what substance they possess. Here he sees the industry of his native country displayed in a new manner, and traces in their works the embryos of all the arts, sciences, and ingenuity which flourish in Europe. Here he beholds fair cities, substantial villages, extensive fields, an immense country filled with decent houses, good roads, orchards, meadows, and bridges, where a hundred years ago all was wild, woody, and uncultivated!

What a train of pleasing ideas this fair spectacle must suggest! It is a prospect which must inspire a good citizen with the most heartfelt pleasure. The difficulty consists in the manner of viewing so extensive a scene. He is arrived on a new continent; a modern society offers itself to his contemplation, different from what he had hitherto seen. It is not composed, as in Europe, of great lords who possess everything, and of a herd of people who have nothing. Here are no aristocratical families, no courts, no kings, no bishops, no ecclesiastical dominion, no invisible power giving to a few a very visible one, no great manufacturers employing thousands, no great refinements of luxury. The rich and the poor are not so far removed from each other as they are in Europe.

Some few towns excepted, we are all tillers of the earth, from Nova Scotia to West Florida. We are a people of cultivators, scattered over an immense territory, communicating with each other by means of good roads and navigable rivers, united by the silken bands of mild government, all respecting the laws without dreading their power, because they are equitable. We are all animated with the spirit of industry, which is unfettered and unrestrained, because each person works for himself. If he travels through or rural districts, he views not the hostile castle and the haughty mansion, contrasted with the clay-built hut and miserable cabin, where cattle and men help to keep each other warm, and dwell in meanness, smoke, and indigence. A pleasing uniformity of decent competence appears throughout our habitations. The meanest of our log houses is a dry and comfortable habitation.

Lawyer or merchant are the fairest titles our towns afford; that of a farmer is the only appellation of the rural inhabitants of our country. It must take some time before he can reconcile himself to our dictionary, which is but short in words of

NAME ______ CLASS ______ DATE ______ SCORE ______

dignity and names of honor. There, on a Sunday, he sees a congregation of respectable farmers and their wives, all clad in neat homespun, well mounted, or riding their own humble wagons. There is not among them an esquire, saving the unlettered magistrate. There he sees a parson as simple as his flock, a farmer who does not riot on the labor of others. We have no princes for whom we toil, starve, and bleed; we are the most perfect society now existing in the world. Here man is free as he ought to be; nor is this pleasing equality so transitory as many others are. Many ages will not see the shores of our great lakes replenished with inland nations, nor the unknown bounds of North America entirely peopled. Who can tell how far it extends? Who can tell the millions of men whom it will feed and contain? For no European foot has as yet traveled half the extent of this mighty continent!

Vocabulary Skills *(25 points; 5 points each)*

On the line provided, write the letter of the *best* answer to each of the following items.

______ **1.** People who are "convulsed by factions" are —

- **A** violently agitated
- **B** denied upward mobility
- **C** given extra responsibility
- **D** ignored as troublemakers

______ **2.** Equitable laws may be considered —

- **F** misleading
- **G** heartfelt
- **H** just and impartial
- **J** cruel

______ **3.** An unfettered spirit of industry is —

- **A** devious
- **B** not restricted
- **C** imaginary
- **D** unworthy of serious attention

______ **4.** A person's appellation is his or her —

- **F** reputation
- **G** political organizations
- **H** name or title
- **J** equipment or gear

______ **5.** Aristocratical families are —

- **A** of an elite, land-owning class
- **B** skilled painters and sculptors
- **C** the original Americans
- **D** Puritans

COMPREHENSION *(25 points; 5 points each)*

On the line provided, write the letter of the *best* answer to each of the following items.

______ **6.** Crèvecoeur believes an English person arriving in North America would probably feel —

F envy

G pride

H hostility

J anger

______ **7.** The "national genius" that Crèvecoeur believes the Americans inherited from the British lies *mainly* in Americans' —

A artistic taste

B literary ability

C industriousness

D sense of humor

______ **8.** According to Crèvecoeur, *most* people in America during this period —

F were wealthy landowners

G experienced abject poverty

H traveled constantly

J lived modestly and comfortably

______ **9.** Crèvecoeur describes the North American continent *mainly* as —

A beautiful and inspiring

B vast and unexplored

C heavily populated

D dangerous

______ **10.** According to Crèvecoeur, an important difference between Europe and North America is that the latter lacks —

F humble farmers

G aristocratic families

H lawyers or merchants

J religious leaders

Reading Skills and Strategies

Understanding Cultural Characteristics *(5 points)*
On the line provided, write the letter of the *best* answer to the following item.

______ **11.** Crèvecoeur admires all of the following qualities about Americans *except* —

A the rich and the poor are far removed from one another

B they respect the laws without dreading the power of government

C their industry is unrestricted

D they are industrious

Making Inferences About Main Ideas *(15 points)*
On the line provided, write the letter of the *best* answer to the following item.

______ **12.** From the following statements, choose the one you think *best* states the implicit and explicit assumptions that Crèvecoeur makes about America in this passage. On a separate sheet of paper, indicate the letter of the answer you choose, and briefly defend your choice with supporting passages from the essay.

F North America is a land of equality.

G North America is a land of danger.

H North America is a land of great manufacturers.

J North America is a land of luxury.

Analyzing Tone *(10 points)*

13. A writer's tone may be either subjective or objective. Decide which of these two words best describes the tone of "What Is an American?" On a separate sheet of paper, state whether the writer's tone is objective or subjective. Then, list three phrases from the text that indicate this tone and explain briefly why each phrase indicates a subjective or objective tone.

LITERARY FOCUS: CONSTRUCTED RESPONSE *(20 points)*

Analyzing Style: Emotional Appeal and Parallelism

14. Crèvecoeur writes in a style very different from the plain style of the Puritans. The Puritans used everyday language and avoided rich imagery and elaborate figures of speech. This selection uses language that is more literary and ornamental, employing both parallelism and rhetorical appeals to the readers' emotions. On the chart below, list examples found in the excerpt of parallelism on one side, and examples of emotional appeals on the other. List at least two examples of each form of rhetoric.

Rhetoric in "What Is an American?"

Parallelism	Emotional Appeal

NAME ______ CLASS ______ DATE ______ SCORE ______

COLLECTION 2 DIAGNOSTIC TEST

LITERATURE
INFORMATIONAL TEXT
VOCABULARY

American Romanticism: 1800–1860

On the line provided, write the letter of the *best* answer to each of the following items. *(100 points; 10 points each)*

______ **1.** Writers use **mood** to —

A convey an overall feeling in a literary work

B establish an external conflict

C create believable characters

D give a narrator a distinct personality

______ **2.** A metrical unit in a line of poetry is called a —

F rhyme

G foot

H stressed syllable

J refrain

______ **3.** Which of the following sentences contains a **figure of speech**?

A Advances in technology have transformed the lives of ordinary citizens.

B All night long we could hear the waves crashing against the rocky shore.

C My aunt's house was like a museum filled with precious objects from the past.

D The smell of freshly baked cookies made me hungry.

______ **4.** A literary work in which characters, settings, and events stand for abstract ideas is a(n) —

F satire

G tragedy

H epic

J allegory

______ **5.** The **symbolic meaning** of a story —

A is a summary of factual details

B goes beyond the story's literal meaning

C is its universal theme

D describes the reader's reactions to events in the story

______ **6.** What is **alliteration**?

F A pause or break in a line of a poem

G The repetition of the same consonant sounds in words that are close together

H Vowel sounds that are repeated in a line of poetry

J Words whose sounds echo their sense

______ **7.** When you make a **generalization** about a writer's beliefs, you —

A critique the writer's ideas by presenting opposing arguments

B draw a conclusion based on information in a text

C elaborate on the writer's ideas using your personal experiences

D compare the writer's views with established opinion

______ **8.** **Emotional appeals** are a persuasive technique consisting of —

F attacks on opponents

G exaggerated claims

H loaded language and anecdotes

J questions directed to the reader

______ **9.** A **word analogy** is a —

A synonym for a word

B clue to a word's meaning

C word's antonym

D type of comparison

______ **10.** Which of the following statements about **suffixes** is *false*?

F The definition of *suffix* is "a word part that comes from Greek."

G Suffixes can change the tense of a base word.

H Suffixes are word parts that are attached to the end of a base word.

J Suffixes are attached to a base word to create a new word.

NAME ______ CLASS ______ DATE ______ SCORE ______

LITERARY PERIOD INTRODUCTION TEST **Student Edition page 138**

American Romanticism: 1800–1860

COMPREHENSION *(100 points; 10 points each)*

On the line provided, write the letter of the *best* answer to each of the following items.

______ **1.** Romanticism celebrated all of the following *except* —

A the future growth of industry

B feeling over reason

C imagination over science

D nature over civilization

______ **2.** A group of Romantics called the Transcendentalists believed that —

F America was destined to conquer the world

G everything in the physical world is a reflection of the Divine Soul

H true art could only be created by Americans on American soil

J art was the best way to bring about social change

______ **3.** The movement that furthered American education, self-improvement, and cultural development was called —

A rationalism

B the Fireside Poetic movement

C Romanticism

D the lyceum movement

______ **4.** Which of the following is an opinion held by the American Romantic writers?

F Cities are centers of corruption and ugliness.

G European literature has no traditions worth considering.

H Westward expansion is dangerous.

J Ordinary readers do not appreciate Romantic ideals.

______ **5.** American Romantic writers rejected rationalism because they believed that —

A logical thought is not possible

B scientific thinking hadn't been fully developed

C the rationalist tradition had not produced any worthwhile writers

D intuition and imagination yield greater truths

______ **6.** The writings of James Fenimore Cooper explored —

F the subconscious

G frontier communities and Native Americans

H the danger and evil of urban America

J intuition

______ **7.** Cooper's best-known character, Natty Bumppo, represents —

A a worldly, sophisticated hero

B the American rationalist hero

C the American Romantic hero

D a person uncomfortable in nature

______ **8.** The American Romantic poets —

F used typically English themes and forms

G created a uniquely "American" voice

H emphasized sophisticated real-life figures

J valued logic over emotion

______ **9.** As literary models, American Romantic poets used —

A ideas drawn from the novels of the American Romantics

B poetic traditions established by European Romantics

C the rhythms and rhymes of folk songs

D experimental forms created by younger poets

______ **10.** The Dark Romantics explored —

F the reasons for the decay of European society and growth of American society

G the civilization of the Goths

H the psychological effects of sin and guilt as well as the conflict between good and evil

J lessons to be drawn from traditional religions

The Devil and Tom Walker Washington Irving

COMPREHENSION *(40 points; 4 points each)*

On the line provided, write the letter of the *best* answer to each of the following items.

______ **1.** What is the story's setting?

A A Midwestern frontier pine forest, circa 1608

B The New Orleans, Louisiana, riverfront, circa 1680

C A forest near Boston, Massachusetts, circa 1727

D A pond deep in the Maine forest, circa 1850

______ **2.** Tom Walker might *best* be described as —

F having been beaten down by bad luck

G basically kind but misunderstood

H crafty but very lazy

J stingy and cruel but courageous

______ **3.** Tom Walker's wife is *best* described as —

A very generous and much loved by her neighbors

B kind toward her husband, but cruel to others

C yearning for companionship

D a fierce shrew, always nagging and yelling

______ **4.** In this story the woods are used to symbolize —

F evil

G goodness

H isolation

J greed

______ **5.** Which of the following phrases is an example of Irving's use of humor?

A "Tom consoled himself for the loss of his property, with the loss of his wife, for he was a man of fortitude."

B "He knows how to play his cards when pretty sure of his game."

C "He insisted that the money found through his means should be employed in his service."

D " 'You shall extort bonds, foreclose mortgages, drive the merchants to bankruptcy—.' "

______ **6.** What does Irving use to symbolize hypocrisy and hidden evil?

F The devil's deal with Tom

G Mrs. Walker's heart and liver, wrapped in the checked apron

H The flourishing trees that are rotten to the core

J The Walkers' silver teapots and spoons

______ **7.** What enabled you to predict that the figure that appears to Tom in the forest is the devil?

A He appears when Tom kicks the skull.

B He has large red eyes.

C He has a hoarse, growling voice.

D Tom is instantly frightened.

______ **8.** Tom's wife decides to go into the forest because she —

F wants to escape from Tom's unkindness

G decides to make her own deal with the devil

H gets lost on her way to the market

J wants to pick some herbs and wild mushrooms for their meager meal

______ **9.** How does Tom die?

A The people he has cheated rise up against him.

B He falls off his horse and gets trampled.

C The devil is tricked by his own words.

D He is killed by Native Americans.

______ **10.** What happens to Tom Walker's money at the end of the story?

F It is given to the townspeople.

G The townspeople seize it.

H It goes to Mrs. Walker.

J It turns into cinders and ashes.

LITERARY FOCUS: MOOD *(15 points; 5 points each)*

On the line provided, write the letter of the *best* answer to each of the following items.

______ **11.** What feeling about the setting does Irving want to arouse?

A fear

B optimism

C anger

D hope

______ **12.** Which item *best* contributes to the story's mood?

F "The swamp was thickly grown with great gloomy pines and hemlocks . . . which made it dark at noonday. . ."

G ". . . stepping from tuft to tuft of rushes and roots . . ."

H "At length he arrived at a firm piece of ground, which ran like a peninsula into the deep bosom of the swamp."

J "Nothing remained of the old Indian fort but a few embankments, gradually sinking to the level of the surrounding earth."

______ **13.** "The Devil and Tom Walker" is based on the archetype of a person who —

A is unhappy in marriage

B lives in New England

C sells his soul to the devil

D hunts for treasure

READING SKILLS: MAKING PREDICTIONS *(5 points)*

On the line provided, write the letter of the *best* answer to the following item.

______ **14.** Like Tom Walker, no doubt you weren't surprised by the appearance of the devil. You were prepared because you knew that Tom —

F had read or heard about other people meeting with the devil

G had met the devil before

H is the kind of man who is not surprised by anything

J took the shortcut in order to meet the devil

NAME ______ CLASS ______ DATE ______ SCORE ______

VOCABULARY DEVELOPMENT *(20 points; 4 points each)*

Match each Vocabulary word on the left with its definition on the right. On the line provided, write the letter of the definition.

______ **15.** prevalent

______ **16.** stagnant

______ **17.** precarious

______ **18.** impregnable

______ **19.** melancholy

a. sad; gloomy

b. incapable of being captured or entered by force

c. widely existing

d. uncertain

e. not flowing or moving

CONSTRUCTED RESPONSE *(20 points)*

20. Explain the story's mood. How does Irving create humor in a story in which there are few happy events? On a separate sheet of paper, write a paragraph that explains your answer. Support your ideas with details from the selection.

NAME ______ CLASS ______ DATE ______ SCORE ______

Thanatopsis William Cullen Bryant

COMPREHENSION *(60 points; 6 points each)*

On the line provided, write the letter of the *best* answer to each of the following items.

______ **1.** In the beginning of the poem, Nature speaks to —

A the dead

B infants and old people

C wild animals in the forest

D the person who thinks about Nature

______ **2.** According to the poem, what should people do when they feel afraid of death?

F Keep very busy and think about life.

G Spend plenty of time with their friends and family.

H Go into Nature and listen to what Nature teaches.

J Read poetry about Nature outdoors under the sky.

______ **3.** In this poem, Nature urges the poet to find comfort in the —

A fact that he is young and death is far off

B promise of an afterlife

C knowledge that death joins us with all other people

D idea that he will be famous after he dies

______ **4.** What does the poet mean in the following quotation?

"The oak / Shall send his roots abroad, and pierce thy mold."

F Oak trees will send roots through your corpse.

G Oak trees will unite you with people in other countries.

H Nature, represented by an oak tree, will change you.

J Nature, represented by an oak tree, will preserve your corpse.

______ **5.** According to the last stanza, how should people regard death?

A Calmly, with trust

B Angrily, as though being betrayed by Nature

C Fiercely, like a slave being forced to do something against his or her will

D Nicely, with good manners

______ **6.** According to the poet, all humans come from —

F hidden quarries

G the sky

H Nature

J phantoms

______ **7.** Which image *most* strongly appeals to the sense of touch?

A "she speaks / A various language . . ."

B "and a smile / And eloquence of beauty . . ."

C "The all-beholding sun shall see no more . . ."

D "nor yet in the cold ground . . ."

______ **8.** Which of the following quotations from "Thanatopsis" *could* be considered a consolation?

F "Yet a few days, and thee / The all-beholding sun shall see no more . . ."

G "sad images / Of the stern agony, and shroud, and pall . . ."

H "Yet not to thine eternal resting place / Shalt thou retire alone . . ."

J "And, lost each human trace, surrendering up / Thine individual being, shalt thou go . . ."

______ **9.** Which statement *best* summarizes the cycle described in this poem?

A The dead are replaced by the living, who die in turn.

B The natural world is destructive.

C We move from cheerfulness to sorrow and back again.

D Nature speaks to us gently, then harshly.

______ **10.** "Thanatopsis" is a good example of Romantic poetry because —

F the poem is written in unrhymed lines and focuses on the supernatural

G the poem is concerned with thoughts of dying

H nature arouses emotions and insights in the speaker

J the poet applies logic and rational thinking to human concerns about life and death

LITERARY FOCUS: THEME *(15 points; 5 points each)*
On the line provided, write the letter of the *best* answer to each of the following items.

______ **11.** In the first half of the poem, death is described as —

A a great gift

B a neutral event

C a destructive force

D something welcome

______ **12.** In the second half of the poem, death is described as a(n) —

F artificial process that lacks reality

G natural process for everyone who ever lived

H brutal wrenching from loved ones

J vicious betrayal of our expectations

______ **13.** The theme of "Thanatopsis" strongly suggests that human beings are —

A the highest form of living things

B an ongoing part of the earth itself

C doomed to live in dread of death

D not capable of improving their lives

READING SKILLS: READING INVERTED SENTENCES *(5 points)*

On the line provided, write the letter of the *best* answer to the following item.

______ **14.** Which of the following quotations is the *best* example of an inverted sentence?

F "The oak / Shall send his roots abroad . . ."

G "the dead reign there alone . . ."

H "All that breathe / Will share thy destiny . . ."

J "and thee / The all-beholding sun shall see no more . . ."

CONSTRUCTED RESPONSE *(20 points)*

15. In "Thanatopsis," Bryant expresses his views on both the process of life and the nature of individual lives. On a separate sheet of paper, write a paragraph describing Bryant's views on individual lives. Support your ideas with details from the poem.

NAME ______ CLASS ______ DATE ______ SCORE ______

SELECTION TEST **Student Edition pages 172, 174** LITERARY RESPONSE AND ANALYSIS

The Tide Rises, the Tide Falls Henry Wadsworth Longfellow
The Cross of Snow Henry Wadsworth Longfellow

COMPREHENSION *(60 points; 6 points each)*

On the line provided, write the letter of the *best* answer to each of the following items.

______ **1.** You can infer from details in "The Tide Rises, the Tide Falls" that the traveler —

A dies

B drowns

C disappears

D is Longfellow

______ **2.** In "The Tide Rises, the Tide Falls," the rising and falling of the tide suggests —

F waves of despair

G the end of summer

H the passage of time

J the joy of life

______ **3.** The repeated last line in "The Tide Rises, the Tide Falls" is intended to suggest the —

A traveler's footsteps

B unceasing motion of the tides

C great difficulty of travel in the 19th century

D dawn following each night

______ **4.** You can infer from "The Tide Rises, the Tide Falls" that Longfellow —

F accepts the fact that life goes on after someone dies

G believes that people should fight against death

H believes that he will live forever through his poetry

J was very afraid of death

______ **5.** The theme of "The Tide Rises, the Tide Falls" is *best* stated as —

A humans have little control over their fate

B human life is long and part of an endless cycle

C the sea is dangerous yet sustains human life and hope

D the ocean goes on, but human life is limited

_____ **6.** The mood of "The Cross of Snow" is *best* described as —

F joyful

G eerie

H grieving

J romantic

_____ **7.** In "The Cross of Snow," the images of a halo, fire, and sunlight contrast with the —

A image of a snowy, sun-capped mountain

B face of the speaker's dead wife

C image of a sunless mountain ravine

D memory of a happy marriage

_____ **8.** In "The Cross of Snow," the cross the speaker wears is —

F guilt about the accident that killed his wife

G an emotional pain

H a medal that his wife gave him

J a memory of a trip he took with his family

_____ **9.** Readers can conclude that the female subject of "The Cross of Snow" is —

A remembered fondly and deeply missed by the speaker

B a lonely person who lives isolated from society

C one of the speaker's few childhood friends

D very spiritual and in touch with the ways of nature

_____ **10.** What is surprising about the image of the cross in "The Cross of Snow" is that it —

F gets dirty with time

G is very large

H appears and disappears with the seasons

J lasts through time

LITERARY FOCUS: METER AND SONNET *(20 points; 5 points each)*

On the line provided, write the letter of the *best* answer to each of the following items.

______ **11.** The pattern of stressed and unstressed syllables in poetry is called —

A meter

B scanning a poem

C a foot

D an iamb

______ **12.** Longfellow used an iambic meter in "The Tide Rises, the Tide Falls" to —

F capture the ebbing and rising tide

G create a sing-song effect

H avoid a predictable rhythm

J express his feelings about death

______ **13.** "The Cross of Snow" is a type of poem called —

A a spondee

B the Shakespearean sonnet

C free verse

D the Italian sonnet

______ **14.** Which of the following statements is *not* true regarding this line from "The Tide Rises, the Tide Falls"?

"The little waves, with their soft, white hands . . ."

F The line is in strict iambic meter.

G The line has end rhyme with one line in the same stanza.

H The line shows personification.

J The line repeats initial consonant sounds.

Constructed Response *(20 points)*

15. Choose what you believe is the strongest response to the following item. Note that there is more than one possible answer. Then, on a separate sheet of paper, briefly defend your answer. Use at least one example from each poem to support your ideas.

Longfellow's imagery serves the following purpose:

A To balance the positive aspects of the human condition with the negative ones

B To express the speaker's reactions to personal experiences

C To call attention to the inevitable sadness of life

D To point out what can be learned from studying nature

from Nature Ralph Waldo Emerson

COMPREHENSION *(40 points; 4 points each)*

On the line provided, write the letter of the *best* answer to each of the following items.

______ **1.** According to *Nature*, where should a person go to be alone?

A To his chamber, his private room in the house

B To the city's streets

C To a house of worship

D Outside to look at the stars

______ **2.** What does Emerson mean by "nature"?

F People who have not been corrupted or disappointed

G The impressions we get from different natural objects

H Outer space

J Flowers, animals, and mountains

______ **3.** The third paragraph of the excerpt ends with this sentence: "This is the best part of these men's farms, yet to this their warranty deeds give no title." In the context of the paragraph, this sentence means —

A the most valuable quality of the land is something that cannot be owned

B the deeds to the majority of the farms do not list the owners' names

C the work the farmers perform does not entitle them to own the land

D poets should be given all the land because only they can understand its worth

______ **4.** According to Emerson, the person who can truly see nature is like a child because he or she —

F is free from the burden of thought

G perceives nature as being a kind of toy

H sees with the heart as well as the eye

J no longer needs to rely on either reason or faith

______ **5.** When Emerson crosses the "bare common," he is —

A sad at considering his mortality

B completely happy

C upset when he realizes his unimportance

D lonely

______ **6.** In the woods, Emerson finds —

F abundant fish and game

G trees one can talk to

H a peaceful place to write

J love and the joy of youth

______ **7.** Emerson describes himself as a "transparent eyeball" because he —

A feels that he sees everything

B is young again and totally virtuous

C regrets his past mistakes and petty cruel acts

D feels complete communion with nature

______ **8.** According to Emerson, nature wears the colors of —

F autumn

G man's spirit

H childhood

J vegetables

______ **9.** Which of the following statements *best* describes Emerson's attitude toward society?

A He believes that society always has humanity's best interests at heart.

B He thinks that societies are becoming increasingly civilized.

C He values nature highly and has some contempt for society.

D He hopes that nature will someday destroy all societies.

______ **10.** Emerson's purpose in this essay is to —

F express his disappointment in the society of his time

G explain and analyze how nature works

H describe a profound way of seeing nature

J argue that everyone should leave the cities and live in nature

LITERARY FOCUS: IMAGERY *(15 points; 5 points each)*
On the line provided, write the letter of the *best* answer to each of the following items.

______ **11.** **Imagery** can be described as —

A word pictures

B sensory naturalism

C words that have a pleasing sound

D the tone of a literary work

_____ **12.** Which of the following quotations from the selection does *not* contain an example of imagery?

F "The stars awaken a certain reverence, because though always present, they are always inaccessible. . . ."

G "The sun illuminates only the eye of the man, but shines into the eye and the heart of the child."

H "Standing on the bare ground—my head bathed by the blithe air, and uplifted into infinite space—all mean egotism vanishes."

J "the same scene which yesterday breathed perfume and glittered as for the frolic of the nymphs . . ."

_____ **13.** Emerson says, "For, nature is not always tricked in holiday attire, but the same scene which yesterday breathed perfume and glittered as for the frolic of the nymphs, is overspread with melancholy today." To what senses does this imagery appeal?

A touch and taste

B sight and taste

C sight and smell

D smell and sound

Reading Skills: Monitoring Your Reading *(5 points)*

On the line provided, write the letter of the *best* answer to the following item.

_____ **14.** Which item contains the *best* paraphrase of the following statement?

"The sun illuminates only the eye of the man, but shines into the eye and the heart of the child."

F The sun favors children over adults.

G Adults have developed an immunity to the rays of the sun.

H Children are better able to see the sun than adults are.

J Adults can see nature, but they don't truly appreciate it the way children do.

NAME ______ CLASS ______ DATE ______ SCORE ______

VOCABULARY DEVELOPMENT *(20 points; 4 points each)*

Complete each analogy with a Vocabulary word from below. Use each Vocabulary word only once.

admonishing **integrate** **blithe** **perennial** **occult**

15. CONSOLIDATE : CONCENTRATE :: UNIFY : ______

16. CHEERFUL : LIVELY :: ELATED : ______

17. PRAISING : EXHORTING :: COMMENDING : ______

18. INTERRUPTS : CONSTANT :: DISCONTINUES : ______

19. MANIFEST : COVERT :: APPARENT : ______

CONSTRUCTED RESPONSE *(20 points)*

20. On a separate sheet of paper, write a paragraph explaining how Emerson uses imagery in *Nature* to explore his ideas about society and nature. Support your ideas with details from the selection.

from Self-Reliance Ralph Waldo Emerson

COMPREHENSION *(40 points; 4 points each)*

On the line provided, write the letter of the *best* answer to each of the following items.

______ **1.** What is the point of the comparison Emerson makes between the kernel of corn and human effort?

- **A** You must work hard to grow corn just as you must work hard to achieve your potential.
- **B** People cannot survive without food, so we must all work very hard.
- **C** As corn grows slowly, so it takes a long time for people to realize their potential.
- **D** A kernel of corn is small and hard to see. In a similar way, our potential is often hidden and hard to see.

______ **2.** According to Emerson, how do we feel after we have worked hard for a goal?

- **F** Angry and cheated
- **G** Relieved and happy
- **H** Annoyed and tired
- **J** Despairing and gloomy

______ **3.** What truth must we all accept?

- **A** We all need friends.
- **B** We must stay childlike to appreciate the world.
- **C** We must accept the place that providence has found for us.
- **D** It is acceptable to be a coward.

______ **4.** What is Emerson's opinion of society?

- **F** Society helps people achieve their potential.
- **G** We must accept society's rules.
- **H** Society is all that stands between us and the forces of chaos.
- **J** Society conspires to deny people their freedom.

______ **5.** Emerson states that the most sacred part of a person is —

- **A** the work that they accomplish
- **B** their courage to be a nonconformist
- **C** the shadow that they cast on the world
- **D** the integrity of their individual mind

______ **6.** What does Emerson call "the hobgoblin of little minds"?

- **F** Consistency
- **G** Society
- **H** Cowardice
- **J** Conspiracy

______ **7.** According to Emerson, what makes someone a fully realized person?

- **A** Fitting in with others
- **B** Achieving their potential
- **C** Following their own conscience
- **D** Staying pure and wise in spirit

______ **8.** Emerson says we are "ashamed of that divine idea which each of us represents." Which of the following items *best* describes what he means by "that divine idea"?

- **F** An image of the world
- **G** God
- **H** Each person's unique character, as conceived by God
- **J** A wonderful and exciting plan of action

______ **9.** The tone of Emerson's essay is *best* described as —

- **A** neutral
- **B** uplifting
- **C** despairing
- **D** gloomy

______ **10.** Which of the following statements *best* states one of Emerson's philosophies?

- **F** Turnabout is fair play.
- **G** Keep your head in the clouds.
- **H** Misery loves company.
- **J** Be true to yourself.

LITERARY FOCUS: FIGURES OF SPEECH *(10 points; 5 points each)*
On the line provided, write the letter of the *best* answer to each of the following items.

______ **11. Figures of speech** are —

- **A** the beat, or set pattern of syllables, in a literary work
- **B** a pattern of internal rhyme
- **C** different ways that people speak to each other
- **D** not intended to be taken literally

______ **12.** Emerson uses the following metaphor: ". . . no kernel of nourishing corn can come to him but through his toil bestowed on that plot of ground which is given to him to till." Which of the following best describes what that "plot of ground" represents?

F The land a person has been given

G A person's food

H A person's individual duties

J The circumstances an individual is born into

READING SKILLS: UNDERSTANDING FIGURES OF SPEECH *(10 points; 5 points each)*

On the line provided, write the letter of the *best* explanation of each of the figures of speech below.

______ **13.** "Trust thyself: Every heart vibrates to that iron string."

A If you trust yourself, you will come up against a steel wall.

B Trust yourself, and you will be strong.

C If you trust yourself, you will be broken as easily as a string.

D Trust yourself, and you will become a musician.

______ **14.** "Speak what you think now in hard words, and tomorrow speak what tomorrow thinks in hard words again. . . ."

F It is difficult to speak eloquently and correctly.

G Telling the truth is dangerous, so don't do it.

H Say what's on your mind in the strongest way you can.

J Say what you want regardless of whether you have thought about it.

VOCABULARY DEVELOPMENT *(20 points; 4 points each)*

Write a synonym or antonym for each Vocabulary word, as directed.

15. conviction *synonym:* ______________________

16. imparted *antonym:* ______________________

17. manifest *synonym:* ______________________

18. transcendent *antonym:* ______________________

19. integrity *synonym:* ______________________

NAME ______ CLASS ______ DATE ______ SCORE ______

Constructed Response *(20 points)*

20. On a separate sheet of paper, state the theme of Emerson's essay, and explain how he develops his theme with figures of speech. Support your ideas with details from the selection.

from Walden, or Life in the Woods Henry David Thoreau

COMPREHENSION *(40 points; 4 points each)*

On the line provided, write the letter of the *best* answer to each of the following items.

______ **1.** How long did Thoreau live in the woods at Walden Pond?

- A A few days
- B A few months
- C One year
- D About two years

______ **2.** In the section called "Economy," which of the following activities *best* illustrates Thoreau's doctrine of simplicity?

- F Hosting social gatherings for his neighbors
- G Writing books about forest plants
- H Building his own house
- J Keeping a journal and doing research about the animals he encounters

______ **3.** In the section called "Where I Lived, and What I Lived For," Thoreau says he wants to live at Walden because he —

- A wants to withdraw from life and prove that he can make it on his own
- B wants to live life more fully
- C wants to prove that he does not need other people
- D dislikes people and wants to get away from them

______ **4.** In the section called "Where I Lived, and What I Lived For," Thoreau gives his opinion of progress when he —

- F argues that progress is essential for a country's survival
- G believes that progress is superficial and imaginary
- H admires progress in all its forms
- J maintains that people should not follow their dreams because dreams are not real

______ **5.** In the section called "Where I Lived, and What I Lived For," what is Thoreau's attitude toward individuality and conformity?

- A A certain amount of conformity is necessary if people are to get along.
- B We live best when we conform to society.
- C Only certain people are really individuals; the others are best off conforming.
- D People must follow their inner voice in order not to be tyrannized by conformity.

______ **6.** In the section called "Solitude," Thoreau —

F explains that he does not feel lonely

G argues that people should live near conveniences such as the post office

H admits that it is tough being alone during big storms

J explains that he would feel lonely in outer space but never on earth

______ **7.** In the section called "The Bean Field," Thoreau shows his feelings about working in the fields. He —

A enjoys the work and comes to love his beans

B resents the time that gardening takes from his writing

C is annoyed that the insects eat so much of his crop

D is surprised that the beans look so nice in their neat rows

______ **8.** In the section called "Brute Neighbors," what do the ants symbolize?

F The people he does not like or respect

G The historical conflicts of the Greeks and Romans

H Human warfare

J Conflict between animals

______ **9.** In the section called "Conclusion," Thoreau says that he is leaving Walden because he —

A is lonely and misses the company of other people

B did not find what he was seeking at Walden

C wishes to move on to other experiences

D has become tired of working so hard for the essentials of life

______ **10.** With which of the following statements would Thoreau *most* likely agree?

F Most people's lives are too simple.

G Most people forfeit their lives by doing what society tells them to do.

H The chief purpose of everyone's life should be to glorify God.

J People need to learn to compromise to get along.

LITERARY FOCUS *(15 points; 5 points each)*
On the line provided, write the letter of the *best* answer to each of the following items.

______ **11.** When Thoreau uses the metaphor, "I wanted to live deep and suck out all the marrow of life," he means that he —

A never wants to go hungry
B wants to dive into the ocean and explore caves
C wants to get the most from life that he possibly can
D wants to live deliberately and get ahead of his neighbors

______ **12.** Which of the following statements is a metaphor?

F "I left the woods for as good a reason as I went there."
G "Time is but the stream I go a-fishing in."
H "Shall a man go and hang himself because he belongs to the race of pygmies, and not be the biggest pygmy that he can?"
J "Why should we be in such desperate haste to succeed and in such desperate enterprises?"

______ **13.** Which statement is the *best* paraphrase of the following metaphor: "We do not ride on the railroad; it rides upon us"?

A People are primitive and need technology to succeed.
B Life is uncertain; therefore, we must toil to support ourselves.
C In order to communicate with nature, we must become self-reliant.
D People are controlled by what they create rather than controlling their creations.

READING SKILLS: MAKING GENERALIZATIONS ABOUT A WRITER'S BELIEFS *(5 points)*
On the line provided, write the letter of the *best* answer to the following item.

______ **14.** Which of the following generalizations *best* summarizes Thoreau's opinions about life?

F Solitude is tedious and boring.
G Intelligent people need many friends.
H A simple life is a happy life.
J The mind can be stimulated only by reading.

NAME ______________________ CLASS ______________ DATE ______________ SCORE ______________

VOCABULARY DEVELOPMENT *(20 points; 4 points each)*

On the line provided, write the Vocabulary word that *best* completes each sentence.

pertinent **encumbrance** **impervious** **temporal** **superfluous**

15. The hut was so well constructed that it was ______________________ to rain and stayed dry even in fierce rainstorms.

16. As much as possible, Thoreau disdains the ______________________, or worldly, aspects of civilization and concentrates on simplicity.

17. Thoreau took only what he needed with him to the woods, leaving

______________________, needless items behind.

18. Unnecessary objects would just be a(n) ______________________, a burden to him.

19. Thoreau's point about living simply is especially ______________________ today, when we question how to conduct a meaningful life.

CONSTRUCTED RESPONSE *(20 points)*

20. Cite at least two metaphors that Thoreau uses to explain his philosophy of life. On a separate sheet of paper, write a paragraph that explains your answer. Support your ideas with details from the selection.

from Resistance to Civil Government

Henry David Thoreau

COMPREHENSION *(40 points; 4 points each)*

On the line provided, write the letter of the *best* answer to each of the following items.

______ **1.** What view of government does Thoreau express in the opening paragraph?

- **A** Government should govern as little as possible.
- **B** All government should be abolished.
- **C** People need government to protect them from foreign invasions.
- **D** The best government is a democracy.

______ **2.** What is Thoreau's opinion of the Mexican war that was being fought when he wrote this essay?

- **F** The war is necessary to repel invasion.
- **G** The war will help America assert its world superiority.
- **H** The Mexicans will welcome American education and freedoms.
- **J** A few people caused the war by using the government as their tool.

______ **3.** In the second paragraph, to what does Thoreau compare the government?

- **A** India rubber
- **B** A wooden gun
- **C** A smoking gun
- **D** A big machine

______ **4.** In Thoreau's view, the practical reason the majority rules in a democracy is that the —

- **F** system satisfies most people
- **G** majority opinion is always the right opinion
- **H** majority has more physical power on its side
- **J** majority opinion is more likely to be correct than the minority system

______ **5.** What does Thoreau ask for instead of *no* government?

- **A** An end to all taxes
- **B** Increased trade and commerce
- **C** A better government at once
- **D** New elected officials

______ **6.** Thoreau thinks that if people want a better government, they should —

F withhold all tax payments until government improves

G go to jail to protest poor government

H speak out about the kind of government they want

J write to their elected officials

______ **7.** Thoreau's *main* hope for the democracy of his time was that it would —

A disappear as people stopped voting

B progress from an absolute to a limited monarchy

C abolish poll taxes

D be one step along the route to a more perfect state

______ **8.** Thoreau suggests that slavery could be abolished in America by —

F slaves rebelling against their masters all throughout the country

G one man refusing to support slavery and going to jail for it

H a group of honest men stepping in and abolishing slavery

J a compromise reached between the government and slaveholders

______ **9.** After Thoreau is jailed, he —

A loses all respect for the government and pities it

B is appalled that he is punished

C is angry about losing his freedom

D worries that he will lose his voting privileges

______ **10.** Thoreau's *primary* purpose in this essay is to persuade people to —

F call for an immediate end to the government

G rebel against an unjust war

H follow their individual conscience

J devote themselves to eliminating all wars

NAME ______ CLASS ______ DATE ______ SCORE ______

LITERARY FOCUS: PARADOX *(20 points; 5 points each)*

On the line provided, write the letter of the *best* answer to each of the following items.

______ **11.** What is a **paradox**?

- **A** A statement that appears self-contradictory but reveals a truth
- **B** The repetition of initial consonant sounds in several words in a sentence
- **C** A reference to a well-known place, event, person, work of art, or other work of literature
- **D** A brief story that gets the reader's interest and sheds light on the writer's main idea and theme

______ **12.** Which of the following statements describes a paradoxical situation in the selection?

- **F** "For it matters not how small the beginning may seem to be. . . ."
- **G** "I felt as if I alone of all my townsmen had paid my tax."
- **H** "*It* does not keep the country free. *It* does not settle the West."
- **J** "I think that we should be men first, and subjects afterward."

______ **13.** What does Thoreau mean by the following paradox: "That government is best which governs not at all"?

- **A** All government must be immediately abolished.
- **B** All government is inherently bad for the people being governed.
- **C** Effective governments allow people to rule themselves.
- **D** Government can never really control people; all power is an illusion.

______ **14.** Thoreau uses paradoxes because he believes that —

- **F** contradictory statements never reveal the truth
- **G** life is complex, so complicated statements should be used to reveal the truth about it
- **H** the truth can always be revealed by using descriptive details
- **J** truth can be revealed by examining contradictions

VOCABULARY DEVELOPMENT *(20 points; 4 points each)*

Match each Vocabulary word on the left with its definition on the right. On the line provided, write the letter of the definition.

______ **15.** expedient
______ **16.** perverted
______ **17.** posterity
______ **18.** alacrity
______ **19.** inherent

a. convenience; means to an end
b. eagerness
c. inborn; built-in
d. generations to come
e. misdirected; corrupted

NAME ______________ CLASS ______________ DATE ______________ SCORE ______________

CONSTRUCTED RESPONSE *(20 points)*

20. Do you agree with Thoreau's statement "That government is best which governs not at all"? Why or why not? On a separate sheet of paper, write a paragraph that explains your answer. Support your ideas with details from the selection.

NAME ______________________ CLASS ______________________ DATE ______________ SCORE ______________

SELECTION TEST **Student Edition pages 220, 221** **INFORMATIONAL READING**

from On Nonviolent Resistance Mohandas K. Gandhi
from Letter from Birmingham City Jail
Martin Luther King, Jr.

COMPREHENSION *(100 points; 10 points each)*
On the line provided, write the letter of the *best* answer to each of the following items.

_____ **1.** According to Gandhi, what are the two ways of countering injustice?

- **A** Violence and jail
- **B** Nonviolence and writing
- **C** Smashing in the head of a lawbreaker and getting the police to arrest the person
- **D** Violence and nonviolence

_____ **2.** What does Gandhi mean when he says: "No clapping is possible without two hands to do it. . . ."?

- **F** It takes more than one person to govern a country fairly.
- **G** You cannot have a government if the people refused to be ruled by it.
- **H** You cannot accomplish anything without the help of many people.
- **J** If at first you don't succeed, try again.

_____ **3.** Gandhi argues that government exists only —

- **A** to determine and administer fair punishments for lawbreakers
- **B** through the approval of those being governed
- **C** to control unruly mobs
- **D** to help people avoid unnecessary suffering and pain

_____ **4.** The tone of Gandhi's essay is *best* described as —

- **F** calmly defiant
- **G** furiously rebellious
- **H** arrogantly superior
- **J** sadly resigned

_____ **5.** King justifies breaking some laws but upholding other laws when he —

- **A** argues that the laws made by whites do not apply to blacks
- **B** maintains that the existing laws are unjust because they are not applied equally
- **C** argues that an unjust law does not have to be upheld
- **D** claims that only laws made by the majority are valid

______ **6.** According to King, an unjust law is a law that —

F is applied unfairly

G harms some people

H cannot be enforced

J does not agree with moral law

______ **7.** King develops his arguments *primarily* though —

A comparison and contrast

B time order

C advantages and disadvantages

D telling a personal story

______ **8.** What paradox does King use to conclude his essay?

F Advocating the overthrow of the government strengthens the government.

G Respectfully breaking an unjust law expresses the highest regard for law.

H Anarchy is a healthy way to maintain a democracy.

J Laws that are not written down are not laws.

______ **9.** On hearing King's argument, Gandhi *most* likely would —

A disagree because King advocates violence

B disagree because King talks only about unjust laws

C agree because both leaders say that you should be willing to die for your convictions

D agree because King advocates the right of people to resist

______ **10.** Gandhi's arguments differ from King's arguments in that Gandhi —

F does not give examples of unjust laws; King does

G argues that everyone is obligated to participate in government; King speaks to blacks only

H claims that protest is immoral; King says that it is moral

J talks about unfair governments; King talks about fair governments

Dr. Heidegger's Experiment Nathaniel Hawthorne

COMPREHENSION *(40 points; 4 points each)*

On the line provided, write the letter of the *best* answer to each of the following items.

______ **1.** In the beginning of the story, the characters are alike in every way *except* one. It cannot be said that they —

- **A** are all unhappy with their lives
- **B** have all wasted their youth
- **C** are all old and frail
- **D** have all been famous and respected

______ **2.** What happened to Dr. Heidegger's fiancée?

- **F** She ran off with another man.
- **G** Dr. Heidegger magically imprisoned her in the mirror.
- **H** She married Dr. Heidegger but died soon after.
- **J** She died before they were married.

______ **3.** What is the strangest object in Dr. Heidegger's study?

- **A** The mirror
- **B** A large book of magic
- **C** A small round table, as black as ebony
- **D** A beautiful cut glass vase

______ **4.** Hawthorne builds suspense by —

- **F** not explaining that Dr. Heidegger does many strange experiments
- **G** withholding information about Dr. Heidegger's wife
- **H** not revealing at first why Dr. Heidegger has called his friends together
- **J** misrepresenting each character's background

______ **5.** According to the narrator, what does Dr. Heidegger give his friends to drink?

- **A** Water from the Fountain of Youth
- **B** Rare old wine from his cellar
- **C** Bubbly spring water
- **D** A magical potion he has cooked up

______ **6.** From the guests' reactions to the drink, you can infer that they —

- **F** sincerely repent their past misdeeds
- **G** are greedy, vain, and selfish
- **H** have learned not to trust Dr. Heidegger, because his experiments rarely work
- **J** appreciate Dr. Heidegger's efforts on their behalf

______ **7.** What do Dr. Heidegger's friends resolve to do the next day?

A Live better lives because of the lesson they learned

B Make fun of the infirmity of old age, especially the doctor

C Apologize to Dr. Heidegger for doubting his genius

D Immediately set off for Florida

______ **8.** How long do the effects of the drink last?

F A few minutes

G A day

H A year

J Forever

______ **9.** What lesson does Dr. Heidegger learn from his friends?

A People don't learn from their mistakes.

B Youth is wasted on the young.

C It is foolish to give away great secrets for free.

D People can reform, if given the chance.

______ **10.** What do his friends learn from their experience?

F That scientists can do good and evil

G To take care of yourself when you are young

H Never to take a drink unless everyone does

J Little or nothing at all

LITERARY FOCUS: ALLEGORY *(15 points; 5 points each)*
On the line provided, write the letter of the *best* answer to each of the following items.

______ **11.** An **allegory** might be *best* defined as a —

A reference to a well-known place, event, person, work of art, or other work of literature

B person's story of his or her own life

C literary work in which characters, setting, and events stand for abstract ideas and moral qualities

D piece of literature written to be performed in front of an audience

______ **12.** What weakness does the Widow Wycherly represent?

- **F** Sin
- **G** Vanity
- **H** Greed
- **J** Corruption

______ **13.** If Hawthorne had named his characters after their weaknesses, what would Mr. Gascoigne be called?

- **A** Conniving Politician
- **B** Arrogant Investor
- **C** Dull Leader
- **D** Casanova

READING SKILLS: IDENTIFYING DETAILS *(5 points)*

On the line provided, write the letter of the *best* answer to the following item.

______ **14.** Which of the following details does *not* support the moral: People would continue to make the same mistakes even if given a second chance?

- **F** The Widow Wycherly acts like a coquette.
- **G** The three rivals exchange threatening glances.
- **H** Dr. Heidegger does not drink the liquid.
- **J** The four struggle and overturn the table with the vase holding the water.

VOCABULARY DEVELOPMENT *(20 points; 4 points each)*

On the line provided, write the Vocabulary word that *best* completes each sentence.

venerable **infamous** **ponderous** **veracious** **effervescent**

15. Murderers, thieves, and corrupt politicians often become ______________ for their corrupt acts.

16. Dr. Heidegger had trouble lifting the ______________ book because it was so heavy.

17. He poured a(n) ______________ drink, and the bubbles tickled everyone's noses.

18. Old people are ______________ and worthy of our respect.

19. People like Mr. Gascoigne are not ______________ since they often do not tell the truth.

NAME CLASS DATE SCORE

CONSTRUCTED RESPONSE *(20 points)*

20. In what ways is "Dr. Heidegger's Experiment" an allegory? On a separate sheet of paper, provide at least two examples from the story that show that Hawthorne's story is allegorical. Support your ideas with details from the selection.

The Minister's Black Veil Nathaniel Hawthorne

COMPREHENSION *(40 points; 4 points each)*

On the line provided, write the letter of the *best* answer to each of the following items.

______ **1.** Mr. Hooper's sudden adoption of a black veil makes his congregation uneasy because —

- **A** they think he means to do them harm
- **B** they can't decide what would explain his action
- **C** the veil immediately reminds them of his sinfulness
- **D** they believe he had a terrible accident

______ **2.** Wearing the veil changes Mr. Hooper's sermon in that it makes the sermon —

- **F** more difficult to understand
- **G** less frightening
- **H** more interesting
- **J** more powerful

______ **3.** After the end of services on the first Sunday that Mr. Hooper wears the black veil, —

- **A** no one wants to walk next to him or invite him to dinner
- **B** the parishioners quickly adjust to Mr. Hooper's changed appearance
- **C** two of the younger children start to laugh at the strange sight of the minister in his veil
- **D** Mr. Hooper goes directly home rather than greeting his parishioners in front of the church

______ **4.** The veil changes Mr. Hooper's personality in that it makes him —

- **F** kinder and more gentle
- **G** cruel and heartless
- **H** seem ghostlike from head to foot
- **J** more patient with small children

______ **5.** No one will ask Mr. Hooper why he is wearing the veil because —

- **A** no one cares why he is wearing the veil
- **B** everyone already knows the reason
- **C** they are afraid that if they ask, he will make them wear veils, too
- **D** they are afraid of what his answer might be

______ **6.** Mr. Hooper tells his fiancée, Elizabeth, "There is an hour to come . . . when all of us shall cast aside our veils." He means that —

F everyone's soul will be revealed on the Judgment Day

G everyone will soon be wearing veils but only for a short time

H everyone is already wearing a veil in the privacy of the home

J everyone should be wearing a veil to hide his or her shame

______ **7.** When Mr. Hooper refuses to remove the veil, Elizabeth —

A breaks their engagement

B breaks down crying and hugs him

C runs from the room, but returns soon after

D screams at him in a rage, telling him about the embarrassment he is causing her

______ **8.** After permanently adopting the black veil, Mr. Hooper —

F ignores his responsibilities as a minister

G tends his congregation with his usual care

H frequently cries and flies into rages

J accuses his congregation of terrible sins

______ **9.** When the Reverend Mr. Clark tries to remove his veil, Mr. Hooper —

A lets the veil slip between his fingers

B struggles to keep the veil but is overpowered by the Reverend Mr. Clark

C begs the Reverend to help him remove the veil

D grabs the veil and refuses to allow it to be removed

______ **10.** "The Minister's Black Veil" is a parable *mainly* because the —

F characters and setting are made up

G story is based on a true event

H moral themes form the center of the story

J story is sad and depressing

LITERARY FOCUS: SYMBOL *(15 points; 5 points each)*

On the line provided, write the letter of the *best* answer to each of the following items.

______ **11.** The black veil has such a powerful effect on people for all of the following reasons *except* —

A it is creepy looking

B it reminds them of their own sins and shortcomings

C it makes them think Mr. Hooper is hiding something awful

D only women wore veils in Colonial America

______ **12.** What does the black veil symbolize?

- **F** Sin and guilt
- **G** A facial deformity
- **H** Death and destruction
- **J** Misfortune and sorrow

______ **13.** Mr. Hooper chooses to look physically different from other people. This symbolic act is meant to —

- **A** reveal how he is more sinful than other people
- **B** display that he suffers a condition shared by all people
- **C** protect him from other people's sins
- **D** highlight his role as an agent of holiness in a world of sin

Reading Skills: Drawing Inferences *(5 points)*

On the line provided, write the letter of the *best* answer to the following item.

______ **14.** From Elizabeth's talk with Mr. Hooper, you can infer that —

- **F** Mr. Hooper is doomed to be lonely
- **G** Mr. Hooper wants to end the relationship
- **H** Elizabeth understands why Mr. Hooper wears the veil
- **J** Elizabeth rejects Mr. Hooper only because she worries about a scandal

Vocabulary Development *(20 points; 4 points each)*

Write a synonym or antonym for each Vocabulary word, as directed.

15. semblance *synonym:* ______________________

16. iniquity *antonym:* ______________________

17. sagacious *antonym:* ______________________

18. portend *synonym:* ______________________

19. obscurity *antonym:* ______________________

CONSTRUCTED RESPONSE *(20 points)*

20. Hawthorne could have made the main character of this story a banker, a teacher, a shopkeeper, or a person with any other job. On a separate sheet of paper, write a paragraph discussing how the parable is affected by Hawthorne's decision to make the main character a minister. Support your ideas with details from the selection.

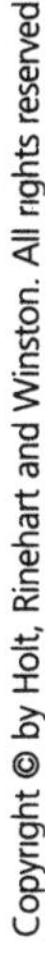

The Pit and the Pendulum Edgar Allan Poe

COMPREHENSION *(40 points; 4 points each)*

On the line provided, write the letter of the *best* answer to each of the following items.

______ **1.** The story is told from which point of view?

A Third-person-limited view of a member of the French army

B Omniscient view of the author

C Third-person view of the inquisitor

D First-person view of the prisoner

______ **2.** What might explain how the candles seem to change shape from "slender angels" to "meaningless spectres"?

F The candles are magical and can change shape.

G The narrator is hallucinating.

H Inquisitors have changed the candles.

J The candles are imaginary.

______ **3.** When he comes to after fainting, what does the narrator remember?

A Shadowy figures carrying him to a strange damp place

B His childhood and his parents

C His wife and children back home

D His previous stay in the dungeon

______ **4.** You can infer that the narrator is frightened about being in the dark because —

F he has always been afraid of the dark

G he knows exactly what torture awaits him

H the unseen is more terrifying than the seen

J he can hear the bats and rats but not see them

______ **5.** The narrator is afraid that he will find himself in a tomb because he —

A fears that he will be taken from the tomb and tortured

B fears that he has been buried alive

C has always been afraid of tombs

D suspects the tomb will plunge into a bottomless pit

______ **6.** What fate does the narrator think awaits him?

F Starvation

G The torture of his family

H Public execution

J Many months in the dungeon

______ **7.** When the narrator is sentenced to die, the authorities provide him with food because they —

A feel very sorry for him

B left the food there by mistake

C plan more punishments before he dies

D always feed their prisoners until the end

______ **8.** The prisoner frees himself when he —

F waits until the pendulum cuts the bonds and quickly rolls out of the way

G screams and screams until they release him

H pays a great deal of money and is released

J smears meat on the bonds that hold him, and the rats chew through them

______ **9.** At the end of the story, the —

A narrator plunges to his death in the pit

B narrator is saved from the pit by a French general

C inquisitors release him because he is really innocent

D prison burns, and in the turmoil the prisoner is able to escape

______ **10.** The mood of this story is *best* described as —

F neutral

G romantic

H terrifying

J confusing

LITERARY FOCUS: SYMBOLIC MEANING *(20 points; 5 points each)*
On the line provided, write the letter of the *best* answer to each of the following items.

______ **11.** A **symbol** is —

A a person, place, thing, or event that has meaning in itself and also stands for something beyond itself

B a speech one character speaks while alone on the stage

C words that appeal to the five senses: sight, hearing, taste, touch, or smell

D the time and place where the events take place

______ **12.** To infer the symbolic meaning of a story, you use all of the following methods *except* —

F adding what you already know to story clues to make inferences about the characters and theme

G interpreting the story's symbols

H ignoring the dialogue

J drawing conclusions based on hints in the plot

______ **13.** The pit in which the prisoner is kept can be read to symbolize —

A salvation

B hell

C hope

D escape

______ **14.** What could be the symbolic meaning of the French Army?

F Military might

G New trouble

H Betrayal

J Divine intervention

VOCABULARY DEVELOPMENT *(20 points; 4 points each)*

Complete each analogy with a Vocabulary word from below. Use each Vocabulary word only once.

potent **tumultuous** **averted** **lucid** **imperceptible**

15. VAGUE : APPARENT :: INDISTINCT : ______

16. LARGE OBJECT : DETECTABLE :: SMALL OBJECT : ______

17. LION : POWERFUL :: GORILLA : ______

18. SLEEP : CALM :: RIOT : ______

19. ALLOWED : PERMITTED :: PREVENTED : ______

CONSTRUCTED RESPONSE *(20 points)*

20. Based on "The Pit and the Pendulum," in what ways can Poe be considered a Dark Romantic? Write your answer on a separate piece of paper. Support your ideas with details from the selection.

NAME _______________ CLASS _______________ DATE _______________ SCORE _______________

The Raven Edgar Allan Poe

COMPREHENSION *(60 points; 6 points each)*
On the line provided, write the letter of the *best* answer to each of the following items.

______ **1.** At first, the speaker thinks the noise he hears is —
- **A** his enemy stalking him
- **B** the wind blowing the door open
- **C** someone at the door
- **D** his friends playing tricks on him

______ **2.** When the narrator opens the door and looks out, he half expects to find —
- **F** a Greek god come to life in the form of a bird
- **G** a group of angels
- **H** the woman he had loved, who has died
- **J** the image of his own death

______ **3.** Why does the poet have the Raven perch on the bust of the Greek goddess Pallas?
- **A** Ravens were sacred to the Greeks.
- **B** This association suggests that the Raven is wise.
- **C** The speaker associates Pallas with his dead love, Lenore.
- **D** The poet is suggesting that this poem takes place in ancient Greece.

______ **4.** At *first* encounter, the speaker's reaction to the Raven is —
- **F** revulsion
- **G** fear
- **H** anger
- **J** amusement

______ **5.** When the Raven says, "Nevermore," the speaker takes this response to be —
- **A** the bird's name
- **B** a prophecy
- **C** a message from Lenore
- **D** the words of an evil spirit

______ **6.** The narrator guesses that the Raven says, "Nevermore," because —
- **F** it had been listening to the narrator mourning for Lenore
- **G** its former master was an unhappy person
- **H** Lenore had originally kept it as a pet
- **J** the narrator's enemy had taught it this word to torture the narrator

______ **7.** Near the end of the poem, the narrator asks the Raven two questions to which the bird answers, "Nevermore." These questions concern —

A the success of the speaker's literary works

B Lenore's love for the speaker

C what will happen after death

D the bird's purpose in visiting the speaker

______ **8.** Readers can infer from the poem's conclusion that the speaker will —

F be reunited with Lenore

G die soon

H never escape his despair

J make his sorrow the subject of a great poem

______ **9.** The speaker can *best* be described as a —

A lonely, elderly man longing for visitors

B magician conjuring up evil spirits

C poet seeking inspiration for a new work

D melancholy person trying to forget a great tragedy

______ **10.** What is the poem's mood?

F Reassuring

G Romantic

H Soothing

J Despairing

LITERARY FOCUS: SOUND EFFECTS *(20 points; 5 points each)*

On the line provided, write the letter of the *best* answer to each of the following items.

______ **11.** In which quotation below are the underlined words an example of sound effects created by alliteration?

A "What this grim, ungainly, ghastly, gaunt, and ominous bird of yore / Meant in croaking 'Nevermore.'"

B "Leave no black plume as a token of that lie thy soul hath spoken! / Leave my loneliness unbroken!—quit the bust above my door!"

C "Back into the chamber turning, all my soul within me burning, / Soon again I heard a tapping somewhat louder than before."

D "On this home by Horror haunted—tell me truly, I implore— / Is there—is there balm in Gilead?—tell me—tell me, I implore!"

_____ **12.** Which word in the following passage is an example of onomatopoeia?

"This I whispered, and an echo murmured back the word, 'Lenore!'" / Merely this and nothing more."

F murmured

G echo

H merely

J Lenore

_____ **13.** Which of the following lines does *not* have internal rhyme?

A "Then this ebony bird beguiling my sad fancy into smiling . . ."

B "Startled at the stillness broken by reply so aptly spoken . . ."

C "And each separate dying ember wrought its ghost upon the floor."

D "Till I scarcely more than muttered 'Other friends have flown before— . . .'"

_____ **14.** What does the word *croaking* suggest in the following lines:

"What this grim, ungainly, ghastly, gaunt and ominous bird of yore / Meant in croaking 'Nevermore'"?

F eating

G flying

H dying

J repeating

CONSTRUCTED RESPONSE *(20 points)*

15. On a separate sheet of paper, write a paragraph explaining how the poem's mood reinforces its theme. First, identify the mood and the theme. Then, show how the poem's mood serves to intensify the theme. Support your ideas with details from the poem.

Eldorado Edgar Allan Poe

COMPREHENSION *(60 points; 6 points each)*

On the line provided, write the letter of the *best* answer to each of the following items.

______ **1.** What is the only location actually mentioned in the poem?

A Florida

B Africa

C Colombia

D California

______ **2.** In which item are the underlined words an example of alliteration?

F "Gaily bedight, / A gallant knight"

G "Had journeyed long, / Singing a song"

H "But he grew old— / This knight so bold—"

J "A gallant knight, / In sunshine and in shadow . . ."

______ **3.** As the knight sets off on his quest, he is —

A fierce and determined

B discouraged

C cheerful and optimistic

D weak and brokenhearted

______ **4.** According to details in the poem, the knight's search for his goal lasts a —

F few days

G few months

H few years

J very long time

______ **5.** Who helps the knight on his quest?

A A "gallant knight"

B The knight's queen

C The people of Eldorado

D A "pilgrim shadow"

______ **6.** The knight receives all the following advice *except* —

F "Turn around and return to your home."

G go "Over the Mountains / Of the Moon."

H go "Down the Valley of the Shadow."

J "Ride, boldly ride."

NAME ______ CLASS ______ DATE ______ SCORE ______

______ **7.** How might the advice be *best* described?

A Clear and useful

B Foolish but helpful

C Ambiguous and difficult to follow

D Useless because the knight already knows it

______ **8.** Which couplet is an example of end rhyme?

F "He met a pilgrim shadow— / 'Shadow,' said he"

G "No spot of ground / That looked like Eldorado."

H "But he grew old— / This knight so bold—"

J "And o'er his heart a shadow / Fell as he found"

______ **9.** What *probably* happens at the end of the poem?

A The knight completes his quest, with great success.

B The knight continues his quest, without success.

C A shadow leads him to the gold.

D The knight gets some friends to help him.

______ **10.** Whom does the knight symbolize?

F Everyone who knows that Eldorado is a myth

G People who go on a quest for great wealth

H All people who succeed in their search for great wealth

J People who set high goals for themselves

LITERARY FOCUS: ARCHETYPE *(20 points; 5 points each)*

On the line provided, write the letter of the *best* answer to each of the following items.

______ **11.** What is an **archetype**?

A An original, imaginative pattern that appears across cultures and is repeated through the ages

B The repetition of initial consonant sounds in several words in a sentence or line of poetry

C A reference to a well-known place, event, person, work of art, or other work of literature

D A brief story that gets the reader's interest and sheds light on the writer's main idea and theme

______ **12.** On his quest, the knight is headed to —

F the Mountains of the Moon

G Eldorado

H the Valley of Shadow

J his home in England

______ **13.** The knight's quest is not successful because he —

A does not try hard enough

B does not have clear directions

C has a goal that is imaginary, not real

D gives up too soon

______ **14.** What is the archetype in this poem?

F Helpful people

G Failure

H The Mountains of the Moon

J A quest for great wealth

Constructed Response *(20 points)*

15. On a separate sheet of paper, describe a story, film, or television show in which a character sets off on a quest for a lofty goal. The goal might be great wealth, love, happiness, or eternal life, for example. Explain how the goal is an archetype. Support your ideas with details from the selection.

American Romanticism: 1800–1860

This test asks you to use the skills and strategies you have learned in this collection. Read the following passage, and answer the questions that follow it.

Inscription for the Entrance to a Wood
by William Cullen Bryant

Stranger, if thou hast learned a truth which needs
No school of long experience, that the world
Is full of guilt and misery, and hast seen
Enough of all its sorrows, crimes, and cares
To tire thee of it, enter this wild wood
And view the haunts of Nature. The calm shade
Shall bring a kindred calm, and the sweet breeze
That makes the green leaves dance, shall waft a balm
To thy sick heart. Thou wilt find nothing here
Of all that pained thee in the haunts of men,
And made thee loathe thy life. The primal curse
Fell, it is true, upon the unsinning earth,
But not in vengeance. God hath yoked to guilt
Her pale tormentor, misery. Hence, these shades
Are still the abodes of gladness; the thick roof
Of green and stirring branches is alive
And musical with birds, that sing and sport
In wantonness of spirit; while below
The squirrel, with raised paws and form erect,
Chirps merrily. Throngs of insects in the shade
Try their thin wings and dance in the warm beam
That waked them into life. Even the green trees
Partake the deep contentment; as they bend
To the soft winds, the sun from the blue sky
Looks in and sheds a blessing on the scene.
Scarce less the cleft-born wildflower seems to enjoy
Existence, than the wingèd plunderer
That sucks its sweet. The mossy rocks themselves,
And the old and ponderous trunks of prostrate trees
That lead from knoll to knoll a causey rude
Or bridge the sunken brook, and their dark roots,
With all their earth upon them, twisting high,
Breathe fixed tranquillity. The rivulet
Sends forth glad sounds, and tripping o'er its bed
Of pebbly sands, or leaping down the rocks,
Seems, with continuous laughter, to rejoice
In its own being. Softly tread the marge,
Lest from her midway perch thou scare the wren
That dips her bill in the water. The cool wind,

That stirs the stream in play, shall come to thee,
Like one that loves thee nor will let thee pass
Ungreeted, and shall give its light embrace.

VOCABULARY SKILLS *(25 points; 5 points each)*
Each of the underlined words below has also been underlined in the selection. Re-read those passages in which the underlined words appear. Then, use context clues and your prior knowledge to select an answer. On the line provided, write the letter of the meaning of the underlined word.

______ **1.** When something wafts down from the sky, it —

A sinks heavily

B evaporates

C transmits a message

D floats

______ **2.** If you loathe your job, you —

F adore it

G like it somewhat

H strongly dislike it

J are indifferent to it

______ **3.** A wantonness of spirit suggests —

A spontaneity

B restraint

C neutrality

D indifference

______ **4.** People who feel contentment are —

F fair

G apathetic

H wretched

J happy

______ **5.** A ponderous footstep is —

A muddy

B light

C heavy

D little

NAME ______ CLASS ______ DATE ______ SCORE ______

COMPREHENSION *(25 points; 5 points each)*
On the line provided, write the letter of the *best* answer to each of the following items.

______ **6.** "Inscription for the Entrance to a Wood" focuses *mainly* on —

- **F** the premature death of heroes
- **G** ambition as the highest human goal
- **H** the comfort that nature offers humanity
- **J** guilt as the cause of human misery

______ **7.** The poem portrays various elements of nature as —

- **A** living in a fragile state of coexistence with each other
- **B** rejoicing in the comfort of their existence
- **C** part of the ongoing pattern of life and death
- **D** constantly battling the human world in order to survive

______ **8.** The insects in the poem are described as —

- **F** annoying but hard-working creatures
- **G** reflections of beauty and grace
- **H** the lowest form of living beings
- **J** harmful and sneaky

______ **9.** The speaker suggests that human beings should approach nature —

- **A** only when absolutely necessary
- **B** with fear and caution
- **C** with total abandon
- **D** with openness and optimism

______ **10.** At the end of the poem, the stranger is welcomed into the world of nature through —

- **F** the trees
- **G** riddles
- **H** reason
- **J** love

NAME ______ CLASS ______ DATE ______ SCORE ______

READING SKILLS AND STRATEGIES: CONSTRUCTED RESPONSE *(30 points; 10 points each)*

Monitoring Your Reading

11. Paraphrase each of these passages from "Inscription for the Entrance to a Wood" in your own words.

Original Passage

"Stranger, if thou hast learned a truth which needs / No school of long experience, that the world / Is full of guilt and misery, and hast seen / Enough of all its sorrows, crimes, and cares / To tire thee of it, enter this wild wood / And view the haunts of Nature."

______

______

______

______

______

"Thou wilt find nothing here / Of all that pained thee in the haunts of men, / And made thee loathe thy life."

______

______

______

______

______

"Hence, these shades / Are still the abodes of gladness; the thick roof / Of green and stirring branches is alive / And musical with birds . . . "

______

______

______

______

Understanding Figures of Speech

12. Identify each of the following types of figures of speech. Then, provide a definition of the specific figure of speech.

Example

"the sweet breeze / That makes the green leaves dance . . ."

"Society is a joint-stock company in which the members agree for the better securing of his bread to each shareholder. . . . "

"The life in us is like the water in the river."

"The rivulet / Sends forth glad sounds. . . ."

Drawing Inferences

13. What does Bryant imply about the effect of a walk in the woods? From the following options, choose the one you think is the best answer to the question. Then, on a separate piece of paper, write the letter of the answer you chose and briefly defend your choice. Use at least one example from the selection to support your ideas.

A A walk in the woods will awaken a person to the pleasures of physical exercise.

B A walk in the woods will bring forgiveness for sins.

C A walk in the woods will prepare a person for death.

D A walk in the woods will ease the pain of living in the world.

LITERARY FOCUS: CONSTRUCTED RESPONSE *(20 points)*

14. To show how "Inscription for the Entrance to a Wood" by William Cullen Bryant is part of the the Romantic literary tradition, explain how the poem exhibits each characteristic listed below or provide an example from the poem illustrating that characteristic.

1. Values feeling and intuition over reason

2. Celebrates unspoiled nature

3. Contemplates nature's beauty as a path to spiritual and moral development

4. Prefers youthful, naive innocence to educated sophistication

NAME ______ CLASS ______ DATE ______ SCORE ______

COLLECTION 3 DIAGNOSTIC TEST

LITERATURE

American Masters: Whitman and Dickinson

On the line provided, write the letter of the *best* answer to each of the following items. *(100 points; 10 points each)*

______ **1.** Poetry that does not conform to a regular meter and rhyme scheme is called —

A blank verse

B free verse

C haiku

D lyric poetry

______ **2.** Which of the following statements about **symbols** is *false*?

F The purpose of symbols is to create ambiguity.

G While a symbol suggests a wider meaning, it also functions as itself in a literary work.

H To understand a symbol, the reader often has to make inferences based on evidence in the text.

J Some symbols have a universal meaning.

______ **3.** Words that do not rhyme exactly are called —

A rhyme scheme

B internal rhyme

C end rhyme

D slant rhyme, or approximate rhyme

______ **4.** The **tone** of a literary work is *most* often revealed by the —

F reader's opinion of the work

G writer's choice of words

H subject of the work

J characters' actions

______ **5.** What is **irony**?

A A negative or critical remark

B A style of writing characterized by the use of humor

C A contrast between what we expect to happen and what actually occurs

D A work that mocks traditional literary conventions

______ **6.** Which of the following statements about **theme** is *true*?

F Theme is an element of prose, not poetry.

G A story's theme can usually be stated in one word.

H A work of literature has only one theme.

J The theme of a literary work is often implied, not stated.

______ **7.** Writers use **imagery** to —

A evoke pictures in the mind of the reader

B give their writing a pleasing sound

C convey the multiple meanings of words

D make their writing more abstract

______ **8.** The word *fizz* is an example of —

F onomatopoeia

G diction

H cliché

J assonance

______ **9.** **Personification** can *best* be described as the —

A creation of vivid characters

B use of realistic dialogue

C connection between a writer's life and a literary work

D giving of human characteristics to an object or animal

______ **10.** "Life is a carnival" is an example of a(n) —

F simile

G archetype

H idiom

J metaphor

NAME ______ CLASS ______ DATE ______ SCORE ______

LITERARY PERIOD INTRODUCTION TEST **Student Edition page 302**

American Masters: Whitman and Dickinson

COMPREHENSION *(100 points; 10 points each)*

On the line provided, write the letter of the *best* answer to each of the following items.

______ **1.** Walt Whitman's writing style can *best* be described as —

A bold and confident

B folksy and charming

C elegant and refined

D elevated and sublime

______ **2.** Unlike Walt Whitman, Emily Dickinson was —

F a world traveler

G private and shy

H people-oriented

J involved in social causes

______ **3.** An important similarity shared by Whitman and Dickinson is their —

A fondness for big-city living

B obscurity during their lifetime

C rejection by the literary community

D abandonment of literary conventions

______ **4.** Whitman saw the purpose of his poetry as a —

F message to the future

G relic of his childhood

H religious duty

J tool of social reform

______ **5.** Whitman's feelings about his own poems are *best* revealed by his —

A instructions to have them destroyed

B refusal to publish them until after his death

C decision to self-publish at his own expense

D pursuit of other occupations he considered more worthwhile

______ **6.** Whitman's style and technique are based on **cadence,** which can be defined as the —

F regular rhyme and rhythm used in ballads and epic poems

G rhythm and long sweeps of sound used by great speakers

H use of exact rhymes, as in Romantic poetry

J use of iambic pentameter, in the manner of William Shakespeare

______ **7.** Whitman's use of **cadence** forms the basis of his —

A rhymes

B essays

C sonnets

D free verse

______ **8.** Dickinson's poetry is noted for its —

F historical value

G errors in word usage

H precise language

J epic sweep

______ **9.** Dickinson did not achieve fame in her lifetime largely because —

A she disagreed with the way her work was edited

B her poetry was published only after her death

C her poetry was banned

D she believed poetry was not meant to be published

______ **10.** Which of the following statements *best* describes the influence of Dickinson and Whitman on later poets?

F Later poets felt inferior and stopped writing.

G After Dickinson and Whitman's time, poets were treated with great respect.

H The poetry of Dickinson and Whitman moved people to social action.

J Later poets were more open to experimentation.

NAME ______ CLASS ______ DATE ______ SCORE ______

SELECTION TEST **Student Edition page 311**

I Hear America Singing Walt Whitman

COMPREHENSION *(60 points; 6 points each)*

On the line provided, write the letter of the *best* answer to each of the following items.

______ **1.** The Americans the speaker refers to in the poem are —

- **A** ordinary working people
- **B** wounded soldiers
- **C** great figures in United States history
- **D** doctors and nurses

______ **2.** Which of the following statements is true about the songs America is singing?

- **F** The songs are out of tune.
- **G** Each person has a different song.
- **H** People are singing songs no one can hear.
- **J** People are singing out of sorrow.

______ **3.** The speaker does *not* suggest that American women —

- **A** are full participants in society
- **B** work as hard as the men do
- **C** are unfulfilled in their jobs
- **D** do many kinds of work

______ **4.** You can infer that Whitman chose to write about these Americans because —

- **F** these were the people he had only read about
- **G** he wanted them to have better working conditions
- **H** he wanted to make up for his life of privilege
- **J** he thought they were the true American heroes

______ **5.** What literary device is evident in this poem?

- **A** Historical allusion
- **B** Simile
- **C** Repetition
- **D** Rhyme

______ **6.** What does this poem suggest about "America singing"?

- **F** Americans do not understand one another.
- **G** People know that singing makes work go faster.
- **H** Americans take pride in the work they do.
- **J** Each person's song reflects his or her ethnic heritage.

______ **7.** What can you conclude is Whitman's attitude toward work?

A Work is a waste of a person's intellect.

B Some people are meant to be laborers.

C All honest work is fulfilling.

D Manual labor is more valuable than other kinds of work.

______ **8.** As used in this poem, what does the word *singing* symbolize?

F Complaining

G Slacking off

H Celebrating

J Communicating

______ **9.** What is the overall tone of this poem?

A Joyous

B Sarcastic

C Dismal

D Eerie

______ **10.** Which repeated word serves to unify this poem?

F carols

G worker

H strong

J singing

LITERARY FOCUS: CATALOG *(20 points; 5 points each)*
On the line provided, write the letter of the *best* answer to each of the following items.

______ **11.** When used to refer to a poetic technique, the word *catalog* refers to —

A two related lines of poetry that rhyme

B a list of related people, places, or events

C a comparison between two unlike things

D a reference to another work of literature

______ **12.** To fully appreciate Whitman's use of catalogs, readers should read the poem —

F aloud

G as rapidly as possible

H silently

J without emotion

______ **13.** In "I Hear America Singing" Whitman uses a catalog to —

A organize details

B clarify ideas

C show relationships

D create rhyme

______ **14.** Whitman favored the catalog as a technique because it expressed his —

F English-Dutch heritage

G knowledge of poetic devices

H tendency to repeat himself

J unbounded love for all things

Constructed Response *(20 points)*

15. Explain how using the catalog technique allowed Whitman to express his ideas about workers and America. On a separate sheet of paper, write a paragraph that explains your answer. Support your ideas with details from the selection.

from Song of Myself, Numbers 10 and 33 Walt Whitman

COMPREHENSION *(60 points; 6 points each)*

On the line provided, write the letter of the *best* answer to each of the following items.

_____ **1.** The first scene of *Song of Myself,* number 10, depicts the speaker —

- **A** hunting alone in the woods
- **B** setting up a trading post
- **C** sheltering a runaway slave
- **D** hearing about a shipwreck and its victims

_____ **2.** In the second scene of *Song of Myself,* number 10, the speaker spends time with —

- **F** his extended family
- **G** boatmen and clam-diggers
- **H** great military heroes
- **J** Civil War veterans

_____ **3.** In *Song of Myself,* number 10, the speaker describes the marriage of a trapper and a Native American girl. In this section the speaker's role can be *best* described as that of a(n) —

- **A** interpreter
- **B** dancing guest
- **C** participant
- **D** observer

_____ **4.** From his description of the runaway slave, you can infer that Whitman —

- **F** strongly opposed slavery
- **G** wanted to stay neutral on the slavery issue
- **H** felt guilty about owning slaves himself
- **J** had never met a slave before

_____ **5.** In *Song of Myself,* number 33, the skipper of the boat is depicted as —

- **A** cowardly
- **B** heroic
- **C** misunderstood
- **D** unlucky

_____ **6.** In *Song of Myself,* number 33, Whitman —

- **F** refuses to help the skipper
- **G** is repulsed by the suffering he describes
- **H** takes on the suffering of the victims
- **J** ponders matters of life and death

______ **7.** In *Song of Myself*, number 33, Whitman catalogs all the following heroes *except* —

A assassinated world leaders

B women condemned as witches

C runaway slaves being chased by slave catchers

D firefighters trapped in burning buildings

______ **8.** In *Song of Myself*, number 33, Whitman lists heroes who are —

F well-known Americans

G ordinary people

H famous figures from world history

J poets and writers

______ **9.** When the speaker in *Song of Myself*, number 33, writes that agonies are "changes of garments," he means that —

A he wants to suffer so that happiness will be more meaningful

B he cannot decide on his role in life

C he identifies deeply with others and takes on their emotions

D agony is a superficial emotion

______ **10.** Number 10 and number 33 of *Song of Myself* are united by the —

F strong sense of rhyme

G repeated phrases

H use of alliteration

J common themes

LITERARY FOCUS: FREE VERSE *(20 points; 5 points each)*
On the line provided, write the letter of the *best* answer to each of the following items.

______ **11. Free verse** is *best* described as —

A poetry written without regular rhyme schemes and meter

B words and expressions not meant to be taken literally

C clues that hint at what will happen later on in the poem

D exaggeration used for a literary effect such as emphasis, drama, or humor

______ **12.** Whitman achieved his specific purposes with all of the following poetic techniques *except* —

F alliteration

G rhyme

H assonance

J onomatopoeia

______ **13.** Which of the following quotations is the *best* example of Whitman's use of alliteration to unify his ideas?

A "My eyes settle the land, I bend at her prow or shout joyously from the deck."

B "I saw the marriage of the trapper in the open air in the far west. . . ."

C "The Yankee clipper is under her sky-sails, she cuts the sparkle and scud. . . ."

D "On a bank lounged the trapper, he was drest mostly in skins, his luxuriant beard and curls protected his neck. . . ."

______ **14.** In *Song of Myself,* number 33, Whitman personifies death as something chasing a ship. This figure of speech —

F suggests that the victims were doomed from the start

G shows that death is always present, even when we are not aware of it

H makes death seem to be a justified end

J shows death's enormous and persistent power

CONSTRUCTED RESPONSE *(20 points)*

15. In *Song of Myself,* Whitman says that he understands people by imaginatively participating in their experiences. Explain how Whitman uses poetic techniques and stylistic devices to encourage readers to participate in the experiences and images he describes. On a separate sheet of paper, write a paragraph that explains your answer. Support your ideas with details from the poem.

NAME ________________ CLASS ________________ DATE ________________ SCORE ________

from Song of Myself, Number 52 Walt Whitman

COMPREHENSION *(60 points; 6 points each)*

On the line provided, write the letter of the *best* answer to each of the following items.

_____ **1.** In, *Song of Myself,* number 52, Whitman —

A suggests that poetry will save the world

B explains that all poets deserve equal respect

C proclaims his own importance as a poet

D discusses the difference between poetry and prose

_____ **2.** The tone in this section of *Song of Myself* is *best* described as —

F lighthearted

G bombastic

H detached

J intimate

_____ **3.** Which phrase from this poem *best* expresses the way Whitman characterizes his own poetry?

A "drift it in lacy jags"

B "shadow'd wilds"

C "loitering"

D "barbaric yawp"

_____ **4.** Which image *best* appeals to the sense of hearing or sound?

F "The spotted hawk swoops by and accuses me, he complains / of my gab and my loitering."

G "I too am not a bit tamed, I too am untranslatable. . ."

H "The last scud of day holds back for me . . ."

J "I depart as air, I shake my white locks at the runaway sun. . . ."

_____ **5.** In this poem, Whitman uses the first-person point of view to make his poem more —

A unconventional

B like a factual report

C of an expression of himself

D lively and amusing

______ **6.** Which of the following quotations from the poem has the *best* example of alliteration?

F "I shake my white locks at the runaway sun"

G "The last scud of day holds back for me"

H "The spotted hawk swoops by and accuses me"

J "It coaxes me to the vapor and the dusk."

______ **7.** Which phrase from the poem is a simile?

A "He complains of my gab and my loitering."

B "I shake my white locks at the runaway sun."

C "If you want me again look for me under your boot-soles"

D "I depart as air"

______ **8.** In this poem, Whitman uses parallel structure to —

F help readers visualize key images

G link related images and unify his poem

H show stressed and unstressed syllables

J mimic a regular rhyme scheme

______ **9.** At the end of the poem, the speaker —

A proclaims his love for democracy

B encourages us to read more of his poetry

C reaffirms his link to the reader

D makes ironic comments about his own work

______ **10.** How could you *best* demonstrate Whitman's use of cadence in this poem?

F Discuss the imagery.

G Explain the theme.

H Point out the rhyming pattern.

J Read the poem aloud.

READING SKILLS: COMPARING THEMES ACROSS TEXTS *(20 points; 5 points each)*

On the line provided, write the letter of the *best* answer to each of the following items.

______ **11.** A common theme that runs through all the sections of *Song of Myself* is Whitman's own —

A belief in his power as a poet

B failure to change the world

C love of solitude

D inability to trust people

______ **12.** To sum up all the parts of *Song of Myself*, Whitman uses a literary technique called a —

F conflict

G climax

H couplet

J coda

______ **13.** In *Song of Myself*, Whitman's theme is *best* demonstrated by —

A the "last scud of day holds back for me"

B the "spotted hawk swoops by and accuses me"

C "look for me under your boot-soles"

D "coaxes me to the vapor and the dusk"

______ **14.** A common theme in the Whitman poems you have read is that —

F the natural world is becoming corrupt

G people should delight in their thoughts and spirit

H once people have died, they are soon forgotten

J the people of the world struggle without hope

CONSTRUCTED RESPONSE *(20 points)*

15. How does Whitman's theme in *Song of Myself*, number 52, reflect the themes and concerns of the time in which he lived? On a separate sheet of paper, write a paragraph that explains your answer. Support your ideas with details from the poem.

NAME ______ CLASS ______ DATE ______ SCORE ______

SELECTION TEST **Student Edition pages 322, 323, 325** LITERARY RESPONSE AND ANALYSIS

A Sight in Camp in the Daybreak Gray and Dim

Walt Whitman

from Specimen Days **Walt Whitman**

from Hospital Sketches **Louisa May Alcott**

COMPREHENSION *(60 points; 6 points each)*

On the line provided, write the letter of the *best* answer to each of the following items.

______ **1.** What is the "sight" that the speaker sees "in the daybreak gray and dim"?

- **A** The outbreak of another battle
- **B** Soldiers on stretchers
- **C** His brother George
- **D** A beautiful sunrise

______ **2.** Which of the following images from "A Sight in Camp in the Daybreak Gray and Dim" is *not* a visual image?

- **F** "ample brownish woolen blanket"
- **G** "flesh all sunken about the eyes"
- **H** "in the daybreak gray and dim"
- **J** "in the cool fresh air"

______ **3.** In "A Sight in Camp in the Daybreak Gray and Dim," Whitman emphasizes the —

- **A** fierceness of the fighting between North and South
- **B** reasons the war had to be fought
- **C** hardships he endured as a nurse during the war
- **D** connection between all people affected by the war

______ **4.** In the last stanza, Whitman implies that the Christlike soldier's death is —

- **F** meaningless
- **G** horrific
- **H** a sacrifice
- **J** beautiful

______ **5.** The tone of this poem is —

- **A** detached
- **B** gentle
- **C** despairing
- **D** inflamed

NAME ______ CLASS ______ DATE ______ SCORE ______

______ **6.** Based on Whitman's comments in *Specimen Days*, you can conclude that he —

F resented the President for plunging the country into war

G believed that Lincoln was a good man rather than a good leader

H greatly admired the President's strength of character

J believed that Lincoln was an opportunist

______ **7.** You can infer that one reason Whitman wrote *Specimen Days* was to —

A record what he saw as the truth

B advance his reputation as a major American poet

C leave a favorable impression of the war

D argue that hospitals must be upgraded

______ **8.** In *Hospital Sketches*, Alcott describes a scene of —

F horror and suffering

G calm readiness

H hopelessness

J false hope

______ **9.** From her account of serving as an army nurse, Alcott emerges as —

A self-serving and hypocritical

B useless and frightened

C brave and compassionate

D cold and distant

______ **10.** "A Sight in Camp in the Daybreak Gray and Dim," *Specimen Days*, and *Hospital Sketches* all contain —

F the theme of betrayal

G the argument that America has been hopelessly harmed by the Civil War

H attempts to explain why the North won the Civil War

J descriptions of soldiers wounded in the Civil War

LITERARY FOCUS: SYMBOL *(20 points; 5 points each)*
On the line provided, write the letter of the *best* answer to each of the following items.

______ **11.** As used in literature, a **symbol** is —

A the feeling of anticipation a writer creates

B a group of lines in a poem linked by theme

C a person, place, or object used to represent an abstract idea

D the writer's general tone and attitude about life

______ **12.** Whitman uses symbols for all of the following reasons *except* to —

F make the poem simpler to comprehend

G represent important abstract ideas

H convey his theme indirectly

J pack a great deal of meaning into his writing

______ **13.** In "A Sight in Camp in the Daybreak Gray and Dim," Whitman uses the three dead soldiers to symbolize the —

A futility of war

B universality of sacrifice

C importance of self-determination

D fear of injury and death

______ **14.** The fact that the events take place at daybreak may symbolize —

F broken promises of peace

G the entry of the soldiers' souls into eternal life

H an end to Whitman's old way of life

J the dawn of a new era for the United States

CONSTRUCTED RESPONSE *(20 points)*

15. Why do you think Whitman concentrates on describing the soldiers rather than commenting on the philosophical issues raised by the Civil War? Explain your opinion by referring to the influences of the historical period that shaped his thought. On a separate sheet of paper, write a paragraph that explains your answer. Support your ideas with details from the selections

Full Powers Pablo Neruda *translated by* Ben Belitt *and* Alastair Reid

COMPREHENSION *(60 points; 6 points each)*

On the line provided, write the letter of the *best* answer to each of the following items.

______ **1.** As he writes the first stanza, the poet is in —

- **A** a busy cafe
- **B** a dark cavern
- **C** a sunny street
- **D** Walt Whitman's birthplace

______ **2.** Which quotation from the poem uses alliteration and assonance to create musical effects?

- **F** "There is no way of explaining what does happen"
- **G** "And so I am made up of a non-being, / and, as the sea goes battering at a reef . . ."
- **H** "while my eyes meanwhile take measure of the meadows"
- **J** "Sometimes I puzzle over origins—. . . ."

______ **3.** What does the poet mean when he says "I forge the keys"?

- **A** He writes poetry to unlock life's mysteries.
- **B** He wants to bring his poetry to a wider audience.
- **C** The world conspires against artists, especially poets.
- **D** Like most poets, he is an impostor.

______ **4.** Which image *most* strongly appeals to the sense of touch?

- **F** "And I do not weary of going and returning."
- **G** "and keep on opening broken doors to the sea / for it to fill the wardrobes with its foam"
- **H** "Sometimes I puzzle over origins—. . . ."
- **J** "And I know that I keep on going for the going's sake. . . ."

______ **5.** The phrase "the fine threads spreading from a sea on fire" is an example of a(n) —

- **A** anecdote
- **B** paradox
- **C** couplet
- **D** simile

______ **6.** Where do the two lost channels carry the speaker?

- **F** The first toward non-being and the second toward death
- **G** The first toward the waves and the second toward the sky
- **H** The first toward the window and the second toward the shade
- **J** The first toward death and the second toward singing

______ **7.** In this poem the poet uses a great deal of imagery related to —

A industrialization

B the desert

C the forest

D water

______ **8.** What might the sea symbolize in this poem?

F Conscious forces

G The power of life and regeneration

H The diversity of human experience

J The passing of time

______ **9.** The poet's singing symbolizes —

A hope

B the sea

C life

D music

______ **10.** *Unlike* Walt Whitman, the speaker —

F believes that people are individuals

G lives a public as well as a private life

H lacks Whitman's exuberant self-assurance

J does not use poetry as a form of self-expression

READING SKILLS: COMPARING AND CONTRASTING POEMS *(20 points; 5 points each)*
On the line provided, write the letter of the *best* answer to each of the following items.

______ **11.** Through their poetry both Whitman and Neruda express their —

A awareness of their physical environment

B privileged backgrounds

C lack of education

D hidden motives

______ **12.** In the poem "Full Powers," Pablo Neruda pays homage to Walt Whitman with the phrase —

F "I recover space"

G "I do not weary"

H "I can sing"

J "I puzzle over origins"

______ **13.** Both Whitman and Neruda write in a style known as —

A sonnet

B free verse

C ballad

D epic

______ **14.** The works of Whitman and Neruda do *not* reflect similar attitudes about —

F the function of poetry

G the importance of success

H their connection to nature

J their love for humankind

CONSTRUCTED RESPONSE *(20 points)*

15. Explain several ways that the poems of Walt Whitman and Pablo Neruda qualify as classics of world literature. On a separate sheet of paper, write a paragraph that explains your answer. Support your ideas with details from the poems.

The Soul selects her own Society Emily Dickinson
If you were coming in the Fall Emily Dickinson

COMPREHENSION *(60 points; 6 points each)*

On the line provided, write the letter of the *best* answer to each of the following items.

______ **1.** In "The Soul selects her own Society," the soul shuts her door when —

- **A** she is commanded to by her divine Majority
- **B** the emperor asks her to do so
- **C** she has chosen with whom she belongs
- **D** she is crushed by responsibilities

______ **2.** In "The Soul selects her own Society," how does the soul react to the chariots and the emperor?

- **F** The soul is unmoved.
- **G** The soul is very impressed.
- **H** The soul bows to the pressure to react.
- **J** The soul rebels in fury.

______ **3.** In "The Soul selects her own Society," after the soul chooses one society, she sometimes —

- **A** blooms with renewed strength
- **B** dies without regret
- **C** makes everyone feel welcome
- **D** shuts herself off from others

______ **4.** What can you infer about the soul from the words *shuts*, *unmoved*, and *close*?

- **F** The soul detests all people.
- **G** The soul controls her own fate.
- **H** Once hurt, the soul can never recover.
- **J** The soul requires divine intervention to change.

______ **5.** In "The Soul selects her own Society," the soul determines a person's —

- **A** desire for change
- **B** deepest relationships
- **C** happiness
- **D** self-confidence

______ **6.** In "If you were coming in the Fall," whom is the speaker addressing?

F A stranger

G Her mother

H An enemy

J Her beloved

______ **7.** The tone of "If you were coming in the Fall" can *best* described as —

A hopeful

B sarcastic

C tragic

D hysterical

______ **8.** In the last stanza of "If you were coming in the Fall," the speaker expresses the idea that —

F she is not to blame for what went wrong

G lovers who part should never be reunited

H a lover should also be a friend

J uncertainty is frustrating

______ **9.** When the speaker says that she will count centuries until her "fingers dropped," she is using a figure of speech called —

A personification

B alliteration

C hyperbole

D symbolism

______ **10.** "The Soul selects her own Society" and "If you were coming in the Fall" both demonstrate the poet's —

F reliance on classical forms

G love for everyday language

H use of elaborate imagery and figures of speech

J strong sense of end rhyme

NAME ____________________ CLASS ____________ DATE ________ SCORE ______

LITERARY FOCUS: SLANT RHYME *(20 points; 5 points each)*

On the line provided, write the letter of the *best* answer to each of the following items.

______ **11. Slant rhyme** is created by —

A words that rhyme exactly

B words that have a close, but imprecise, rhyme

C rhymes that occur in the last two lines of the poem

D rhymes that are unintentional

______ **12.** Which of the following words from "The Soul selects her own Society" does *not* contain slant rhyme?

F door/more

G one/stone

H society/majority

J nation/attention

______ **13.** In which quotation from "If you were coming in the Fall"does the poet use a simile?

A "I'd brush the summer by / With half a smile, and half a spurn, / As Housewives do, a Fly."

B "If I could see you in a year, / I'd wind the months in balls—"

C "And put them each in separate Drawers, / For fear the numbers fuse—"

D "If only Centuries, delayed, / I'd count them on my Hand"

______ **14.** In "If you were coming in the Fall," the speaker compares "this life" to a(n) —

F poem

G rind

H eternity

J hand

CONSTRUCTED RESPONSE *(20 points)*

15. Explain how Dickinson uses figures of speech to help readers feel compassion for her situation in "If you were coming in the Fall." Give at least two examples from the poem to make your point. On a separate sheet of paper, write a paragraph that explains your answer. Support your ideas with details from the poem.

NAME ____________ CLASS ____________ DATE ____________ SCORE ____________

Tell all the Truth but tell it slant Emily Dickinson
Apparently with no surprise Emily Dickinson
Success is counted sweetest Emily Dickinson

COMPREHENSION *(60 points; 6 points each)*
On the line provided, write the letter of the *best* answer to each of the following items.

______ **1.** What does the frost do to the flower in "Apparently with no surprise"?

A Plays with it
B Makes it look beautiful
C Makes it stronger
D Kills it

______ **2.** Which pair of words from "Apparently with no surprise" show end rhyme?

F flower/power
G surprise/play
H unmoved/day
J day/God

______ **3.** In "Apparently with no surprise" Dickinson portrays a world in which God is —

A weak
B neutral
C cruel
D distracted

______ **4.** According to the speaker in "Tell all the Truth but tell it slant," the truth is —

F a lie
G awesome
H present in everything
J poetic

______ **5.** How does the speaker believe the truth should be revealed?

A Gradually
B All at once
C Not at all
D Often

_____ **6.** According to the speaker, a slant truth is a —

F social lie

G major falsehood

H major truth

J partial truth

_____ **7.** According to the speaker in "Success is counted sweetest," the people that value success the most are the ones who have —

A already achieved it

B failed at everything

C never attempted anything

D been successful early in life

_____ **8.** The "nectar" in "Success is counted sweetest" symbolizes —

F a drink

G poison

H failure

J an achievement

_____ **9.** Which is the *best* statement of the theme of "Success is counted sweetest"?

A Failure helps you appreciate success.

B Those who have experienced failure are doomed to repeat it.

C Success often takes you by surprise.

D Success is the best value to pursue.

_____ **10.** Dickinson may have written "Success is counted sweetest" as an ironic comment on her own —

F lack of publishing success

G longing for companionship

H dependence on her family

J anger towards her beloved

LITERARY FOCUS: TONE *(20 points; 5 points each)*

On the line provided, write the letter of the *best* answer to each of the following items.

______ **11.** A writer's attitude toward his or her subject is called —

A alliteration

B tone

C symbolism

D pitch

______ **12.** In "Tell all the Truth but tell it slant," Dickinson uses a straightforward, neutral tone to emphasize the fact that the speaker is —

F speaking from the heart

G not telling the whole truth

H trying to be dramatic

J pleading with the reader

______ **13.** What is the tone of "Success is counted sweetest"?

A Arrogant

B Sorrowful

C Optimistic

D Ironic

______ **14.** Which image appeals most strongly to the sense of sound?

F "To comprehend a nectar / Requires sorest need."

G "As he defeated—dying—/ On whose forbidden ear"

H "The Truth must dazzle gradually / Or every man be blind—"

J "The distant strains of triumph / Burst agonized and clear!"

CONSTRUCTED RESPONSE *(20 points)*

15. Select one of the three poems by Dickinson, and describe the feelings it evokes in you. Cite at least two figures of speech the poet uses to evoke this emotion. On a separate sheet of paper, write a paragraph that explains your answer. Support your ideas with details from the poem.

Because I could not stop for Death Emily Dickinson
I heard a Fly buzz—when I died Emily Dickinson
Much Madness is divinest Sense Emily Dickinson

COMPREHENSION *(60 points; 6 points each)*

On the line provided, write the letter of the *best* answer to each of the following items.

______ **1.** Death's carriage in "Because I could not stop for Death" holds all of the following *except* —

- **A** the speaker
- **B** Death
- **C** the reader
- **D** immortality

______ **2.** The things the carriage passes are noteworthy because they —

- **F** represent modern industrialization
- **G** embody the society that Dickinson avoided
- **H** were the only places besides home that she knew well
- **J** show that Dickinson regretted her seclusion

______ **3.** In the fifth stanza the horses pause at the House because —

- **A** it is the only familiar place
- **B** they are too frightened to proceed
- **C** they are in need of food and water
- **D** it is the speaker's grave

______ **4.** In "I heard a Fly buzz—when I died," the speaker prepared for death by —

- **F** catching a fly
- **G** offering the King her room
- **H** writing to everyone she loved
- **J** willing away her possessions

______ **5.** In "I heard a Fly buzz—when I died," the Fly's buzzing —

- **A** terrifies the speaker
- **B** soothes the speaker
- **C** intensifies the quiet
- **D** makes life more precious

NAME ______________________ CLASS ______________ DATE ____________ SCORE ________

______ **6.** How does the speaker feel about death in "I heard a Fly buzz—when I died"?

F She is angry to be taken so soon.

G She accepts death quietly.

H She vows to overcome her illness.

J She strikes a bargain with God.

______ **7.** In "Much Madness is divinest Sense" Dickinson compares —

A conformity and nonconformity

B methods of treating the mentally ill

C sense and the majority

D madness and a chain

______ **8.** The speaker in "Much Madness is divinest Sense" uses madness to mean a(n) —

F unwillingness to follow society's rules

G chemical imbalance

H incurable illness

J endearing personality trait

______ **9.** In "Much Madness is divinest Sense" Dickinson argues that —

A people must conform if the society is to function

B for the sake of society, insane people must be treated

C society tries to force people to conform

D poets are the only truly sane people

______ **10.** Which of the following poetic devices is not used in these three poems?

F Tone

G Metaphor

H Symbolism

J Refrain

NAME ______ CLASS ______ DATE ______ SCORE ______

LITERARY FOCUS: IRONY AND PARADOX *(15 points; 5 points each)*

On the line provided, write the letter of the *best* answer to each of the following items.

______ **11.** The way Death is portrayed in "Because I could not stop for Death" is ironic because Death is seen as —

A inevitable

B comforting

C avoidable

D an adventure

______ **12.** What is ironic about the buzzing of the fly in "I heard a Fly buzz—when I died"?

F Unlike the speaker, the fly is aware of death.

G The beauty of the fly distracts the speaker from the reality of death.

H Although the fly is a trivial sign of life, it signals the speaker's death.

J The buzzing of the fly makes the speaker cling harder to life.

______ **13.** In "Much Madness is divinest Sense" defining madness as the "divinest Sense" is an example of a(n) —

A paradox

B allusion

C metaphor

D illusion

READING SKILLS: SUMMARIZING A TEXT *(5 points)*

On the line provided, write the letter of the *best* answer to the item below.

______ **14.** In "Because I could not stop for Death," the speaker —

F does not take time to mourn a relative's death

G resists dying

H accompanies Death to a tomb

J observes Death taking a friend

CONSTRUCTED RESPONSE *(20 points)*

15. Explain how Emily Dickinson uses irony and tone to demystify death in "I heard a Fly buzz—when I died" or "Because I could not stop for Death." On a separate sheet of paper, write a paragraph that explains your answer. Support your ideas with details from the poems.

NAME ______ CLASS ______ DATE ______ SCORE ______

COLLECTION 3 SUMMATIVE TEST

American Masters: Whitman and Dickinson

This test asks you to use the skills and strategies you have learned in this collection. Read the two poems below, and answer the questions that follow them.

Aboard at a Ship's Helm
by Walt Whitman

Aboard at a ship's helm,
A young steersman steering with care.
Through fog on a sea-coast dolefully ringing,
An ocean-bell—O a warning bell, rock'd by the waves.
O you give good notice indeed, you bell by the sea-reefs ringing,
Ringing, ringing, to warn the ship from its wreck-place.

For as on the alert O steersman, you mind the loud admonition,
The bows turn, the freighted ship tacking speeds away under her gray sails,
The beautiful and noble ship with all her precious wealth speeds away gayly
and safe.
But O the ship, the immortal ship! O ship aboard the ship!
Ship of the body, ship of the soul, voyaging, voyaging.

The Moon is distant from the Sea
by Emily Dickinson

The Moon is distant from the Sea—
And yet, with Amber Hands—
She leads Him—docile as a Boy—
Along appointed Sands—

He never misses a Degree—
Obedient to Her Eye
He comes just so far—toward the Town—
Just so far—goes away—

Oh, Signor, Thine, the Amber Hand—
And mine—the distant Sea—
Obedient to the least command
Thine eye imposes on me—

VOCABULARY SKILLS *(25 points; 5 points each)*
Each of the underlined words below has also been underlined in the poems. Re-read those passages in which the underlined words appear, and then use context clues and your prior knowledge to help you select an answer. On the line provided, write the letter of the word or words that *best* answers each question.

______ **1.** In the Whitman poem a bell is ringing dolefully, or —

- **A** cheerfully
- **B** hopelessly
- **C** mournfully
- **D** slowly

______ **2.** The bell's admonition ____________ sailors about a nearby reef.

- **F** warns
- **G** puzzles
- **H** scolds
- **J** nags

______ **3.** When applied to a ship, the word *tacking* means —

- **A** striking
- **B** moving toward land
- **C** suddenly sinking
- **D** changing directions

______ **4.** In the Dickinson poem the sea is called docile because it is —

- **F** helpful
- **G** indifferent
- **H** hostile
- **J** submissive

______ **5.** The degree referred to in the Dickinson poem is an —

- **A** academic title
- **B** official rank
- **C** assigned direction
- **D** unofficial designation

NAME ______ CLASS ______ DATE ______ SCORE ______

COMPREHENSION *(25 points; 5 points each)*

On the line provided, write the letter of the *best* answer to each of the following items.

______ **6.** Both the Whitman poem and the Dickinson poem are examples of poetry that —

- **F** stresses the pangs of love that are not returned
- **G** praises the work of ordinary people
- **H** abandons conventional rhyme and meter
- **J** captures the cadence of public speakers

______ **7.** In the first stanza of the Whitman poem, the speaker describes —

- **A** the fog-bound ship approaching the reef
- **B** the fear in the heart of the inexperienced sailor
- **C** a rocky shore that inevitably wrecks ships
- **D** the deceptive nature of many warnings

______ **8.** In the last two lines of the Whitman poem, the speaker suggests that —

- **F** the ship is loaded with pirate gold
- **G** ocean voyages are filled with excitement
- **H** danger can be avoided if we heed the warnings
- **J** the human soul faces a difficult journey

______ **9.** In the Dickinson poem the moon and sea are metaphors for the —

- **A** rising and falling of the tide
- **B** relationship between teacher and pupil
- **C** cruelty of nature
- **D** loved one and the speaker

______ **10.** An example of slant rhyme in the Dickinson poem is —

- **F** Hands / Sands
- **G** Eye / away
- **H** Sea / me
- **J** Along / appointed

READING SKILLS AND STRATEGIES: CONSTRUCTED RESPONSE *(30 points; 15 points each)*

Summarizing a Text

11. From the following options, choose the one you think is the best summarization of "The Moon is distant from the Sea." On a separate sheet of paper, write the letter of the answer you chose, and briefly defend your choice. Use at least two examples from Dickinson's poem to justify your ideas.

- **A** Just as the sea is "led" by the moon, so the speaker is led by the sea.
- **B** Just as the sea is "led" by the moon, so the speaker is led by God.
- **C** Just as the sea is "led" by the moon, so the speaker is led by an inner direction.
- **D** Just as the sea is "led" by the moon, so the speaker is led by his or her father.

NAME ____ CLASS ____ DATE ____ SCORE ____

Comparing Themes Across Texts

12. On a separate sheet of paper, write a brief paragraph in which you agree or disagree with the following statement. Be sure to support your opinion with at least two examples from the poems.

Both "Aboard at a Ship's Helm" and "The Moon is distant from the Sea" deal with finding a direction in life; however, Whitman sees the force for that direction as coming from an internal source, while Dickinson sees it coming from an external one.

LITERARY FOCUS: CONSTRUCTED RESPONSE *(20 points)*

Literary Elements: Free Verse

13. What elements of free verse do you find in "Aboard at a Ship's Helm"? In the left side of the following chart, identify three elements of free verse Whitman used. One the right side, give an example of each element from the poem.

Elements of Free Verse	Example
1.	
2.	
3.	

NAME ______ CLASS ______ DATE ______ SCORE ______

COLLECTION 4 DIAGNOSTIC TEST

LITERATURE
INFORMATIONAL TEXT
VOCABULARY

The Rise of Realism: The Civil War to 1914

On the line provided, write the letter of the *best* answer to each of the following items. *(100 points; 10 points each)*

______ **1.** Which of the following sentences describes an **internal conflict**?

- **A** Two brothers, fighting for opposing sides in a war, face each other in battle.
- **B** A soldier must confront his fear in order to help his comrades conquer the enemy.
- **C** As a fierce snowstorm threatens their regiment, soldiers must overcome frostbite and starvation to survive.
- **D** A young man argues with his parents about enlisting in the army.

______ **2.** In the **third-person-limited point of view,** the narrator —

- **F** is all-knowing and enters the minds of all the characters
- **G** is the main character who tells the story
- **H** focuses on the thoughts and feelings of one character
- **J** is the author writing about him- or herself

______ **3.** **Situational irony** occurs when —

- **A** what actually happens differs from what the reader expects will happen
- **B** the reader is more knowledgeable than the characters
- **C** a character says one thing but means something different
- **D** one character reveals the truth about an event to another character

______ **4.** What is **satire**?

- **F** A technique used to suggest two or more meanings in a work
- **G** A type of comedy in which characters are involved in ridiculous situations
- **H** A story in which characters and events stand for moral qualities
- **J** A type of writing that ridicules people or institutions in an attempt to bring about change

______ **5.** **Motivation** refers to —

- **A** the narrator's attitude toward characters
- **B** the way a literary work affects the reader
- **C** the lessons an author wants to teach
- **D** the reasons for a character's actions

______ **6.** Which of the following statements about the **historical period** in which a story is written is *false*?

F The historical period can influence the attitudes expressed in a story.

G Classic literature is not influenced by the period in which it is written.

H The author's choice of a setting can be affected by the time period in which the author lives.

J A story's plot can be shaped by the historical period during which the story is written.

______ **7.** Poets rely on the **connotations** of words to —

A state their theme directly

B create rhythm

C suggest meaning

D establish a rhyme scheme

______ **8.** One device used in speeches to reinforce a message is —

F repetition

G foreshadowing

H description

J stereotype

______ **9.** Unlike a **synonym,** an **antonym** has —

A a different figurative meaning than another word

B the opposite, or nearly the opposite, meaning of another word

C a similar literal meaning as another word

D a different part of speech than another word

______ **10.** The **affixes** *–tion* and *–ment* are examples of —

F suffixes that can change words into nouns

G prefixes used to create new words

H archaic language

J word parts that carry the core meaning of a word

NAME ______________________ CLASS ______________ DATE ____________ SCORE __________

LITERARY PERIOD INTRODUCTION TEST **Student Edition page 382**

The Rise of Realism: The Civil War to 1914

COMPREHENSION *(100 points; 10 points each)*

On the line provided, write the letter of the *best* answer to each of the following items.

_____ **1.** Having seen the horrors of the Civil War firsthand as a Union camp hospital volunteer, Walt Whitman —

- **A** kept his optimistic attitude about the American character
- **B** became a bitter old man
- **C** was crushed by the death of his brother
- **D** decided to enlist in the army himself

_____ **2.** In response to the Civil War, Melville did *not* —

- **F** believe the fighting was both heroic and useless
- **G** write a great novel about the Civil War
- **H** write war poems that reveal his belief that humanity was basically evil
- **J** write war poems that show a respect for the soldiers on both sides

_____ **3.** Because few major American writers fought in the war, —

- **A** most people thought they were cowards and unpatriotic
- **B** they did not pay attention to the war
- **C** there were no realistic accounts of the war
- **D** very little important poetry and fiction emerged directly from this war

_____ **4.** A great novel of the Civil War was not written until long after the war had ended because —

- **F** the form of the realistic novel had not yet been fully developed
- **G** no one wanted to read a novel about the Civil War
- **H** none of the American writers were willing to go to the battlefields
- **J** the writers who saw the fighting firsthand were not willing to write about it

_____ **5.** The naturalistic novel has all the following characteristics *except* —

- **A** ordinary, everyday people as characters
- **B** a belief than human behavior was determined by biology and environment
- **C** the view that life was a grim, losing battle
- **D** larger-than-life, idealistic heroes

_____ **6.** After the Civil War, realistic writers sought to —

- **F** use romance to entertain readers and reveal truth
- **G** accurately portray real life without filtering it through Romanticism
- **H** heal the wounds of the war
- **J** soften the harsh edges of reality

_____ **7.** Although regional writers realistically described the speech patterns and mannerisms of a relatively small geographical area, these writers —

A were even more realistic in showing life as a losing battle

B were most interested in the impact of social forces on people

C were often unrealistic in depicting character and social environment

D mocked the people they described

_____ **8.** Naturalistic writers often showed human life as —

F crude and subject to the natural laws of the universe

G all working out for the best in the end

H an unlimited journey of body and spirit

J determined by a person's own choice

_____ **9.** The psychological novels of Henry James might *best* be described as —

A showing people driven by animal instincts

B showing the characters' inner lives

C tending to describe innocent Europeans

D all taking place in the United States

_____ **10.** The writings of an **ironist** may typically —

F describe the war and its outcome

G tell stories with happy endings

H show the indifference of the universe

J show how the universe helps people achieve their goals

NAME ______ CLASS ______ DATE ______ SCORE ______

SELECTION TEST **Student Edition page 399** LITERARY RESPONSE AND ANALYSIS

from Narrative of the Life of Frederick Douglass

Frederick Douglass

COMPREHENSION *(40 points; 4 points each)*

On the line provided, write the letter of the *best* answer to each of the following items.

______ **1.** In the first paragraph of this selection, Douglass explains that his purpose is to —

- **A** show how a slave was made a man
- **B** show how a man was made a slave
- **C** get revenge on Mr. Covey for his brutal treatment
- **D** explain how difficult life was for slaves

______ **2.** While fanning wheat, Douglass collapses because —

- **F** he wants to get out of working
- **G** Mr. Covey beats him and kicks him
- **H** the work is very difficult and requires a lot of concentration
- **J** the heat and work has made him ill

______ **3.** Douglass leaves the plantation to —

- **A** escape from slavery
- **B** get help from Master Thomas, his owner
- **C** visit with Sandy Jenkins
- **D** get some magic powder to help himself recover from the abuse

______ **4.** Jenkins advises Douglass to carry a root that will —

- **F** heal the wounds Douglass got from the beating
- **G** make Covey kinder and more compassionate
- **H** make it impossible for any white man to whip Douglass
- **J** help Douglass become a free man

______ **5.** Douglass thinks the root may bring him good luck because Covey —

- **A** could not find him in the cornfield
- **B** ignored Douglass when he returned to the plantation
- **C** sets Douglass free
- **D** treats him kindly upon his return

______ **6.** When Covey tries to bind Douglass's legs with a rope, Douglass —

- **F** fights back by grabbing Covey by the throat
- **G** bows down and begs Covey for mercy
- **H** asks other people for help
- **J** escapes and runs away to St. Michael's

______ **7.** When Covey calls out and asks Bill to help subdue Douglass, Bill —

A will not help unless Covey pays him

B immediately tackles Douglass

C refuses to get involved

D helps Douglass tie up Covey

______ **8.** For six months after this incident, —

F Covey gives Douglass the worst jobs on the plantation

G Covey never touches Douglass

H Douglass and Covey never speak

J Douglass does not regain his strength

______ **9.** During the course of this selection, Douglass shows how he —

A moves from fear to defiance

B is consumed by fear

C is reduced to total submission

D comes to respect Covey

______ **10.** At the end of the selection, Douglass —

F is still enslaved

G vows that he will be revenged

H regularly suffers abuse from white men

J regains his sense of freedom and dignity

LITERARY FOCUS: METAPHOR *(15 points; 5 points each)*

On the line provided, write the letter of the *best* answer to each of the following items.

______ **11.** By using a metaphor comparing his appearance to that of a "man who had escaped a den of wild beasts," Douglass suggests that —

A Covey had little control over his land and slaves

B slaves are treated like beasts, but the slaves' owners are the real beasts

C he is very near to death

D being a beast is preferable to being a slave

______ **12.** Which of the following sets of images does Douglass use in the metaphor that concludes the selection?

F Embers, a whip, and the arm of slavery

G A whip, a tomb, and a rope

H A tomb, a bloody arm, and an irritated wound

J Embers, a tomb, and heaven

NAME ______ CLASS ______ DATE ______ SCORE ______

______ **13.** This extended metaphor represents —

A freedom and the abolition movement

B youth and beauty

C rebirth and resurrection

D Douglass's decreasing willpower

READING SKILLS: ANALYZING AN AUTHOR'S ARGUMENT *(5 points)*

On the line provided, write the letter of the *best* answer to the following item.

______ **14.** Douglass achieves his purpose by —

F using only persuasive devices to make his case

G relying only on his personal story to make his case

H using description, narration, and persuasion

J using mostly persuasive techniques but also some description

VOCABULARY DEVELOPMENT *(20 points; 4 points each)*

Match each Vocabulary word on the left with its definition on the right. On the lines provided, write the letter of the definition.

______ **15.** intimated

______ **16.** comply

______ **17.** interpose

______ **18.** afforded

______ **19.** render

a. make

b. gave; provided

c. hinted

d. put forth in order to interfere

e. obey

CONSTRUCTED RESPONSE *(20 points)*

20. Explain how Douglass uses literary devices such as imagery, personification, figures of speech, and sounds to make his experiences vivid for his readers. On a separate sheet of paper, write a paragraph that explains your answer. Support your ideas with details from the selection.

NAME ______ CLASS ______ DATE ______ SCORE ______

SELECTION TEST **Student Edition page 407** LITERARY RESPONSE AND ANALYSIS

from Incidents in the Life of a Slave Girl

Harriet A. Jacobs

COMPREHENSION *(40 points; 4 points each)*

On the line provided, write the letter of the *best* answer to each of the following items.

______ **1.** After she escapes, Linda does not enter her grandmother's house because —

A she and her grandmother do not get along

B she knows that her grandmother will turn her in to Mr. Flint

C her grandmother is old and very ill, so she cannot help Linda

D she does not want to upset her grandmother and bring her harm

______ **2.** Instead, Linda decides to —

F immediately run to a free state

G ask her friend Sally for help

H hide in the basement of her brother's house

J ask Mr. Sands for help

______ **3.** As she leaves her children, Linda —

A kisses them and prays for them

B gives all her savings for their support

C clips a lock of each child's hair as a keepsake

D writes them a note so that they will never forget her

______ **4.** From her actions toward her children, you can conclude that Linda —

F realizes that she and her children will never be close

G understands that her children will never be free

H knows that her children will not understand why she has left them

J loves her children very much

______ **5.** To get Linda back, Mr. Flint promises all of the following options *except* —

A giving a reward for her recapture

B lashing any slaves who helped Linda escape

C granting Linda's brother William his freedom

D letting Linda keep her children with her

______ **6.** As explained in this account, Linda hides at her friend's house for about —

F a week

G a month

H a year

J five years

______ **7.** To force Linda out of hiding, Flint —

A sells her children

B puts her children in jail

C forces Linda's aged aunt to take care of her children

D kills her children

______ **8.** Harriet Jacobs probably chose to call Dr. James Norcom "Mr. Flint" to suggest that —

F he is vicious and violent

G his character is hard and inflexible

H other people in the neighborhood despise him

J he keeps many slaves and treats them all poorly

______ **9.** Harriet Jacobs *most* likely changed the names of her characters to —

A protect her relatives against retribution and revenge

B make her story more compelling

C maintain the traditions of nineteenth-century literature

D fool reporters from newspapers and magazines

______ **10.** Which of the following mottoes would Linda be *most* likely to adopt?

F "A bird in hand is worth two in the bush."

G "Learn to accept what you cannot change."

H "Never give up."

J "Good things come to people who wait."

LITERARY FOCUS: INTERNAL AND EXTERNAL CONFLICT *(20 points; 5 points each)*
On the line provided, write the letter of the *best* answer to each of the following items.

______ **11.** The *primary* conflicts in this story were all caused by —

A the system of slavery

B a weakness in Jacobs's character

C Mr. Flint's extreme cruelty

D Mr. Flint's harassment

______ **12.** All of the following situations are external conflicts in this narrative *except* Jacobs's —

F disagreement with her friend Sally over involving Jacobs's grandmother in the escape

G anguish over leaving her children

H attempt to escape from her owner

J efforts to avoid recapture

______ **13.** One indicator of an internal conflict that Jacobs faced is her —

A argument with Mr. Flint about closing the house at night

B brother's inability to read and write well

C guilt over leaving her children in jail

D inability to pray and receive comfort from prayer

______ **14.** The internal conflict that Jacobs finds *most* difficult to resolve is her —

F argument with Sally

G struggle with Mr. Flint

H decision to involve her friends and family in her escape

J attempts to avoid being recaptured

Vocabulary Development *(20 points; 4 points each)*

Write a synonym or antonym for each Vocabulary word, as directed.

15. malice *antonym:* ______

16. fervently *synonym:* ______

17. provocation *synonym:* ______

18. distressed *antonym:* ______

19. impulse *synonym:* ______

Constructed Response *(20 points)*

20. Which do you think was the *strongest* force in Jacobs's life: the institution of slavery, her religious beliefs, or her ethical standards? On a separate sheet of paper, write a paragraph that explains your answer. Support your ideas with details from the narrative.

NAME ______ CLASS ______ DATE ______ SCORE ______

SELECTION TEST **Student Edition pages 413, 415, 416, 418** LITERARY RESPONSE AND ANALYSIS

from My Bondage and My Freedom Frederick Douglass
Go Down, Moses
Follow the Drinking Gourd
Swing Low, Sweet Chariot
The Most Remarkable Woman of This Age
from Commonwealth *and* Freeman's Record

COMPREHENSION *(60 points; 6 points each)*
On the line provided, write the letter of the *best* answer to each of the following items.

_____ **1.** According to Frederick Douglass, slaves sang while they worked because —
- A their masters did not like it when slaves were silent
- B singing made the work go faster
- C they wanted to keep their heritage alive
- D they were exuberant on allowance day

_____ **2.** Douglass compares the slaves' songs to songs that —
- F he himself had learned while enslaved
- G were sung by the Israelites while they were enslaved by the Egyptians
- H people hear while lost deep in the woods
- J he heard in Ireland during the great famine

_____ **3.** When he hears the songs, Douglass always feels —
- A cheerful that he is no longer enslaved
- B proud that his people are rebelling
- C so sad that he often cries
- D amazed that people can endure so much adversity and still sing

_____ **4.** The "drinking gourd" of the song refers to —
- F the shape of Chesapeake Bay
- G the constellation of the Big Dipper
- H a code phrase for the "thirst for freedom"
- J the fact that safe houses were marked by a gourd by the door

_____ **5.** In "Go Down, Moses" and "Swing Low, Sweet Chariot," the slaves' experience is —
- A told in terms borrowed from the Old Testament tales of the Israelites' captivity
- B very difficult to understand
- C disguised in lighthearted melodies
- D exactly the same as the experience of the Israelites in biblical times

______ **6.** In "Go Down, Moses" all of the following demands are made *except* —

F asking the Pharaoh to speak to Moses on his behalf

G giving directions to the Pharaoh's location

H imploring the Pharaoh to grant the people freedom

J making threats if the Pharaoh will not let the people be free

______ **7.** What does "home" represent in "Swing Low, Sweet Chariot"?

A The speaker's birthplace in Africa

B Jordan

C The plantation

D Heaven

______ **8.** The tone of "Swing Low, Sweet Chariot" is *best* described as —

F neutral

G sorrowful

H joyful

J rebellious

______ **9.** "Follow the Drinking Gourd" is *most* likely intended to —

A convince slaves that it is safe to escape

B give directions to escaping slaves by pointing out stars and landmarks

C remind escaping slaves to take plenty of water and food with them

D caution slaves against escaping without being fully prepared for hardships

______ **10.** The writer of "The Most Remarkable Woman of This Age" —

F admires Harriet Tubman very much

G argues that Harriet Tubman learned about bravery from Moses

H knows very little about Harriet Tubman's life

J criticizes Harriet Tubman for being ruthless

LITERARY FOCUS: POLITICAL POINTS OF VIEW *(20 points; 5 points each)*
On the line provided, write the letter of the *best* answer to each of the following items.

______ **11.** In the passage from *My Bondage and My Freedom*, Douglass asserts that one common element in the songs of slaves is —

A hidden messages to their loved ones who have escaped

B open criticism of their masters

C flattery for their owners in order to draw a favorable glance

D many references to Greek and Roman myths

______ **12.** You can infer that Douglass wrote this selection to —

F encourage slaves to keep singing to relieve their hardship

G remind people of the soul-killing power of slavery

H invite historians to collect slave songs to preserve this unique heritage

J convince people of the power of song to affect the human soul

______ **13.** The article, "The Most Remarkable Woman of This Age," is an effective political tool because —

A the author includes details about Harriet Tubman's youth

B people often re-read periodicals for years

C it exposed the conditions of slavery to a large audience

D it describes Harriet Tubman's time in Philadelphia

______ **14.** Spirituals express concerns with —

F both spiritual salvation and physical freedom from slavery

G only spiritual salvation

H only physical freedom from slavery

J the condition of the ancient Israelites

CONSTRUCTED RESPONSE *(20 points)*

15. How do Frederick Douglass's words on spirituals affect your political understanding of slavery today? On a separate sheet of paper, write a paragraph that explains your answer. Support your ideas with details from the passage.

An Occurrence at Owl Creek Bridge Ambrose Bierce

COMPREHENSION *(40 points; 4 points each)*

On the line provided, write the letter of the *best* answer to each of the following items.

______ **1.** This story is set in Alabama during —

A the Revolutionary War, circa 1780

B the Civil War, circa 1864

C the Vietnam War, circa 1967

D World War I, circa 1919

______ **2.** Peyton Farquhar is *best* described as a —

F spy posing as a farmer

G middle-aged sentinel in the army

H thirty-five-year-old planter

J young and enthusiastic captain in the army

______ **3.** Peyton Farquhar —

A is tricked by a scout for the opposition

B betrays his own people for money

C turns his back on his wife and children

D lives a long and prosperous life

______ **4.** Early in the story, what interrupts Farquhar's thoughts about his wife and children?

F A train heading toward the bridge

G A hail of bullets

H The arrival of more troops

J The ticking of his watch

______ **5.** While Farquhar is underwater, he thinks that he is going to die, but —

A the current is so strong that the ropes break

B his hands seem to work independently of his will and free themselves

C he only loses consciousness

D the soldiers take pity on him and rescue him

______ **6.** After the board is kicked out from under him, Farquhar experiences —

F an intense sharpening of his senses

G despair and grief

H a surprising burst of happiness

J relief that he is going to live

NAME ________________ CLASS ________________ DATE ________ SCORE ________

______ **7.** After Farquhar appears to have escaped from the gunfire while in the river, he —

A is too exhausted to swim

B is picked up by a passing riverboat

C is recaptured and shot at once

D lands on a bank and runs through the woods

______ **8.** How much time passes in the story?

F A few minutes

G A few hours

H One day

J A day and a night

______ **9.** What actually happens in this story?

A Farquhar escapes hanging and is reunited with his family.

B The officers imagine that Farquhar is hanged.

C Farquhar dies by hanging.

D Farquhar drowns under the Owl Creek Bridge.

______ **10.** In part, this story illustrates —

F the importance of staying true to your values

G how all reality is an illusion

H the price people pay for being traitors

J our deep attachment to life

LITERARY FOCUS: POINT OF VIEW *(15 points; 5 points each)*
On the line provided, write the letter of the *best* answer to each of the following items.

______ **11.** When Farquhar hears his watch ticking with an exaggerated intensity, Bierce is using the point of view known as —

A second person limited

B first person

C objective

D third person limited

______ **12.** Which of the following details from the story *best* describes the author's use of the omniscient point of view?

F Bierce objectively describes the plantation.

G The narrator reports that the gray-clad horseman was a Federal scout.

H Bierce focuses only on Farquhar and his thoughts.

J The narrator gives a first-person account of the events.

_______ **13.** Bierce uses the omniscient point of view to —

A allow readers to view events through the eyes of only one character

B give readers the widest possible vantage point

C show Farquhar's innermost thoughts from Farquhar's own viewpoint

D limit the range of his narrative

READING SKILLS: ANALYZING SEQUENCE OF EVENTS *(5 points)*

On the line provided, write the letter of the *best* answer to the following item.

_______ **14.** Bierce plays with time in all of the following ways *except* by —

F including a flashback

G starting the story only minutes before it ends

H flashing forward to tell you what will happen to Farquhar ten years later

J telling about events that happen only in Farquhar's mind

VOCABULARY DEVELOPMENT *(20 points; 4 points each)*

On the line provided, complete each analogy with a Vocabulary word. Use each Vocabulary word only once.

sentinel **deference** **perilous** **encompassed** **pivotal**

15. TORNADO : HAZARDOUS :: HURRICANE : _______________

16. INSOLENCE : RESPECT :: IMPERTINENCE : _______________

17. ENCIRCLED : ENCLOSED :: ENVELOPED : _______________

18. TRIVIAL : CENTRAL :: IRRELEVANT : _______________

19. GUARD : DEFENDER :: WATCHMAN : _______________

CONSTRUCTED RESPONSE *(20 points)*

20. Throughout the story, Bierce uses stylistic devices to suggest Farquhar's real fate. Explain how the author uses elements of style to achieve his purpose. On a separate sheet of paper, write a paragraph that explains your answer. Support your ideas with details from the story.

A Mystery of Heroism Stephen Crane
War Is Kind Stephen Crane

COMPREHENSION *(40 points; 4 points each)*

On the line provided, write the letter of the *best* answer to each of the following items.

______ **1.** When the story opens, the battle —

A is in a brief lull while the soldiers reload their rifles

B has ended for the day

C has calmed down significantly

D is raging fiercely

______ **2.** Collins wants to get a drink of water because —

F he is thirsty

G the other men dare him to go

H it is his job to get water for the other men

J he does not want to fight any more

______ **3.** By the time Collins asks for permission to go to the well, —

A the soldiers have teased him so much that he feels he cannot back out

B the lieutenant has died

C the troops are preparing to charge

D his extreme thirst is dictating his actions

______ **4.** You can infer that Collins's superior officers —

F very much want him to get the water because they are also thirsty

G understand Collins's need to become a hero

H are afraid that Collins will gain all the fame for himself

J do not want him to go because the risk is not worth taking

______ **5.** Once Collins reaches the well, he —

A has time to fill each canteen

B is hit by a bullet but continues to fill the canteens

C grows impatient and fills a bucket instead of the canteens

D is trapped by the well and cannot return to his company

______ **6.** Collins does not consider himself a hero because he —

F believes heroes lead shameless lives, and he regrets some of his actions

G was just going to the well to get some water

H was terrified by the risk he took

J turns his back on the wounded lieutenant

______ **7.** When the dying lieutenant asks Collins for a drink of water, Collins's first reaction is to —

A carry the wounded man back to his regiment
B refuse the request and keep on running
C leave the officer a canteen of water and keep on running
D stop at once and give the man some water

______ **8.** Upon his return to his regiment, Collins is greeted by —

F a burst of gunfire
G absolute quiet
H a roar of approval
J his colonel's angry outburst

______ **9.** The story's title probably includes the word *mystery* because —

A Collins wonders whether there is water in the well
B Collins behaves more like a coward than a hero
C the story is a mystery
D heroic behavior is not easy to define

______ **10.** The title of the poem, "War Is Kind," is an example of verbal irony because the author —

F is using sarcasm and means the opposite
G is using an understatement and means that war is loving
H is using exaggeration
J wants to trick the reader

LITERARY FOCUS: SITUATIONAL AND VERBAL IRONY *(20 points; 5 points each)*
On the line provided, write the letter of the *best* answer to each of the following items.

______ **11.** In "A Mystery of Heroism," it is ironic that —

A the bucket is empty in the end
B Collins really does go to the well
C the battle continues even though Collins has stopped fighting
D the well is dry

______ **12.** Crane also uses situational irony when —

F Collins is killed after he returns, not during his mad dash across the field

G the lieutenant dies on the battlefield

H Collins survives his foolhardy escapade

J the water is not fit to drink

______ **13.** Which of the following examples from the story is the *strongest* example of situational irony?

A The colonel and the captain can't decide to let Collins get the water.

B In the midst of the battle an officer screams an order so loudly that it comes out as a shriek.

C The soldiers' roar of laughter greets Collins on his return.

D Collins returns to give the dying lieutenant a drink of water but spills the water all over the lieutenant's face.

______ **14.** When the speaker of "War Is Kind" says, "Do not weep, maiden, for war is kind," what technique is he using to make his point?

F Exaggeration

G Situational irony

H Rhythm and rhyme

J Verbal irony

VOCABULARY DEVELOPMENT *(20 points; 4 points each)*

On the line provided, write the Vocabulary word that *best* completes each sentence.

conflagration **stolidity** **ominous** **gesticulating** **provisional**

15. The ______________________ sound of marching soldiers caused the unarmed men to scurry for cover from the menacing approach.

16. Since no one could hear over the roar of the gunfire, the soldiers communicated by

______________________ with their hands.

17. They quickly built a ______________________ hiding place to shelter themselves for a few minutes.

18. A huge ______________________ started when a small fire spread to a nearby village.

19. The soldiers showed no emotion at all, and their ______________________ frightened the attackers.

Constructed Response *(20 points)*

20. Is Collins's act ultimately heroic, foolish, or a combination of both? How do Collins's actions reinforce Crane's purpose in this story? On a separate sheet of paper, write a paragraph that explains your answer. Use details from the story to support your ideas.

NAME ______ CLASS ______ DATE ______ SCORE ______

SELECTION TEST **Student Edition pages 446, 447, 448, 449, 450** LITERARY RESPONSE AND ANALYSIS

Letter to His Son Robert E. Lee
Letter to Sarah Ballou Maj. Sullivan Ballou
The Gettysburg Address Abraham Lincoln
from A Diary from Dixie Mary Chesnut
from Men at War: An Interview with Shelby Foote Ken Burns

COMPREHENSION *(60 points; 6 points each)*

On the line provided, write the letter of the *best* answer to each of the following items.

______ **1.** According to Lee in "Letter to His Son," the greatest disaster the country could face would be —

A the dissolution of the Union

B a state of anarchy

C our loss of honor

D government by Lincoln

______ **2.** Lee wrote this letter to thank his son for a gift and to —

F state that he should be commander in chief of the Confederate Army

G explain his reasons for not supporting the Union

H argue that secession would be a terrible mistake

J insist that the South must be avenged for Northern aggression

______ **3.** In view of Major Ballou's strong attachment to his family, his service as a soldier might *best* be described as the act of a —

A leader

B traitor

C coward

D patriot

______ **4.** Major Ballou offers his wife all of the following *except* —

F his ability to survive the battles unharmed

G their eventual reunion

H his eternal love

J his apologies for having been thoughtless and foolish

______ **5.** As he stated in Gettysburg, Lincoln believed that the Civil War would affect the entire world because —

A so many people died

B the war would eradicate slavery

C the war would show if a democracy could prevail

D his words would never be forgotten

______ **6.** The tone of Lincoln's speech is *best* described as —

F colloquial and informal

G formal and dignified

H abstract and hypothetical

J casual and relaxed

______ **7.** In *A Diary from Dixie* Dr. Palmer, the minister, tells his listeners that the South —

A could still be victorious with their support

B will lose the war and the institution of slavery is doomed

C is losing the war because of poor leadership

D needs slavery to survive economically

______ **8.** From her diary entries, Mary Chesnut emerges as —

F stubborn and optimistic

G totally devoted to the Southern cause

H not very concerned about the future

J perceptive and intelligent

______ **9.** According to Shelby Foote, the Civil War —

A defined America as a nation

B is not as important as many people think

C affected people in the nineteenth century but not the twentieth century

D was second in importance to the Revolutionary War

______ **10.** Shelby Foote argues that —

F Southerners could have won the Civil War if they had been better organized

G young men in the North had a greater motivation to fight in the war

H the South never had a chance of winning the war

J the country was essentially unchanged by the Civil War

READING SKILLS: ANALYZING POLITICAL POINTS OF VIEW *(20 points; 5 points each)*

On the line provided, write the letter of the *best* answer to each of the following items.

______ **11.** Lee tells his son that he will only raise his sword in —

A revolution

B anarchy

C civil war

D defense

______ **12.** Major Ballou thinks that he will —

F be killed in action

G soon be walking again

H soon arrive in Rhode Island

J return home safely

______ **13.** Lincoln tells his audience that they must do all of the following *except* —

A remember the task before them

B increase their devotion to the rebirth of freedom

C dedicate and consecrate the battlefield

D remember what he says in his address

______ **14.** According to Shelby Foote, after the Civil War the United States —

F was not as united as before the war

G turned its attention to the Homestead Act

H punished the Confederate states for trying to secede

J truly became one nation

CONSTRUCTED RESPONSE *(20 points)*

15. Compare and contrast the political assumptions in Robert E. Lee's "Letter to His Son" with those in Lincoln's famous speech at Gettysburg. On a separate sheet of paper, write a paragraph that explains your answer. Support your ideas with details from the narrative.

NAME ______ CLASS ______ DATE ______ SCORE ______

SELECTION TEST **Student Edition page 455** LITERARY RESPONSE AND ANALYSIS

"I Will Fight No More Forever" Chief Joseph

COMPREHENSION *(60 points; 10 points each)*

On the line provided, write the letter of the *best* answer to each of the following items.

______ **1.** Chief Joseph vows that he "will fight no more forever" for all of the following reasons *except* —

A he has been advised by his chiefs to surrender

B the chiefs have been killed

C his people lack blankets and food

D he feels sick and sad with loss

______ **2.** Chief Joseph states that he now wants to spend his time —

F finding a new place to live

G planting next summer's crops

H looking for his children

J negotiating with General Howard

______ **3.** You can infer that Looking Glass and Toohoolhoolzote were —

A Chief Joseph's wives

B enemy warriors

C responsible for the tribe's current problems

D chiefs in the tribe

______ **4.** Chief Joseph says that many members of the tribe —

F have joined other tribes

G are being educated at Indian schools

H have turned their backs on Chief Joseph, believing that he is a weak leader

J have run away to the hills

______ **5.** What feelings does this speech evoke in readers?

A Hostility and anger

B Neutrality and objectivity

C Sadness and sympathy

D Cool restraint

______ **6.** You can conclude from this speech that Chief Joseph —

F had no recourse but to surrender

G didn't really have to surrender

H and General Howard were bitter enemies

J and General Howard had never met each other

Literary Focus: American Indian Oratory *(20 points; 5 points each)*

On the line provided, write the letter of the *best* answer to each of the following items.

______ **7.** The tone of this speech is *best* described as —

A arrogant
B dignified
C detached
D whiny

______ **8.** Chief Joseph's purpose in this speech was to accomplish all of the following objectives *except* —

F surrender his tribe to the federal government
G warn pioneers that they must leave the tribe's land or face attack
H explain why he will stop fighting
J describe his tribe's current situation

______ **9.** You can conclude that Chief Joseph —

A is a very weak leader
B cannot decide which path his people should take
C is too proud to negotiate with the federal government
D cares deeply about his people and is trying to safeguard them

______ **10.** To convey his ideas and achieve his purpose, Chief Joseph uses —

F colloquial language and complex sentences
G elevated diction and dialogue
H difficult words and long sentences
J repetition of key words and parallelism

Constructed Response *(20 points)*

11. Why do you suppose this speech continues to affect people today? On a separate sheet of paper, analyze the qualities that make it so powerful.

NAME ______ CLASS ______ DATE ______ SCORE ______

SELECTION TEST **Student Edition page 460**

The Celebrated Jumping Frog of Calaveras County

Mark Twain

COMPREHENSION *(40 points; 4 points each)*

On the line provided, write the letter of the *best* answer to each of the following items.

______ **1.** The narrator calls on Simon Wheeler to —

A find out about a friend's childhood friend, Rev. Leonidas W. Smiley

B hear the story of Jim Smiley

C learn more about the Old West and its humorous characters

D place some bets on horses, dogs, and frogs

______ **2.** Why does the narrator listen to Simon Wheeler's long story?

F The narrator is collecting material for his writing.

G The narrator is waiting for Rev. Leonidas W. Smiley, so he can't leave.

H Simon has backed the narrator into a corner and won't let him escape.

J Simon and the narrator are old friends, so the narrator doesn't want to be rude.

______ **3.** Jim Smiley's horse wins races by —

A attacking all the other horses in the race

B raising a lot of dust so the other horses can't see where to go

C barreling past the other horses, after having a head start

D making so much noise that she scares all the other horses

______ **4.** Andrew Jackson, the bull pup, wins fights by —

F tricking all the bettors with his fake asthma attacks

G rolling over and playing dead

H biting other dogs and throwing them over his shoulder

J holding his opponent's hind leg until the other dog collapses

______ **5.** The bull pup finally loses a fight when he —

A starts wheezing and can't breathe

B is attacked by a fierce, heavy dog

C is filled with buckshot and can't move

D is pitted against a dog that doesn't have hind legs

______ **6.** Is the stranger as innocent as he appears?

F No, because he tricks Smiley.

G No, because he has a racing frog hidden in his coat.

H Yes, because he doesn't know anything about frog races.

J Yes, because he is a stranger in town.

______ **7.** How does the frog lose the race?

A The other frog attacks him.

B When he realizes that he can't win, he just gives up and dies.

C The stranger fills him with lead pellets, so the frog is too heavy to hop.

D He gets confused and hops in the wrong direction.

______ **8.** Simon Wheeler is *best* described as —

F dishonest and corrupt

G long-winded and unintentionally funny

H concise and intentionally funny

J greedy but unlucky

______ **9.** Jim Smiley is *best* described as a —

A gullible gambler

B good storyteller

C skilled risk taker

D minister

______ **10.** The story ends when —

F Smiley finds the stranger and gets his money back

G Smiley bets on a banana that looks like a cow

H Simon and the narrator bet on a yellow, one-eyed cow

J Wheeler starts telling another story, and the narrator leaves

LITERARY FOCUS: COMIC DEVICES *(15 points; 5 points each)*

On the line provided, write the letter of the *best* answer to each of the following items.

______ **11.** The purpose of this story is to —

A warn readers about the evils of gambling

B entertain readers

C teach readers about famous public figures from the past

D describe life in an Old West mining camp

_____ **12.** Twain accomplishes his purpose *chiefly* through —

F telling a story within a story, also called a "frame story"

G using several different narrators

H specific examples of wrongdoing

J outrageous exaggeration and word play

_____ **13.** Daniel Webster was the most famous public speaker of his day. Twain uses Webster's name to create humor when he —

A misspells Webster's first and last names

B pokes fun at Webster's appearance by naming a dog after him

C makes fun of Webster's voice by naming a frog after him

D satirizes Webster's stubbornness by naming a horse after him

READING SKILLS: UNDERSTANDING VERNACULAR *(5 points)*

On the line provided, write the letter of the *best* answer to the following item.

_____ **14.** All of the following excerpts contain vernacular language that vividly captures the characters in Calaveras County *except* —

F "At the door I met the sociable Mr. Wheeler returning . . ."

G "There couldn't be no solit'ry thing mentioned but that feller'd offer to bet on it. . . ."

H "Thish-yer Smiley has a mare—the boys called her the fifteen-minute nag, but that was only in fun, you know. . . ."

J "always fetch up at the stand just about a neck ahead, as near as you could cipher it down . . ."

VOCABULARY DEVELOPMENT *(20 points; 4 points each)*

Write a synonym or antonym for each Vocabulary word, as directed.

15. garrulous *antonym:* ____________________

16. infamous *antonym :*____________________

17. dilapidated *synonym :*____________________

18. interminable *antonym:* ____________________

19. conjecture *synonym:* ____________________

NAME ______ CLASS ______ DATE ______ SCORE ______

CONSTRUCTED RESPONSE *(20 points)*

20. Explain three ways that Twain creates humor in "The Celebrated Jumping Frog of Calaveras County." Consider the form of the story as well as its content. On a separate sheet of paper, write a paragraph that explains your answer. Support your ideas with details from the story.

The Lowest Animal Mark Twain

COMPREHENSION *(40 points; 4 points each)*

On the line provided, write the letter of the *best* answer to each of the following items.

_____ **1.** What is Twain's theory of humanity?

- **A** People descended from animals.
- **B** Animals descended from people.
- **C** People and animals are on the same level.
- **D** Animals are more cruel and vicious than people.

_____ **2.** To give his theory credence, Twain claims that —

- **F** he heard about it from a famous scientist
- **G** he read about it in scientific books and studies
- **H** he drew his conclusions from his own experiments
- **J** it was created by Charles Darwin

_____ **3.** Twain concludes that English earls are cruel because they —

- **A** like to hunt, but anacondas do not hunt
- **B** eat wild animals while anacondas prefer domesticated animals
- **C** eat far more than they need to survive
- **D** kill animals for fun rather than for food

_____ **4.** You can infer from the example of the earl and the anaconda that Twain —

- **F** had never met an English earl
- **G** knew a lot about anacondas
- **H** was a vegetarian, a person who does not eat meat
- **J** was not a supporter of hunting for sport

_____ **5.** What example does Twain *not* cite to make his point that humanity is cruel?

- **A** Native Americans have gouged out prisoners' eyes.
- **B** King John burned his nephew with a hot iron.
- **C** Americans have hanged their neighbors.
- **D** Zealots in the Middle Ages skinned captives alive, pouring salt on the wounds.

_____ **6.** According to Twain, human beings are inferior to animals in all of the following ways *except* —

- **F** animals cannot show love, while humans can
- **G** people wage war
- **H** humans are intolerant of different religions
- **J** we enslave others of our kind, while animals do not

______ **7.** The tone of Twain's essay is *best* described as —

A light
B bitter
C uproariously funny
D neutral

______ **8.** Twain's last example demonstrates that —

F we should eliminate all religion if we want to get along
G people are foolish and intolerant
H some animals can get along peacefully, while others cannot
J animals need to be tamed before they can live together

______ **9.** When Twain says, "Man is the Animal that Blushes . . . or has occasion to," he means that —

A men and jackasses both laugh
B animals get embarrassed
C the animals laugh at man's foolishness
D man has reason to be ashamed

______ **10.** Twain says that of all the animals, man alone is —

F happy
G reasonable
H cruel
J noble

LITERARY FOCUS: SATIRE *(15 points; 5 points each)*
On the line provided, write the letter of the *best* answer to each of the following items.

______ **11.** Twain satirizes all of the following human foibles *except* —

A love
B greed
C vengeance
D intolerance

______ **12.** In Twain's example of people refusing to be seen undressed in public, Twain is satirizing —

F religious intolerance

G false modesty

H avarice

J cruelty

______ **13.** What is ironic about Twain's assertion that humans are the "Reasoning Animal"?

A People *are* the most intelligent creatures on earth.

B Many animals are just as smart as people.

C We rarely get a chance to display the full range of our intelligence.

D Our actions show that we are irrational and unreasoning.

READING SKILLS: RECOGNIZING A WRITER'S PURPOSE *(5 points)*

On the line provided, write the letter of the *best* answer to the following item.

______ **14.** Twain wrote his satire "The Lowest Animal" *mainly* to —

F bemoan the degeneration of the human race

G criticize people for their cruelty and viciousness

H force people to reexamine their attitudes and behavior

J inspire confidence and hope among despairing people

VOCABULARY DEVELOPMENT *(20 points; 4 points each)*

On the line provided, complete each analogy with a Vocabualry word. Use each Vocabulary word only once.

allegiance **atrocious** **appease** **avaricious** **sordid**

15. GENEROUS : GREEDY :: CHARITABLE : ______________________

16. BABY : PACIFY :: DICTATOR : ______________________

17. SQUALID : FILTHY :: FOUL : ______________________

18. COUNTRY : LOYALTY :: FLAG : ______________________

19. WORTHY : ABOMINABLE :: DESIRABLE : ______________________

NAME ______ CLASS ______ DATE ______ SCORE ______

CONSTRUCTED RESPONSE *(20 points)*

20. Which of Twain's arguments are *most* effective? Why? Select two of Twain's arguments to evaluate. On a separate sheet of paper, write a paragraph that explains your answer. Support your ideas with details from the essay.

NAME ______ CLASS ______ DATE ______ SCORE ______

SELECTION TEST **Student Edition pages 481, 493**

To Build a Fire Jack London
from Left for Dead Beck Weathers

COMPREHENSION *(40 points; 4 points each)*
On the line provided, write the letter of the *best* answer to each of the following items.

______ **1.** How cold is it when "To Build a Fire" opens?
- **A** 30 degrees above zero
- **B** 0 degrees
- **C** 32 degrees below zero
- **D** 75 degrees below zero

______ **2.** The man is *best* described as —
- **F** intelligent and highly organized
- **G** brave and heroic
- **H** foolish and unimaginative
- **J** very knowledgeable about surviving in Alaskan winters

______ **3.** What does the man fear from the beginning of his journey?
- **A** Falling through the snow and getting his feet wet
- **B** The strange color of the sky
- **C** The dog's strange behavior
- **D** Getting caught in a sudden avalanche

______ **4.** The man makes all the following mistakes *except* —
- **F** deciding to traveling alone
- **G** forgetting to bring matches with him
- **H** not listening to people who know more about the North
- **J** not understanding the danger he faces

______ **5.** After he falls into the spring, the man —
- **A** cannot build a fire
- **B** succeeds in building a fire
- **C** kills the dog to stay warm
- **D** builds a roaring fire and dries out completely

______ **6.** When the bough full of snow falls, the man —
- **F** realizes that he is likely to die
- **G** starts the fire easily
- **H** huddles with the dog to warm his hands and feet
- **J** immediately panics and starts running toward camp

_____ **7.** Why is the man unable to reach the camp?

A He lacks the endurance to run that far.

B He gets lost.

C He trips and breaks his legs.

D The trail has been covered over by fresh snow.

_____ **8.** You can infer that London —

F feels great sympathy for the man

G believes that no one should travel in the Yukon

H realizes that the man could have saved himself

J thinks that the man is a fool

_____ **9.** When Beck Weathers falls, he holds his hands close to his body so that —

A he will land flat and not fall through the snow

B his arms stay warm

C he won't damage his hands with further frostbite

D his head will be protected from frostbite

_____ **10.** All of the following things happen to Weathers *except* —

F his right arm is frozen over his head

G he eats his own boot to stay alive

H Todd Burleson finds him

J he doesn't want to believe the "blue rocks" are tents

LITERARY FOCUS: NATURALISM *(15 points; 5 points each)*
On the line provided, write the letter of the *best* answer to each of the following items.

_____ **11.** In London's story, nature is portrayed as —

A indifferent to humanity

B warm and kind

C helpful but ignored

D misunderstood and misused

_____ **12.** **Naturalism,** as shown in this story, holds that —

F animals and humans can learn to respect each other

G nature is a source of comfort and inspiration

H human beings are subjected to forces beyond their control

J close observation of nature requires a scientific approach

______ **13.** London's story shows the naturalist belief that people are at the mercy of —

- **A** a spiritual entity
- **B** animals and other creatures
- **C** other people
- **D** heredity and environment

READING SKILLS: ANALYZING TEXT STRUCTURES: CAUSE AND EFFECT *(5 points)*
On the line provided, write the letter of the *best* answer to the following item.

______ **14.** In "To Build a Fire" the man's final predicament is caused when he —

- **F** does not pay enough attention to his immediate surroundings
- **G** steps into a hidden spring and does not stop to dry his feet
- **H** chooses to travel when everything is thawing
- **J** stops for lunch and uses up all his matches

VOCABULARY DEVELOPMENT *(20 points; 4 points each)*
Match each Vocabulary word on the left with its definition on the right. On the lines provided, write the letter of the definition.

______ **15.** intangible	**a.** absolutely necessary
______ **16.** undulations	**b.** firmness
______ **17.** protruding	**c.** difficult to define; vague
______ **18.** solidity	**d.** sticking out
______ **19.** imperative	**e.** wavelike motions

CONSTRUCTED RESPONSE *(20 points)*

20. Which of the following statements about "To Build a Fire" do you think *best* reflects naturalist theory? On a separate sheet of paper, write a paragraph that explains your answer. Support your ideas with details from the story.

- **A** The man dies because he underestimates the force of the bitter cold.
- **B** The man's survival depends on factors over which he has no control.
- **C** The dog is better suited to the Yukon's environment than the man is.
- **D** Even with a companion along, it would have been dangerous for the man to travel through the Yukon.

What Do You Feel Underground?

Gabriela Mistral *translated by* Maria Giachetti

COMPREHENSION *(60 points; 6 points each)*

On the line provided, write the letter of the *best* answer to each of the following items.

______ **1.** The "you" in the poem's title is —

A the speaker's dead lover

B the speaker

C nature

D worms

______ **2.** What emotions does the speaker feel *most* strongly?

F Fury and passion

G Confusion and astonishment

H Regret and sorrow

J Joy and satisfaction

______ **3.** In which season does the poem take place?

A Fall

B Spring

C Summer

D Winter

______ **4.** The poem is set in —

F the ocean

G a beautiful place bordering a river

H heaven

J the city

______ **5.** The poet develops her ideas largely through —

A irony

B sarcasm

C questions

D inversion

______ **6.** The speaker asks if the person being addressed recalls all of the following events *except* —

F singing together

G the sky

H water flowing down the mountain

J walking through the woods with the speaker

______ **7.** The speaker wishes that the "you" could enjoy —

A traveling with the speaker
B the beautiful fragrances all around
C seeing the children play in the clear mountain stream
D swimming in the clear, cool lake

______ **8.** The speaker would also like to —

F hug the person being addressed
G kiss the person being addressed
H silence the person being addressed
J ask advice of the person being addressed

______ **9.** The person being addressed cannot respond because he or she —

A refuses to speak to the poet anymore
B moved far away from the poet
C has died
D deliberately deserted the speaker

______ **10.** The poem might be *best* summarized by saying that the speaker —

F wishes that she had someone with whom to share nature's glory
G expresses anger that her lover has left her without even saying goodbye
H expresses sorrow that her lover cannot savor the beauty of the world
J wants to go underground to escape her sorrow and isolation

LITERARY FOCUS: IMAGERY *(20 points; 5 points each)*
On the line provided, write the letter of the *best* answer to each of the following items.

______ **11.** To which sense does the following image appeal: "Underground do you feel / the delicate warmth of this spring?"

A smell
B touch
C sight
D taste

______ **12.** Which image *most* strongly appeals to the sense of smell?

F "Do you remember the sky"

G "Does the sharp perfume of honeysuckle / reach you through the earth?"

H "Do you remember the deep-tapestried path, / my still hand in your trembling hand?"

J "But you are underground—/your tongue silenced by dust"

______ **13.** With the lines, "You might like the ambivalent warmth / of my mouth, its soft violence," the speaker —

A conveys the passion of love, its combination of tenderness and power

B suggests that all love is doomed to fail

C infers that her love was unsure and tentative, never firm

D communicates her undying passion for her lover

______ **14.** Which image appeals to both taste and sound?

F "This spring perfumes and refines / the sweet liquor of veins."

G "If only underground your beautiful / closed mouth could savor it!"

H "there is no way that you can sing with me / the sweet and fiery songs of this spring."

J "Do you remember the sky, / the clear jets of mountain water"

CONSTRUCTED RESPONSE *(20 points)*

15. What feelings does this poem evoke? Identify the emotion or emotions conveyed in this poem and describe two ways the speaker creates this feeling. On a separate sheet of paper, write a paragraph that explains your answer. Support your ideas with details from the poem.

NAME ______ CLASS ______ DATE ______ SCORE ______

SELECTION TEST **Student Edition pages 504, 510**

A Pair of Silk Stockings Kate Chopin
Now and Then, America Pat Mora

COMPREHENSION *(40 points; 4 points each)*

On the line provided, write the letter of the *best* answer to each of the following items.

______ **1.** At first, Mrs. Sommers thinks that she will spend her fifteen dollars on —

A fine leather gloves for herself
B a good lunch
C a matinee at the theater
D clothing for her children

______ **2.** At the beginning of the story, Mrs. Sommers is characterized as a —

F neglectful mother
G flighty, irresponsible person
H dutiful, caring parent
J cheerful woman

______ **3.** What can you infer about Mrs. Sommers's past?

A She had more money and lived a more gracious life.
B Her husband deserted her a few years ago.
C She had grown up in poverty.
D She did not want to get married and have children.

______ **4.** How do the silk stockings affect Mrs. Sommers?

F She is ashamed that she cannot afford them.
G She is put off by their extravagance.
H She is repelled by their slimy feeling.
J When she touches them, she wants more things.

______ **5.** You can conclude from the events in this story that —

A when this story takes place, women wore pants most of the time
B in the past nearly all women had silk stockings
C silk stockings were an expensive luxury
D in the past, women rarely shopped

______ **6.** After Mrs. Sommers buys the stockings, what is her next purchase?

F A pair of beautiful leather shoes
G Two magazines
H Shoes for her children
J A dress for her daughter

______ **7.** Mrs. Sommers also allows herself the luxury of a —

A visit to a museum and a few newspapers

B meal at a nice restaurant and a play

C new hat and a play

D box of chocolates

______ **8.** Mrs. Sommers's new clothes make her feel —

F guilty and ashamed of her extravagance

G self-confident

H fearful of her family's reaction

J convinced that she will have to return everything

______ **9.** At the matinée, Mrs. Sommers —

A is distracted by guilty thoughts of her spending spree

B leaves early because she does not like the play

C decides to leave her family and become an actress

D very much enjoys the performance

______ **10.** Pat Mora wants America to accept her —

F pinstriped suit

G death

H silk tie

J difference

LITERARY FOCUS: MOTIVATION *(15 points; 5 points each)*

On the line provided, write the letter of the *best* answer to each of the following items.

______ **11.** Before she buys herself some luxuries, Mrs. Sommers is likely motivated by all of the following forces *except* —

A political forces to vote

B social pressure for women to be self-sacrificing

C philosophical beliefs that women do not deserve their own money

D ethical forces that spark her deep-seated guilt about indulging herself

_____ **12.** What motivates Mrs. Sommers to treat herself to some luxuries?

F She wants to spend all the money that she has saved.

G She thinks she deserves some luxuries after all her sacrifices.

H She is likely acting on an impulse.

J Her husband's departure makes her want to live for the moment.

_____ **13.** Each of the objects that Mrs. Sommers buys is —

A against her religious beliefs

B an unnecessary extravagance

C essential to maintain her social status, given her husband's good salary

D a political statement of defiance at her second-class status

READING SKILLS: ANALYZING HISTORICAL CONTEXT *(5 points)*
On the line provided, write the letter of the *best* answer to the following item.

_____ **14.** Analyzing the historical context of "A Pair of Silk Stockings" is *most* important for understanding why Mrs. Sommers —

F is filled with importance when she gets fifteen dollars

G patches her children's old clothes

H likes to shop for bargains

J takes the elevator to the ladies waiting room

VOCABULARY DEVELOPMENT *(20 points; 4 points each)*
Write a synonym or antonym for each Vocabulary word, as directed.

15. judicious *antonym:* ____________________

16. appreciable *synonym:* ____________________

17. veritable *synonym:* ____________________

18. acute *antonym:* ____________________

19. judicious *synonym:* ____________________

CONSTRUCTED RESPONSE *(20 points)*

20. Why does Mrs. Sommers spend the fifteen dollars the way she does rather than the way she had planned? On a separate sheet of paper, write a paragraph that explains your answer. Support your ideas with details from the story.

NAME ______ CLASS ______ DATE ______ SCORE ______

SELECTION TEST **Student Edition page 514**

LITERARY RESPONSE AND ANALYSIS

A Wagner Matinée Willa Cather

COMPREHENSION *(40 points; 4 points each)*

On the line provided, write the letter of the *best* answer to each of the following items.

______ **1.** On greeting his aunt, Clark notices how —

A eager she is to see Boston again

B shabby she looks and how exhausted she seems

C easily she adjusts to life in Boston

D unfriendly and distant she acts

______ **2.** In regard to his aunt, Clark —

F is ashamed by her appearance

G feels a combination of admiration, gratitude, and pity

H is shocked by her poor speech and narrow attitudes

J feels annoyed that she gave him so little notice about her visit

______ **3.** As far as Uncle Howard is concerned, Clark —

A feels that Howard is cruel and treats Georgiana badly

B realizes that Howard is a cultured man who got trapped on the prairie

C admires Howard's ambition and ability to work hard

D is sad that Howard did not give his wife a comfortable life

______ **4.** Georgiana is primarily a victim of the decision she made when she —

F chose to set aside her music and become active in her community

G married a good man who became unable to work

H fell in love with Howard and moved with him to an isolated farm

J chose to continue studying music on her own

______ **5.** When Clark was a boy, Georgiana warned him not to —

A love something too much, or it might be taken from him

B choose a wife too quickly, for he might be hurt

C return to Boston, because he might be unhappy with city life

D give up his studying, because he could end up poor and miserable

______ **6.** Clark decides to take Georgiana to a concert to —

F awaken in her all the beauty that she has missed

G show her how city life is better than country life

H force her to take up her music again

J persuade her to leave Howard and move back to Boston

______ **7.** At first, Clark is afraid to take Georgiana to the concert because she might —

A embarrass him by her unsophisticated behavior and appearance

B be embarrassed at returning to the world she had left for so long

C fall asleep and snore

D not understand what she would be hearing

______ **8.** When the horns play during the *Tannhäuser*, Georgiana clutches Clark's sleeve and he —

F remembers how much Georgiana dislikes brass instruments

G remembers how silent the Nebraska plains are

H realizes that Georgiana is ill

J realizes that Georgiana's hands are too crippled to play the piano

______ **9.** Georgiana cries during the concert *primarily* because she —

A remembers how important music is to her

B is suddenly homesick for Nebraska and her family

C dislikes being with so many snobby people

D is happy that she gave up her career as a pianist

______ **10.** Clark sympathizes with his aunt because —

F he remembers his own difficulties returning to the city

G Howard had written to him about Georgiana's decline

H she passed on her love of music to him long ago

J he doesn't like classical music either

LITERARY FOCUS: SETTING *(20 points; 5 points each)*
On the line provided, write the letter of the *best* answer to each of the following items.

______ **11.** What two settings form the basis of this story?

A Boston and New York

B Nebraska and New York

C Boston and Nebraska

D New York and Franz Josef Land

______ **12.** In describing the two settings, the narrator —

F explains his aunt's reasons for returning to her birthplace

G contrasts the bleakness of one with the liveliness of the other

H contrasts the purity of one with the decadence of the other

J explains the major reasons for the Westward Expansion movement

______ **13.** Georgiana's reaction to the setting of the concert reveals that she —

A does not enjoy the concert

B never really enjoyed music

C is furious with Howard

D misses the cultural opportunities of the East

______ **14.** The setting has a major influence on all of the following elements *except* —

F point of view

G characters

H plot

J theme

Vocabulary Development *(20 points; 4 points each)*

Match each Vocabulary word on the left with its definition on the right. On the line provided, write the letter of the definition.

______ **15.** legacy	**a.** devoted to one's religion
______ **16.** grotesque	**b.** inheritance
______ **17.** eluding	**c.** deeply respectful
______ **18.** reverential	**d.** escaping
______ **19.** pious	**e.** strange; absurd

Constructed Response *(20 points)*

20. How does the setting influence Georgiana's major life choices? On a separate sheet of paper, write a paragraph that explains your answer. Support your ideas with details from the story.

NAME ______ CLASS ______ DATE ______ SCORE ______

SELECTION TEST **Student Edition pages 523, 524**

Richard Cory Edwin Arlington Robinson
Miniver Cheevy Edwin Arlington Robinson

COMPREHENSION *(40 points; 4 points each)*

On the line provided, write the letter of the *best* answer to each of the following items.

______ **1.** Richard Cory has all of the following qualities *except* —

A wealth
B good clothes
C good manners
D happiness

______ **2.** The narrator of "Richard Cory" is —

F Richard Cory
G Richard Cory's best friend
H Richard Cory's wife
J a person in the town

______ **3.** "Richard Cory" contains strong visual images of —

A life in a small town
B poor people living on the street
C life in a big city about fifty years ago
D people working in a factory

______ **4.** Richard Cory's eventual fate —

F results from his business failures
G shows his true criminal nature
H comes as a surprise to the townspeople
J was predictable, given his everyday behavior

______ **5.** The final mystery of Richard Cory's life concerns —

A why he took frequent strolls into town
B what unspeakable sadness he kept hidden
C how he managed to impress other people
D what kind of treasures he had

______ **6.** Miniver Cheevy *best* loves —

F thinking of glorious civilizations from the past
G spending time with his friends and family
H working hard to earn money
J serving in the army

______ **7.** Miniver Cheevy can *best* be characterized as the type of person who —

A blames himself for all his problems

B finds happiness in even the smallest pleasures

C feels that he is out of place and misunderstood

D strikes out violently when he is criticized

______ **8.** The irony of Miniver Cheevy's story is that he —

F enjoys thinking about ancient days

G dreams of great deeds while failing to act

H knows nothing about medieval history

J fails to use his wealth wisely

______ **9.** To comfort himself, Miniver Cheevy —

A relies on alcohol

B writes about knighthood

C teaches Greek history

D dresses in royal clothing

______ **10.** Richard Cory and Miniver Cheevy are similar in that they both have —

F comfortable homes

G great fortunes

H secret miseries

J good jobs

LITERARY FOCUS: LANGUAGE AND STYLE: CONNOTATIONS *(20 points; 5 points each)*
On the line provided, write the letter of the *best* answer to each of the following items.

______ **11.** In "Richard Cory" all of the following words connote kingliness or royalty *except* —

A crown

B imperially

C glittered

D bread

_____ **12.** The poet uses words that connote royalty to —

F create a contrast between the townspeople and Richard Cory

G show that Richard Cory really was a king

H suggest that Richard Cory didn't deserve his good fortune

J mock Richard Cory's behavior toward the townspeople

_____ **13.** The words *Thebes*, *Camelot*, and *Priam* in "Miniver Cheevy" —

A connote failure and despair

B connote the glory and glamour of the distant past

C suggest that Miniver Cheevy is very ambitious and heroic

D imply a bright future for Miniver Cheevy

_____ **14.** Robinson describes the "medieval grace / Of iron clothing" to —

F show that today's armor is lightweight and comfortable

G foreshadow Miniver Cheevy's death in war

H create an image of success

J create an ironic tone

VOCABULARY DEVELOPMENT *(20 points; 4 points each)*

Match each Vocabulary word on the left with its definition on the right. On the line provided, write the letter of each definition.

_____ **15.** imperially

_____ **16.** arrayed

_____ **17.** assailed

_____ **18.** vagrant

_____ **19.** renown

a. fame

b. homeless

c. clothed

d. royally

e. attacked

CONSTRUCTED RESPONSE *(20 points)*

20. In both "Richard Cory" and "Miniver Cheevy," the characters yearn for things they feel they lack in life. How does Robinson use irony and tone to convey his themes? On a separate sheet of paper, write a paragraph that explains your answer. Support your ideas with details from both poems.

NAME CLASS DATE SCORE

COLLECTION 4 SUMMATIVE TEST

The Rise of Realism: The Civil War to 1914

This test asks you to use the skills and strategies you have learned in this collection. Read the following passage from Mark Twain's novel *Adventures of Huckleberry Finn.* At this point in the novel, Huck has been taken away from his irresponsible, drunken father and placed with a pious widow who is attempting to civilize him. Huck's father, known as "Pap," has heard that Huck has received some money, and Pap comes creeping into Huck's room one night in search of it. When Huck goes into his room and lights his candle, "there sat Pap—his own self!" After you read the passage, answer the questions that follow it.

Pap Starts in on a New Life
by Mark Twain

I had shut the door. Then I turned around, and there he was. I used to be scared of him all the time, he tanned[1] me so much. I reckoned I was scared now, too; but in a minute I see I was mistaken—that is, after the first jolt, as you may say, when my breath sort of hitched, he being so unexpected; but right away after I see I warn't scared of him worth bothering about.

He was most fifty, and he looked it. His hair was long and tangled and greasy, and hung down, and you could see his eyes shining through like he was behind vines. It was all black, no gray; so was his long, mixed-up whiskers. There warn't no color in his face, where his face showed; it was white; not like another man's white, but a white to make a body sick, a white to make a body's flesh crawl—a tree-toad white, a fish-belly white. As for his clothes—just rags, that was all. He had one ankle resting on t'other knee; the boot on that foot was busted, and two of his toes stuck through, and he worked them now and then. His hat was laying on the floor—an old black slouch with the top caved in, like a lid.

I stood a-looking at him; he set there a-looking at me, with his chair tilted back a little. I set the candle down. I noticed the window was up; so he had clumb in by the shed. He kept a-looking me all over. By and by he says:

"Starchy clothes—very. You think you're a good deal of a big-bug, *don't* you?"

"Maybe I am, maybe I ain't," I says.

"Don't give me none o' your lip," says he. "You've put on considerable many frills since I been away. *I'll* take you down a peg before I get done with you. You're educated, too, they say—can read and write. You think you're better'n your father, now don't you, because he can't? I'll take it out of you. Who told you you might meddle with such hi-falut'n foolishness, hey?—who told you you could?"

"The widow. She told me."

"The widow, hey?—and who told the widow she could put in her shovel about a thing that ain't none of her business?"

"Nobody told her."

"Well, I'll learn her how to meddle. And looky here—you drop that school, you hear? I'll learn people to bring up a boy to put on airs over his own father and let on to be better'n what *he* is. You lemme catch you fooling around that school again, you hear? Your mother couldn't read, and she couldn't write, nuther, before she died. None of the family couldn't before *they* died. I can't, and here you're

1. **tanned:** whipped

a-swelling yourself up like this. I ain't the man to stand it—you hear? Say, lemme hear you read."

I took up a book and begun something about General Washington and the wars. When I'd read about half a minute, he fetched the book a whack with his hand and knocked it across the house. He says:

"It's so. You can do it. I had my doubts when you told me. Now looky here; you stop that putting on frills. I won't have it. I'll lay for you, my smarty; and if I catch you about that school I'll tan you good. First you know you'll get religion, too. I never see such a son."

He took up a little blue and yaller picture of some cows and a boy, and says: "What's this?"

"It's something they give me for learning my lessons good."

He tore it up, and says:

"I'll give you something better—I'll give you a cowhide."

He set there a-mumbling and a-growling a minute, and then he says:

"*Ain't* you a sweet-scented dandy, though? A bed; and bed-clothes, and a look'n'-glass; and a piece of carpet on the floor—and your own father got to sleep with the hogs in the tanyard. I never see such a son. I bet I'll take some o' these frills out o' you before I'm done with you. Why, there ain't no end to your airs—they say you're rich. Hey?—how's that?"

"They lie—that's how."

"Looky here—mind how you talk to me; I'm a-standing about all I can stand now—so don't gimme no sass. I've been in town two days, and I hain't heard nothing but about you bein' rich. I heard about it away down the river, too. That's why I come. You git me that money tomorrow—I want it."

"I hain't got no money."

"It's a lie. Judge Thatcher's got it. You git it. I want it."

"I hain't got no money, I tell you. You ask Judge Thatcher; he'll tell you the same."

"All right. I'll ask him; and I'll make him pungle,[2] too, or I'll know the reason why. Say, how much you got in your pocket? I want it."

"I hain't got only a dollar, and want that to—"

"I don't make no difference what you want it for—you just shell it out."

He took it and bit it to see if it was good, and then he said he was going downtown to get some whiskey, said he hadn't had a drink all day. When he had got out on the shed he put his head in again, and cussed me for putting on frills and trying to do better than him; and when I reckoned he was gone he came back and put his head in again, and told me to mind about that school, because he was going to lay for me and lick me if I didn't drop that.

Next day he was drunk, and he went to Judge Thatcher's and bullyragged him, and tried to make him give up the money; but he couldn't, and then he swore he'd make the law force him.

The judge and the widow went to law to get the court to take me away from him and let one of them be my guardian; but it was a new judge that had just come, and he didn't know the old man; so he said courts mustn't interfere and separate families if they could help it; said he'd druther not take a child away from its father. So

2. **pungle:** pay the money.

Judge Thatcher and the widow had to quit on the business.

That pleased the old man till he couldn't rest. He said he'd cowhide me till I was black and blue if I didn't raise some money for him. I borrowed three dollars from Judge Thatcher, and Pap took it and got drunk, and went a-blowing around and cussing and whooping and carrying on; and he kept it up all over town, with a tin pan, till most midnight; then they jailed him, and the next day they had him before the court, and jailed him again for a week. But he said *he* was satisfied; said he was boss of his son, and he'd make it warm for *him*.

When he got out the new judge said he was a-going to make a man of him. So he took him to his own house, and dressed him up clean and nice, and had him to breakfast and dinner and supper with the family; and was just old pie to him, so to speak. And after supper he talked to him about temperance and such things till the old man cried, and he said he'd been a fool, and fooled away his life; but now he was a-going to turn over a new leaf and be a man nobody wouldn't be ashamed of, and he hoped the judge would help him and not look down on him. The judge said he could hug him for them words; so *he* cried, and his wife she cried again; Pap said he'd been a man that had always been misunderstood before, and the judge said he believed it. The old man said that what a man wanted that was down was sympathy, and the judge said it was so; so they cried again. And then it was bed-time the old man rose up and held out his hand, and says:

"Look at it, gentlemen and ladies all; take a-hold of it; shake it. There's a hand that was the hand of a hog; but it ain't so no more; it's the hand of a man that's started in on a new life, and I'll die before he'll go back. You mark them words—don't forget I said them. It's a clean hand now; shake it—don't be afeared."

So they shook it, one after the other, all around, and cried. The judge's wife she kissed it. Then the old man he signed a pledge—made his mark. The judge said it was the holiest time on record, or something like that. Then they tucked the old man into a beautiful room, which was the spare room, and in the night some time he got powerful thirsty and clumb out on the porch roof and slid down a stanchion and traded his new coat for a jug of forty-rod, and clumb back again and had a good old time; and toward daylight he crawled out again, drunk as a fiddler, and rolled off the porch and broke his left arm in two places, and was most froze to death when somebody found him after sun-up. And when they come to look at that spare room they had to take soundings before they could navigate it.

The judge felt kind of sore. He said he reckoned a body could reform the old man with a shotgun, maybe, but he didn't know no other way.

VOCABULARY SKILLS *(25 points; 5 points each)*

Each of the underlined words below has also been underlined in the selection. Re-read those passages in which the underlined words appear, and then use context clues and your prior knowledge to help you select an answer. On the line provided, write the letter of the word or words that *best* answers each question.

______ **1.** A dandy is a man who pays too much attention to his ______.

A appearance

B education

C diet

D friends' business

NAME ______ CLASS ______ DATE ______ SCORE ______

______ **2.** If you serve as a child's guardian, you are his or her ______.

F captor
G guide
H legal caretaker
J coach

______ **3.** A person who believes in temperance practices ______ in regard to alcoholic beverages.

A overindulgence
B recklessness
C sociability
D abstinence

______ **4.** Someone who yearns for sympathy typically wants ______.

F education
G congruity
H discipline
J compassion

______ **5.** To navigate is to ______ a course.

A avoid
B divert
C steer
D mobilize

COMPREHENSION *(25 points; 5 points each)*

On the line provided, write the letter of the *best* answer to each of the following items.

______ **6.** When Huck's father appears, at first Huck —

F is furious
G is frightened
H panics and screams for help
J does not care one way or the other

______ **7.** The *main* reason that Pap has come to see his son is that Pap —

A has heard that Huck is rich
B is concerned about Huck's well-being
C wants to warn Huck about getting too fancy in his dress and education
D wants to give Huck a beating for not attending school

______ **8.** When Pap finds out that Huck can read, Pap —

F is angry that Huck is trying to improve himself

G is proud of his son and wants Huck to teach him how to read

H tries to prove that he can read better than Huck can

J says that he will approve of Huck's reading if Huck will give him money

______ **9.** After Pap's conversion, Pap does all of the following things *except* —

A cry openly and proclaim that he is going to get a job

B sign a paper saying that he will no longer drink

C trade his new coat for a jug of whiskey

D join the church and get a job

______ **10.** When Pap breaks his arm and the judge sees the condition of his room, —

F Huck feels sorry for Pap and gives him more money

G the judge and his wife invite Pap to live with them until his arm heals

H the judge is angry because he has been fooled

J the court awards custody of Huck to Judge Thatcher

READING SKILLS AND STRATEGIES *(15 points; 5 points each)*

Analyzing Sequence of Events

11. In the boxes below, briefly describe the chronology of Pap's actions after he leaves Huck's room and before the judge invites him to dinner. Be sure to record the events in the order in which they occur. The first box has been filled in for you.

Sequence of Pap's Actions

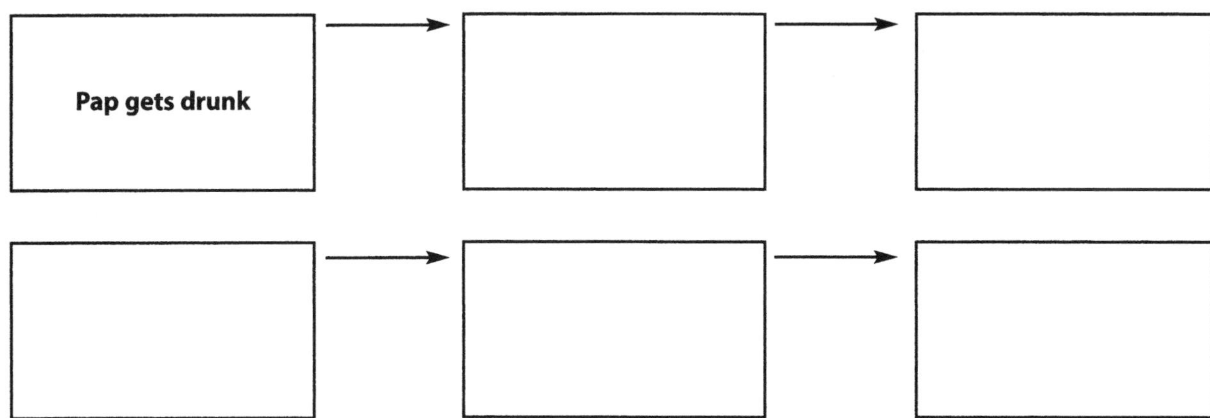

NAME ______ CLASS ______ DATE ______ SCORE ______

Analyzing Text Structures: Cause and Effect

12. Trace the causes and effects in "Pap Starts in on a New Life" by completing the following chart.

Cause	Effect
Pap hears that Huck has money.	______
Pap takes a dollar from Huck.	______
______	______
______	______
______	Pap tries to bully Judge Thatcher into giving him Huck's money.

Recognizing the Vernacular

On the line provided, write the letter of the *best* answer to the following item.

______ **13.** Which item below is *not* written in the vernacular?

- **A** "I hain't got no money."
- **B** "I had my doubts when you told me."
- **C** "Looky here—mind how you talk to me."
- **D** "Well, I'll learn her how to meddle."

LITERARY FOCUS: CONSTRUCTED RESPONSE

Analyzing Comic Devices *(10 points)*

14. Twain uses humor to recount a dramatic series of events. Identify the comic devices Twain uses, and explain how these devices create humor. On a separate sheet of paper, write a paragraph that explains your answer. Use at least two examples from the selection.

Analyzing Figures of Speech *(10 points)*

15. Complete the following chart to see how Mark Twain uses imagery, figures of speech, and sounds to evoke readers' emotions in "Pap Starts in on a New Life."

Literary Device	Example	Emotion Evoked
Imagery		
Metaphor		
Simile		
Sounds		

Analyzing Point of View *(15 points)*

16. Which of the following statements *best* captures why Twain chose to use Huck's point of view in the novel? Choose what you believe is the *strongest* response. Circle the letter of the answer you chose. Then, on a separate sheet of paper, briefly defend your choice. Use at least one example from the selection to support your ideas.

F Huck's casual, conversational style lightens up otherwise serious events.

G Twain wants the reader to see events through Huck's eyes.

H The story would not keep the reader's interest if it were told from the third-person-limited point of view.

J Using an objective voice is not natural for Twain.

COLLECTION 5 DIAGNOSTIC TEST

LITERATURE
VOCABULARY

The Moderns: 1914–1939

On the line provided, write the letter of the *best* answer to each of the following items. *(100 points; 10 points each)*

_____ **1.** What is **imagery**?

A Words whose sounds suggest their meanings

B A list appearing in a poem of objects, people, or events

C The overall feeling evoked in a poem

D Language that appeals to the senses

_____ **2.** A poem in which a character speaks directly to one or more listeners is called a(n) —

F ballad

G elegy

H sonnet

J dramatic monologue

_____ **3.** The character who initiates or drives a story's action is called the —

A speaker

B foil

C protagonist

D antagonist

_____ **4.** **Setting** includes all of the following elements *except* the —

F time period in which a story takes place

G location of a story

H conflicts between main and subordinate characters

J customs and social conditions of the time when a story's action takes place

_____ **5.** When poets use **allusions,** they —

A make references to something well known from literature, history, or art

B express a common truth in a short statement

C draw comparisons between two things to show how they are alike

D reverse the normal word order in a sentence or phrase

______ **6.** Writers use **ambiguity** when they want to —

F explain the theme of their work

G describe something abstract

H leave their meaning open to several interpretations

J create dynamic characters

______ **7.** A **narrative poem** contains —

A a description of events from the poet's own life

B a story about the gods, goddesses, and heroes of a particular culture

C an expression of the speaker's views about life

D characters and a series of related events

______ **8.** What is **blank verse**?

F Poetry that does not contain rhythm or rhyme

G Unrhymed iambic pentameter

H Poetry that rhymes but has no regular meter

J Two consecutive rhyming lines

______ **9.** Groups of words with the same **root** are called —

A idioms

B loaded words

C word families

D prefixes

______ **10.** Which of the following relationships is *not* typically found in a **word analogy**?

F degree

G characteristic of

H synonyms

J literal and figurative meanings

NAME ______ CLASS ______ DATE ______ SCORE ______

LITERARY PERIOD INTRODUCTION TEST **Student Edition page 562**

The Moderns: 1914–1939

COMPREHENSION *(100 points; 10 points each)*

On the line provided, write the letter of the *best* answer to each of the following items.

______ **1.** Until the beginning of the twentieth century, all of the following attitudes were part of the American dream *except* —

A respect for the mysterious workings of the subconscious mind

B belief in the United States as a new Eden with limitless resources

C trust in the ultimate triumph of any self-reliant individual

D faith in the country's progress toward prosperity

______ **2.** In the period after World War I, American writers began to —

F tighten their connections with the past

G grow cynical about traditional authority and values

H urge the country to "build, build, build!"

J abandon art and look for new ways of making a living

______ **3.** The modernist movement challenged American writers to —

A reflect Marxist values in their work

B set their stories in the South or Midwest

C find new themes, styles, and subjects

D avoid the influence and ideas of European writers

______ **4.** American modernists created a literature that —

F avoided basic questions asked by writers of the past

G was too dependent on European styles

H reflected a variety of American voices

J focused only on the positive side of American culture

______ **5.** A growing interest in psychoanalysis led writers to —

A doubt the value and sincerity of literature

B rely on doctors to help them find meaning in life

C avoid describing characters' feelings

D try to capture characters' thought processes

______ **6.** During the Jazz Age many American writers and artists —

- **F** wrote persuasively in favor of Prohibition
- **G** became saxophonists or singers
- **H** lived as expatriates in France
- **J** embraced the idea of America as Eden

______ **7.** Ernest Hemingway created major characters who —

- **A** are talkative and flamboyant
- **B** avoid the difficult challenges of life
- **C** are willing to do anything to achieve their selfish goals
- **D** behave honorably in a world without purpose

______ **8.** Some American poets found inspiration in the work of European painters and began to use their imagery and symbolism. Other American poets found inspiration in —

- **F** colonial American painting
- **G** the rhythms and vocabulary of ordinary speech
- **H** ancient Greek and Roman myths
- **J** the forms of Shakespearean drama

______ **9.** According to the imagists, what aspect of a poem should carry its meaning and emotions?

- **A** Rhyme and meter
- **B** Wordplay
- **C** Prettiness and sentimentality
- **D** Sensory images

______ **10.** Poets of the Harlem Renaissance often used —

- **F** obscure images and symbols
- **G** jazz and blues rhythms and African American dialect
- **H** references to the history of Africa
- **J** discussions of the decline of American cities

NAME ______ CLASS ______ DATE ______ SCORE ______

SELECTION TEST **Student Edition pages 576, 578, 579** LITERARY RESPONSE AND ANALYSIS

The River-Merchant's Wife: A Letter Ezra Pound
The Garden Ezra Pound
A Few Don'ts by an Imagiste Ezra Pound

COMPREHENSION *(40 points; 4 points each)*

On the line provided, write the letter of the *best* answer to each of the following items.

______ **1.** In "The River-Merchant's Wife: A Letter" the speaker recalls how she first met her husband —

A when they were children

B on their wedding day

C during courtship

D five months before

______ **2.** The speaker describes her behavior during the early days of the marriage as —

F coy and flirtatious

G joyful and lighthearted

H shy and somber

J reckless and nervous

______ **3.** The couple became separated when the husband —

A fell ill and went to a hospital

B left home on business

C died unexpectedly

D was kidnapped

______ **4.** In her loneliness the speaker finds it painful even to watch —

F a pair of butterflies

G purple plums

H the swirling river

J chattering monkeys

______ **5.** What is the *main* emotion the speaker expresses in the poem?

A Anger that her husband has abandoned her

B Emptiness at knowing she will never find true love

C Nostalgia to return to the home of her youth

D Longing for the beloved from whom she is separated

______ **6.** In "The Garden" the line "Like a skein of loose silk" describes —

F how the woman is dressed

G how the woman walks

H what the poet feels toward the woman

J the way the "rabble" looks at the woman

______ **7.** Who is "dying piecemeal" in "The Garden"?

A Plants and flowers

B The speaker of the poem

C The walking woman

D The children on the street

______ **8.** The woman's *main* problem seems to be that she is —

F bored

G hungry

H poor

J ill

______ **9.** In "A Few Don'ts by an Imagiste," Pound writes, "Use no superfluous word, no adjective, which does not reveal something." Which of the following adjectives in "The Garden" reveals the woman's disrespect for the poor?

A round

B poor

C sturdy

D unkillable

______ **10.** What is the speaker thinking of doing?

F Speaking to the woman

G Helping the poor children

H Asking the woman to marry him

J Robbing the woman of her money

Literary Focus: Imagery and the Objective Correlative *(40 points; 10 points each)*
On the line provided, write the letter of the *best* answer to each of the following items.

______ **11.** In line 2 of "The River-Merchant's Wife: A Letter," the image of the wife pulling flowers as a child is meant to express that —

A she dislikes flowers

B she is mischievous

C she will marry a merchant

D her life will be sorrowful

_____ **12.** In line 18, the image of the monkeys making sorrowful sounds is meant to communicate that —

F the monkeys are angry

G good fortune awaits

H the wife is sad

J life is difficult

_____ **13.** According to "A Few Don'ts by an Imagiste," how important are images in poetry?

A Images are not as important as the careful use of rhyme and meter.

B Images are less important than the "music" of the poem.

C One genuine image is worth more than "voluminous works."

D Only critics can decide how successful an image is.

_____ **14.** Which of the following images from "The River-Merchant's Wife: A Letter" is the *best* example of an objective correlative?

F The butterflies

G Cho-fu-Sa

H The bamboo stilts

J The village

CONSTRUCTED RESPONSE *(20 points)*

15. Various images in the two Ezra Pound poems contribute to the poems' overall moods. Choose one of the two poems and, on a separate sheet of paper, describe what you think the overall mood of the poem is. Select two images and explain how you think they help create that mood. Be sure to identify the poem you are discussing.

NAME ______ CLASS ______ DATE ______ SCORE ______

SELECTION TEST **Student Edition page 584**

LITERARY RESPONSE AND ANALYSIS

The Love Song of J. Alfred Prufrock T. S. Eliot

COMPREHENSION *(40 points; 4 points each)*
On the line provided, write the letter of the *best* answer to each of the following items.

______ **1.** Which of the following statements *best* reflects Prufrock's view of himself?
- **A** I am a victim of bad luck.
- **B** I am unable to take risks.
- **C** Women have always admired me.
- **D** I am an adventurous youth.

______ **2.** Prufrock seems to be a man who has —
- **F** suffered a hard life in working-class London
- **G** had a happy home and family
- **H** avoided opportunities for change
- **J** treated others cruelly and has withheld forgiveness

______ **3.** The epigraph to the poem can be found —
- **A** before the first line
- **B** at the end
- **C** in the biography of T. S. Eliot
- **D** in the repeated lines

______ **4.** When the speaker compares the evening to "a patient etherized upon a table," he is emphasizing the —
- **F** excitement that lies ahead
- **G** human quality of the evening and the patient
- **H** lifelessness of the night
- **J** doctor-patient relationship

______ **5.** To which of the following works does the poem *not* make an **allusion**?
- **A** The Bible
- **B** A play by Shakespeare
- **C** A poem by Walt Whitman
- **D** A great Italian artist

______ **6.** Which of the following phrases or lines is *not* repeated in the poem?
- **F** "Scuttling across the floors of silent seas."
- **G** "And would it have been worth it, after all . . ."
- **H** "That is not what I meant, at all."
- **J** "There will be time. . . ."

_____ **7.** Which of the following lines *is* repeated in the poem to poetic effect?

A "Do I dare?"

B "In a minute there is time. . . ."

C "Of restless nights in one-night cheap hotels . . ."

D "In the room the women come and go . . ."

_____ **8.** Prufrock thinks of the frolicking mermaids as creatures who —

F know that the ocean is safer than land

G crawl on the bottom of the sea

H laugh at Romanticism

J live in a world of freedom and beauty

_____ **9.** Which image *most* clearly shows Prufrock's timidity and his inability to make a decision?

A "After the novels, after the teacups, after the skirts that trail along the floor — . . ."

B "Shall I part my hair behind? Do I dare to eat a peach?"

C "Human voices wake us, and we drown."

D "To have squeezed the universe into a ball . . ."

_____ **10.** What does Prufrock mean when he says, "I am not Prince Hamlet, nor was meant to be; / Am an attendant lord . . ."?

F I am a villain, not a hero.

G I am no hero, but just a minor character on the stage of my own life.

H The mermaids will never sing to me.

J I am the lord of all around me.

LITERARY FOCUS: DRAMATIC MONOLOGUE *(30 points; 10 points each)*
On the line provided, write the letter of the *best* answer to each of the following items.

_____ **11.** Prufrock's dramatic monologue enables the reader to —

A see logical, sequential connections between ideas

B understand the lives of many characters at once

C witness the key events of Prufrock's childhood

D follow the stream of Prufrock's rambling thoughts

______ **12.** Which line immediately tells the reader that "The Love Song of J. Alfred Prufrock" is a dramatic monologue?

F "Let us go then, you and I . . ."

G "To lead you to an overwhelming question . . ."

H "Like a patient etherized upon a table . . ."

J "The yellow fog that rubs its back upon the window-panes . . ."

______ **13.** Like all dramatic monologues, "The Love Song of J. Alfred Prufrock" —

A contains allusions

B uses figures of speech

C relies heavily on images

D is told in the first person

READING SKILLS: IDENTIFYING THE MAIN IDEA AND SUPPORTING DETAILS *(10 points)*
On the line provided, write the letter of the *best* answer to the following item.

______ **14.** Which of the following sentences *best* states the *main* idea of the poem?

F Love is impossible to find.

G Modern life is spiritually empty.

H People no longer yearn for heroes.

J Modern people are generous and kind.

CONSTRUCTED RESPONSE *(20 points)*

15. Prufrock expresses a general sense of despair. On a separate sheet of paper, identify one figure of speech, one nonfigurative, or literal, image, and one other aspect of style that you think vividly communicates the despair. Explain why these passages or aspects of style impress you.

NAME ______________________ CLASS ______________________ DATE ______________ SCORE ______________

SELECTION TEST **Student Edition pages 593, 594, 595** LITERARY RESPONSE AND ANALYSIS

The Red Wheelbarrow William Carlos Williams
The Great Figure William Carlos Williams
This Is Just to Say William Carlos Williams

COMPREHENSION *(40 points; 4 points each)*

On the line provided, write the letter of the *best* answer to each of the following items.

______ **1.** "The Red Wheelbarrow" depicts a —

A realistic scene

B series of fantastic images

C character's sorrow

D historically important event

______ **2.** The speaker in "The Red Wheelbarrow" —

F makes allusions to musical compositions

G emphasizes the importance of ordinary things

H regrets past actions

J offers a philosophy of life

______ **3.** "The Red Wheelbarrow" has all the following characteristics *except* —

A ordinary speech

B a focus on images

C rhyme and meter

D free verse

______ **4.** To what does the title "The Great Figure" actually refer?

F Vast size

G The numeral 5 on a firetruck

H A famous person

J A Greek statue

______ **5.** The setting of "The Great Figure" is a —

A dense forest in New Jersey

B beautiful but deserted town

C rainy night on a city street

D busy day in a shopping mall

______ **6.** The poem "The Great Figure" creates an overall impression of —

F dramatic action

G peace and quiet

H wartime intrigue

J an ordinary workday

______ **7.** "This Is Just to Say" is both a poem and a(n) —

A note of apology

B valentine to the poet's wife

C excuse for leaving the office early

D joke at the reader's expense

______ **8.** The *main* images in "This Is Just to Say" are ones of —

F heat and dust

G snow and ice

H sweetness and cold

J bitterness and regret

______ **9.** "This Is Just to Say" is *mainly* about —

A the courage to eat peaches

B making bad decisions and instantly regretting them

C the fear of being punished

D the wonder of everyday things

______ **10.** William Carlos Williams's poems can *best* be described as —

F ornate

G surrealistic

H sophisticated in rhyme scheme

J deceptively simple

LITERARY FOCUS: IMAGERY *(40 points; 10 points each)*
On the line provided, write the letter of the *best* answer to each of the following items.

______ **11.** Williams's poems can be called **imagist** because they —

A express the poet's imagination

B use a lot of figurative language

C use images only as symbols of other things

D give imagery primary importance

______ **12.** To describe the images in "The Red Wheelbarrow," Williams uses —

F colors and simple language

G references to imagist theory

H elaborate figures of speech

J a strong, steady beat

______ **13.** The images in "The Great Figure" *primarily* appeal to readers' senses of —

A touch and hearing

B smell and taste

C sight and hearing

D smell and sight

______ **14.** Williams uses all of the following images in "The Great Figure" *except* —

F clanging gongs

G glaring sunlight

H howling sirens

J rumbling wheels

Constructed Response *(20 points)*

15. William Carlos Williams's "The Red Wheelbarrow," "The Great Figure," and "This Is Just to Say" share an ability to surprise the reader by initially creating a sense of expectation or curiosity. On a separate sheet of paper, describe how two of the poems evoke emotions of curiosity or surprise. Refer to at least one image in each poem to support your ideas.

NAME ______ CLASS ______ DATE ______ SCORE ______

SELECTION TEST **Student Edition pages 598, 599**

LITERARY RESPONSE AND ANALYSIS

Poetry Marianne Moore
Ars Poetica Archibald MacLeish

COMPREHENSION *(40 points; 4 points each)*

On the line provided, write the letter of the *best* answer to each of the following items.

______ **1.** In the first line of "Poetry" the speaker makes the surprising claim that she —

- **A** is not a poet
- **B** hates critics
- **C** is a baseball fan
- **D** dislikes poetry

______ **2.** The speaker claims that grasping hands, dilating eyes, and rising hair are important because —

- **F** a sophisticated interpretation can be given to them
- **G** they are derivative and unoriginal
- **H** they are useful
- **J** they are new and exotic

______ **3.** In "Poetry" the upside-down bat can be seen as a metaphor for —

- **A** school books and business letters
- **B** derivative and unintelligible poetry
- **C** baseball fans, critics, and statisticians
- **D** hands that grasp and eyes that dilate

______ **4.** According to "Poetry," a good poet would —

- **F** symbolize love as a heart
- **G** read Homer for inspiration
- **H** deny the importance of textbooks and papers
- **J** use realistic details to describe imaginary places

______ **5.** According to "Poetry," the *best* subject matter for poetry is —

- **A** bats, elephants, and wolves
- **B** raw and genuine
- **C** gardens and nature
- **D** unintelligible

______ **6.** Marianne Moore's term for trivial, mediocre poets is —

F junior poets

G lesser poets

H half poets

J bad poets

______ **7.** Good poets, Moore claims, are "literalists of the imagination." In other words, good poets —

A never use figures of speech

B shun real life, living instead in their own private worlds

C try to describe exactly what their imaginations show them

D use difficult words to describe ordinary things

______ **8.** In "Ars Poetica" Archibald MacLeish compares the silence of poetry to all of the following *except* —

F a flight of birds

G a globed fruit

H old medallions

J the moon

______ **9.** What does MacLeish mean by "A poem should be wordless"?

A The shortest poems are best.

B People should dislike poems because they do not say anything.

C The reader of a poem should be more aware of images and emotions than of the words used to evoke them.

D Painting, sculpture, dance, music, and other nonliterary arts can also be called poetry.

______ **10.** In "Ars Poetica" MacLeish asserts that "A poem should not mean / But be." Which statement in Moore's "Poetry" says much the same thing?

F "I, too, dislike it: there are things that are important beyond all this fiddle."

G "These things are important not because a / high-sounding interpretation can be put upon them. . . ."

H "The same thing may be said for all of us. . . ."

J "We / do not admire what / we cannot understand. . . ."

NAME ______________________ CLASS ______________ DATE __________ SCORE __________

LITERARY FOCUS: IMAGERY *(40 points; 10 points each)*
On the line provided, write the letter of the *best* answer to each of the following items.

______ **11.** The *most* original image in "Poetry" is found in the phrase —

A "literalists of the imagination"

B "the raw material of poetry"

C "a perfect contempt for it"

D "imaginary gardens with real toads in them"

______ **12.** An image Moore does *not* use in "Poetry" is —

F a poet leaning her head in her hands

G a critic twitching

H a horse feeling a flea

J a wolf under a tree

______ **13.** Moore uses imagery from all of the following areas of experience *except* —

A nature

B sports

C education

D fashion

______ **14.** What image does MacLeish use to describe "the history of grief"?

F "leaning grasses"

G "night-entangled trees"

H "An empty doorway"

J "two lights above the sea"

Constructed Response *(20 points)*

15. Which of the following statements best describes the meaning of Moore's "Poetry"? There is more than one possible answer. Write the letter of the answer(s) you choose, and then defend your choice. In supporting your ideas, use at least one example of Moore's imagery, style, or tone.

A All poetry should only focus on the natural world.

B If you say you dislike poetry, you probably dislike only certain types of poetry.

C Poets should write with imagination about topics that are useful or emotionally powerful.

what if a much of a which of a wind E. E. Cummings
"Miracles are to come" E. E. Cummings
somewhere i have never travelled, gladly beyond E. E. Cummings

COMPREHENSION *(40 points; 4 points each)*

On the line provided, write the letter of the *best* answer to each of the following items.

______ **1.** In E. E. Cummings's poem "what if a much of a which of a wind," the images describe —

A a tornado in the Midwest

B the destruction of the universe

C a gravitational problem

D global weather changes

______ **2.** Cummings's "what if a much of a which of a wind" expresses confidence in —

F natural phenomena

G poetry

H humanity

J the rational, scientific mind

______ **3.** The image "blow king to beggar and queen to seem" implies that events will —

A overturn political systems

B establish a king and queen in the United States.

C force nations to borrow money

D have little effect on the rich and powerful

______ **4.** The figure of speech "sprinkles nowhere with me and you" literally means —

F "does nothing to me and you"

G "lights up the darkness with the light of life"

H "kills the two of us"

J "plants seeds of love throughout the world"

______ **5.** In "Miracles are to come" Cummings says that poems "are not for mostpeople." How does "what if a much of a which of a wind" seem to contradict that statement?

A Most people have read that poem.

B The poem is only about the life of one person—the poet himself.

C The poem is about a disaster happening to most, or even all, people.

D The poem praises selfishness at the expense of togetherness.

______ **6.** The poem "somewhere i have never travelled,gladly beyond" is *mainly* about the —

F speaker's desire to travel to new places

G speaker's wish to avoid arguments with his beloved

H power of words to make people fall in love

J speaker's thoughts and feelings about his beloved

______ **7.** The speaker of "somewhere i have never travelled,gladly beyond" compares himself to —

A a flower

B a small, frail hand

C silent eyes

D the color red

______ **8.** The speaker of "somewhere i have never travelled,gladly beyond" seems fascinated *most* by his beloved's —

F voice and hair

G eyes and hands

H hands and feet

J laughter and weeping

______ **9.** Which of the following does the speaker of "somewhere i have never travelled,gladly beyond" *not* compare his beloved to?

A A place he has never traveled

B Spring

C The snow

D A golden gown

______ **10.** In "Miracles are to come" Cummings claims that his poems "are by somebody who can love." Which aspect of his poems *best* supports that claim?

F The speaker of "somewhere i have never travelled,gladly beyond" tenderly describes his beloved.

G In "somewhere i have never travelled,gladly beyond" there is nature imagery.

H The speaker of "what if a much of a which of a wind" is self-confident.

J In "what if a much of a which of a wind" there is great destruction.

NAME ______ CLASS ______ DATE ______ SCORE ______

READING SKILLS: READING CUMMINGS *(40 points; 10 points each)*

On the line provided, write the letter of the *best* answer to each of the following items.

______ **11.** Nonstandard **syntax,** or sentence structure, is part of E. E. Cummings's style. If the first two lines of "somewhere i have never travelled,gladly beyond" were rewritten as a sentence that used standard syntax and mechanics, they would be —

A Somewhere I have travelled gladly beyond any experience, your eyes have their silence.

B Somewhere I have never travelled, gladly beyond any experience, your eyes have their silence.

C Somewhere I have never travelled. Gladly beyond all experience, your eyes have their silence.

D Somewhere I have never travelled. Gladly beyond all experience. Your eyes have their silence.

______ **12.** Wordplay is part of Cummings's style. Which passage from "what if a much of a which of a wind" uses the spellings of words to make a clever point?

F "blow friend to fiend"

G "bites this universe in two"

H "yanks immortal stars awry"

J "blow pity to envy"

______ **13.** Inventive grammar is part of Cummings's style. If a Cummings sentence were given standard capitalization and punctuation, it would still include nonstandard syntax and grammar. Which rewritten sentence below still uses nonstandard grammar?

A Nobody, not even the rain, has such small hands.

B Your slightest look will easily enclose me.

C The most who die, the more we live.

D I do not know what it is about you that closes and opens.

______ **14.** In the figure of speech, "nobody,not even the rain,has such small hands," —

F the woman is compared to rain

G the rain is personified as if it has human hands

H size is attributed to something nonexistent: the rain's hands

J all of the above

NAME CLASS DATE SCORE

Constructed Response *(20 points)*

15. The poems "what if a much of a which of a wind" and "somewhere i have never travelled,gladly beyond" are clearly the work of the same poet. Yet despite their similarities, they are also different. On a separate sheet of paper, discuss at least two ways in which the poems are similar and two ways in which they are different. At least two of your reasons should involve the poet's use of style, imagery, figures of speech, or sounds.

Soldier's Home Ernest Hemingway
Nobel Prize Acceptance Speech, 1954 Ernest Hemingway

COMPREHENSION *(40 points; 4 points each)*

On the line provided, write the letter of the *best* answer to each of the following items.

______ **1.** Which of the following sentences *best* states the theme of "Soldier's Home"?

- A Family and friends want returning soldiers to find good jobs.
- B Most civilians don't appreciate the heroism of soldiers.
- C Wartime combat can be so devastating that it changes one completely.
- D Most soldiers return home with little respect for their neighbors.

______ **2.** Krebs can *best* be described as a person who —

- F deeply mistrusts everyone around him
- G looks forward to rejoining his boyhood friends
- H has lost his goals and the energy to pursue them
- J has suffered injuries that leave him physically disabled

______ **3.** When he returns home, Krebs finds that he —

- A can talk about the war only to his sister
- B must lie to be listened to
- C wants to read adventure books
- D does not want a girlfriend

______ **4.** Krebs has returned home too late to —

- F find a comfortable apartment
- G feel any interest in wartime events
- H receive news of the whereabouts of his fellow soldiers
- J receive an elaborate welcome from his hometown

______ **5.** Krebs's sister Helen seems to —

- A need his love and approval
- B grow embarrassed by his behavior
- C resent his long absence from home
- D be jealous of the attention he gets

______ **6.** Krebs's father finally agrees that Krebs —

- F is lazy and should be kicked out of the house
- G should re-enlist in the army
- H may take the car out from time to time
- J should come to work for him

NAME ______ CLASS ______ DATE ______ SCORE ______

______ **7.** After the conversation with his mother, Krebs decides to go away because he —

- **A** wants to avoid any kind of conflict
- **B** hears of a good job waiting for him in Kansas City
- **C** realizes that his parents no longer love him
- **D** yearns to find a rural area and settle down

______ **8.** What does Krebs seem to need *most* when he returns home from the war?

- **F** An executive job at his father's office
- **G** Solitude and understanding
- **H** Further military training
- **J** Stimulation and excitement

______ **9.** Judging from "Soldier's Home" and Hemingway's 1954 Nobel Prize acceptance speech, what do writers have in common with combat veterans who have returned home?

- **A** Literary skill
- **B** A yearning for something unattainable
- **C** An "alchemy"
- **D** Loneliness

______ **10.** In his 1954 Nobel Prize acceptance speech, Hemingway expresses both an awareness of great writers who came before him and a need to exceed their accomplishments. In "Soldier's Home" Hemingway succeeded by writing one of the first realistic descriptions of —

- **F** postwar disillusionment
- **G** war
- **H** the Midwest
- **J** family life

LITERARY FOCUS: PROTAGONISTS—THE ANTIHERO *(15 points; 5 points each)*
On the line provided, write the letter of the *best* answer to each of the following items.

______ **11.** What is a **protagonist**?

- **A** A character who contrasts with the hero archetype
- **B** The main character, the one who initiates the story's action
- **C** A character who opposes the hero
- **D** An antihero

NAME ______________ CLASS ______________ DATE ______________ SCORE ______________

______ **12.** How is an **antihero** different from a hero?

- **F** Actually they are the same.
- **G** The hero is a protagonist; the antihero isn't.
- **H** Heroes are more interesting than antiheroes.
- **J** The antihero is a nonheroic protagonist.

______ **13.** What traits mark Krebs as an antihero rather than a hero?

- **A** He was not a very good soldier during the war.
- **B** He decides to leave home at the end of the story.
- **C** He loves his sisters more than he loves his parents.
- **D** He is disillusioned and has lost a sense of purpose.

Reading Skills: Reading for Details *(5 points)*

On the line provided, write the letter of the *best* answer to the following item.

______ **14.** Which detail of his past is Krebs *most* nostalgic about?

- **F** The Rhine River Valley
- **G** The library
- **H** Being in Europe
- **J** Playing pool

Vocabulary Development *(20 points; 4 points each)*

Match the definition on the left with the Vocabulary word on the right. On the line provided, write the letter of the Vocabulary word.

______ **15.** overstatement	**a.** alliances
______ **16.** results of an action	**b.** atrocity
______ **17.** horrible; brutal	**c.** consequences
______ **18.** close associations for mutual benefit	**d.** exaggeration
______ **19.** scheming	**e.** intrigue

Constructed Response *(20 points)*

20. "Soldier's Home" is more than a portrait of one character. It is also a portrait of modern society at a specific point in its history. On a separate sheet of paper, describe how Krebs has been shaped by his historical period. Cite several details from the story that show those effects.

Winter Dreams F. Scott Fitzgerald
A Letter to His Daughter F. Scott Fitzgerald

COMPREHENSION *(40 points; 4 points each)*

On the line provided, write the letter of the *best* answer to each of the following items.

______ **1.** Dexter Green can *best* be described as —

A ambitious and full of desires

B judgmental and comical

C courageous and helpful

D honest and trustworthy

______ **2.** Which of the following word pairs describes Judy Jones?

F Sensitive and compassionate

G Confident and condescending

H Uneducated and poor

J Sophisticated and kind

______ **3.** Dexter quits his job as a caddy when he —

A joins the Army

B is told to caddy for the young girl Judy Jones

C gets into an argument with the nurse

D wins the championship

______ **4.** Dexter wants *most* to —

F associate with the rich and famous

G marry a woman who truly loves him

H become a great golfer

J have the best things in life

______ **5.** What happens to Dexter and Judy's engagement?

A Dexter breaks off the engagement.

B Dexter reveals that he never intended to marry Judy.

C Judy breaks off the engagement.

D Judy discovers that Dexter is married.

______ **6.** At the end of the story, Devlin tells Dexter that —

F Judy cannot stand her husband

G Judy and her husband are divorced

H Judy still dates a number of men

J Judy's husband does not treat her well

_____ **7.** What is Dexter's eventual attitude toward Judy's flirtations with men?

- **A** He is outraged.
- **B** He often criticizes Judy to her face.
- **C** He enjoys watching Judy flirt with other men.
- **D** He does not condemn Judy for her flirtations.

_____ **8.** At the end of the story, tears stream down Dexter's face because —

- **F** Judy has told him she never loved him
- **G** he is mourning the loss of a dream or ideal
- **H** Judy's slap stung him painfully
- **J** he realizes that Judy had never truly been beautiful

_____ **9.** In "A Letter to His Daughter" Fitzgerald —

- **A** tells his daughter that he can no longer afford her favorite luxuries
- **B** tries to mold his daughter's character
- **C** confesses that he is not the writer he wishes he could have been
- **D** warns his daughter not to go out with the wrong boys

_____ **10.** One reason Judy Jones could have benefited from Fitzgerald's letter to his daughter is that Judy —

- **F** needed to be told she was spending too much money
- **G** needed advice on how to become a writer
- **H** could have used someone to teach her a better set of values
- **J** neglected her body and needed to be told not to

LITERARY FOCUS: MOTIVATION AND PARADOXES *(15 points; 5 points each)*
On the line provided, write the letter of the *best* answer to each of the following items.

_____ **11.** What is Dexter's motivation for pursuing Judy?

- **A** He wants to work for her father.
- **B** He sees her as a symbol of "the best."
- **C** He is the only man she is interested in.
- **D** She seems shy and lonely.

______ **12.** Which of the following expressions describes a **paradox**?

F Winter dreams

G Tremendous superiority

H Affordable luxuries

J Reverberating sound

______ **13.** Which of the following items contains a paradox?

A "May one year back had been marked by Judy's poignant, unforgivable, yet forgiven turbulence. . . ."

B "Judy Jones, a slender enameled doll in cloth of gold . . ."

C "She was watching him closely and the silence was embarrassing. . . ."

D "Two tears had rolled down her wet face and trembled on her upper lip."

Reading Skills: Making Inferences About Characters *(5 points)*
On the line provided, write the letter of the *best* answer to the following item.

______ **14.** On Dexter's return to the golf course as a golfer, what do his actions suggest about his feelings?

F He is uncomfortable with his new, privileged position.

G Proud and arrogant, he looks down on the caddies.

H He wishes he had learned the course better in his youth.

J He has gone golfing only in the hope of impressing Judy.

Vocabulary Development *(20 points; 4 points each)*
Write the letter of the choice that is the *best* synonym for the Vocabulary word.

______ **15.** malicious

A kindly

B nasty

C wild

D tame

______ **16.** mirth

F sorrow

G hope

H despair

J joy

______ **17.** ludicrous

A ridiculous

B uncommon

C sensible

D direct

______ **18.** divergence

- **F** difference
- **G** exactness
- **H** width
- **J** height

______ **19.** reserve

- **A** folly
- **B** restraint
- **C** creativity
- **D** sentimentality

CONSTRUCTED RESPONSE *(20 points)*

20. Based on your reading of "Winter Dreams" and "A Letter to His Daughter," what was F. Scott Fitzgerald's view of life? How was it a product of a particular historical era? On a separate sheet of paper, write your answers, supporting them with specifics from the texts.

NAME ______ CLASS ______ DATE ______ SCORE ______

SELECTION TEST **Student Edition pages 646, 654** LITERARY RESPONSE AND ANALYSIS

A Rose for Emily William Faulkner
Nobel Prize Acceptance Speech, 1950 William Faulkner

COMPREHENSION *(40 points; 4 points each)*

On the line provided, write the letter of the *best* answer to each of the following items.

______ **1.** The emotions a reader might be expected to feel toward Emily include —

A amusement and gratitude

B pity and horror

C contempt and disappointment

D approval and satisfaction

______ **2.** After her father dies, Emily —

F moves to another town

G sees many suitors

H becomes a supporter of the arts

J refuses to acknowledge his death

______ **3.** The last time the townspeople see Homer Barron alive, he is —

A buying a suit of clothes

B drinking with other men

C proposing marriage to Emily

D entering Emily's house

______ **4.** The strand of gray hair discovered at the end of the story implies that —

F Emily has lain beside the skeleton

G Homer Barron had gray hair

H Homer Barron kept a lock of Emily's hair

J Emily was much older than Homer

______ **5.** Colonel Sartoris influences Emily by making her —

A think about future suitors

B feel as if she is above the law

C feel as if the world is ending

D think about military matters

______ **6.** To influence the development of her character, Emily's father —

F drives off suitors and prevents her from marrying

G refuses to allow her to use the family name

H forces her to work in the family business

J forgets to leave anything to her in his will

______ **7.** Which of Homer Barron's actions has the *greatest* effect on the development of Emily's character?

A Taking her to visit the North

B Sometimes going drinking without her

C Returning to town after an absence

D Enraging her by rejecting her

______ **8.** The narrator generalizes about people by saying that "we knew that with nothing left, she would have to cling to that which had robbed her, as people will." Miss Emily's behavior supports this generalization because she —

F refuses to pay her taxes

G gains a lot of weight

H goes out with Homer Barron

J refuses to admit that her father is dead

______ **9.** Judging from William Faulkner's Nobel Prize acceptance speech, what aspect of Miss Emily would he have admired *most*?

A Her love for Homer Barron

B Being out of touch with reality

C Having an "inexhaustible voice"

D Her enduring from generation to generation

______ **10.** In his speech, Faulkner says that "the human heart in conflict with itself" is the only thing worth writing is about. "A Rose for Emily" portrays the human heart in conflict with itself by showing that Emily —

F felt both love and hate for Homer Barron

G performed all her actions with an aristocratic sense of sureness

H kept the same black servant throughout her life

J was a Grierson through and through

LITERARY FOCUS: SETTING *(15 points; 5 points each)*
On the line provided, write the letter of the *best* answer to each of the following items.

______ **11.** The small-town setting of the story helps the reader understand —

A why the thwarting of Emily's desire to marry mattered so much

B the history of the Civil War

C why Emily's father did not let her marry

D the tolerant attitudes of the townspeople toward African Americans

______ **12.** The town described in the story is a(n) —

- **F** idealized view of Southern society
- **G** unnecessary backdrop to the action
- **H** distraction from more important things
- **J** crucial part of the story's plot

______ **13.** All of the following factors are important aspects of this story's setting *except* —

- **A** Colonel Sartoris's death
- **B** the old, decaying house
- **C** customs for treating the upper classes
- **D** attitudes toward African Americans

READING SKILLS: MAKING INFERENCES ABOUT CHARACTERS *(5 points)*

On the line provided, write the letter of the *best* answer to the following item.

______ **14.** All of the following details help you make the inference that Miss Emily is a murderer *except* the —

- **F** smell in the house
- **G** disappearance of Homer Barron
- **H** arsenic she buys
- **J** market basket

VOCABULARY DEVELOPMENT *(20 points; 4 points each)*

On the line provided, write the Vocabulary word that *best* completes each sentence.

pauper **tranquil** **acrid** **archaic** **perverse**

15. The odor issuing from Emily's house was ______________ and unpleasant.

16. Emily inherited the house, but in terms of money she was left a virtual ______________.

17. Emily's actions ranged from the merely odd and ______________ to the outright murderous.

18. The era of the Griersons seems so distant to us today, it is almost ______________.

19. Although horrible things were happening behind closed curtains, the town was outwardly

______________ and calm.

NAME ______ CLASS ______ DATE ______ SCORE ______

Constructed Response *(20 points)*

20. In what ways is Emily affected by the shadows of the past? On a separate sheet of paper, explain how Emily has been shaped by the culture and historical period in which she lives. Discuss her family's sense of its position in society, and cite details from the story to support your ideas.

NAME ______ CLASS ______ DATE ______ SCORE ______

SELECTION TEST **Student Edition page 659**

LITERARY RESPONSE AND ANALYSIS

The Feather Pillow

Horacio Quiroga *translated by* Margaret Sayers Peden

COMPREHENSION *(40 points; 4 points each)*

On the line provided, write the letter of the *best* answer to each of the following items.

______ **1.** At the beginning of "The Feather Pillow," what gives the young bride "hot and cold shivers"?

A Her honeymoon

B Her husband's mustache

C The idea of living in the jungle

D Fear of insects and spiders

______ **2.** Jordan and Alicia's house is described as a —

F cozy forest cottage

G sturdy pioneer homestead

H cold, white enchanted palace

J typical South American rancho

______ **3.** During a typical day, Alicia —

A visits friends

B cooks and cleans

C talks on the phone and writes in her journal

D waits for Jordan to return from work

______ **4.** Alicia first becomes ill with —

F chickenpox

G the flu

H smallpox

J polio

______ **5.** The doctors —

A are not called in time to do anything for Alicia

B are unable to find out what is wrong with Alicia

C make things worse by prescribing the wrong medicine

D make things worse by "bleeding" Alicia

______ **6.** In the depths of her illness, Alicia imagines she sees —

F an anthropoid, or humanlike creature

G a slithering serpent

H her husband trying to kill her

J her childhood home

______ **7.** During Alicia's illness, it becomes clear that Jordan —

A hates his wife

B is responsible for the illness

C loves his wife deeply

D cares only for money

______ **8.** What causes Alicia's death?

F Her husband

G Sheer exhaustion and weakness

H A horrible little creature

J The flu

______ **9.** What does the feather pillow have to do with Alicia's death?

A She is smothered with it in her sleep.

B In the feathers lives a parasite that sucks Alicia's blood.

C Jordan keeps the feather pillow as a reminder of his wife's tragic death.

D The pillow is soaked through with Alicia's blood.

______ **10.** The tale of Alicia and the pillow *most* closely resembles —

F stories about women who are imprisoned in castles

G legends about earwigs that burrow into people's brains

H folk tales about witches who curse newborn children

J epics about heroes who kill giants or dragons

LITERARY FOCUS: COMPARING THEMES ACROSS TEXTS *(15 points; 5 points each)*

On the line provided, write the letter of the *best* answer to each of the following items.

______ **11.** One Gothic theme that can be found in both "The Feather Pillow" and "A Rose for Emily" is the —

A haunted house

B murdered spouse

C innocent young woman

D house with a secret evil

______ **12.** Unlike the Gothic fiction of Faulkner, Poe, or Hawthorne, Horacio Quiroga's story —

F is a product of Latin American culture

G involves a mysterious death

H is intended to be scary

J is superbly written

______ **13.** "The Feather Pillow" and "A Rose for Emily" both use the Gothic form to show the —

A importance of communication between husband and wife

B defects of early twentieth-century medicine

C oppressiveness of nosy, snoopy, intrusive neighbors

D ill effects of isolation for women in old-fashioned communities

READING SKILLS: MAKING PREDICTIONS *(5 points)*

On the line provided, write the letter of the *best* answer to the following item.

______ **14.** Which item below contains a detail that helps you predict the outcome of this story?

F "She cast a furtive glance at the impressive stature of her Jordan. . . ."

G "The carpet swallowed his steps."

H "The lights were lighted all day long in her bedroom. . . ."

J "Then her sobs subsided, and she stood a long while, her face hidden in the hollow of his neck, not moving or speaking a word."

VOCABULARY DEVELOPMENT *(20 points; 4 points each)*

Match the definition on the left with the Vocabulary word on the right. On the line provided, write the letter of the Vocabulary word.

______ **15.** tiny	**a.** inert
______ **16.** motionless	**b.** inexplicable
______ **17.** unable to be explained	**c.** furtive
______ **18.** lessened	**d.** diminutive
______ **19.** stealthy; hidden	**e.** subsided

CONSTRUCTED RESPONSE *(20 points)*

20. Horacio Quiroga, like Edgar Allan Poe, believed that every word and action in a short story should build to a unified emotional effect. What effect do you think Quiroga was trying to achieve in "The Feather Pillow"? What aspects of his style show him trying to achieve that effect. How well do you think he achieved the effect, and why? On a separate sheet of paper, answer these questions, giving specific examples from the text to support your ideas.

NAME ______ CLASS ______ DATE ______ SCORE ______

SELECTION TEST **Student Edition page 670** **LITERARY RESPONSE AND ANALYSIS**

The Leader of the People John Steinbeck

COMPREHENSION *(40 points; 4 points each)*

On the line provided, write the letter of the *best* answer to each of the following items.

______ **1.** Throughout the story, Jody is concerned with hunting what animals?

A Buffaloes

B Coyotes

C Mice

D Deer

______ **2.** Jody's grandfather's greatest achievement was that he —

F lived to a very old age

G led a wagon train west to California

H was the father of a fine family

J was the most skillful hunter in his community

______ **3.** Why doesn't Jody's father, Carl, like Jody's grandfather?

A Carl is tired of hearing Grandfather's stories about the past.

B Grandfather is critical of the way Carl runs the ranch.

C Carl's wife prefers her father to her husband or son.

D Carl feels that Grandfather has sponged off others all his life.

______ **4.** To characterize Jody's feelings about his grandfather, you could say that Jody —

F shares his father's view

G wishes his grandfather would not tell the same stories over and over

H is ashamed of his grandfather's weaknesses

J idolizes and admires his grandfather

______ **5.** Evidently Jody's father —

A requires that Jody ask his permission before doing anything on the ranch

B never goes back on something he has said, not even within the family

C will not allow Jody to have any fun, despite Jody's constant pleading

D is rather carefree, an attitude that annoys his family when there is work to be done

______ **6.** Which character in the story is the "leader of the people"?

F Jody

G Carl

H Grandfather

J Billy Buck

______ **7.** At the end of John Steinbeck's story, Grandfather says that the *most* important thing he wants to tell about is —

A the way it felt to come to the end of the frontier

B massacres of Indian villages

C the discovery of gold in California

D the westward movement of a large mass of people

______ **8.** According to Grandfather, some men hated the ocean because in the past —

F it prevented them from continuing westward

G men preferred farming or ranching to fishing

H men were afraid of the unpredictability of floods

J it did not provide drinking water

______ **9.** Which of the following statements *best* describes the climax, or dramatic high point, of the story?

A Grandfather overhears Carl saying he doesn't want to hear the stories.

B Jody's mother says that the stories might be all that Grandfather has left.

C Grandfather accepts the fact that he has to settle at the edge of the continent.

D Jody's father gives in by agreeing to listen to the stories again and again.

______ **10.** At the end of the story, why does Jody offer to make lemonade for Grandfather?

F Jody wants to annoy his mother by asking for a lemon.

G Upset by Grandfather's sadness, Jody wants to cheer himself and his grandfather.

H Jody has been ordered by his father to make sure Grandfather is treated well.

J Jody wants his parents to stop thinking ill of him.

LITERARY FOCUS: CONFLICT *(20 points; 5 points each)*
On the line provided, write the letter of the *best* answer to each of the following items.

______ **11.** All of the following pairs are in conflict throughout "The Leader of the People" *except* —

A the past versus the present

B Billy Buck versus his fear of mice

C Jody versus his father

D Grandfather versus Carl Tiflin

NAME ______ CLASS ______ DATE ______ SCORE ______

______ **12.** The difference between **internal** and **external conflict** is that —

F external conflict is more serious

G internal conflict is more serious

H internal conflict occurs within a character, while external conflict occurs between a character and the outside world

J an external conflict can be resolved, while an internal conflict usually remains unchanged

______ **13.** In "The Leader of the People," the central conflict between Carl and Mrs. Tiflin is that they —

A disagree over how Jody should be raised

B argue about how to run the ranch

C have differing views of Grandfather and his stories

D have different responses to the rugged life of the West

______ **14.** An **archetype** is a kind of —

F plot device

G character trait

H point of view

J basic symbol or image

Vocabulary Development *(20 points; 4 points each)*

On the line provided, write the letter of the *best* answer to each of the following items.

______ **15.** If a storyteller relates a story listlessly, he or she tells it —

A with humor, wit, and gesture

B a different way each time

C without much energy or interest

D expressively but naturally

______ **16.** If you retract something you have said, you —

F emphasize it more strongly

G take it back

H clarify it for the listener

J ask for feedback

______ **17.** An arrogant person would be *most* likely to —

A always believe his or her actions were correct

B ask for permission before going anywhere

C ask directions when traveling in an unfamiliar place

D be hesitant about criticizing others

______ **18.** "His father looked down at him contemptuously," says the narrator of the story. The father —

F scorns the child

G respects the child

H loves the child

J fears the child

______ **19.** An animal that is immune to a certain disease —

A dies from the disease

B catches the disease but recovers

C catches the disease and spreads it

D does not catch the disease

CONSTRUCTED RESPONSE *(20 points)*

20. On a separate sheet of paper, describe a conflict in "The Leader of the People" that involves an archetype. State what the archetype is. Remember that an archetype may be an idea or attitude rather than a character. State whether the conflict is internal or external, whether it is resolved or not, and how it is resolved (or why it is not resolved).

NAME ______ CLASS ______ DATE ______ SCORE ______

SELECTION TEST **Student Edition pages 686, 692**

A Worn Path Eudora Welty

"Is Phoenix Jackson's Grandson Really Dead?" Eudora Welty

COMPREHENSION *(40 points; 4 points each)*

On the line provided, write the letter of the *best* answer to each of the following items.

______ **1.** Phoenix Jackson's goal for her journey is to —

- **A** beg for money on the streets
- **B** get medicine for her grandson's throat
- **C** go for her yearly medical checkup
- **D** assist a hunter in the woods

______ **2.** In this story, Natchez is a —

- **F** dog
- **G** person
- **H** city
- **J** steamboat

______ **3.** On her journey, Phoenix comes upon a(n) —

- **A** old woman with a cane
- **B** hunter and his dog
- **C** feast under a tree in the forest
- **D** alligator under a log

______ **4.** The incidents with the thorn bush and the scarecrow indicate that Phoenix —

- **F** has trouble seeing
- **G** fears nothing
- **H** has trouble walking
- **J** drifts in and out of consciousness

______ **5.** Throughout her journey, Phoenix —

- **A** wants to turn back
- **B** tries to remember where she is going
- **C** is determined to keep going
- **D** thinks only of her grandson

_______ **6.** How is Phoenix able to remember the way to her destination?

- **F** There are signs at regular intervals along the path.
- **G** She asks several helpful people for directions.
- **H** She is able to find her way with the help of a large black dog.
- **J** After many trips there, her feet remember where to take her.

_______ **7.** When Phoenix arrives at the doctor's office, the attendant thinks that Phoenix is —

- **A** in the wrong building
- **B** insane
- **C** from the country
- **D** a charity case

_______ **8.** Phoenix plans to use her two nickels to buy —

- **F** a paper windmill
- **G** throat medicine
- **H** a new dress
- **J** a new cane

_______ **9.** According to Eudora Welty, what question do students ask *most* frequently about "A Worn Path"?

- **A** "How did you get the idea for this story?"
- **B** "Did this really happen, or did you make it up?"
- **C** "Is Phoenix Jackson's grandson really dead?"
- **D** "Was Phoenix Jackson based on a real person?"

_______ **10.** According to Welty, what is her *best* answer to this popular question?

- **F** Phoenix Jackson was based on the woman who raised her as a child.
- **G** Phoenix Jackson is alive.
- **H** Some of the story was based on reality, but the plot was mostly invented.
- **J** The grandson is actually alive.

NAME ______________ CLASS ______________ DATE ______________ SCORE ______________

LITERARY FOCUS: THEME *(20 points; 5 points each)*
On the line provided, write the letter of the *best* answer to each of the following items.

______ **11.** The **theme** of a story is —
- A never stated directly
- B something the main character agrees with
- C the identity of the storyteller
- D an important idea or insight evoked by the story

______ **12.** Which of the following statements expresses a theme?
- F The story takes Phoenix through the woods, across a river, and into a city.
- G Phoenix Jackson is an old woman living in the South several decades ago.
- H Life can be compared to an eventful journey.
- J A path is a long, usually narrow route for travel.

______ **13.** The *main* theme of "A Worn Path" can *best* be expressed as —
- A the temptation to steal is a powerful test of faith
- B incredible physical strength can result from age and wisdom
- C an overwhelming presence of nature can threaten human lives
- D strong devotion helps people continue on a difficult journey

______ **14.** One theme of this story can *best* be compared to a particular archetype of the journey, which might be characterized as a(n) —
- F endless road to nowhere
- G long trail with obstacles and challenges
- H high-speed chase down a freeway
- J bumpy dirt road through a cornfield

VOCABULARY DEVELOPMENT *(20 points; 4 points each)*
On the line provided, write the Vocabulary word that *best* completes each sentence.

persistent **illumined** **intent** **appointed** **solemn**

15. Phoenix Jackson is ______________________ on going to the doctor's office time after time, despite obstacles.

16. The streets are ______________________ by hundreds of Christmas lights in many colors.

17. For Phoenix, her journey on the path is a(n) ______________________ and important duty.

18. Phoenix believes that all creatures, including dogs, people, and thorn bushes, were put on earth to fulfill certain ______________________ tasks.

19. As Phoenix loosens her dress from the thorns, her fingers are busy and ____________________.

CONSTRUCTED RESPONSE *(20 points)*

20. Based on Phoenix Jackson's archetypal journey and on themes you perceive in "A Worn Path," what do you think is Eudora Welty's view of life? On a separate sheet of paper, explain your response, referring to specific details from the story.

NAME ______ CLASS ______ DATE ______ SCORE ______

SELECTION TEST **Student Edition page 697**

The Jilting of Granny Weatherall

Katherine Anne Porter

COMPREHENSION *(40 points; 4 points each)*

On the line provided, write the letter of the *best* answer to each of the following items.

______ **1.** Which phrase *best* describes Granny Weatherall's life?

- **A** Long years of hard work on a homestead
- **B** A youthful romance that blossomed into a lifelong loving marriage
- **C** One early tragedy followed by sixty years of untroubled good fortune
- **D** Frustration after frustration with no silver linings in the clouds

______ **2.** The title "The Jilting of Granny Weatherall" reflects an event from Granny's past. A title reflecting Granny's present would be —

- **F** "The Death of Granny Weatherall"
- **G** "Fencing the Hundred Acres"
- **H** "Hapsy and Hapsy's Child"
- **J** "The Uncut Wedding Cake"

______ **3.** Granny Weatherall's attitude can *best* be described as —

- **A** sweetly nostalgic
- **B** resolute and determined
- **C** sarcastic and tart
- **D** gently humorous

______ **4.** The story is told from the point of view of —

- **F** Doctor Harry
- **G** Cornelia
- **H** Ellen Weatherall
- **J** George

______ **5.** Granny Weatherall's marriage to John was evidently —

- **A** filled with conflict
- **B** bitter but outwardly polite
- **C** disappointing and dreary
- **D** emotionally and materially successful

______ **6.** When Granny sees Hapsy coming into the room, others around her perceive that —

- **F** Granny is very ill
- **G** Hapsy is actually leaving the room
- **H** Granny's daughter Lydia is entering the room
- **J** the weather is starting to get worse

_____ **7.** Granny has a desire to find George because she wants —
- **A** to tell him that she will always love him
- **B** him to know that she had a fine life without him
- **C** her children to get to know him
- **D** to let him know that she forgives him

_____ **8.** When Granny feels her feet being tickled, it is because —
- **F** Cornelia is playfully tickling her
- **G** the doctor is checking her reflexes
- **H** a sudden breeze has uncovered her feet
- **J** the priest is anointing her feet with oil in the last rites

_____ **9.** Granny Weatherall views Doctor Harry as if he were —
- **A** her husband
- **B** the man who deceived her
- **C** a mere boy
- **D** a great medical pioneer

_____ **10.** Which character is *not* physically present at Granny Weatherall's deathbed?
- **F** Cornelia
- **G** Hapsy
- **H** Father Connolly
- **J** Lydia

LITERARY FOCUS: STREAM OF CONSCIOUSNESS *(15 points; 5 points each)*
On the line provided, write the letter of the *best* answer to each of the following items.

_____ **11.** Katherine Anne Porter uses the stream-of-consciousness technique to —
- **A** express the feelings of relatives gathered around a deathbed
- **B** point out the injustices Granny Weatherall has suffered
- **C** vividly describe the hard life of a pioneer
- **D** allow the reader to get inside Granny's head

_____ **12.** Porter's use of stream of consciousness allows the reader to —
- **F** admire Granny Weatherall's accurate memory
- **G** contrast Granny Weatherall's thoughts with reality
- **H** sympathize with Hapsy and Lydia
- **J** realize that the doctor was absent for five minutes

______ **13.** A passage in the story that could *only* be part of the stream of consciousness is —

A "So, my dear Lord, this is my death and I wasn't even thinking about it."

B "The tall black dresser gleamed with nothing on it but John's picture. . . ."

C "I'm not going, Cornelia. I'm taken by surprise. I can't go."

D "Doctor Harry spread a warm paw like a cushion on her forehead. . . ."

READING SKILLS: READING CLOSELY *(5 points)*

On the line provided, write the letter of the *best* answer to the following item.

______ **14.** When Granny notes that the doctor has returned after only five minutes, what has really happened is that —

F the doctor never actually returned

G an entire day has passed

H it was actually the doctor's brother

J she had imagined the first visit

VOCABULARY DEVELOPMENT *(20 points; 4 points each)*

Match the definition on the right with the Vocabulary word on the left. On the line provided, write the letter of the definition.

______ **15.** jilted

______ **16.** tactful

______ **17.** dwindled

______ **18.** disputed

______ **19.** vanity

a. skilled in saying the right thing

b. excessive pride

c. rejected (as a lover)

d. contested

e. diminished

CONSTRUCTED RESPONSE *(20 points)*

20. At the end of the story, Katherine Anne Porter uses stream of consciousness to show that two major events of Granny Weatherall's life are being confused in her mind. On a separate sheet of paper, name the two events. Then, give examples of key passages, and analyze how both events are present in Granny's stream of consciousness.

The Secret Life of Walter Mitty James Thurber
The New Yorker's Farewell E. B. White

COMPREHENSION *(40 points; 4 points each)*

On the line provided, write the letter of the *best* answer to each of the following items.

______ **1.** Walter Mitty might be *best* described as a —

A bold, dashing hero
B writer with a vivid imagination
C timid, humdrum man who imagines himself as brave
D cruel husband who habitually berates his wife

______ **2.** Mrs. Mitty might be *best* described by saying that she —

F does all the shopping for the household
G cannot make decisions
H is always working
J constantly tells Walter what to do

______ **3.** When Walter imagines that he is on the witness stand, he —

A brilliantly argues for his innocence in the murder of Gregory Fitzhurst
B proudly admits that he could have killed Gregory Fitzhurst with his left hand
C successfully demonstrates that the district attorney murdered Fitzhurst
D acts as his own lawyer in the trial for the murder of Fitzhurst

______ **4.** Walter imagines that he fixes an anesthetizer machine in the operating room using a —

F fountain pen
G glove
H puppy biscuit
J pencil

______ **5.** In all of his fantasies, Walter imagines that he is a(n) —

A outlaw who narrowly escapes from the authorities
B man who shows control in tough situations
C person who knows exactly how to follow orders
D pilot who saves his passengers' lives

______ **6.** When Walter imagines being questioned about his gun, he sees himself as —

F arrogant and fearless
G frightened and intimidated
H confused and depressed
J excited and hysterical

______ **7.** Which of the following statements *best* describes the relationship of Mr. and Mrs. Mitty?

A She is deeply in love with him, but he no longer loves her.

B He makes all the decisions, and she meekly goes along with them.

C She is domineering, and he submits to her wishes.

D He is realistic, and she lives in a fantasy world.

______ **8.** Walter's courtroom drama is triggered by —

F his sudden recollection of what he needs at the store

G his overhearing a newsboy talking about a trial

H an article he reads in the hairdresser's shop

J something that goes wrong during surgery

______ **9.** James Thurber's statement, "The clocks that strike in my dreams are often the clocks of Columbus," means that —

A like Walter Mitty, Thurber lived in a fantasy world

B Thurber had a lifelong interest in the history of great explorers

C his boyhood home remained an important part of Thurber's inner life

D Thurber had the uncanny ability to remember all of his dreams in detail

______ **10.** E. B. White's statement about Thurber, "His pencil was connected to his mind by the best conductive tissue I have ever seen in action," means that —

F Thurber was White's favorite writer of all time

G Thurber often wished he could stop writing but could not

H White's opinion of Thurber differed from most critics' opinions

J White admired how easily Thurber was able to express his thoughts in writing

LITERARY FOCUS: PARODY *(15 points; 5 points each)*
On the line provided, write the letter of the *best* answer to each of the following items.

______ **11.** Thurber's descriptions of Mitty's fantasies can be seen as parodies because they —

A humorously mimic real life

B humorously imitate action-adventure stories

C seriously criticize modern drama

D seriously imitate mystery novels

_____ **12.** Which of the following details is part of one parody in the story?

F Walter waits for his wife to get her hair done.

G Walter asks for puppy biscuits at the A&P.

H Walter attempts to take the chains off his car.

J Walter hits the district attorney.

_____ **13.** Which detail of parody in "The Secret Life of Walter Mitty" involves irony?

A Mitty imagines himself as the brave commander of an airplane.

B Mitty's response to the pressures of life is to retreat into fantasy.

C Mitty, who has been defeated by life, imagines himself as "Mitty the Undefeated."

D Mitty's wife does not show up in his fantasies.

READING SKILLS: ANALYZING CAUSE AND EFFECT *(5 points)*

On the line provided, write the letter of the *best* answer to the following item.

_____ **14.** The use of cause and effect in "The Secret Life of Walter Mitty" is unusual in that —

F Walter's wife is often the cause

G the effects often come before the causes

H the causes are everyday events and the effects are wild fantasies

J most of the action happens without any cause

VOCABULARY DEVELOPMENT *(20 points; 4 points each)*

On the line provided, write the letter of the word that *best* completes each item.

_____ **15.** Distraught means —

A troubled

B calm

C poorly educated

D not respected

_____ **16.** A haggard-looking person is probably —

F healthy-looking

G in the prime of life

H just back from the gym

J tired or ill

_____ **17.** Two people who are bickering are *not* —

A related

B in agreement

C business partners

D being active

______ **18.** It is insolent to —

F ask for help when you need it

G give directions to someone who is lost

H show disrespect to one's elders

J cooperate with a peer on schoolwork

______ **19.** Which of the following words means cowardly?

A bedlam

B pandemonium

C rending

D craven

CONSTRUCTED RESPONSE *(20 points)*

20. On a separate sheet of paper, discuss how James Thurber uses fantasy to convey ideas about reality in "The Secret Life of Walter Mitty." Cite specific events and details from the story, and name two or more subgenres of fiction that Thurber uses.

NAME ______ CLASS ______ DATE ______ SCORE ______

SELECTION TEST **Student Edition pages 717, 719** LITERARY RESPONSE AND ANALYSIS

Common Diction Robert Frost
Design Robert Frost

COMPREHENSION *(40 points; 4 points each)*

On the line provided, write the letter of the *best* answer to each of the following items.

______ **1.** Which description *best* sums up the action of "Design"?

A A spider sits by its web, waiting for something to drop into its clutches.

B A sensitive poet rescues a harmless creature from being killed by a predator.

C A poet sees a moth trapped by a spider and thinks about what it all means.

D A man sees a design in nature and decides to duplicate it in art.

______ **2.** What word is used five times in the poem?

F design

G spider

H dead

J white

______ **3.** What is compared to a paper kite in the poem?

A The flower

B Death

C A witches' broth

D The moth's wings

______ **4.** Which of the following questions *best* paraphrases the question asked in the poem's sestet (the last six lines)?

F What power created beauty and evil?

G What nutrients does a moth provide to a spider?

H Why are moths usually pale in color rather than dark?

J What ailments can be treated with the heal-all flower?

______ **5.** In line 13, the speaker suggests that the purpose of design in nature is to —

A make people feel good in times of doubt or grief

B conceal and then reveal a horrifying ugliness beneath the surface

C enable some creatures to camouflage themselves

D provide relief from the grimness of everyday life

______ **6.** In line 14, the speaker suggests that —

F the spider may be innocent after all

G there may be no purpose behind the design of nature

H the moth could have escaped the spider

J the belief in human goodness is an illusion

______ **7.** Is "Design" essentially a pessimistic poem or an optimistic one?

A It is pessimistic, because it suggests that the universe is either evil or indifferent.

B It is pessimistic, because the last line offers an alternative to the rest of the poem.

C It is optimistic, because all the creatures in the poem are fulfilling their natural roles.

D It is optimistic, because the poet created a beautiful design—this poem—from his experience.

______ **8.** The imagery throughout "Design" suggests that —

F the moth is not actually dead

G evil may masquerade as innocence

H the spider is aware of the speaker

J all of nature is beautiful

______ **9.** The feature "Common Diction" is about Robert Frost's —

A dislike of common, everyday speech

B desire to create a separate style of English for poetry

C preference for simple words

D use of "dictionary words" that have to be looked up by the reader

______ **10.** Which word choice in the poem *best* reflects the view presented in "Common Diction"?

F "steered the white moth thither . . ."

G "What brought the kindred spider to that height?"

H "Mixed ready to begin the morning right . . ."

J "What but design of darkness to appall?"

LITERARY FOCUS: SONNET *(40 points; 10 points each)*

On the line provided, write the letter of the *best* answer to each of the following items.

______ **11.** Every **sonnet** must have —

A fourteen lines

B rhyme and meter

C iambic pentameter

D philosophical ideas

______ **12.** The last two lines of a sonnet are called the —

F sestet

G couplet

H quatrain

J octave

______ **13.** How are the **Petrarchan,** or Italian, sonnet and the **Shakespearean,** or English, sonnet different?

A They have different numbers of lines.

B They are written in different languages.

C One is usually serious; the other usually comic.

D They have different internal structures.

______ **14.** The words *white, blight, right, kite, height,* and *night; moth, cloth, broth,* and *forth*; and *heal-all, appall,* and *small,* tell you that Frost's sonnet, —

F unlike most sonnets, is in free verse

G like most sonnets, uses wordplay

H like most sonnets, contains rhyme

J unlike most sonnets, contains rhyme

CONSTRUCTED RESPONSE *(20 points)*

15. What philosophical views are expressed in the sonnet "Design"? How can you tell? On a separate sheet of paper, write your answer, refering to specific views and to specific aspects of the text.

NAME ______ CLASS ______ DATE ______ SCORE ______

SELECTION TEST **Student Edition pages 721, 722** LITERARY RESPONSE AND ANALYSIS

Nothing Gold Can Stay Robert Frost
Trying to Name What Doesn't Change Naomi Shihab Nye

COMPREHENSION *(40 points; 4 points each)*
On the line provided, write the letter of the *best* answer to each of the following items.

______ **1.** In "Nothing Gold Can Stay," gold symbolizes, or stands for, —
- **A** the color of autumn leaves
- **B** human greed and selfishness
- **C** sunrise on a spring morning
- **D** fleeting beauty and perfection

______ **2.** The meaning of the title "Nothing Gold Can Stay" can be paraphrased as —
- **F** "Easy Come, Easy Go"
- **G** "Beauty Always Fades"
- **H** "The More You Earn, the More You Spend"
- **J** "Great Poetry Lasts Forever"

______ **3.** "Nothing Gold Can Stay" contains eight lines of verse. Which pair of lines rhymes?
- **A** 1 and 2
- **B** 1 and 3
- **C** 2 and 3
- **D** 2 and 4

______ **4.** Which of the following groups of words from the poem does *not* use alliteration?
- **F** gold/hold
- **G** dawn/down/day
- **H** green/gold
- **J** subsides/so/sank

______ **5.** How many stressed, or accented, syllables are there in each line of the poem?
- **A** two
- **B** three
- **C** four
- **D** five

______ **6.** Which of the following real aspects of gold does *not* fit in with the theme of the poem?
- **F** Gold is rare.
- **G** Gold is valuable.
- **H** Gold does not tarnish.
- **J** Gold is shiny.

______ **7.** The tone of "Nothing Gold Can Stay" can *best* be described as —

A mocking

B hostile

C sad

D angry

______ **8.** Which statement accurately expresses how this poem's style reflects its theme?

F The poem uses rhyme because rhyme is often associated with light, comic verse.

G The poet has deliberately limited himself to a small set of sounds and images.

H The poem says that beauty is fleeting, and the poem itself is both beautiful and brief.

J *Subsides* is probably the hardest word in the poem.

______ **9.** In "Trying to Name What Doesn't Change," what idea or theme is implied about change?

A Living things change, but nonliving things do not.

B Everything changes, even if the change is slow.

C Memory is the only thing in life that doesn't change.

D Nothing really changes; change is an illusion.

______ **10.** How are "Nothing Gold Can Stay" and "Trying to Name What Doesn't Change" different in their use of sounds and other techniques of poetry?

F Actually, they are similar in most ways.

G "Nothing Gold Can Stay" is free verse, while "Trying to Name What Doesn't Change" is not.

H The two poems use different rhyme schemes, meters, and types of alliteration.

J "Nothing Gold Can Stay" uses rhyme and meter, while "Trying to Name What Doesn't Change" is free verse.

LITERARY FOCUS: ALLUSION *(40 points; 10 points each)*
On the line provided, write the letter of the *best* answer to each of the following items.

______ **11.** An **allusion** is —

A a reference to something well-known

B something that seems to be there but isn't

C the use of several words beginning with the same consonant

D an idea that is stated or implied throughout a poem

______ **12.** In "Nothing Gold Can Stay" the allusion that would be understood *best* by an ancient Greek would be the —

F idea of seasons changing

G biblical account of the Garden of Eden

H verse form Robert Frost has chosen

J idea of a passing Golden Age

______ **13.** Which phrase in "Trying to Name What Doesn't Change" is an allusion to the biblical story of the burning bush?

A "weeds that grow up spidery . . ."

B "The wood was split. . . ."

C "fire in the petals"

D "Butchers crack the necks of a hundred hens."

______ **14.** Which phrase in "Trying to Name What Doesn't Change" is an allusion to some current scientific knowledge?

F "Nature's first green is gold. . . ."

G "Stars explode."

H "A track without a train / is a changed track."

J "The widow . . . / spices her soup with cinnamon."

CONSTRUCTED RESPONSE *(20 points)*

15. Choose either "Nothing Gold Can Stay" or "Trying to Name What Doesn't Change." On a separate sheet of paper, name the emotions you think the poet tries to evoke in the reader. What specific aspects of the poem's style, tone, sounds, and contents convey those emotions?

NAME ______ CLASS ______ DATE ______ SCORE ______

SELECTION TEST **Student Edition page 724** **LITERARY RESPONSE AND ANALYSIS**

Birches Robert Frost

COMPREHENSION *(40 points; 4 points each)*

On the line provided, write the letter of the *best* answer to each of the following items.

______ **1.** The image that starts the speaker onto the train of thought that guides the poem is a(n) —

A pile of cut logs on the edge of the woods
B stand of trees in which some of the trees curve down to the earth
C orchard in which young saplings are sprouting
D young man who has injured himself climbing trees

______ **2.** Why couldn't this poem be about oaks or maples?

F Birches are especially slender and bendable.
G Oaks and maples don't grow in Robert Frost's part of the world.
H The words *oaks* and *maples* wouldn't sound right in the poem.
J The trees Frost saw were birches, so he had to write about them.

______ **3.** According to the speaker, what has caused the birches to bend?

A A sudden windstorm
B Boys swinging from the treetops
C Ice during a winter storm
D A problem in the growth of the seedling

______ **4.** The metaphor "heaps of broken glass" in line 12 describes —

F a boy's injury
G sawdust lying at the foot of tree stumps
H the speaker's eyeglasses, which change his view of the trees
J shattered ice

______ **5.** The poet compares the trees' trailing their leaves on the ground to —

A boys playing in the trees
B girls drying their hair
C the inner dome of heaven
D boys playing baseball

______ **6.** The speaker of the poem —

F is a man who swung birches when he was a boy
G is a boy who is nervous about swinging his first birch
H speaks with no personal authority on the subject of birch swinging
J is the father of a boy who has injured himself in a tree

______ **7.** Birches, ice, snow, and dark branches tell you that the visual imagery in "Birches" is —

A rainbow hued

B tinged with the pink and violet of twilight

C loud and clattering

D mostly black and white

______ **8.** According to the poem, a boy who swings birches experiences —

F a terrifying near-death vision

G the pleasures of both heaven and earth

H the anger of the farmer who owns the land

J a number of minor injuries

______ **9.** The speaker dreams of becoming a birch swinger once again when —

A he is tired of the cares of human life

B he reaches a stumbling block in his writing

C the days are beautiful and everything seems perfect

D it is painful to walk through the pathless forest

______ **10.** What view of life does the speaker express in lines 53–59?

F Earthly life is a sham.

G The only wisdom lies in seeking heaven.

H Pleasure is the only worthwhile pursuit.

J A good life combines earthly life with spiritual yearnings.

READING SKILLS: READING POETRY *(40 points; 10 points each)*
On the line provided, write the letter of the *best* answer to each of the following items.

______ **11.** Because "Birches" is written in blank verse —

A it contains neither rhyme nor meter

B every other line rhymes

C its lines vary widely in length

D it contains meter but not rhyme

______ **12.** The best description of the way "Birches" is written would be to say that it —

F has a very stilted style

G contains a lot of dialect

H sounds exactly like a sonnet

J is close to conversational English

______ **13.** At the end of which of the following lines would you pause briefly?

A "When I see birches bend to left and right . . . "

B "I like to think some boy's been swinging them."

C "Loaded with ice a sunny winter morning . . ."

D "Across the lines of straighter darker trees . . ."

______ **14.** At the end of which of the following lines would you stop?

F "With all her matter of fact about the ice storm . . ."

G "Shattering and avalanching on the snow crust— . . ."

H "As the stir cracks and crazes their enamel."

J "And so not carrying the tree away . . ."

CONSTRUCTED RESPONSE *(20 points)*

15. The emotions of the speaker in "Birches" are complex and subtle. On a separate sheet of paper, name the emotions, and tell how the sound of the poem helps to express them.

NAME ______ CLASS ______ DATE ______ SCORE ______

SELECTION TEST **Student Edition pages 727, 729** LITERARY RESPONSE AND ANALYSIS

Mending Wall Robert Frost
Mending Test Penelope Bryant Turk
To the Editor Jeffrey Meyers

COMPREHENSION *(40 points; 4 points each)*

On the line provided, write the letter of the *best* answer to each of the following items.

______ **1.** The wall in this poem is on —

A the boundary between two farms

B the border between states

C an obstacle course in the woods

D the side of a farmhouse

______ **2.** What happens to the wall every winter?

F Because of the cold, it becomes more solid.

G The speaker tries fruitlessly to rebuild it.

H A crowd of citizens tears it down.

J Freezing and thawing makes some of the stones fall.

______ **3.** What happens every spring?

A The neighbor threatens to sue the speaker unless he helps mend the wall.

B The speaker's cows cross over and tear up the neighbor's pasture.

C The speaker reminds his neighbor that it is time to mend the wall.

D Rabbits, foxes, and hunters damage the wall.

______ **4.** Which line from the poem *best* expresses the speaker's attitude toward the wall?

F "Where they have left not one stone on a stone . . ."

G "To each the boulders that have fallen to each."

H "'Good fences make good neighbors.'"

J "There where it is we do not need the wall . . ."

______ **5.** If you were looking at the two neighbors' fields from above, what would you see?

A Two identical fields separated by a stone wall

B A fallow, unplanted field next to a thriving, growing one

C A grove of pines and a grove of apple trees, with a wall between them

D A rich man's prosperous field next to a poor man's meager field

______ **6.** What do line 28, "Spring is the mischief in me," and line 36, "I could say 'Elves' to him," tell you about the speaker?

F He believes in elves and other spirits.

G He is a playful sort of person.

H He hates his neighbor.

J He does not understand the true causes of wall damage.

______ **7.** What is implied in lines 37–38, "I'd rather / He said it for himself"?

A The speaker wishes his neighbor would understand on his own why it is good for walls to come down.

B The speaker wishes his neighbor would say, "Good fences make good neighbors."

C The speaker wishes his neighbor would warn him when the cows are coming through.

D The speaker wishes his neighbor would be the first one to mention wall mending.

______ **8.** What does the wall in this poem *not* stand for?

F Itself

G Barriers between people

H Understanding and communication

J The difficulties of human relationships

______ **9.** What is one difference between Robert Frost's "Mending Wall" and Penelope Bryant Turk's "Mending Test"?

A They have different metrical patterns.

B "Mending Test" does not have a serious point to make.

C "Mending Test" uses rhyme, and "Mending Wall" does not.

D "Mending Wall" is a work of art, while "Mending Test" is a comic imitation of it.

______ **10.** In "Mending Wall," what does "he will not go behind his father's saying" mean in line 43?

F The speaker, although a grown man, is still afraid of his father.

G The neighbor is afraid to do anything unless his father approves.

H The speaker disapproves of the neighbor's independent ways.

J The neighbor is unwilling to examine critically the wisdom of authorities.

NAME ______ CLASS ______ DATE ______ SCORE ______

LITERARY FOCUS: AMBIGUITY *(40 points; 10 points each)*

On the line provided, write the letter of the *best* answer to each of the following items.

______ **11.** If a poem's meaning is **ambiguous,** it is —

A impossible to understand

B open to interpretation

C plain to the average reader

D too complex to be published

______ **12.** In the first line of "Mending Wall," the word *something* is ambiguous. What *can't* the word *something* refer to in this context?

F An unknown power

G The speaker of the poem

H The wall-loving neighbor

J Winter weather

______ **13.** Jeffrey Meyers claims to have resolved the ambiguity of the word *something* in "Mending Wall." What does he say the word means?

A Frost

B Water

C Humanity

D Elves

______ **14.** The "gaps" the speaker refers to in lines 9–11 might refer to gaps in a stone wall. What else might they refer to in this context?

F Gaps between teeth

G Distance between people

H Omissions in a text

J Rivers that must be jumped

CONSTRUCTED RESPONSE *(20 points)*

15. Does ambiguity make good poems? On a separate sheet of paper, evaluate "Mending Wall" and decide how its ambiguities affect its literary greatness. Provide specific reasons and examples.

NAME ______ CLASS ______ DATE ______ SCORE ______

SELECTION TEST **Student Edition pages 731, 736** LITERARY RESPONSE AND ANALYSIS

The Death of the Hired Man Robert Frost

"I must have the pulse beat of rhythm . . ." Robert Frost

COMPREHENSION *(40 points; 4 points each)*

On the line provided, write the letter of the *best* answer to each of the following items.

______ **1.** Mary waits for her husband to tell him that —

A the mortgage is due

B she needs more things from the market

C Silas is back

D the hired man is sick

______ **2.** Mary reveals that the hired man is —

F dead

G working in the fields

H conversing with a neighbor

J asleep by the stove

______ **3.** The *main* conflict between Warren and Mary is whether —

A to pay the hired man fairly

B to take in the hired man even though he can no longer work

C the hired man is dead or only asleep

D to hire more help for the season

______ **4.** The hired man tries to "save his self-respect" by telling Mary —

F that he's come to ditch the meadow

G about all the other places he has worked

H that someone else has offered him a job

J that he is sick

______ **5.** Silas can't erase from his mind thoughts of —

A the time he has wasted working on a farm

B his ill health

C his need for money and security

D the arguments he used to have with Harold

______ **6.** Mary seems to believe that —

F her husband is cruel

G the hired man lived a rich, full life

H people should be able to think of their past with pride

J people should earn their keep

______ **7.** According to Mary, home is the place where —

A you were born

B people have to take you in

C your dog lives

D your relatives reside

______ **8.** Silas does not go to his brother's because —

F he wants to teach Harold to load hay

G his brother thinks him worthless

H he needs to pay off his debt to Warren and Mary

J his brother's farm is too far away

______ **9.** Based on the ***Primary Source,*** "I must have the pulse beat of rhythm . . . ," what was Robert Frost's opinion of free verse?

A He liked it, which was why he used it in "The Death of the Hired Man."

B He despised it and refused to read it.

C Although he didn't respect it as much as blank verse, he occasionally enjoyed reading it.

D He felt that all verse forms were equally worthy, depending on the skill of the poet.

______ **10.** In what ways does "The Death of the Hired Man" contain "the pulse beat of rhythm . . . beating under the things" Frost wrote"?

F The poem uses blank verse to create the feeling of real speech.

G As a ballad, the poem has a strong, repetitive beat.

H "The Death of the Hired Man" uses musical devices, such as rhyme.

J Frost wrote the poem while listening to the jazz that was all the rage in his era.

NAME ______ CLASS ______ DATE ______ SCORE ______

LITERARY FOCUS: NARRATIVE POETRY AND BLANK VERSE *(30 points; 10 points each)*

On the line provided, write the letter of the *best* answer to each of the following items.

______ **11.** Who says, "Someone else can," in line 24?

- **A** Mary
- **B** Warren
- **C** The hired man
- **D** Robert Frost

______ **12.** How is it that the dialogue in the poem sounds realistic even though it is poetry?

- **F** Frost used an unrhymed metrical form that closely mirrors the rhythms of speech.
- **G** In Frost's day, New England farmers spoke a more elegant kind of English than most Americans do today.
- **H** Frost was not very concerned about sticking to the rules of blank verse.
- **J** Because "The Death of the Hired Man" is in free verse, it can have any rhythm the poet desires.

______ **13.** Which of the following lines is written in strict iambic pentameter?

- **A** "Mary sat musing on the lamp-flame at the table . . ."
- **B** "'All right,' I say, 'I can't afford to pay. . . .'"
- **C** "'Someone else can.' 'Then someone else will have to.'"
- **D** "Which showed how much good school had ever done him."

READING SKILLS: MAKING INFERENCES ABOUT CHARACTER *(10 points)*

On the line provided, write the letter of the *best* answer to the following item.

______ **14.** In "The Death of the Hired Man" the characters' feelings are revealed by —

- **F** how the characters react to death
- **G** the characters' different definitions of death
- **H** the observations of a third-person narrator
- **J** what the characters say to one another

CONSTRUCTED RESPONSE *(20 points)*

15. On a separate sheet of paper, explain how the idea of home is important thematically in "The Death of the Hired Man." Support your answer by referring to specific details in the poem.

SELECTION TEST **Student Edition pages 745, 747**

LITERARY RESPONSE AND ANALYSIS

Tableau Countee Cullen
Incident Countee Cullen

COMPREHENSION *(40 points; 8 points each)*
On the line provided, write the letter of the *best* answer to each of the following items.

______ **1.** In "Tableau" the two boys are walking together because they —
- A are trying to cause trouble
- B hope to cause social change
- C are following local custom
- D enjoy each other's company

______ **2.** Other people react to the behavior of the boys by —
- F cheering them on
- G becoming upset
- H ignoring their presence
- J quietly approving of the friendship

______ **3.** In the last stanza of "Tableau," the boys —
- A angrily confront the adults of the town
- B happily continue walking
- C sadly go their separate ways
- D speak to each other loudly

______ **4.** "Incident" seems to present a simple picture, but the larger focus of the poem is the —
- F boys at play
- G reaction of a boy to an adult
- H state of race relations
- J poet's childhood dreams

______ **5.** In the last stanza of "Incident," the poet describes the —
- A harm a word can cause
- B power of friendship
- C courage of two boys
- D enlightened attitude of two boys

LITERARY FOCUS: METAPHOR *(40 points; 10 points each)*

On the line provided, write the letter of the *best* answer to each of the following items.

______ **6. Metaphor** is one kind of —

F simile

G figure of speech

H personification

J symbolism

______ **7.** Unlike simile, metaphor —

A uses the linking words *like* or *as* to signal comparison

B uses fewer words to say the same thing

C uses fancy poetic words rather than everyday ones

D does not use linking words to make the comparison

______ **8.** An example of metaphor in "Tableau" is —

F "From lowered blinds the dark folk stare"

G "They pass, and see no wonder"

H "The sable pride of night"

J "Locked arm in arm they cross the way"

______ **9.** The words *lightning* and *thunder* in "Tableau" suggest that the friendship of the two boys —

A is somehow related to the weather

B is a danger to the safety of the community

C is a powerful natural force

D cannot do anyone any harm

CONSTRUCTED RESPONSE *(20 points)*

10. On a separate sheet of paper, analyze "Tableau" and "Incident," discussing all of the following elements: the author's purpose, the emotions the poem evokes, the poem's tone, the figures of speech used, and any other aspects of style or sound that you feel are relevant.

NAME _______________ CLASS _______________ DATE _______________ SCORE _______________

SELECTION TEST **Student Edition pages 751, 754, 756**

LITERARY RESPONSE AND ANALYSIS

The Weary Blues Langston Hughes
Harlem Langston Hughes
Heyday in Harlem Langston Hughes

COMPREHENSION *(40 points; 4 points each)*

On the line provided, write the letter of the *best* answer to each of the following items.

_____ **1.** The song performed in "The Weary Blues" addresses —

A all people who are unhappy

B the plight of underpaid musicians

C the musician's poor health

D men without children

_____ **2.** Who utters lines 25–26, "'I got the Weary Blues / And I can't be satisfied'"?

F The speaker of the poem

G Langston Hughes

H The musician

J A man in the audience

_____ **3.** The lines in quotation marks in the poem come from —

A dialogue between the speaker and the musician

B the lyrics of the song the speaker hears

C the title "The Weary Blues"

D a conversation between members of the audience

_____ **4.** At the end of "The Weary Blues," the musician —

F sleeps like the dead

G meets the poet

H smiles at the audience

J passes a hat around for money

_____ **5.** Which of the following elements does the poem "The Weary Blues" *not* have in common with blues songs?

A Emotionally powerful words

B Rhythmic lines

C Instrumental accompaniment

D Clever use of repetition

______ **6.** In the poem "Harlem" the speaker uses the pronoun *we* to refer to —

F residents of New York

G poets and other artists

H people who remember the Depression

J African Americans in Harlem

______ **7.** In "Harlem" the phrase "what / We remember" in lines 22–23 does *not* refer to —

A dishonest acts committed against African Americans

B the end of legal segregation in the United States

C delays in achieving equality and justice

D increasing hardship during the Depression

______ **8.** What solution does the speaker of the poem offer for the problems of Harlem?

F Violent rebellion

G Peaceful protest against unjust laws

H Hard work and ambition

J No clear solution

______ **9.** "Heyday in Harlem" accomplishes all of the following purposes *except* to —

A describe Harlem during the period of its renaissance

B sketch how blacks and whites interacted, or did not interact, at that time

C explain house-rent parties

D state why Langston Hughes came to Harlem and why he left

______ **10.** Both "Harlem" and "Heyday in Harlem" —

F offer optimistic views of Harlem

G show a realistic understanding of Harlem life

H are cheerful in the face of prejudice

J are written in free verse

LITERARY FOCUS: RHYTHM AND MOOD *(40 points; 10 points each)*
On the line provided, write the letter of the *best* answer to each of the following items.

______ **11.** In poetry, **rhythm** refers to —

A the rise and fall of stressed and unstressed syllables

B vowel sounds repeated at the ends of words

C free (unmetered) verse as opposed to formal verse

D formal verse as opposed to free verse

NAME ______ CLASS ______ DATE ______ SCORE ______

______ **12.** Rhythms in "The Weary Blues" —

F are unvarying from line to line

G reflect the rhythms of song and speech

H require a piano accompaniment in order to really be felt

J are those of the traditional sonnet

______ **13.** The **mood** of a work is the —

A way in which the writer uses language

B author's emotional state

C attitude of the poet

D atmosphere or dominant feeling

______ **14.** The mood of "Harlem" does *not* include —

F an ominous sense of future conflict

G simple joy in being alive

H anger about present conditions

J bitterness about the past

CONSTRUCTED RESPONSE *(20 points)*

15. On a separate sheet of paper, compare and contrast the moods of "The Weary Blues" and "Harlem." Be sure to find similarities as well as differences, and to cite specific images, figures of speech, and sound devices.

NAME ______ CLASS ______ DATE ______ SCORE ______

The Negro Speaks of Rivers Langston Hughes
the mississippi river empties into the gulf Lucille Clifton

COMPREHENSION *(40 points; 4 points each)*

On the line provided, write the letter of the *best* answer to each of the following items.

_____ **1.** One river that is *not* mentioned in "The Negro Speaks of Rivers" is the —

A Rio Grande
B Congo
C Nile
D Mississippi

_____ **2.** What do the rivers named in "The Negro Speaks of Rivers" have in common?

F They are in Africa.
G They are historically important to the speaker.
H They have yearly floods.
J Famous dams have been built on them.

_____ **3.** According to the speaker, his soul is like a river because it —

A flows gently wherever it can
B dries up at times or rushes in torrents at others
C has grown deep over time
D is hard to contain

_____ **4.** What aspect of human biology does the speaker compare to rivers?

F Digestion
G Reproduction
H Respiration
J Circulation

_____ **5.** The line "I looked upon the Nile and raised the pyramids above it" shows that the speaker —

A identifies himself with his cultural ancestors
B lived thousands of years ago
C could not possibly have also seen Abe Lincoln on the Mississippi
D is Egyptian

______ **6.** The words *muddy, golden, dusky,* and *dawns* evoke images of —

F sight

G hearing

H smell

J touch

______ **7.** What form is "The Negro Speaks of Rivers" written in?

A Sonnet

B Ballad

C Free verse

D Blank verse

______ **8.** In "the mississippi river empties into the gulf," some people "mistakenly" —

F go sailing in bad weather

G trust too much in the future

H live solely in the present

J are afraid to risk entering the water

______ **9.** What quality of rivers is examined in *both* "The Negro Speaks of Rivers" and "the mississippi river empties into the gulf"?

A Unpredictability

B Timeless flow

C Danger

D Economic importance

______ **10.** The first line of "the mississippi river empties into the gulf," "and the gulf enters the sea and so forth," shows you that Lucille Clifton's poem —

F is a narrative

G describes the experiences of African Americans

H was written earlier than "The Negro Speaks of Rivers"

J uses the rhythms of colloquial speech

LITERARY FOCUS: REPETITION *(40 points; 10 points each)*

On the line provided, write the letter of the *best* answer to each of the following items.

______ **11.** One type of repetition is a **refrain,** which is a(n) —

A event that recurs in several parts of a ballad

B repeated consonant sound at the beginnings of words

C repeated pattern of stressed syllables

D repeated line or lines in a poem or song

______ **12.** What is one refrain in "The Negro Speaks of Rivers"?

F "ancient as the world and older than the flow"

G "I built my hut near the Congo and it lulled me to sleep."

H "I've known rivers."

J "Ancient, dusky rivers."

______ **13.** What is another refrain in "The Negro Speaks of Rivers"?

A "I've seen its muddy bosom turn all golden in the sunset."

B "I bathed in the Euphrates."

C "I heard the singing of the Mississippi."

D "My soul has grown deep like rivers."

______ **14.** Which of the following statements describes another type of repetition in the second stanza of "The Negro Speaks of Rivers"?

F A different river is named in each of the first four lines.

G It has four lines that begin with the pronoun *I* and a past-tense verb.

H The first three lines each end with a period.

J The speaker talks about Abe Lincoln.

CONSTRUCTED RESPONSE *(20 points)*

15. On a separate sheet of paper, tell what emotions you think Langston Hughes was trying to evoke in the reader of "The Negro Speaks of Rivers." Be sure to mention the words, sounds, and images in the poem that help to evoke those emotions.

from Dust Tracks on a Road Zora Neale Hurston

COMPREHENSION *(40 points; 4 points each)*

On the line provided, write the letter of the *best* answer to each of the following items.

______ **1.** Where and when did Zora Neale Hurston grow up?

- **A** The South during the days of slavery
- **B** Florida during the era of segregation
- **C** Harlem during its Renaissance
- **D** The North during the civil rights movement

______ **2.** Upon seeing cars and carriages pass by her house, Zora Neale would —

- **F** ask the travelers for a ride
- **G** follow them on her bike
- **H** run to inform her parents
- **J** try to race the cars on foot

______ **3.** Zora Neale's grandmother feared that Zora Neale's boldness would —

- **A** cause her to fall off the gatepost
- **B** make her unpopular at school
- **C** provoke white people to harm her
- **D** one day cause a traffic accident

______ **4.** The students' good behavior in school is *mostly* influenced by —

- **F** their wish to impress their teachers
- **G** the threat of Mrs. Calhoun's palmetto switch
- **H** the absence of visitors in the classroom
- **J** the hope that visitors will recognize them

______ **5.** What is Zora Neale's reaction to the *first* gift given to her by the visitors from Minnesota?

- **A** She is grateful but disappointed because she had hoped for more.
- **B** She is embarrassed that the women singled her out.
- **C** It is one of the most joyful experiences of her life.
- **D** She is suspicious of the women's generosity.

______ **6.** The visitors' gifts do *not* include —

- **F** money
- **G** books
- **H** clothing
- **J** eyeglasses

_____ **7.** By ignoring her grandmother's warning, Zora Neale shows that she is —

A outgoing, independent, and brazen
B ignorant, uneducated, and closed minded
C frightened, weak, and insecure
D irritable, angry, and impatient

_____ **8.** By reading the class reader from cover to cover, Zora Neale shows that she is —

F worried that the other students will mock her
G obsessed with pleasing her parents and teacher
H afraid she won't get straight A's
J self-motivated and ambitious

_____ **9.** What got Zora Neale interested in reading the Bible?

A The military exploits of King David
B The moral lessons of the Gospels
C The description of the Garden of Eden
D The beautiful poetry of the Psalms

_____ **10.** In what way was Zora Neale's school similar to most schools in the United States today?

F The teachers hoped for the success of their students.
G Physical punishment was used.
H Many grades were taught in the same room.
J It was legally segregated.

LITERARY FOCUS: AUTOBIOGRAPHY *(20 points; 5 points each)*
On the line provided, write the letter of the *best* answer to each of the following items.

_____ **11.** The difference between **biography** and **autobiography** is that —

A biography involves research and interviews
B autobiography is written by the person the book is about
C biography is not about living people
D autobiography is often written by authors

______ **12. Subjective details —**

F must be verified by outside observers

G show how the autobiographer feels

H are not truthful or trustworthy

J are rarely found in autobiographies

______ **13.** Which adjective does *not* fit Zora Neale as she portrays herself in her autobiography?

A Mild mannered

B Bold

C Brilliant

D Observant

______ **14.** Which of the following details is purely subjective?

F Hurston's grandmother's reaction to Zora's behavior at the roadside

G Hurston's date and place of birth

H Hurston's witty description of her thoughts concerning the visitors' hands

J The details of the gifts the visitors gave Zora Neale

VOCABULARY DEVELOPMENT *(20 points; 4 points each)*

Match the definition on the left with the Vocabulary word on the right. On the line provided, write the letter of the Vocabulary word.

______ **15.** think; imagine — **a.** exalted

______ **16.** deeply — **b.** realm

______ **17.** kingdom — **c.** profoundly

______ **18.** lifted up — **d.** resolved

______ **19.** made a decision; determined — **e.** conceive

CONSTRUCTED RESPONSE *(20 points)*

20. On a separate sheet of paper, use subjective details as the basis for an analysis of Zora Neale Hurston's view of herself and the world around her. In your opinion, did her view of life help or hinder her in becoming a writer?

NAME CLASS DATE SCORE

COLLECTION 5 SUMMATIVE TEST

The Moderns: 1914–1939

This test asks you to use the skills and strategies you have learned in this collection. Read the poems and answer the questions that follow.

Daybreak in Alabama
by Langston Hughes

When I get to be a composer
I'm gonna write me some music about
Daybreak in Alabama
And I'm gonna put the purtiest songs in it
Rising out of the ground like a swamp mist
And falling out of heaven like soft dew.
I'm gonna put some tall trees in it
And the scent of pine needles
And the smell of red clay after rain
And long red necks
And poppy colored faces
And big brown eyes
Of black and white black white black people
And I'm gonna put white hands
And black hands and brown hands and yellow hands
And red clay earth hands in it
Touching everybody with kind fingers
And touching each other natural as dew
In that dawn of music when I
Get to be a composer
And write about daybreak
In Alabama.

The Planet on the Table
by Wallace Stevens

Ariel was glad he had written his poems.
They were of a remembered time
Or of something seen that he liked.
Other makings of the sun
Were waste and welter
And the ripe shrub writhed.
His self and the sun were one
And his poems, although makings of his self,
Were no less makings of the sun.

It was not important that they survive.
What mattered was that they should bear
Some lineament or character,
Some affluence, if only half-perceived
In the poverty of their words,
Of the planet of which they were part.

VOCABULARY SKILLS *(15 points; 3 points each)*
On the line provided, write the letter of the *best* answer to each of the following items.

_____ **1.** A composer is a —
- **A** trumpet player
- **B** painter
- **C** songwriter
- **D** collector

_____ **2.** Welter could be —
- **F** a disordered jumble
- **G** rich growth
- **H** brightly colored paper
- **J** useful products

_____ **3.** A snake that writhed probably —
- **A** became stronger
- **B** twisted and turned
- **C** grew heartily
- **D** stood out

_____ **4.** Lineament is *best* described as a —
- **F** type of cloth
- **G** muscle pain
- **H** healing balm
- **J** distinctive feature

_____ **5.** Affluence refers to the planet's —
- **A** abundance
- **B** rivers
- **C** land mass
- **D** size

COMPREHENSION *(15 points; 3 points each)*

On the line provided, write the letter of the *best* answer to each of the following items.

______ **6.** In Langston Hughes's poem, which of the following is *not* something the composer says he is going to put into his music?

F Tall trees

G Gravel roads

H The smell of red clay after rain

J The scent of pine needles

______ **7.** To what does Hughes compare the color of people's faces?

A Daybreak

B Music

C Clay

D Poppies

______ **8.** In Hughes's poem, what could "Daybreak in Alabama" stand for?

F A beautiful sunset

G Westward migration

H Natural disaster

J A change for the better

______ **9.** The subject of Wallace Stevens's poem is the —

A writing of poetry

B solar system

C speaker's disillusionment

D richness of language

______ **10.** In "The Planet on the Table," which of the following statements is *not* true about the poems that Ariel writes?

F It is not essential that they survive.

G They were of a forgotten time.

H Ariel is happy that he wrote them.

J They were partly creations of the sun.

READING SKILLS AND STRATEGIES: CONSTRUCTED RESPONSE *(15 points)*

Identifying Main Ideas and Supporting Details

On the line provided, write the letter of the *best* answer to the following item.

______ **11.** From the following options, choose the statement that *best* expresses the *main* idea of "The Planet on the Table." Then, on a separate sheet of paper, write the letter of the answer you choose, and briefly defend your choice. Use at least two details from the poem to support your ideas.

A The makings of the sun are the things of the natural world, while the makings of the poet are poems that reflect the imaged world.

B The poet should write about pleasant things instead of "waste and welter."

C The makings of the sun will die and decompose, but the makings of the poet's mind will be eternal.

D Poems should be true to the inner world of the poet's mind.

LITERARY FOCUS: CONSTRUCTED RESPONSE *(5 points)*

Recognizing Theme

On the line provided, write the letter of the *best* answer to the following item.

______ **12.** The speaker in "Daybreak in Alabama" seems to believe that —

F relationships between people of all races can improve

G hatred is part of the human character

H Alabama is the most beautiful place to live

J music is the best form of expression

IDENTIFYING AND ANALYZING IMAGERY *(10 points)*

13. In the chart below, list three images from "Daybreak in Alabama" that appeal to different senses. Note the sense to which each image appeals. Then, offer your analysis of how the images contribute to the poem's meaning, mood, or tone.

Image	Sense

Interpretation

NAME ______ CLASS ______ DATE ______ SCORE ______

COMPARING AND CONTRASTING POEMS *(20 points)*

14. Based on "Daybreak in Alabama" and "The Planet on the Table" and on what you have learned in this chapter, compare and contrast the ways in which Langston Hughes and Wallace Stevens both represent the modern era in American literature.

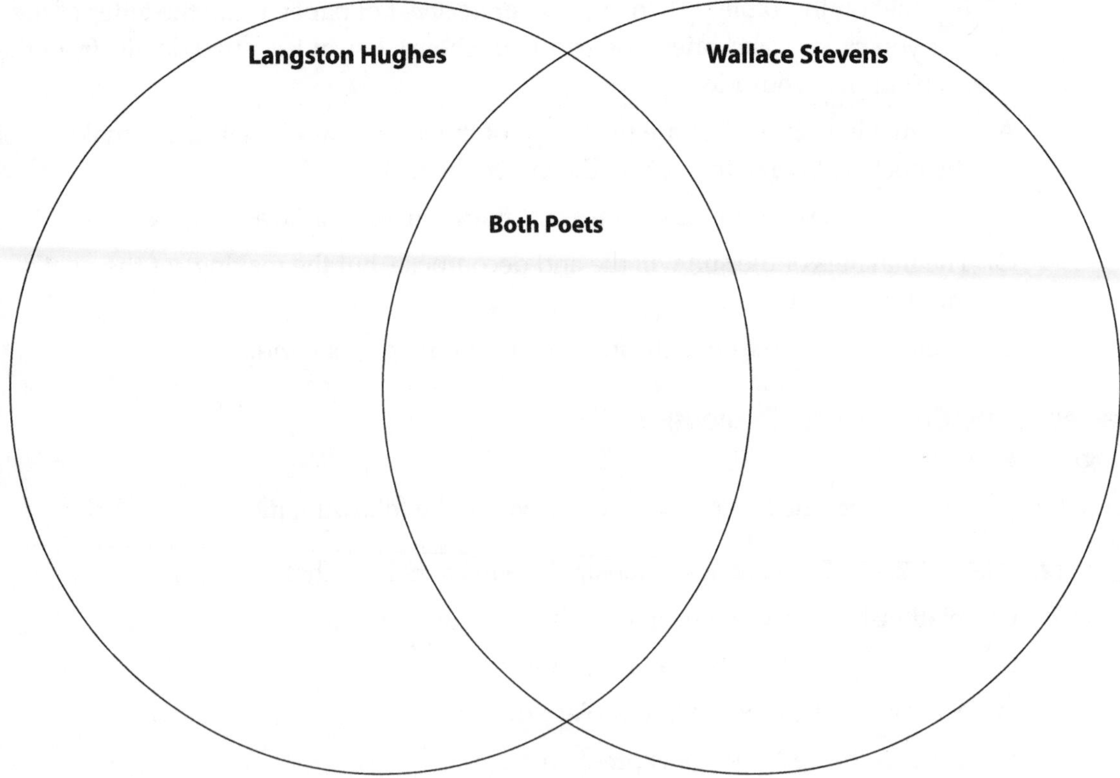

ANALYZING STYLE *(20 points)*

15. On a separate sheet of paper, discuss the idea or ideas about poetry that you think Wallace Stevens is developing in "The Planet on the Table." What specific words and passages express or imply those ideas? In interpreting the poem, identify specific devices—figures of speech, irony, sound devices, and other aspects of style—which help convey the poet's views.

COLLECTION 6 DIAGNOSTIC TEST

LITERATURE
INFORMATIONAL TEXT
VOCABULARY

Contemporary Literature: 1939 to Present

On the line provided, write the letter of the *best* answer to each of the following items. *(100 points; 5 points each)*

______ **1.** "Fear nipped at my heels and followed me everywhere" is an example of a(n) —

A extended metaphor
B simile
C implied metaphor
D symbol

______ **2.** A **memoir** is —

F a true account of a personal experience
G a novel written in the first person
H another term for a biography
J a long speech made by a character in a play

______ **3.** Which of the following statements about **conflict** is *true*?

A A character can experience both internal and external conflict in a story.
B The conflict in a story is revealed in the opening of the work.
C Conflicts are always resolved in the course of a story.
D External conflicts affect characters more deeply than internal conflicts do.

______ **4.** The purpose of **theme** is to —

F teach the reader a moral lesson
G convey the author's attitude toward a subject
H clarify the topic of a literary work
J reveal an insight about human life

______ **5.** Through **satire,** writers hope to —

A gain insight into themselves
B bring about reform
C capture the beauty of the natural world
D pay tribute to someone

______ **6.** **Style** in literature refers to —

F the format of a poem

G the distinctive way in which a writer uses language

H the manner in which characters dress and speak

J the genre, or type, of a literary work

______ **7.** A character's **motivation** —

A is a result of his or her actions

B must sometimes be inferred

C is dependent on the story's point of view

D never changes in the course of a story

______ **8.** A character who uses **verbal irony** —

F says one thing but means another

G knows less than the reader

H intentionally deceives the reader

J uses exaggeration to emphasize a point

______ **9.** Which of the following elements do writers rely on the *most* to reveal character?

A Mood

B Dialogue

C Epithets

D Stereotypes

______ **10.** Which of the following statements about **characterization** is *false*?

F Both fiction and nonfiction writers use techniques of characterization.

G To reveal character, writers show how a particular character affects other people.

H Showing what other people think of another character does not help to reveal that character's personality.

J The character of a first-person narrator is revealed through his or her private thoughts and feelings.

______ **11.** The social and political environment unique to a story's time and place is its —

A tone

B main idea

C exposition

D historical context

______ **12.** **Rhythm** is —

F used only in poetry

G the alternation of stressed and unstressed syllables

H always accompanied by rhyme

J consistent throughout a work

______ **13.** The **speaker** of a poem —

A is all-knowing

B does not make personal observations

C is always the voice of the poet

D addresses the reader directly, using the pronoun *I*

______ **14.** Which of the following phrases contains **alliteration** and **assonance**?

F He could see me by the tree.

G The curtain was made of silk.

H The black bird flew by us.

J The willows seemed to whisper in the wind.

______ **15.** Which of the following statements about **archetypes** is *false*?

A Archetypes are specific to a particular culture.

B Archetypes recur in literature through the ages.

C Plots and settings can be archetypes.

D Some archetypes are characters or images.

_______ **16.** A scene that interrupts the chronological sequence of events in a story to depict something that happened earlier is called —

F a climax

G an aside

H a flashback

J foreshadowing

_______ **17.** In **persuasive writing**, authors would *most likely* include both facts and loaded language to —

A make their writing sound better

B give their work the characteristics of fiction

C appeal to the reader's heart and mind

D simplify their argument

_______ **18.** What is an **assertion**?

F A factual statement

G A statement that expresses an opinion about an issue

H Evidence provided to support a point

J A belief that a writer implies through word choice and imagery

_______ **19.** A word's **connotation** is —

A its part of speech

B its dictionary definition

C its context in a sentence

D the emotions or associations that are evoked by the word

_______ **20.** If you wanted to research the **etymology** of a particular word in a dictionary, you should —

F note any synonyms listed for the word and read the entries for those words

G review any sample sentences provided in the entry for the word

H check the entry for alternate spellings of the word

J read the information in the entry that explains the origin of the word

NAME ______ CLASS ______ DATE ______ SCORE ______

LITERARY PERIOD INTRODUCTION TEST **Student Edition page 796**

Contemporary Literature: 1939 to Present

COMPREHENSION *(100 points; 10 points each)*

On the line provided, write the letter of the *best* answer to each of the following items.

______ **1.** Contemporary writers such as Kurt Vonnegut and Joseph Heller have described war as —

A an expression of patriotic loyalty

B a reflection of the madness of modern life

C the ultimate test of masculinity

D a logical response to personal frustrations

______ **2.** According to the introduction, the chief drawback of the spread of technology is —

F the extinction of some animal species

G a decreased life expectancy

H dehumanization of the individual

J a sluggish economy prone to recession

______ **3.** U.S. involvement in the Vietnam War —

A established the concept of war as glorious

B lasted for two years

C sharply divided the American public

D greatly enhanced America's image abroad

______ **4.** In general, **postmodern literature** —

F is lacking in meaning other than what the reader brings to it

G closely resembles modernist works of the 1930s

H is realistic and known for its reliance on the past

J comments on itself and is open to multiple interpretations

______ **5.** Short stories such as Donald Barthelme's "Sentence" and novels such as Walter Abish's *Alphabetical Africa* are notable for their —

A nontraditional forms and structures

B conventional viewpoints and detached tones

C familiar characters and themes

D focus on different worlds and cultures

______ **6.** One of the characteristics of **postmodern fiction** is the use of —

F linear, chronological plots and standard methods of character development

G nontraditional forms blurring the boundaries between fiction and nonfiction

H themes advancing the idea that life is limited

J imitation and the nostalgic pursuit of the past

______ **7.** **New journalists** such as Truman Capote and Joan Didion attracted attention by —

A using historical characters in fictional stories

B asserting the writer's personal presence in nonfiction pieces

C using old-fashioned language to describe cultural events

D mixing realistic narrative devices with elements of magic and dreams

______ **8.** **Contemporary nonfiction** has become as much of an art form as fiction or poetry because —

F journalists and other nonfiction writers now receive improved training in writing

G writers care more about accuracy than providing an entertaining story

H critics and the general public have become disillusioned with other forms of entertainment

J it often incorporates literary elements such as suspense, symbolism, and characterization

______ **9.** **Postmodern poetry** can be described as a(n) —

A rebellion against impersonal poetry that emphasizes intellectual analysis

B attempt to follow Ezra Pound's insistence that the image is the core of the poem

C reflection of the conformity and boredom that is seen in society as a whole

D frank and brutal re-creation of the poet's travel experiences

______ **10.** Since the 1970s, American poetry has —

F been characterized by diverse voices and styles

G become increasingly narrow in subject matter

H reflected a more elitist perspective

J been appreciated for its simplicity and earnestness

NAME ______ CLASS ______ DATE ______ SCORE ______

SELECTION TEST **Student Edition page 814** LITERARY RESPONSE AND ANALYSIS

The Death of the Ball Turret Gunner Randall Jarrell

COMPREHENSION *(60 points; 6 points each)*
On the line provided, write the letter of the *best* answer to each of the following items.

______ **1.** From which point of view is the poem told?
- A Third person
- B First person
- C Omniscient
- D All knowing

______ **2.** You can infer that the ball turret gunner is —
- F a vastly experienced soldier
- G much decorated for bravery
- H young, probably eighteen years old
- J from a family of soldiers

______ **3.** Jarrell's ball turret gunner entered the armed forces —
- A as a fierce patriot
- B under protest
- C after careful decision
- D without much thought

______ **4.** The poet capitalizes the word "State" in line 1 to —
- F show the ball turret gunner's fear of war
- G refer to the army, navy, and marines
- H stand for all countries that have wars
- J show the government's indifferent power

______ **5.** When the speaker says that he was "loosed from its dream of life," he means that he —
- A realized that he was about to die
- B was not ready to die
- C desperately tried to escape and parachute to safety
- D was long dead

______ **6.** This poem is told as a —
- F sonnet
- G flashback
- H flash-forward
- J nonfiction narrative

______ **7.** The first three words of the last line —

A illustrate the speaker's growing confusion

B clarify that the poem is a work of nonfiction

C confirm a chilling sense of doom

D are an example of figurative language

______ **8.** The ball turret gunner views life as a "dream" because he —

F is removed from everyday life in the airplane

G recalls his mother's love and care

H knows he will die and cannot imagine his former life

J does not want to live after what he has experienced

______ **9.** The tone of this poem is *best* described as —

A humorous

B patriotic

C condescending

D elegiac

______ **10.** A ball turret is a —

F special high-speed ammunition made of titanium

G type of heat seeking missile with a homing device

H transparent plastic hemisphere set in the bottom of a bomber

J type of cannon mounted on top of the wings of a fighter

LITERARY FOCUS: IMPLIED METAPHOR *(20 points; 5 points each)*
On the line provided, write the letter of the *best* answer to each of the following items.

______ **11.** An **implied metaphor** is a(n) —

A suggested comparison between two unlike things

B overt comparison between two unlike things

C comparison between two closely linked people, places, or things

D comparison that uses "like" or "as" to link the two parts

______ **12.** Writers use **implied metaphors** to —

F give their poems a musical tone

G help readers see ideas in new ways

H make references to works of literature, art, and music

J talk about war and other major conflicts

NAME ______ CLASS ______ DATE ______ SCORE ______

______ **13.** In the poem's implied metaphor the ball turret gunner is compared to a(n) —

A hose

B fierce bomber pilot

C unborn animal

D handsome young man

______ **14.** The poem's implied metaphor adds to its impact by —

F emphasizing the soldier's youth and innocence

G arguing against all wars

H showing that everyday life is unreal during wartime

J conveying the need for alertness during battle

CONSTRUCTED RESPONSE *(20 points)*

15. How does Randall Jarrell use figurative language in "The Death of the Ball Turret Gunner" to rouse readers' emotions? What does his attitude toward his topic suggest about his political stance? On a separate sheet of paper, write a paragraph that explains your answer. Support your ideas with details from the selection.

SELECTION TEST **Student Edition page 818** LITERARY RESPONSE AND ANALYSIS

from Night Elie Wiesel *translated by* Stella Rodway

COMPREHENSION *(40 points; 4 points each)*

On the line provided, write the letter of the *best* answer to each of the following items.

_____ **1.** Why do Madame Schächter's actions trouble the people in the boxcar?

A She awakens them to the terror of their situation.

B The people cannot stand the noise and disturbance.

C Everyone is trying to get some sleep.

D The people are worried that the boxcar is on fire.

_____ **2.** The people in the boxcar do all of the following to silence Madame Schächter *except* —

F bind and gag her

G beat her

H threaten to throw her out

J reason with her

_____ **3.** Wiesel creates a sense of fear and foreboding in the boxcar scene by describing all of the following details *except* —

A a smell of burning flesh

B snarling German shepherds

C the sight of flames

D a tall chimney against a black sky

_____ **4.** The head of the block counsels the prisoners to —

F answer the doctors' questions

G stand up straight and tall

H look directly at the SS guards

J not be afraid

_____ **5.** The prisoners run hard in order to —

A be granted exercise privileges outside the block

B be chosen for special treatment

C not have their numbers noted by Dr. Mengele

D be selected for their positive attitude

_____ **6.** Before Wiesel and his father are separated, his father wants to give him —

F a knife and spoon

G his ration of food

H his pair of boots

J his soup cup

______ **7.** Akiba Drumer asks his fellow prisoners to —

A help him recover his health

B save him from selection

C tell his son what happened

D say prayers after he is dead

______ **8.** Wiesel remembers seeing Rabbi Eliahou's son —

F among the dead outside the shed

G stopping to catch his breath during the run to the camp

H running to distance himself from his father

J being shot by one of the SS guards

______ **9.** Juliek brings with him a —

A violin

B prayer book

C family photograph

D pad and pencils

______ **10.** Wiesel's clawing for air in the cabin conveys a feeling of —

F joy

G doom

H anger

J desperation

READING SKILLS: ANALYZING A READER'S MESSAGE *(20 points; 5 points each)*
On the line provided, write the letter of the *best* answer to each of the following items.

______ **11.** Wiesel suggests that the power of faith —

A cannot sustain in survival situations

B is useless against true evil

C can keep people from giving up hope

D is useful only in times of crisis

______ **12.** From these excerpts, what can you infer is Wiesel's message about the power of evil?

F Evil can only be defeated through luck.

G Only minorities need to fear evil.

H Evil will never be eliminated from the world.

J Evil can be fought in many ways.

NAME ______ CLASS ______ DATE ______ SCORE ______

______ **13.** Wiesel's description of Juliek playing the violin suggests —

A everyone should play an instrument

B that the Nazis hated all music

C how music calms people even in dire straits

D the power of art to express unspeakable emotion

______ **14.** Wiesel wrote *Night* for all of the following purposes *except* —

F as a bulwark against evil

G to create a testament to human endurance

H to get revenge on his Nazi tormentors

J so a Holocaust could never occur again

VOCABULARY DEVELOPMENT *(20 points; 4 points each)*

Match each Vocabulary word on the left with its definition on the right. On the line provided, write the letter of the definition.

______ **15.** abyss	**a.** appearance; likeness
______ **16.** pestilential	**b.** nasty and disgusting
______ **17.** abominable	**c.** bottomless gulf or void
______ **18.** encumbrance	**d.** dangerous and harmful, like a deadly infection
______ **19.** semblance	**e.** hindrance; burden

CONSTRUCTED RESPONSE *(20 points)*

20. Explain why Wiesel includes a description of the prisoners forgetting to say the Kaddish for Akiba and an explanation of Rabbi Eliahou's son running ahead of his father. What message about the Holocaust is Wiesel making by detailing these two incidents? On a separate sheet of paper, write a paragraph that explains your answer. Support your ideas with details from the selection.

A Noiseless Flash *from* Hiroshima John Hersey

COMPREHENSION *(40 points; 4 points each)*

On the line provided, write the letter of the *best* answer to each of the following items.

______ **1.** About how many people were killed by the atomic bomb that exploded in Hiroshima?

A 10,000

B 50,000

C 100,000

D one million

______ **2.** You can infer from Reverend Mr. Tanimoto's feelings before the bomb exploded that —

F the Japanese were completely surprised by the bomb

G few Japanese were concerned about the war or directly affected by it

H the Japanese were secure in their military superiority

J many Japanese worried about retaliatory attacks from the Allies

______ **3.** Reverend Mr. Tanimoto, like most other residents of Hiroshima, is not concerned when the air-raid siren sounds because —

A everyone is well prepared for an attack

B the siren sounds at the same time every day

C he believes the Americans are planning to attack Nagasaki

D his family is safe in the countryside

______ **4.** Ironically, when the bomb struck, almost no one in Hiroshima recalls —

F seeing injured people

G a sudden burst of light

H hearing any sound

J feeling any sense of fear

______ **5.** After the bomb is dropped, —

A medical help is swift

B soldiers quell the panic

C the city explodes in flames

D the sky darkens

______ **6.** Hersey states that Japanese radar operators did not suspect an attack on the morning of August 6, 1945, because —

F they spotted only three planes

G U.S. bombers were flying away from Japan

H a truce with Japan had already been declared

J the American bombers usually attacked at night

______ **7.** Mrs. Nakamura was probably spared because of her decision to —

- **A** evacuate to the local hospital
- **B** go to the East Parade ground
- **C** stay home
- **D** hide in the church basement

______ **8.** Immediately after Father Kleinsorge hears the air raid siren, he —

- **F** wanders in his garden
- **G** stretches out on his cot
- **H** begins to read Mass
- **J** changes into a military uniform

______ **9.** The *main* theme of "A Noiseless Flash" is that —

- **A** chance alone determined who survived the attack
- **B** many people anticipated the nuclear attack and prepared for it
- **C** most people respond methodically in emergencies
- **D** all people suffer equally in a war

______ **10.** The people that John Hersey focuses on can *best* be described as —

- **F** government officials
- **G** ordinary people
- **H** heroic soldiers
- **J** wealthy civilians

LITERARY FOCUS: SUBJECTIVE AND OBJECTIVE REPORTING *(15 points; 5 points each)*

On the line provided, write the letter of the *best* answer to each of the following items.

______ **11.** When writers openly express personal emotions and attitudes toward their subjects, they are using —

- **A** factual reporting
- **B** in-depth analysis
- **C** subjective reporting
- **D** objective reporting

______ **12.** Writers keep their emotions at a distance with —

- **F** subjective reporting
- **G** fictional reporting
- **H** objective reporting
- **J** firsthand reporting

______ **13.** In "A Noiseless Flash," Hersey uses all the following types of objective reporting *except* —

A historical data

B fictional characters

C statistics

D direct quotations

READING SKILLS: READING CLOSELY FOR DETAILS *(5 points)*

On the line provided, write the letter of the *best* answer to the following item.

______ **14.** If "A Noiseless Flash" had been written subjectively, the author —

F would have been required to use the first-person point of view

G could not have used quotations

H would not have been concerned with facts

J could have clearly expressed his own opinions

VOCABULARY DEVELOPMENT *(20 points; 4 points each)*

Complete each analogy with a Vocabulary word from below. Use each Vocabulary word only once.

debris **obsessed** **notorious** **incendiary** **convivial**

15. SOUP : SOOTHING :: FIRECRACKER : ______________

16. REPUTABLE : INFAMOUS :: RESPECTED : ______________

17. ENEMIES : ANTAGONISTIC :: FRIENDS : ______________

18. COLLISION : WRECKAGE :: CRASH : ______________

19. APATHETIC PERSON : INDIFFERENT :: FANATIC : ______________

CONSTRUCTED RESPONSE *(20 points)*

20. Explain how John Hersey blended fiction and nonfiction in Hiroshima. How does this combination of genres help Hersey convey his feelings about the atomic attack on Hiroshima? On a separate sheet of paper, write a paragraph that explains your answer. Support your ideas with details from the selection

"The Arrogance and Cruelty of Power"

from Speech at the Nuremberg Trials, November 21, 1945 Robert H. Jackson

COMPREHENSION *(40 points; 4 points each)*

On the line provided, write the letter of the *best* answer to each of the following items.

______ **1.** According to Jackson, the Nuremberg Trials were held to —

- **A** experiment with justice on an international basis
- **B** conduct abstract speculation in a realistic setting
- **C** defend legalistic theories in an international setting
- **D** use international law to extinguish the greatest evil of our time

______ **2.** Jackson sees the defendants as —

- **F** good men who are misunderstood
- **G** worthy of mercy
- **H** soldiers who merely followed orders
- **J** masterminds of evil

______ **3.** At the time of the trials, Jackson asserts that the prisoners exhibit all of the following characteristics *except* —

- **A** brokenness
- **B** powerlessness
- **C** remorse
- **D** humiliation

______ **4.** By using the words "arrogance," "brutality," and "annihilation," Jackson is appealing to —

- **F** emotion
- **G** reason
- **H** ethics
- **J** authority

______ **5.** Jackson makes his speech convincing by using all of the following techniques *except* —

- **A** a combination of appeals to reason, emotion, and ethics
- **B** addressing his audience's counterclaims
- **C** word choice and syntax
- **D** pattern of organization

______ **6.** Jackson believes that the "first trial in history for crimes against the peace of the world" carries with it a great —

F pleasure

G pain

H responsibility

J temptation

______ **7.** Jackson describes the Nazi leaders on trial as —

A healthy

B remorseful

C pitiful

D sinister

______ **8.** Jackson maintains that the Nazi defendants "directed such a campaign of arrogance, brutality, and annihilation" by —

F blind obedience

G conspiracy

H misjudgment

J ignorance

______ **9.** Jackson accuses the Nazis of all of the following actions *except* —

A ruinous policies of taxation

B planning and waging war

C ruthlessness in the conduct of war

D criminality toward conquered peoples

______ **10.** The defendants were charged with all of the following crimes *except* —

F crimes against peace

G money laundering

H crimes against humanity

J war crimes

LITERARY FOCUS: PERSUASION AND ARGUMENT *(20 points; 5 points each)*
On the line provided, write the letter of the *best* answer to each of the following items.

______ **11.** Jackson uses methods of persuasion to convince the Tribunal of the Nazi defendants' —

A regret
B sorrow
C guilt
D innocence

______ **12.** Jackson begins his argument by setting forth —

F the purpose for the inquest
G what the defendant's represent
H a list of the charges
J the legal basis of the Tribunal's authority

______ **13.** Jackson's appeal is unemotional in all of the following details *except* —

A "These men created in Germany, under the 'Führerprinzip,' a National Socialist despotism"
B "Any tenderness to them is a victory and an encouragement to all the evils"
C "We shall also trace for you the intricate web of organizations which these men formed"
D "We will show how the entire structure of offices and officials was dedicated to the criminal purposes"

______ **14.** Overall, Jackson's argument appeals to —

F emotion
G authority
H pathos
J reason

NAME ______ CLASS ______ DATE ______ SCORE ______

Vocabulary Development *(20 points; 4 points each)*

Write the Vocabulary word that is a synonym or antonym for each word, as directed. Use the Vocabulary word only once.

malignant **vengeance** **vindicate** **magnitude** **arrogance**

15. importance *synonym:* ______

16. humility *antonym:* ______

17. revenge *synonym:* ______

18. good *antonym:* ______

19. blame *antonym:* ______

Constructed Response *(20 points)*

20. On a separate sheet of paper, outline the seven parts of Jackson's argument.

NAME ______ CLASS ______ DATE ______ SCORE ______

SELECTION TEST **Student Edition pages 857, 859, 861** INFORMATIONAL READING

from The Diary of a Young Girl Anne Frank
"The Biggest Battle of All History" John Whitehead
from The Greatest Generation Speaks *by* Tom Brokaw
from April in Germany Margaret Bourke-White

COMPREHENSION *(100 points; 10 points each)*

On the line provided, write the letter of the *best* answer to each of the following items.

_____ **1.** Anne Frank's diary is a primary source because it —

A combines observations from a variety of sources

B is basically optimistic

C was written after the war from historical records

D was created through firsthand observation

_____ **2.** The tone of Anne Frank's diary is *best* characterized as —

F depressed

G excited

H tranquil

J fiery

_____ **3.** Both Anne Frank's account and John Whitehead's letter in *The Greatest Generation Speaks* —

A cover the same day in history

B are narrated in the third person

C are diary entries

D describe the aftermath of World War II

_____ **4.** At the end of the D-day landing, Whitehead's *main* reaction is —

F pride in the United States effort

G despair at his failure to secure the beachhead

H compassion for the dead

J terror at the immediate future

_____ **5.** You can infer that Tom Brokaw included John Whitehead's letter in his anthology *mainly* because —

A Brokaw knew Whitehead personally

B Whitehead was a great military leader and a symbol for all the soldiers

C Brokaw admired Whitehead's bravery and self-sacrifice

D Whitehead's secondary account is convincing because of its details

______ **6.** At Buchenwald, Margaret Bourke-White is overwhelmed when she sees —

F two thousand German civilians in the snow

G General Patton and his liberating armies beating the Germans

H reporters trying to help the concentration camp survivors

J heaps of dead prisoners and starving survivors

______ **7.** Bourke-White is relieved to take photographs because she wants to —

A record the actions of the reporters

B put some distance between herself and the scene

C immortalize Patton's victory

D create a testament so such a horror can never happen again

______ **8.** Bourke-White concludes that the German citizens who were not Jewish —

F deliberately ignored the horrors of concentration camps

G were ignorant of the concentration camps

H were not ashamed of the Nazis' brutality

J did not understand how the Nazis killed so many Jews

______ **9.** These three selections are *different* in that they —

A are not all primary sources

B are not all concerned with the same events

C are not all eyewitness accounts

D each reveal the individual writer's viewpoints

______ **10.** These three selections are *similar* because they —

F show how the war stripped people of their humanity

G downplay the courage it takes to fight injustice

H present a despairing view of World War II

J analyze different responses to the horrors of war

NAME ______ CLASS ______ DATE ______ SCORE ______

SELECTION TEST **Student Edition page 867** LITERARY RESPONSE AND ANALYSIS

Speaking of Courage Tim O'Brien

COMPREHENSION *(40 points; 4 points each)*

On the line provided, write the letter of the *best* answer to each of the following items.

______ **1.** Paul can't share his feelings about the war with his friends because —

A they are tired of listening to his stories

B they cannot understand his feelings because they were not in the war

C he has alienated all of them with his surly attitude

D they have died, moved away from town, or are too busy to talk

______ **2.** Paul can't talk to his father about the war because —

F he is ashamed of the way he acted during combat

G he is afraid of his father

H he and his father do not get along

J his father won't talk about the war

______ **3.** The chilly interior of the air-conditioned car may represent —

A Paul's feelings of isolation

B the Vietnam War

C recent United States history

D the death of Frenchie Tucker

______ **4.** Paul was awarded all the following medals *except* the —

F Good Conduct Medal

G Vietnam Campaign Medal

H Silver Star

J Purple Heart

______ **5.** The descriptions of the stagnant lake and the people going about their business suggest —

A fear of the unknown

B rejection of politics

C indifference to the war

D contempt for veterans

______ **6.** What is the significance of the story taking place on the Fourth of July?

F It is a day for patriotism, but Paul does not feel like a patriot.

G It is typically the most festive holiday in small American towns.

H Paul receives his independence from the tyranny of the town.

J The town's lack of patriotic spirit depresses Paul.

______ **7.** The author is *most* likely using Paul to symbolize —

A everyone who has ever fought in any war

B someone who had serious problems before going to Vietnam

C any survivor of horror

D a generation of young soldiers who returned from Vietnam

______ **8.** Paul's character can *best* be described as —

F lively

G isolated

H fearful

J reckless

______ **9.** Overall, "Speaking of Courage" deals with the subject of —

A freedom

B self-acceptance

C greed

D boredom

______ **10.** His experiences in the war taught Paul —

F the truth behind many lies

G that people who are brave are stupid

H never to ask questions

J important skills he is using in civilian life

LITERARY FOCUS: CONFLICT *(15 points; 5 points each)*
On the line provided, write the letter of the *best* answer to each of the following items.

______ **11.** During the war, Paul faced an external conflict —

A with the enemy

B over his desire to be brave

C as he struggled with himself to win a medal

D over whether or not to finish the job that Frenchie Tucker began

______ **12.** Which of the following statements *best* describes Paul's internal conflict?

F He doesn't want to talk to anyone about the war because he is a coward.

G He needs to talk about the war and his shame, but he cannot find someone to listen or bring himself to face the past.

H The war has made him feel disillusioned about small-town life.

J He feels that he fought a war he does not support.

______ **13.** Paul's internal conflict leads him to —

A speak more to his father

B become involved with the town

C question himself

D seek out an old friend

READING SKILLS: IDENTIFYING HISTORICAL CONTEXT *(5 points)*
On the line provided, write the letter of the *best* answer to the following item.

______ **14.** The conflict that shapes the character of Paul Berlin is between the —

F values his father taught him as a child and the values that his father holds now

G values of small-town Iowa and the progressive values of his father

H repressive values of a small town and the progressive values of a big city

J values of small-town Iowa and the realities of jungle warfare in Vietnam

VOCABULARY DEVELOPMENT *(20 points; 4 points each)*
On the line provided, write the Vocabulary word that *best* completes each sentence.

affluent **tepid** **mesmerizing** **drone** **recede**

15. As he drove around, Paul felt hypnotized by the ____________ sound of the insects buzzing in the heat.

16. Their ____________ was like a steady hum in the hot July air.

17. He knew that the lake would be lukewarm and ____________ in the heat.

NAME ______ CLASS ______ DATE ______ SCORE ______

18. Paul could see the boys ____________ and become more distant as he drove away from them.

19. As with the other townspeople, Paul wasn't ____________ because his family didn't have a lot of money.

CONSTRUCTED RESPONSE *(20 points)*

20. In an attempt to justify the continued United States involvement in Vietnam, President Richard Nixon said that Americans want a peace they can live with; a peace they can be proud of. In what ways does this statement apply to Paul Berlin and his conflicts about his war experiences? On a separate sheet of paper, write a paragraph that explains your answer. Support your ideas with details from the selection.

SELECTION TEST **Student Edition page 878** LITERARY RESPONSE AND ANALYSIS

Game Donald Barthelme

COMPREHENSION *(40 points; 4 points each)*
On the line provided, write the letter of the *best* answer to each of the following items.

______ **1.** Shotwell's obsession with jacks shows his —
- **A** twisted childhood
- **B** love of games
- **C** desire to tease the narrator
- **D** deteriorating mental state

______ **2.** The men in "Game" are upset by —
- **F** the realization that relief is not coming
- **G** the lack of sufficient food and water
- **H** the approaching enemy forces
- **J** their opposing religious beliefs

______ **3.** The narrator's behavior is strange in that he —
- **A** hides all the tacos and chocolate cake
- **B** keeps watching Shotwell's right hand
- **C** writes on the wall with a diamond
- **D** is studying for a Masters of Business Administration

______ **4.** Where are the men?
- **F** A mental hospital
- **G** New York City
- **H** An underground bunker
- **J** A classroom

______ **5.** The keys are designed to —
- **A** free the men from the mental hospital
- **B** honor the men for their bravery
- **C** set off a missile if necessary
- **D** allow them to enter the classroom early

______ **6.** What is the *most* probable reason why has no one come to relieve them?
- **F** Their tour of duty is not yet over.
- **G** They are locked up for their own safety.
- **H** They have been forgotten.
- **J** Everyone who could help them is dead.

______ **7.** The tone of this story is *best* described as —

A overwrought

B calm

C smug

D scornful

______ **8.** The author's use of repetition —

F shows the narrator's increasing instability

G teaches readers to pay close attention to a text

H creates a poetic rhythm

J emphasizes minor points in the story

______ **9.** According on the events in the story, eventually the men will *probably*—

A shoot each other or starve to death

B be relieved by a second shift

C unlock the door, using their two keys

D learn to communicate more openly with each other

______ **10.** Based on the topic and mood of "Game," it was *most* likely written in —

F the 1930s, before the atomic bomb was invented

G 1941, when World War II started

H the 1950s, during cold war hysteria

J the 1990s, after the Vietnam War ended

LITERARY FOCUS: THEME AND TITLE *(20 points; 5 points each)*

On the line provided, write the letter of the *best* answer to each of the following items.

______ **11.** The subject of "Game" can *best* be described as the —

A profound childishness of some adults

B survival of the fittest

C dehumanization of individuals

D need for discipline in the armed forces

______ **12.** Which two meanings of the word *game* does the title convey to suggest the theme?

F Pranks and duty

G Jokes and responsibilities

H Willingness and injuries

J Prey and amusements

______ **13.** How is the title ironic?

A The word *game* usually suggests fun, but the events in this story are serious and deadly.

B Today, war is considered a game.

C Even though the two characters are suspicious of each other, they are actually having fun.

D Each of the characters plays a different game.

______ **14.** The theme of "Game" is *best* stated as —

F people need other people to be truly human

G a friend in need is a friend indeed

H the contemporary world has robbed people of their humanity

J events don't always turn out the way we plan or hope they will

VOCABULARY DEVELOPMENT *(20 points; 4 points each)*

Match each Vocabulary word on the left with its definition on the right. On the line provided, write the letter of the definition.

______ **15.** sated

______ **16.** simultaneously

______ **17.** ruse

______ **18.** scrupulously

______ **19.** precedence

a. at the same time

b. priority

c. satisfied

d. painstakingly; with great care

e. trick

CONSTRUCTED RESPONSE *(20 points)*

20. What comment on modern life does Barthelme make in "Game"? What aspects of our world does he specifically criticize? On a separate piece of paper, write a paragraph that explains your answer. Support your ideas with details from the selection.

NAME ______ CLASS ______ DATE ______ SCORE ______

SELECTION TEST **Student Edition pages 889, 893**

LITERARY RESPONSE AND ANALYSIS

Everything Stuck to Him Raymond Carver
A Still, Small Voice Jay McInerney

COMPREHENSION *(40 points; 4 points each)*

On the line provided, write the letter of the *best* answer to each of the following items.

______ **1.** The setting for the frame, or opening story, is —

A a Thanksgiving a century ago

B a Fourth of July picnic twenty years ago

C in the woods ten years ago

D a Christmas in the present

______ **2.** The inner story takes place —

F about twenty years ago

G in the present

H a century ago

J about fifty years ago

______ **3.** From what point of view is this story told?

A Omniscient point of view

B First-person point of view

C "I" point of view

D "You" point of view

______ **4.** The person listening to the story of the teenage couple is probably —

F a complete stranger to the man speaking

G the new wife of the husband in the story

H the teenage wife in the story

J the baby in the story, all grown up

______ **5.** The phrase that *best* describes the teenage couple in the beginning of the tale within the story is —

A aimless yet hopeful their lives will change

B ambitious yet pessimistic about the future

C ambitious and optimistic about the future

D aimless and pessimistic about the future

______ **6.** As far as the baby is concerned, the man —

F is very sorry that he and his wife had a baby so soon

G resents all the work involved with raising a baby

H loves the baby and marvels at its beautiful tiny body

J does not love the baby yet but hopes that he will soon

______ **7.** The *main* conflict between the boy and girl involves the —

A daughter's conflicting feelings about the couple's divorce

B couple's inability to take care of the baby

C girl's feeling toward her new baby

D question of the boy's commitment to the family

______ **8.** The girl is upset that the boy —

F wants to get divorced

G plans to go hunting

H has taken a second job

J desires her sister Betsy

______ **9.** At the end of the inner story, the young couple assures each other that —

A their baby cannot be sick

B they will not fight again

C their baby will be brilliant

D they will soon leave town

______ **10.** According to Jay McInerney, Raymond Carver believed that literature could be made out of —

F fantasy, folk tales, and myth

G larger-than-life biographies

H quiet reflection on a theme

J strict observation of real life

LITERARY FOCUS: STYLE *(15 points; 5 points each)*
On the line provided, write the letter of the *best* answer to each of the following items.

______ **11.** Carver's writing is distinctive for its —

A deceptive simplicity

B use of alliteration

C long sentences

D exaggerated speech

______ **12.** Which of the following sentences does *not* describe an element of Carver's style?

- **F** He includes lengthy, poetic descriptions.
- **G** Most of the characters don't have names.
- **H** He seems to have deleted all unnecessary words.
- **J** He uses plain language.

______ **13.** Each element of Carver's writing style —

- **A** is similar to most contemporary writers
- **B** is eccentric and unusual
- **C** has a purpose
- **D** is a mere trick

READING SKILLS: LEARNING THROUGH QUESTIONING *(5 points)*

On the line provided, write the letter of the *best* answer to the following item.

______ **14.** Which of the following questions is *not* a legitimate response to "Everything Stuck to Him"?

- **F** What are the characters' feelings?
- **G** What are the characters not saying to each other?
- **H** Where did Raymond Carver go to college?
- **J** Why don't the characters have names?

VOCABULARY DEVELOPMENT *(20 points; 4 points each)*

Use a Vocabulary word from the following list to write a synonym or antonym for each word or phrase on the left, as directed. You will use some of the Vocabulary words more than once.

striking **fitfully** **coincide**

15. happen simultaneously *synonym:* ____________________

16. unattractive *antonym:* ____________________

17. out of sync *antonym:* ____________________

18. regularly *antonym:* ____________________

19. impressive *synonym:* ____________________

Constructed Response *(20 points)*

20. What comment on life does Raymond Carver make in his story? Include a discussion of the characters, setting, and title in your analysis. On a separate sheet of paper, write a paragraph that explains your answer. Support your ideas with details from the selection.

NAME ______ CLASS ______ DATE ______ SCORE ______

SELECTION TEST **Student Edition page 899** **LITERARY RESPONSE AND ANALYSIS**

Daughter of Invention Julia Alvarez

COMPREHENSION *(40 points; 4 points each)*
On the line provided, write the letter of the *best* answer to each of the following items.

_____ **1.** Besides the narrator herself, a *main* character in this story is the —
- A narrator's sister
- B narrator's teacher
- C head nun
- D narrator's mother

_____ **2.** The family in the story has come to the United States to —
- F expand the father's medical practice
- G enroll the narrator and her sisters in an American school
- H help the mother sell her inventions
- J escape the dictator Trujillo

_____ **3.** The mother dreams up all the following inventions *except* —
- A a perpetual-motion machine
- B coffee with creamer already mixed in
- C time-released water capsules for your plants
- D a key-chain timer to let you know when your parking meter expires

_____ **4.** The daughter's attitude toward her mother can *best* be described as —
- F ashamed
- G very resentful
- H affectionate
- J condescending

_____ **5.** What inspires the narrator to write her speech?
- A Her mother's encouragement
- B The poetry of Walt Whitman
- C Her sisters' loving support
- D A desire to be appreciated by the nuns and her classmates

_____ **6.** The narrator thinks her mother's last invention is —
- F the speech for the teachers
- G her daughter's poetry
- H a new kind of language, a combination of Spanish and English
- J a special corkscrew

_____ **7.** Because the narrator's mother stops inventing after reading about the man who creates a suitcase on rollers, we can infer that she —

A thinks her idea about suitcases is better

B wants to learn more about wheels for suitcases

C is frustrated because he was taken seriously and she wasn't

D is going to find manufacturers for her inventions

_____ **8.** The daughter calls her father "Chapita" because she —

F is happy and calls him by his pet nickname

G is angry and calls him the nickname of a dictator

H wants to prove that she understands her father's history

J is too old to sit on his lap and call him "daddy"

_____ **9.** Which of the following statements does *not* explain the title's significance?

A The narrator is the daughter of a famous inventor.

B The mother and daughter are both creative people.

C The mother's inventiveness helps her daughter in a crisis.

D The mother confuses her sayings.

_____ **10.** The narrator's parents symbolically invent a(n) —

F new identity for their daughter

G new brand of suitcase

H new way of solving problems

J new kind of advice

LITERARY FOCUS: CONFLICT *(15 points; 5 points each)*
On the line provided, write the letter of the *best* answer to each of the following items.

_____ **11.** The narrator's argument with her father about the speech is an example of —

A external imagery

B internal dialogue

C internal conflict

D external conflict

_____ **12.** An example of an internal conflict in this story is the —

F mother's constant endeavor to think up inventions

G girl's struggle between her anger at her father and her love for him

H argument over the father being called Trujillo by his daughter

J clash between the father's traditional values and the daughter's opinions

______ **13.** The children who throw stones at the narrator and her sister are part of an —

A external conflict

B internal conflict

C shared dialogues

D interior monologues

Reading Skills: Making Inferences About Characters *(5 points)*

On the line provided, write the letter of the *best* answer to the following item.

______ **14.** We can infer that the narrator's father has a strong reaction to his daughter's speech because he —

F admires his wife's influence over their daughter

G believes that the speech should be published in the local newspaper

H is proud that the nuns have given his daughter an excellent education

J is afraid that his daughter's opinions cause trouble

Vocabulary Development *(20 points; 4 points each)*

Complete each analogy with a Vocabulary word from the following list. Use each Vocabulary word only once.

eulogy **noncommittal** **florid** **ultimatum** **reconcile**

15. WOUND : HEAL :: DIVORCE : ______________________

16. FIRST : PROPOSAL :: LAST : ______________________

17. PLAIN : UNADORNED :: SHOWY : ______________________

18. WEDDING : TOAST :: FUNERAL : ______________________

19. BIASED : TACTFUL :: DOGMATIC : ______________________

CONSTRUCTED RESPONSE *(20 points)*

20. Why do the narrator and her mother have conflicts? Give at least two reasons for their conflicts, using details from the story to support your response. On a separate sheet of paper, write a paragraph that explains your answer. Support your ideas with details from the selection.

NAME ______ CLASS ______ DATE ______ SCORE ______

SELECTION TEST **Student Edition page 913** LITERARY RESPONSE AND ANALYSIS

The Handsomest Drowned Man in the World

Gabriel García Márquez ***translated by*** **Gregory Rabassa**

COMPREHENSION *(40 points; 4 points each)*

On the line provided, write the letter of the *best* answer to each of the following items.

______ **1.** When Esteban's body first washes up on shore, the children react by —

A retreating in terror

B ignoring it

C running to get their parents' help

D burying it and digging it up again

______ **2.** In the beginning of the story, the village is *best* described as —

F a farming community

G large and lush

H small, poor, and plain

J sophisticated and middle-class

______ **3.** After the women clean off Esteban's body, they are shocked to discover that he is —

A badly injured

B large and handsome

C missing his left leg

D their neighbor

______ **4.** When their men come back, the women are happy because —

F they are afraid of Esteban's body

G they want some help handling him

H they want to get his corpse buried, because it is starting to smell

J no neighboring village has claimed the body

______ **5.** The author makes Esteban seem to come to life by —

A revealing his thoughts in the first person

B showing how much the women admire him

C describing his gruesome death

D telling all about his life before he died

______ **6.** The women imagine that Esteban might be described by all of the following qualities *except* —

F cruel

G uncomfortable

H peaceful

J considerate

NAME ______ CLASS ______ DATE ______ SCORE ______

______ **7.** You can infer that the villagers bury Esteban at sea rather than in the village because —

A the village is too small to accommodate his body

B they do not want to dig a grave for him

C it is considered a great honor to be buried at sea

D burial at sea is their custom

______ **8.** What does the drowned man come to symbolize for the villagers?

F The waste of human potential

G Life's richer, deeper possibilities

H Their defects and weaknesses

J Life's savageness

______ **9.** How do the villagers change as they deal with Esteban's corpse?

A They become proud of themselves and their village.

B They argue with one another and bring up past feuds and fights.

C Marriages dissolve and children are ignored.

D Many decide to leave the village and seek their fortunes elsewhere.

______ **10.** Ironically, the *most* vibrant character in this story is the —

F oldest woman

G youngest woman

H dead man

J visiting sea captain

LITERARY FOCUS: MAGIC REALISM *(20 points; 5 points each)*

On the line provided, write the letter of the *best* answer to each of the following items.

______ **11.** How is the story's title an example of magic realism?

A It shows that even handsome people can drown.

B A drowned man is realistic; "handsome" makes him extraordinary.

C It suggests that handsome people are in special danger.

D It shows our need for heroes.

______ **12.** The author's tone in this story is *best* described as —

F sorrowful

G scornful

H eerie

J matter-of-fact

_____ **13.** "The Handsomest Drowned Man in the World" is an example of magic realism because it includes aspects of all of the following elements *except* —

A realism

B myth

C stage directions

D imagination

_____ **14.** Esteban can be interpreted as the archetype of the —

F mistreated child

G henpecked husband

H superhuman hero

J misunderstood genius

VOCABULARY DEVELOPMENT *(20 points; 4 points each)*
On the line provided, write the Vocabulary word that *best* completes each sentence.

bountiful **haggard** **virile** **destitute** **frivolity**

15. The villagers are awed by Esteban because he is so manly and _______________.

16. At first, the men feel that the women's attention to the corpse is mere _______________ and silliness.

17. Even the most worn out and _______________ men and women are delighted by his presence.

18. They give him a generous and _______________ funeral.

19. He may have come to the village a poor, _______________ man, but he left the village far richer from his presence.

CONSTRUCTED RESPONSE *(20 points)*

20. This story can be read as a transformation myth. How does Esteban change as the story progresses to become larger than life? On a separate sheet of paper, write a paragraph that explains your answer. Support your ideas with details from the selection.

Rules of the Game *from* The Joy Luck Club Amy Tan

COMPREHENSION *(40 points; 4 points each)*

On the line provided, write the letter of the *best* answer to each of the following items.

______ **1.** The Jongs acquire a chess set —

A as a birthday present for Vincent

B at a thrift store

C as a school prize

D at a church Christmas party

______ **2.** From the name Mr. and Mrs. Jong give their daughter, you can infer that they —

F do not feel connected to Chinese culture

G want her to blend into American culture

H never want her to forget that she was born on Waverly Place

J did not want a daughter so they gave her a masculine name

______ **3.** Waverly starts playing chess because —

A it seems very interesting to her

B she wants to show up her brothers

C her mother forces her to

D she is bored during vacation

______ **4.** Waverly becomes such a good chess player because —

F she has good luck

G her brothers are excellent teachers

H she does not want to shame her family

J she is curious and intelligent

______ **5.** Mrs. Jong attributes Waverly's success at chess to luck because Mrs. Jong —

A does not want to seem overly proud of her daughter

B does not think that Waverly is working hard enough at learning chess

C is afraid that Waverly will quit if she brags

D knows that success at chess depends on luck

______ **6.** Why does Waverly hate to go shopping with her mother?

F She would rather be home practicing chess moves.

G Her mother refuses to buy her treats.

H She resents her mother showing her off.

J Her mother walks too slowly.

_____ **7.** Mrs. Jong is *best* characterized as all of the following qualities *except* —

A caring

B ambitious

C cruel

D proud

_____ **8.** Waverly runs away from her mother because —

F it is time for her to go to chess practice

G she resents having to share her victory with her mother

H she is cold, tired, and hungry

J she does not like looking at the fish in the windows

_____ **9.** Waverly's relationship to her mother is like a chess game because both —

A are long and boring

B require strategy and cunning

C result in big prizes

D involve other people

_____ **10.** An unspoken but implied point in "Rules of the Game" is —

F traditionally chess has been considered a male enterprise

G there is no such thing as a child prodigy

H chess is a fast-paced game of bluffing

J Waverly is part of a long tradition of famous women chess players

LITERARY FOCUS: MOTIVATION *(20 points; 5 points each)*
On the line provided, write the letter of the *best* answer to each of the following items.

_____ **11.** What does Mrs. Jong mean when she says, "Is shame you fall down nobody push you"?

A She is sorry that Waverly has fallen down.

B Waverly should not quit before she has even tried.

C It's not the mother's fault that Waverly has lost.

D The trouble between them is Waverly's own fault.

_____ **12.** What motivates Mrs. Jong to tell Vincent to throw away the chess set?

F Concern that he will not be able to learn how to play chess

G Worry at the thought of the children fighting over the fine gift

H Pride at accepting a secondhand gift

J Embarrassment at not being able to afford a gift for her son

______ **13.** Waverly asks her brothers many questions about chess because she —

A wants to distract them from their game so she can win

B is trying to be a pest

C thinks the game is a foolish waste of time

D is curious and wants to learn the secrets of the game

______ **14.** Which of the following statements *best* explains one of Waverly's motivations for striving to excel in chess?

F Her talent is a source of anxiety.

G Her chess tournaments often allow her to skip math classes.

H Playing chess is a form of rebelling against authority.

J Her ability at chess makes her popular in school.

VOCABULARY DEVELOPMENT *(20 points; 4 points each)*

Match each Vocabulary word on the left with its definition on the right. On the line provided, write the letter of the definition.

______ **15.** ancestral

______ **16.** intricate

______ **17.** obscured

______ **18.** retort

______ **19.** prodigy

a. concealed; hidden

b. genius; phenomenon

c. inherited

d. complicated; detailed

e. quick, sharp answer

CONSTRUCTED RESPONSE *(20 points)*

20. How does Mrs. Jong's concern for helping her daughter rise in society affect the plot? Cite specific details from the story to make your point. On a separate sheet of paper, write a paragraph that explains your answer. Support your ideas with details from the selection.

NAME ______________________ CLASS ______________________ DATE ______________ SCORE ______________

SELECTION TEST **Student Edition page 934**

LITERARY RESPONSE AND ANALYSIS

When Mr. Pirzada Came to Dine *Jhumpa Lahiri*

COMPREHENSION *(40 points; 4 points each)*

On the line provided, write the letter of the *best* answer to each of the following items.

_____ **1.** Mr. Pirzada is in the United States because he —

- **A** is a scholar doing research in botany
- **B** is a political refugee from Dacca
- **C** is trying to earn enough money to send for his family
- **D** and his wife are getting divorced

_____ **2.** At first, the narrator's parents invite Mr. Pirzada to dinner because they —

- **F** know about his plight and feel sorry for him
- **G** are lonely for familiar companionship
- **H** want him to tutor their daughter
- **J** are cousins

_____ **3.** Why do Lilia's parents say that Mr. Pirzada is no longer Indian?

- **A** He begins to dress as an American and prefers American food.
- **B** He becomes an American citizen.
- **C** India has been partitioned; Mr. Pirzada is Pakistani.
- **D** He loses all interest in East Pakistan's fight for sovereignty.

_____ **4.** You can infer from Lilia's mother's feelings about raising her daughter in America that Lilia's —

- **F** parents do not plan to return to India to live
- **G** parents want to return to their homeland as soon as the war is over
- **H** mother does not appreciate the freedom and openness in America
- **J** mother was not able to receive an education in her homeland

_____ **5.** What gift does Mr. Pirzada bring to Lilia every time he visits her family for dinner?

- **A** Books
- **B** Candy
- **C** Comic books
- **D** Photographs of India

_____ **6.** What does Lilia do with his gifts?

- **F** Give them away
- **G** Share them with her best friend
- **H** Save them in a special box
- **J** Destroy them

_____ **7.** From the way Lilia's parents treat Mr. Pirzada, you can infer that they —

A feel superior to Mr. Pirzada

B consider him only a business friend

C are kind and compassionate people

D are unfeeling and condescending

_____ **8.** All of the following words describe Mr. Pirzada *except* —

F stoical

G generous

H kind

J selfish

_____ **9.** Why does Lilia eat the candies but not brush her teeth?

A The candy is part of her prayer for Mr. Pirzada's family.

B She is testing her parents' rules.

C She does not want the delicious taste of the candies to fade.

D She has lost her toothbrush and is afraid to ask for another one.

_____ **10.** You know that Mr. Pirzada's composure has cracked when he —

F yells at Lilia

G forgets to bring Lilia a gift

H carves a gash in the pumpkin

J understands that his daughters have been killed

LITERARY FOCUS: THEME *(20 points; 5 points each)*
On the line provided, write the letter of the *best* answer to each of the following items.

_____ **11.** Lilia changes when she —

A decides to apply herself to her studies

B begins to understand Mr. Pirzada's pain

C becomes disobedient in school

D discards her native culture and fully adopts America's culture

_____ **12.** From her experiences with Mr. Pirzada, Lilia learns —

F how to celebrate Halloween

G the importance of friendship during times of trouble

H never to trust strangers, even from your birth country

J to love science, especially botany

NAME ______________________ CLASS ______________ DATE __________ SCORE __________

______ **13.** Why do you think the author titled her story "When Mr. Pirzada Came to Dine"?

- **A** Meeting Mr. Pirzada was the single most important event in her childhood.
- **B** Lilia resented Mr. Pirzada's visits because she had less time with her parents when he was there.
- **C** When Mr. Pirzada came to eat dinner with the family, Lilia learned a life lesson.
- **D** The dinners were happy times that Lilia remembers fondly.

______ **14.** Which of the following sentences *best* states the story's theme?

- **F** Troubles that seem insurmountable often resolve on their own.
- **G** We often miss people who are far away, especially family members.
- **H** Other people are often far happier than they seem.
- **J** People can be suffering deeply and not reveal it.

VOCABULARY DEVELOPMENT *(20 points; 4 points each)*

Using the following Vocabulary words, write a synonym or antonym for each word, as directed. Use each Vocabulary word only once.

deplored **placid** **autonomy** **austere** **impeccably**

15. dependence *antonym:* ______________________

16. gaudy *antonym:* ______________________

17. perfectly *synonym:* ______________________

18. approved of *antonym:* ______________________

19. peaceful *synonym:* ______________________

CONSTRUCTED RESPONSE *(20 points)*

20. What message about compassion is revealed in this story? On a separate sheet of paper, write a paragraph that explains your answer. Support your ideas with details from the selection.

NAME ______ CLASS ______ DATE ______ SCORE ______

The Book of the Dead Edwidge Danticat

COMPREHENSION *(40 points; 4 points each)*

On the line provided, write the letter of the *best* answer to each of the following items.

______ **1.** The story's opening sentence, "My father is gone," accomplishes all of the following purposes *except* —

A introduces the themes of death and deception, through the double meaning of "gone"

B provides vivid sensory description

C sparks reader interest

D hints that the speaker's relationship with her father will change

______ **2.** You can infer from the information Annie gives the police officers that —

F she does not love her father

G she respects him

H her father has wandered off before

J her father is slowly losing his mind

______ **3.** The police officers are *best* described as —

A kind and efficient

B indifferent and lazy

C well-meaning but overworked

D cold and arrogant

______ **4.** The *real* reason that Annie's father refuses to have his picture taken is that he —

F is ashamed of his appearance

G thinks taking pictures is a waste of time

H is afraid he will be recognized

J does not want his daughter to think that he is vain

______ **5.** Why is Annie so proud of the sculpture she made of her father?

A It is the first time she has ever tried to sculpt anything.

B It is a revolutionary piece that will win many awards.

C She believes that it captures his heroic nature.

D She thinks that it erases all his terrible deeds from the past.

______ **6.** Annie thinks her parents met —

F on a beach in Haiti

G while working on a TV show

H in prison, as fellow prisoners

J when he escaped from prison

______ **7.** What does Annie's mother mean with the metaphor, "We were like two seeds planted in a rock"?

A They keep secrets locked away from each other.

B They had a hard start but built a good life.

C They are hard, selfish people.

D Their relationship is as strong and pure as rock.

______ **8.** Annie's father looks so happy when he returns to the room because —

F he is relieved to tell Annie the truth about his past

G he knows that Annie was worried

H he enjoyed the time he spent alone on the beach

J the police did not frighten him

______ **9.** The writer imagines her father having a nightmare in which he —

A drowns in the ocean, all alone

B is in prison and his fingernails are being torn out

C is put back into jail and beaten to death

D dips his hands into sand and brings up a fistful of blood

______ **10.** Haiti's political situation shaped the characters in that the —

F government helped people get an education in the arts

G political stability helped people build honest and productive lives

H corrupt government approved violence and deception

J free elections made people feel secure

LITERARY FOCUS: IRONY *(20 points; 5 points each)*
On the line provided, write the letter of the *best* answer to each of the following items.

______ **11.** What is ironic about Gabrielle's father?

A Unlike Annie's father, he really was a political prisoner.

B Gabrielle thinks he likes art, but he really does not.

C He guarded Annie's father in Fort Dimanche.

D He was not punished for criticizing the dictatorship.

______ **12.** One example of **situational irony** in the story is the —

F discovery that Annie's father was a prison guard, not a prisoner

G disclosure that Annie's father was kidnapped

H sculpture is gone, but Gabrielle believes that Annie is delivering it

J admiration Annie's father has for the ancient Egyptians

______ **13.** The luncheon at the Fonteneau's home is an example of —

A verbal irony

B situational irony

C dramatic irony

D allusion

______ **14.** Gabrielle's reason for wanting the sculpture is ironic because she —

F wanted to please her father, but he does not like it

G did not know that the sculpture never existed

H never saw it

J thought it reflected her father, who really was heroic

VOCABULARY DEVELOPMENT *(20 points; 4 points each)*
Write the Vocabulary word that is a synonym or antonym for each word, as directed. Use each Vocabulary word only once.

plain **created** **indestructible** **spellbound** **garish**

15. gaudy *synonym:* ______________

16. mesmerized *synonym:* ______________

17. vulnerable *antonym:* ______________

18. eradicated *antonym:* ______________

19. gaudy *antonym:* ______________

CONSTRUCTED RESPONSE *(20 points)*

20. Explain the story's irony. How does Danticat reverse the reader's expectations? On a separate sheet of paper, write a paragraph that explains your answer. Support your ideas with details from the selection.

from Black Boy Richard Wright

COMPREHENSION *(40 points; 4 points each)*

On the line provided, write the letter of the *best* answer to each of the following items.

______ **1.** At the beginning of the selection, Richard —

- **A** enjoys playing games with his father
- **B** sees his father as a stranger in the house
- **C** feels very close to his father
- **D** respects his father's hard work

______ **2.** The family is plunged into poverty when —

- **F** the family is evicted from their tenement apartment
- **G** Richard's father dies
- **H** Richard's father deserts the family for another woman
- **J** Richard's mother becomes ill

______ **3.** In Memphis, Richard's mother locks him out of the apartment because she wants him to learn —

- **A** good manners
- **B** the importance of honesty
- **C** to defend himself against bullies
- **D** the importance of working hard in school

______ **4.** Richard bitterly resents the preacher for —

- **F** leading his mother on
- **G** taking time and attention away from him
- **H** preaching too long in church on Sundays
- **J** eating a lot of the fried chicken

______ **5.** Richard's mother places him and his brother in an orphanage —

- **A** in desperation
- **B** in anger
- **C** at their father's insistence
- **D** by order of the court

______ **6.** Rather than stay at the orphanage, Richard —

- **F** and his mother ask his father for money
- **G** decides to stay with his father
- **H** lives on the streets
- **J** goes to the judge and asks him for help

______ **7.** Based on the details Wright uses to describe his father and the woman he lives with, we can infer that Richard —

A wants to live with his father and the woman

B wishes the woman was his mother

C admires his father

D dislikes his father

______ **8.** When he meets his father twenty-five years later, Richard realizes that his father —

F and he are more alike than he can admit

G will never understand him

H is admirable after all

J feels very guilty about what happened

______ **9.** All of the following events help create the general mood of this passage *except* —

A at first, Richard is disappointed by the boat to Memphis

B Richard triumphs by beating the gang members

C Richard is offended when his father offers him a nickel

D Richard is hungry much of the time

______ **10.** Wright's *main* subject in this excerpt from his autobiography is —

F danger

G divorce

H racial prejudice

J poverty

LITERARY FOCUS: DIALOGUE AND NONFICTION *(20 points; 5 points each)*

On the line provided, write the letter of the *best* answer to each of the following items.

______ **11.** Which of the following statements does *not* accurately describe **dialogue**?

A It is used only in drama.

B It represents a conversation between two or more people.

C It is used in fiction, nonfiction, and other types of writing.

D It often reveals thoughts and feelings.

______ **12.** In this excerpt you can infer that Wright —

F created the dialogue from his memories and his imagination

G reproduced the characters' words directly from life

H recalled every word he used from an actual conversation

J help readers understand that this is a work of fiction

NAME ______ CLASS ______ DATE ______ SCORE ______

______ **13.** From his dialogue, Richard emerges as having all of the following qualities *except* —

A confusion

B defiance

C fear

D viciousness

______ **14.** Overall, the effect of the dialogue used in this selection is to —

F remind readers that the story is a work of fiction

G surprise readers since it is used so rarely

H reveal how people think and help readers visualize the characters

J emphasize regional accents, making the characters seem realistic

VOCABULARY DEVELOPMENT *(20 points; 4 points each)*

Match each Vocabulary word on the left with its definition on the right. On the line provided, write the letter of the definition.

______ **15.** enthralled	**a.** frantic behavior; wildness
______ **16.** clamor	**b.** fascinated
______ **17.** dispirited	**c.** intensely; eagerly
______ **18.** frenzy	**d.** discouraged
______ **19.** ardently	**e.** loud noise; loud demand or complaint

CONSTRUCTED RESPONSE *(20 points)*

20. In this excerpt, Richard Wright describes a series of difficult situations that he faced as a child. How would you characterize the young Richard? Make at least two references to the passage to support your ideas. On a separate sheet of paper, write a paragraph that explains your answer. Support your ideas with details from the selection.

NAME ______ CLASS ______ DATE ______ SCORE ______

SELECTION TEST **Student Edition page 986** LITERARY RESPONSE AND ANALYSIS

The Girl Who Wouldn't Talk

from The Woman Warrior Maxine Hong Kingston

COMPREHENSION *(40 points; 4 points each)*

On the line provided, write the letter of the *best* answer to each of the following items.

______ **1.** The narrator is a(n) —

A elementary school teacher
B teenage Chinese boy
C young Chinese American girl
D young mother, who recently arrived in America from China

______ **2.** The narrator knows that the quiet girl can talk because she —

F speaks privately with teachers
G whispers during recess
H sings quietly to herself
J reads aloud in class

______ **3.** The narrator and the quiet girl —

A have been fighting with each other for years
B share many similar qualities
C used to be best friends
D eventually resolve their conflict

______ **4.** The narrator stays late after school and —

F gets in trouble with her teachers
G finishes her homework before she has to work
H plays on school grounds
J waits for her parents to pick her up

______ **5.** When she begins to antagonize the quiet girl, the narrator feels that the quiet girl —

A is weak and needs to be toughened up
B is deliberately trying to make the narrator mad
C is not very intelligent
D needs a companion to talk to

______ **6.** To get the quiet girl to talk, the narrator does all of the following actions *except* —

F hits the quiet girl with a stick
G pinches her cheeks
H yells at the quiet girl
J makes the quiet girl cry

______ **7.** The *best* description of the narrator's internal conflict is that she —

A wants everyone to know that she is tough and independent

B wants to blend into the classroom so she can become like a ghost

C wants to be strong, but she sees herself as weak and fragile

D believes that it is her duty to get the quiet girl to talk

______ **8.** The narrator stops picking on the quiet girl when the —

F quiet girl starts to cry

G quiet girl starts talking

H narrator herself starts to cry

J quiet girl's older sister saves her

______ **9.** The story focuses on the subject of —

A racial injustice

B youths' cruelty

C women's rights

D religious persecution

______ **10.** Based on details in the story, readers can infer that the narrator —

F will beg the quiet girl for forgiveness

G becomes ill because she feels guilty

H will buy the quiet girl a gift

J will be harshly punished by her parents

LITERARY FOCUS: CHARACTERIZATION *(15 points; 5 points each)*
On the line provided, write the letter of the *best* answer to each of the following items.

______ **11.** The narrator characterizes American and Chinese girls *primarily* by their —

A grades in school

B family's income

C skill at group sports

D voices

______ **12.** The author characterizes the narrator as —

F kind

G well-meaning

H cruel

J shy and quiet

______ **13.** The younger Chinese sister is a characterized by all of the following qualities *except* —

A timidity

B extroversion

C family-orientation

D determination

READING SKILLS: DRAWING INFERENCES ABOUT CHARACTER *(5 points)*

On the line provided, write the letter of the *best* answer to the following item.

______ **14.** Readers can infer that the older sister is kind by her —

F name

G appearance

H clothing

J actions

VOCABULARY DEVELOPMENT *(20 points; 4 points each)*

Complete each analogy with a Vocabulary word from the list below. Use each Vocabulary word only once.

loitered **nape** **habitually** **sarcastic** **temples**

15. RESPECTFUL : MOCKING :: COURTEOUS : ______

16. TORSO : ARMS :: FOREHEAD : ______

17. HURRIED : RUSHED :: LINGERED : ______

18. SPORADICALLY : OFTEN :: RARELY : ______

19. BACK : SPINE :: NECK : ______

CONSTRUCTED RESPONSE *(20 points)*

20. Why do you think the narrator tries to force the quiet girl to speak? Explain what conflicts could lead her to this action. On a separate sheet of paper, write a paragraph that explains your answer. Support your ideas with details from the selection.

NAME ______________________ CLASS ______________ DATE __________ SCORE __________

SELECTION TEST **Student Edition page 998** LITERARY RESPONSE AND ANALYSIS

from The Way to Rainy Mountain N. Scott Momaday

COMPREHENSION *(40 points; 4 points each)*

On the line provided, write the letter of the *best* answer to each of the following items.

______ **1.** Momaday explains that he returns to Rainy Mountain at first to —

A see how Crow culture affected Kiowa culture

B collect myths and stories of the Kiowas

C take pictures of the region for a book he is preparing

D visit his grandmother's grave

______ **2.** According to the origin myth of the Kiowas, the Kiowas entered the world —

F through the mouth of the Earth Mother

G from the top of Rainy Mountain

H guided by the sun

J through a hollow log

______ **3.** Momaday also returns to the region to —

A understand the journey of his people

B see if he wants to live there full time

C recover from a painful divorce

D visit with his other relatives

______ **4.** The Kiowas learned the culture of the plains from —

F the Comanches

G the legends of the Sun God

H hunting buffalo

J the Crows

______ **5.** The legend of Devils Tower concerns the —

A origin of the mountain

B death of Momaday's grandmother

C origin of the Big Dipper

D origin of the underworld

______ **6.** Momaday says that the legend of Devils Tower is important to the Kiowas because the —

F Kiowas have kinsmen in the sky

G story helped them make a new home

H most important gods were the gods of the earth

J legend helps Kiowa children not fear the dark

______ **7.** Which of the following facts is *not* true of Momaday's grandmother?

A She was there when the Kiowas left the medicine tree.

B She lived in a big, weathered house.

C She knew about things she had seen.

D She became a Christian.

______ **8.** Compared with the other Sun Dances, what was different about the last dance?

F Most of the Kiowas were Christians by then.

G The Kiowas could not find a buffalo bull for the medicine tree.

H The Kiowas invited some white men to observe the dance.

J The dance was held in Montana, not Rainy Mountain.

______ **9.** After the soldiers dispersed the Kiowas at the Sun Dance on July 20, 1890, the Kiowas —

A were put on a reservation near Fort Sill, Oklahoma

B stopped holding the Sun Dance

C discovered that many of their own people had been massacred

D learned that soldiers had shot and killed all the remaining buffalo

______ **10.** The setting of this excerpt from *The Way to Rainy Mountain* takes place —

F in the past and present

G only in the present

H only in the past

J in the future

LITERARY FOCUS: SETTING *(15 points; 5 points each)*

On the line provided, write the letter of the *best* answer to each of the following items.

______ **11.** What distinguishes the setting of Rainy Mountain?

A The weather is very harsh.

B The weather is the same all year around.

C The weather is remarkably mild.

D There is very little rain.

______ **12.** Momaday notes that Rainy Mountain —

F gets rain all year long

G stimulates the imagination

H is in the Rocky Mountain foothills

J is sacred to all Native Americans

NAME ________ CLASS ________ DATE ________ SCORE ________

______ **13.** The setting of Rainy Mountain was important to the Kiowas because —

A they were able to hunt and fish in abundance there

B they felt free in the mountains

C it marked the end of their journey

D they appreciated the beauty of the forests, lakes, and ocean

READING SKILLS: IDENTIFYING MAIN IDEAS AND SUPPORTING DETAILS *(5 points)*

On the line provided, write the letter of the *best* answer to the following item.

______ **14.** One of the main ideas in this excerpt from *The Way to Rainy Mountain* is —

F Kiowas were a mountain people

G Kiowas made friends with the Crows

H seven sisters became the stars of the Big Dipper

J Kiowas changed as they moved south

VOCABULARY DEVELOPMENT *(20 points; 4 points each)*

On the line provided, write the Vocabulary word that *best* completes each sentence.

wariness **opaque** **infirm** **indulge** **tenuous**

15. Momaday's grandmother was healthy until the very end of her life, when she became ill and ____________.

16. The window's were ____________, so you couldn't see in.

17. Momaday's grandmother had firm, not ____________, memories of the past.

18. Momaday would ____________ himself in long, pleasant walks through the cool forest.

19. The only thing that causes him ____________ are bears and other wild animals, so he exercises caution when walking alone.

CONSTRUCTED RESPONSE *(20 points)*

20. Like the Kiowas, Momaday makes a journey. Trace the Kiowas' journey, and explain the purpose of Momaday's journey. On a separate sheet of paper, write a paragraph that explains your answer. Support your ideas with details from the selection.

from In Search of Our Mothers' Gardens Alice Walker

COMPREHENSION *(40 points; 4 points each)*

On the line provided, write the letter of the *best* answer to each of the following items.

______ **1.** Alice Walker's mother —

- **A** won awards for her flowers
- **B** is an artist in the garden
- **C** died when Walker was young
- **D** is a professional gardener

______ **2.** You can infer from Walker's comment that her mother labored "beside—not behind—[her] father in the fields" that Walker's —

- **F** parents did not like field work
- **G** parents spent all their time in the fields
- **H** parents treated each other as equals
- **J** father resented his wife's desire to grow flowers

______ **3.** Walker's description of her mother's daily routine reveals that her mother —

- **A** had a relatively easy life
- **B** was not very efficient
- **C** had a difficult life
- **D** never wanted a career outside her home

______ **4.** The quilt depicting the Crucifixion that hangs in the Smithsonian Institution was made by —

- **F** an anonymous African American woman
- **G** Walker's mother
- **H** Virginia Woolf
- **J** one of Walker's neighbors

______ **5.** Walker agrees with Virginia Woolf's thesis that —

- **A** many working-class women were creative geniuses but remained anonymous
- **B** working-class women cannot be creative because they lack a good education
- **C** many herb sellers were not creative women
- **D** male writers never appreciate their mothers' sacrifices for them

______ **6.** Walker believes that from her mother and previous generations of African American women she inherited —

- **F** the knowledge of many different kinds of plants
- **G** respect for strength and love of beauty
- **H** a dislike for household chores
- **J** appreciation for the importance of relaxation

______ **7.** The author and her mother share a talent for —

A quilt making

B writing poems

C gardening

D storytelling

______ **8.** Which of the following authors is *not* mentioned in this selection?

F Phillis Wheatley

G Virginia Woolf

H Stephen King

J Richard Wright

______ **9.** The *main* idea of Walker's essay can *best* be described as —

A people should make certain their children receive a good education

B efficient housekeeping is the most important skill in life

C all women owe thanks to their creative female relatives and friends

D all women artists have frustrated mothers

______ **10.** Walker supports the main idea of her essay with —

F historical statistics

G descriptions of paintings made by famous women

H several poems

J examples and brief stories

LITERARY FOCUS: PERSONAL ESSAY *(15 points; 5 points each)*
On the line provided, write the letter of the *best* answer to each of the following items.

______ **11.** A **personal essay** is also called a(n) —

A drama

B short story

C work of fiction

D informal essay

______ **12.** A personal essay does *not* normally include —

F prose

G the author's perspective

H imaginary characters and invented plot

J autobiographical elements

______ **13.** This excerpt from *In Search of Our Mothers' Gardens* is considered a personal essay because —

A it is a short work of nonfiction with a personal slant

B it is a work of fiction with a subjective focus

C the author rambles on as in a conversation

D the author reveals intimate details about a person

READING SKILLS: OUTLINING *(5 points)*

On the line provided, write the letter of the *best* answer to the following item.

______ **14.** What is the subject of Walker's personal essay?

F Poverty and its lasting effect on families

G Marriage and children

H Gardening

J Women and creativity

VOCABULARY DEVELOPMENT *(20 points; 4 points each)*

Write the Vocabulary word that is a synonym or antonym for each word, as directed. Use each Vocabulary word only once.

ingenious **vibrant** **medium** **profusely** **conception**

15. material *synonym:* ____________

16. insufficiently *antonym:* ____________

17. foolish *antonym:* ____________

18. imagining *synonym:* ____________

19. active *synonym:* ____________

CONSTRUCTED RESPONSE *(20 points)*

20. Why do you think that Walker searches for her mother's garden? What did she discover in the process? On a separate sheet of paper, write a paragraph that explains your answer. Support your ideas with details from the selection.

NAME ______ CLASS ______ DATE ______ SCORE ______

SELECTION TEST **Student Edition pages 1016, 1020** LITERARY RESPONSE AND ANALYSIS

Autobiographical Notes James Baldwin
from On James Baldwin Toni Morrison

COMPREHENSION *(40 points; 4 points each)*

On the line provided, write the letter of the *best* answer to each of the following items.

______ **1.** In the first part of "Autobiographical Notes," James Baldwin describes his —

A theories regarding the purpose of life

B fondness and aptitude for poetry

C adventures in the French countryside

D early development as a writer

______ **2.** Baldwin considers his first two books —

F unpublishable

G brilliant

H his best work

J better than Faulkner's novels

______ **3.** Baldwin states that it is a writer's duty to —

A examine attitudes in a deep, thoughtful manner

B write about patriotic subjects

C fight for a better world

D focus on a single important issue in every book

______ **4.** Baldwin believes that he has been influenced by all of the following sources *except* —

F Charles Dickens

G the King James Bible

H African American speech patterns

J television

______ **5.** Baldwin believes that it is difficult being an African American writer because —

A no one has written about African Americans before

B the problem of being black in America has been written about so widely

C there are no patterns to follow

D it is almost impossible for African Americans to get their novels published

______ **6.** What is Baldwin's opinion of the past?

F The past is irrelevant when it comes to writers.

G We must discard past experiences to build a new present.

H By understanding the past can we understand the present.

J The past is horrible.

______ **7.** Baldwin insists on continuing to criticize America because he —

A thinks America should be more like Africa

B wants America to be more like France

C has been thrown out of America because of his political activity

D loves America more than any other country

______ **8.** According to Baldwin, all authors write from —

F public pressure

G their own experience

H a deep insecurity

J the words of previous generations of writers

______ **9.** One of Baldwin's main points is the fact that —

A he was shaped by both positive and negative factors

B he had a fellowship when he was twenty-one

C he read to his brothers and sisters

D African American writing is excellent

______ **10.** According to Toni Morrison, James Baldwin gave his friends all of the following gifts *except* —

F language

G courage

H tenderness

J commands

LITERARY FOCUS: TONE *(15 points; 5 points each)*

On the line provided, write the letter of the *best* answer to each of the following items.

______ **11.** **Tone** in writing is *best* described as —

A the writer's attitude on the subject

B an essay's subject

C the atmosphere or mood of a selection

D an essay's topic

______ **12.** In the beginning of the essay, Baldwin says, "In those days my mother was given to the exasperating and mysterious habit of having babies." The tone of this passage is *best* described as —

F humorous

G bitter

H ironic

J vicious

______ **13.** Which of the following words does not describe the tone of "Autobiographical Notes"?

A Direct

B Reflective

C Enraged

D Critical

READING SKILLS: EVALUATING AN AUTHOR'S ARGUMENTS *(5 points)*
On the line provided, write the letter of the *best* answer to the following item.

______ **14.** What is the tone of Toni Morrison's eulogy to James Baldwin?

F Smug

G Condescending

H Loving

J Neutral

VOCABULARY DEVELOPMENT *(20 points; 4 points each)*
Match each Vocabulary word on the left with its definition on the right. On the line provided, write the letter of the definition.

______ **15.** bleak

______ **16.** censored

______ **17.** assess

______ **18.** conundrum

______ **19.** coherent

a. evaluate

b. cheerless

c. clear; logical

d. cut or changed to remove material deemed objectionable

e. riddle

CONSTRUCTED RESPONSE *(20 points)*

20. What tone does Baldwin use to explain his ideas? Give at least two examples from the essay to support your analysis. On a separate sheet of paper, write a paragraph that explains your answer. Support your ideas with details from the selection.

NAME ______________ CLASS ______________ DATE ______________ SCORE ______________

Straw into Gold Sandra Cisneros

COMPREHENSION *(40 points; 4 points each)*

On the line provided, write the letter of the *best* answer to each of the following items.

_____ **1.** At the beginning of her essay, Cisneros recalls —

- **A** having her grandmother teach her how to make tortillas
- **B** being locked in a room and ordered to spin straw into gold
- **C** being asked to make a fancy meal for a dozen people
- **D** being invited to dinner while living in France

_____ **2.** Cisneros compares the challenge of making tortillas to —

- **F** living in a house with six brothers
- **G** writing poetry as a child
- **H** living away from home for a year
- **J** writing a critical essay for an exam

_____ **3.** Cisneros thinks that all the following influences shaped her into becoming a writer *except* her —

- **A** excellent school record
- **B** parents and brothers
- **C** Mexican heritage
- **D** family's poverty

_____ **4.** Cisneros is like her mother in that they both —

- **F** cry while watching Mexican soap operas
- **G** were born and raised in Mexico
- **H** share the same intelligence and artistic talent
- **J** have a sappy heart

_____ **5.** When the family moved into a permanent home in Chicago, Cisneros —

- **A** overcame her shyness and fear of strangers
- **B** met people who would become characters in her writing
- **C** became very homesick for the other places she had lived
- **D** acquired her own room where she could write

_____ **6.** Cisneros's attitude toward her parents' efforts to raise her and her brothers can *best* be described as —

- **F** admiring
- **G** resentful
- **H** bitter
- **J** cynical

______ **7.** Looking back at her childhood, Cisneros believes that she was —

A a serious, competitive student
B very athletic
C a rumpled, skinny, awkward girl
D a popular, sociable girl

______ **8.** Which of the following statements is *not* true about Cisneros's life?

F She left home before her brothers.
G She taught herself to garden.
H She traveled throughout Europe.
J She moved to Texas.

______ **9.** What is the *main* idea of this essay?

A The author's experiences shaped her personality and writing.
B Traveling throughout the world has not changed the author.
C The author is a gifted writer to whom everything has come easily.
D Texas and Mexico are geographically and culturally similar.

______ **10.** Which of the following details does *not* belong in a summary of this essay?

F Cisneros was an excellent student.
G Cisneros has spent a lot of time traveling.
H Cisneros examines her past to find clues to the writer that she has become.
J Cisneros was close to her family, especially her parents and brother Kiki.

LITERARY FOCUS: ALLUSION *(20 points; 5 points each)*

On the line provided, write the letter of the *best* answer to each of the following items.

______ **11.** An **allusion** is *best* described as —

A a comparison of two unlike objects
B writing that contains conflict
C poetic language
D a reference

______ **12.** The title of this essay is an allusion to the fairy tale —

F "The Little Mermaid"
G "Rumpelstiltskin"
H "Snow White"
J "Cinderella"

______ **13.** What does the gold in the title represent?

- **A** The literature Cisneros produced
- **B** Cisneros's mother's gardening skills
- **C** Cisneros's cooking ability
- **D** Cisneros's school record

Reading Skills: Understanding a Writer's Background *(5 points)*

On the line provided, write the letter of the *best* answer to the following item.

______ **14.** What does the straw in the title symbolize?

- **F** Cisneros's lack of success
- **G** The family's lack of food
- **H** The burnt tortillas
- **J** The raw materials of Cisneros's life

Vocabulary Development *(20 points; 4 points each)*

On the line provided, write the Vocabulary word that *best* completes each sentence.

prestigious **intuitively** **flourished** **ventured** **taboo**

15. When Cisneros was a child, it was ____________, or forbidden, for unmarried women to live on their own.

16. Cisneros, however, knew ____________ without conscious reasoning that she had to move out.

17. She took great risks when she ____________ all the way to Europe.

18. Cisneros ____________ and prospered in her new life.

19. Her writing was a great success, and she won many ____________ awards.

Constructed Response *(20 points)*

20. In "Straw into Gold," Cisneros mentions many things she draws upon as subjects for her writing. What do these things have in common? Why do you think she chooses these things over others? On a separate sheet of paper, write a paragraph that explains your answer. Support your ideas with details from the selection.

Night Journey Theodore Roethke

COMPREHENSION *(60 points; 6 points each)*

On the line provided, write the letter of the *best* answer to each of the following items.

_____ **1.** The poem's setting is a —

A train heading east
B train heading west
C plane heading south
D deserted train sitting in the yards

_____ **2.** The poem's speaker is —

F in charge of everyone's safety during the trip
G a porter
H a traveler
J a sales executive

_____ **3.** The speaker cannot sleep because he —

A is afraid of traveling away from home
B is bothered by personal problems
C has sore muscles from sitting so long
D is excited to see the countryside

_____ **4.** The speaker sees all of the following sights *except* —

F bridges
G trees
H mountains shrouded in mist
J cows and sheep grazing

_____ **5.** Readers can infer that the speaker's mood is —

A excited
B depressed
C sorrowful
D bored

_____ **6.** All of the following images create the feeling of the train's movement *except* the —

F beacon's swinging
G rattling of the glass windows
H passengers at rest
J train rushing into the rain

______ **7.** Which of the following images *best* appeals to readers' sense of touch?

- **A** "And gullies washed with light"
- **B** "Mist deepens on the pane; . . ."
- **C** "Wheels shake the roadbed stone, . . ."
- **D** "I watch a beacon swing / From dark to blazing bright; . . ."

______ **8.** The metaphor "bridges of iron lace" make the bridges seem —

- **F** fragile and beautiful
- **G** evil and frightening
- **H** symbolic
- **J** modern

______ **9.** The poet uses alliteration in the line "we rush into the rain" to —

- **A** show that nothing can impede the progress of humankind
- **B** show that the rain slows down the traveler's progress
- **C** suggest that rain depresses people
- **D** help readers feel the speaker's experiences

______ **10.** The overall tone of the poem is *best* described as —

- **F** sarcastic
- **G** ironic
- **H** impressionistic
- **J** bitter

LITERARY FOCUS: RHYME AND RHYTHM *(20 points; 5 points each)*

On the line provided, write the letter of the *best* answer to each of the following items.

______ **11.** **Rhyme** is best defined as the —

- **A** repetition of sounds in accented syllables and all succeeding syllables
- **B** pattern of stressed and unstressed syllables in oral and written language
- **C** beat or tempo of a poem
- **D** repetition of initial consonants or consonant sounds in a line of poetry

______ **12.** Which pair of words from "Night Journey" rhyme?

- **F** pass/pane
- **G** feel/steel
- **H** glass/stone
- **J** shove/night

_____ **13.** Which two lines from the poem show end rhyme?

A "I stare into the night / While others take their rest."

B "Bridges of iron lace, / A suddenness of trees, . . ."

C "Its rhythm rocks the earth, / And from my pullman berth . . ."

D "And gullies washed with light. / Beyond the mountain pass . . ."

_____ **14.** The poet uses rhythm in "Night Journey" to —

F mimic the movement of the journey

G show the speaker's feelings about a time long past

H argue that more people should travel across America

J show the power and fierceness of nature

CONSTRUCTED RESPONSE *(20 points)*

15. What feeling or emotion did you have after reading "Night Journey"? How did Theodore Roethke use sound to create these feelings? On a separate sheet of paper, write a paragraph that explains your answer. Support your ideas with details from the poem.

The Beautiful Changes Richard Wilbur

COMPREHENSION *(60 points; 6 points each)*
On the line provided, write the letter of the *best* answer to each of the following items.

______ **1.** In the first stanza the speaker describes —
- A sailing on a cool blue lake in Switzerland
- B playing with a chameleon
- C walking through a field of fall colors
- D seeing someone hold a rose

______ **2.** To the speaker the thought of "you" evokes the image of —
- F the blue Lucernes
- G a lazy lizard
- H a red, red rose
- J a green praying mantis

______ **3.** The chameleon and mantis create beautiful changes by —
- A adapting to the forest
- B uncovering nature's dark side
- C showing love
- D demonstrating how love remains constant

______ **4.** In the third stanza, how do the hands hold the roses?
- F Jealously
- G Spitefully
- H Carelessly
- J Freely

______ **5.** In the third stanza the way the roses are held is significant because it suggests that —
- A everyone has moments of insecurity and envy
- B beauty belongs to all people, not just individuals
- C some people are incapable of feeling love
- D we change in unpleasant ways

______ **6.** What do the hands represent in the third stanza?
- F Death
- G Someone the speaker loves
- H Nature
- J The speaker himself

______ **7.** According to the third stanza, the beautiful changes in —

A invisible ways

B violent ways

C cruel ways

D kind ways

______ **8.** The speaker *mostly* describes examples of how beauty and change —

F can be found in the natural world

G are created by human efforts

H occur in the spring

J are produced by the speaker

______ **9.** Which of following images is *not* visual?

A "By a chameleon's tuning his skin to it; . . ."

B "As a mantis, arranged / On a green leaf, grows . . ."

C "In such kind ways, . . ."

D "Any greenness is deeper than anyone knows."

______ **10.** The poet uses the colors white, blue, and green to —

F show he is being ironic about change

G symbolize the bad effects of change

H help readers visualize the scene

J encourage people to accept changes

LITERARY FOCUS: AMBIGUITY *(20 points; 5 points each)*

On the line provided, write the letter of the *best* answer to each of the following items.

______ **11.** The word *beautiful* in the title is ambiguous because it —

A can be a noun or an adjective

B has only one meaning

C can be read on one level only

D can be a verb or a preposition

______ **12.** The word *changes* in the title is ambiguous because it —

F has a single definition

G can function as a noun or verb

H can be an adverb, adjective, or pronoun

J it is clear and lucid

NAME ______ CLASS ______ DATE ______ SCORE ______

______ **13.** One of the ambiguities expressed in the title "The Beautiful Changes" and illustrated in Richard Wilbur's poem is that —

A beauty does not exist

B beautiful insects are born

C beautiful transformations occur in nature

D beautiful forests are destroyed

______ **14.** Overall, the title is ambiguous because it —

F has no different shades of meaning

G can be read on one level only

H can mean the beauty of change or changes in beauty

J suggests that nature is constant and never changing

CONSTRUCTED RESPONSE *(20 points)*

15. Based on your reading of "The Beautiful Changes," what do you think the title means? Explain why the title is ambiguous, describe at least two different levels of meaning, and select the meaning you think is *best* supported in the poem. On a separate sheet of paper, write a paragraph that explains your answer. Support your ideas with details from the poem.

NAME ______ CLASS ______ DATE ______ SCORE ______

SELECTION TEST **Student Edition pages 1044, 1047** LITERARY RESPONSE AND ANALYSIS

The Fish Elizabeth Bishop

One Art Elizabeth Bishop

COMPREHENSION *(60 points; 6 points each)*

On the line provided, write the letter of the *best* answer to each of the following items.

______ **1.** After catching the fish, the speaker —

- **A** takes a photograph of it
- **B** is cut by the fish's gills
- **C** watches it thrash in the boat
- **D** examines it closely

______ **2.** The speaker is surprised that —

- **F** the fish had not fought at all
- **G** the fish fought as hard as he did
- **H** other people did not want the fish
- **J** the fish did not taste good

______ **3.** An example of personification in "The Fish" is —

- **A** the fish's skin is compared to old, peeling wallpaper
- **B** a rainbow fills the boat
- **C** the fish is compared to a warrior with medals
- **D** the fish's eyes are bigger than the speaker's eyes

______ **4.** At the end of "The Fish," the speaker's attitude toward the fish can *best* be described as —

- **F** disgusted
- **G** admiring
- **H** disappointed
- **J** indifferent

______ **5.** The ending of "The Fish" is surprising because —

- **A** the speaker lets the fish go
- **B** the fish escapes
- **C** the fish has smaller fish inside it
- **D** other people have also seen the fish

______ **6.** In lines 4–15 of "One Art," the speaker mentions all the following losses *except* —

F keys

G time

H her mother's watch

J her wallet

______ **7.** What has the speaker lost in the last stanza of "One Art"?

A Her broken down car

B Someone she loves

C Her clear voice

D Her little pets

______ **8.** What does the speaker in "One Art" mean when she says she has "lost" a name?

F She changed her name.

G She has forgotten a name.

H She never knew a certain name.

J She gave her name away.

______ **9.** The parenthetical phrases in the last stanza of "One Art" reveal that the speaker —

A is furious about the loss

B is indifferent to the loss

C is delighted about the loss

D has not fully accepted the loss

______ **10.** What is the theme or main idea of "One Art"?

F Dealing with loss is an art.

G Love never lasts.

H People get over loss easily.

J Writing about loss only makes it worse.

LITERARY FOCUS: SYMBOL *(20 points; 5 points each)*
On the line provided, write the letter of the *best* answer to each of the following items.

______ **11.** The fish in "The Fish" is *best* described as —

A aged and battered

B dangerous and ugly

C smooth and graceful

D young and multicolored

_____ **12.** The fish is a symbol for a(n) —

F decaying house

G angry teenager

H young, new writer

J old fighter and survivor

_____ **13.** The rainbow at the end of "The Fish" is *most* likely a symbol for —

A anger

B understanding and happiness

C victory over the forces of nature

D money

_____ **14.** In "The Fish," Elizabeth Bishop uses symbols to —

F show the importance of fish

G make her point directly

H suggest unstated meanings

J imply only one interpretation

CONSTRUCTED RESPONSE *(20 points)*

15. What images and figures of speech did Elizabeth Bishop use to make you admire the fish in "The Fish"? On a separate sheet of paper, write a paragraph that explains your answers. Support your ideas with specific details from the poem

NAME _______________ CLASS _______________ DATE _______________ SCORE _______________

Mirror Sylvia Plath
Mushrooms Sylvia Plath

COMPREHENSION *(60 points; 6 points each)*

On the line provided, write the letter of the *best* answer to each of the following items.

_____ **1.** According to line 2 of "Mirror," what does the mirror do with whatever it sees?

- **A** Shows love and dislike
- **B** Makes it a part of itself
- **C** Swallows it
- **D** Makes it look young and beautiful

_____ **2.** Which of the following claims does the mirror make about itself?

- **F** It is not cruel, only truthful.
- **G** It can allow people to see what they want to see.
- **H** It is something that people do not really see.
- **J** It is lonely and neglected.

_____ **3.** When the woman in "Mirror" sees her reflection, she —

- **A** becomes agitated and upset
- **B** realizes that she must forget her past
- **C** decides to polish the mirror's surface
- **D** is reminded of her grandmother

_____ **4.** At the end of "Mirror," the woman sees —

- **F** a young girl playing happily
- **G** the person she wants to become
- **H** goldfish in a tank
- **J** herself growing older

_____ **5.** Which of the following descriptions from "Mirror" is an example of personification?

- **A** The mirror is silver and exact.
- **B** The candles and the moon are liars.
- **C** The opposite wall is pink with speckles.
- **D** A woman's face replaces the darkness.

_____ **6.** Who sees the mushrooms grow?

- **F** Only people who stay up late at night
- **G** People who betray them
- **H** No one
- **J** Strangers who have opened to door

______ **7.** The mushrooms can be described by all of the following adjectives *except* —

A silent

B determined

C depressed

D humble

______ **8.** One of the main ideas in "Mushrooms" is that quiet people —

F have a lot of strength

G eat a great deal

H are pushy and demanding

J do not work very hard

______ **9.** The tone of "Mushrooms" is *best* described as —

A sorrowful

B fierce

C hopeful

D playful

______ **10.** The mushrooms in "Mushrooms" are personified in all the following ways *except* that —

F their fists push through needles

G they talk quietly

H they diet

J their toes take hold

LITERARY FOCUS: SPEAKER AND TONE *(20 points; 5 points each)*

On the line provided, write the letter of the *best* answer to each of the following items.

______ **11.** In these two poems, the speakers —

A are the same as the poet

B are not the same as the poet

C are clearly named

D do not use the pronoun *I*

______ **12.** The speaker in "Mirror" is —

F Sylvia Plath

G the mirror

H a little four-cornered god

J a lake

______ **13.** The speakers in "Mushrooms" are the —

A mushrooms

B poet

C leaves

D crumbs

______ **14.** The speakers in both poems are alike because they are all —

F the poet herself

G famous places

H well-known people

J not human

Constructed Response *(20 points)*

15. How does Sylvia Plath's choice of speaker in "Mirror" and "Mushrooms" help her achieve her purpose? Explain her purpose in these two poems and explain how she uses tone and style to achieve it. On a separate sheet of paper, write a paragraph that explains your answer. Support your ideas with details from the two poems.

The Bells Anne Sexton
Young Anne Sexton

COMPREHENSION *(60 points; 6 points each)*
On the line provided, write the letter of the *best* answer to each of the following items.

______ **1.** "The Bells" is set in the —

A future, at the place where the circus will be set up
B present, at the circus
C past, in the speaker's memory
D present, at a zoo

______ **2.** In "The Bells" the speaker describes —

F being frightened by the lions at the circus
G feeling protected by a parent
H getting lost at the zoo
J eating popcorn at the circus

______ **3.** In "The Bells" the speaker mentions all the following events *except* —

A feeding the monkeys
B hearing the lions roar
C seeing the trapeze artist
D being in a crowd

______ **4.** You can infer that the speaker of "The Bells" —

F is a performer
G had a unhappy childhood
H loved being with her father
J is afraid of lions and elephants

______ **5.** The tone of "The Bells" is *best* described as —

A angry and resentful
B sweet and loving
C upset but forgiving
D terrifying

______ **6.** The opening line, "A thousand doors ago," in "Young" could describe any of the following topics *except* the —

F places the speaker has lived in or stayed at
G speaker's relationship with the stars
H speaker's experiences
J passage of time

______ **7.** Which of the following lines from "Young" is an example of personification?

A "I lay on the lawn at night, . . ."

B "my mother's window a funnel . . ."

C "my father's window, half shut, . . ."

D "the wise stars bedding over me, . . ."

______ **8.** The child's loneliness in "Young" is reflected in —

F her talking to the stars

G leaves blowing in the wind

H the crickets' ticking

J long winter evenings

______ **9.** Overall, the tone of "Young" is —

A bitter

B furious

C forlorn

D tragic

______ **10.** "Young" describes a —

F young woman having a nervous collapse

G house that is falling down from lack of care

H violent but brief summer storm

J single moment in time

LITERARY FOCUS: IMAGERY *(20 points; 5 points each)*
On the line provided, write the letter of the *best* answer to each of the following items.

______ **11.** The images in "The Bells" that connect father to child include all of the following ones *except* —

A the rings

B the crowds

C the bells

D holding hands

______ **12.** Which of the following images from "The Bells" provides the *best* example of visual imagery?

F "Today the circus poster / is scabbing off the concrete wall. . . ."

G "And the children have forgotten / if they knew at all."

H "This was the sound where it began. . . ."

J "the distant thump of the good elephants, . . ."

______ **13.** What emotion is evoked by the following image from "Young"?

"[I] . . . told the stars my questions
and thought God could really see
the heat and the painted light,
elbows, knees, dreams, goodnight."

A Grief

B Happiness

C Gloom

D Loneliness

______ **14.** "Young" appeals to all of the following senses except —

F hearing

G touch

H smell

J sight

CONSTRUCTED RESPONSE *(20 points)*

15. "The Bells" and "Young" are intended to evoke strong feelings in readers. Identify these feelings, and explain how Anne Sexton uses imagery and sounds to spark feelings in her readers. On a separate sheet of paper, write a paragraph that explains your answer. Support your ideas with details from the two poems.

NAME ______ CLASS ______ DATE ______ SCORE ______

The Bean Eaters Gwendolyn Brooks
In Honor of David Anderson Brooks, My Father
Gwendolyn Brooks

COMPREHENSION *(60 points; 6 points each)*
On the line provided, write the letter of the *best* answer to each of the following items.

______ **1.** Who are the bean eaters described in the poem?
- A A pair of shopkeepers
- B Two African American children
- C A set of dinner plates
- D An elderly couple

______ **2.** Brooks repeats the word *two* in the second stanza to emphasize that —
- F the bean eaters are united
- G the bean eaters have two children
- H everyone needs a friend
- J the bean eaters are usually separated

______ **3.** In the third stanza the poet lists "beads and receipts and dolls and cloths, tobacco crumbs, vases and fringes" to —
- A show objects that have meaning for the bean eaters
- B suggest how the bean eaters' dreams have vanished
- C reveal contempt for the bean eaters' empty lives
- D imply that the bean eaters are messy

______ **4.** Which word *best* describes the bean eaters' feeling about their life together?
- F Bitter
- G Contented
- H Resentful
- J Resigned

______ **5.** You can infer that the poet —
- A holds the bean eaters in contempt
- B admires the bean eaters' heroic endurance
- C believes that she will become a bean eater herself
- D actually knows the bean eaters

______ **6.** In "In Honor of David Anderson Brooks, My Father," what phrase *best* reveals the poet's love for her father?

F "A dryness is upon the house / My father loved and tended."

G "replies / To sun and wind forever."

H "And the fear that strikes and strives."

J "He who was Goodness, Gentleness, / And Dignity is free."

______ **7.** What does the poet suggest by the phrase in the second stanza that her father "walks in valleys now—replies / To sun and wind forever"?

A People feel comfort in nature.

B Her father is in a low period.

C Her father is in paradise.

D The sun and wind help people feel better.

______ **8.** The "cramping chamber's chill" and "hindering fever" in the second stanza symbolize her father's —

F bad case of the flu

G poor housing

H final illness

J heroic battle with sickness

______ **9.** What tone is shown in the third stanza, when the poet describes her father "out upon the wide clean air"?

A Regret

B Joy

C Anger

D Sorrow

______ **10.** The poet's theme reflects —

F her love and admiration for her father

G her belief that her father died too soon

H the importance of honoring your parents

J how love is passed down through the generations

LITERARY FOCUS: THE USES OF RHYME *(20 points; 5 points each)*

On the line provided, write the letter of the *best* answer to each of the following items.

______ **11.** **Rhyme** is *best* defined as the —

- **A** repetition of sounds in accented syllables and all succeeding syllables
- **B** pattern of stressed and unstressed syllables in oral and written language
- **C** beat or tempo of a poem
- **D** repetition of initial consonants or consonant sounds in a line of poetry

______ **12.** Which two words from "The Bean Eaters" rhyme?

- **F** affair/wood
- **G** day/clothes
- **H** good/away
- **J** pair/affair

______ **13.** In "The Bean Eaters," Brooks uses internal rhyme in the phrase "Bean Eaters" to —

- **A** show the poem's setting
- **B** helps readers get a visual image of the characters
- **C** make the phrase flowing and memorable
- **D** suggest how dreams vanish without our knowing it

______ **14.** What feeling does Brooks create in "The Bean Eaters" through her use of rhyme?

- **F** Depression and envy
- **G** Comfort and ease
- **H** Restlessness
- **J** Sorrow and grief

CONSTRUCTED RESPONSE *(20 points)*

15. "In Honor of David Anderson Brooks, My Father" pays homage to the poet's father. Identify at least two ways that Gwendolyn Brooks uses sound to develop this theme. On a separate sheet of paper, write a paragraph that explains your answer. Support your ideas with details from the selection.

NAME ______ CLASS ______ DATE ______ SCORE ______

Elsewhere Derek Walcott

COMPREHENSION *(60 points; 6 points each)*

On the line provided, write the letter of the *best* answer to each of the following items.

______ **1.** What effect does Walcott create in the first stanza by juxtaposing the image of a "white horse" to "barbed wire"?

- **A** He hints that people are like animals.
- **B** He suggests that freedom and innocence are imprisoned by evil.
- **C** He implies that animals are dangerous and should be kept in pens.
- **D** He advises people to escape from evil by running away.

______ **2.** The poet personifies the sea as a woman in the second stanza to —

- **F** suggest that women suffer from oppression more than men
- **G** suggest the unmeasurable tears wept by oppressed people
- **H** shift the setting to overseas
- **J** show that people by the sea suffer more than people who live inland

______ **3.** In the third stanza, what tone does the poet achieve by describing the murders as "a small harvest / of bodies in the truck"?

- **A** Ironic
- **B** Angry
- **C** Peaceful
- **D** Humorous

______ **4.** What sound devices does the poet use in the third stanza in the sentence "Soldiers rest / somewhere by a road, or smoke in a forest"?

- **F** Onomatopoeia and assonance
- **G** Internal rhyme and assonance
- **H** End rhyme and onomatopoeia
- **J** Alliteration and end rhyme

______ **5.** What does the speaker mean in the fourth stanza when he says: "And somehow the foliage / no longer looks like leaves but camouflage"?

- **A** War destroys forests.
- **B** War strikes hardest in tropical areas.
- **C** Forests have become a place where soldiers hide.
- **D** Fighters wear camouflage to protect themselves.

_____ **6.** The images of war and writing in the seventh stanza are *best* described as —

F soothing

G violent

H resentful

J contradictory

_____ **7.** Personifying writing as a person with "throat slit by the paper knife of the state" in the seventh stanza suggests —

A the state hates writers more than revolutionaries

B police states exist only where people are literate

C that even writers cannot combat injustice

D how the state fears the power of writing

_____ **8.** What does the speaker mean when he says, "Last year's massacres" fade like "the faceless numbers / that bewilder you in your telephone / diary"?

F We become numb to the unceasing terror in the world.

G People lose many friends and acquaintances in massacres.

H We don't need to know the people who were killed in mass murders.

J It is difficult to keep track of the different wars around the world.

_____ **9.** Whom does the speaker blame for the world's injustice?

A The world itself

B People who don't grasp the reality of suffering

C Rich people who profit from it

D Evil politicians who create it

_____ **10.** The theme of "Elsewhere" concerns the —

F importance of peace

G poet's personal losses

H powerlessness of writers to combat injustice

J oppression of the world's peoples

LITERARY FOCUS: REPETITION *(15 points; 5 points each)*

On the line provided, write the letter of the *best* answer to each of the following items.

_____ **11.** In poetry, **repetition** includes all of the following elements *except* the repeated use of the same —

- **A** sound
- **B** author
- **C** word
- **D** image or idea

_____ **12.** Poets use repetition to accomplish all of the following effects *except* —

- **F** conveying meaning and clarifying images
- **G** creating moods and evoking emotional responses
- **H** dividing scenes and acts from each other
- **J** building rhythms

_____ **13.** By repeating the word *somewhere,* Derek Walcott —

- **A** suggests that wars take place only in isolated places
- **B** reassures Americans that they are safe from terrorism
- **C** implies that no one is really sure where conflicts will erupt
- **D** suggests that terrorism is not here, for the moment

READING SKILLS: DETERMINING MEANING *(5 points)*

On the line provided, write the letter of the *best* answer to the following item.

_____ **14.** Which question could *best* help you determine the meaning of "Elsewhere"?

- **F** What do I know about Derek Walcott's life and other works?
- **G** What theme do the figures of speech, images, and tone suggest to me?
- **H** Why did Derek Walcott write this poem?
- **J** What feeling did I get when I finished reading this poem?

CONSTRUCTED RESPONSE *(20 points)*

15. "Elsewhere" describes terrible events. On a separate sheet of paper, identify one image, one example of personification, and one figure of speech that help create the poem's mood and meaning. Explain how these elements contribute to the author's philosophical argument in the poem. Support your ideas with details from the selection.

NAME ______ CLASS ______ DATE ______ SCORE ______

The Memory of Elena Carolyn Forché
Bearing Witness: An Interview with Carolyn Forché Bill Moyers

COMPREHENSION *(60 points; 6 points each)*

On the line provided, write the letter of the *best* answer to each of the following items.

______ **1.** In the opening of "The Memory of Elena," the speaker and Elena are —

- **A** in a restaurant
- **B** at a grave
- **C** in jail
- **D** in the flower stalls

______ **2.** What does the poet mean in the first stanza when she refers to waiting for "the silence of an hour"?

- **F** It is so noisy that the speaker and Elena cannot hear themselves talk.
- **G** Elena is waiting for a brief pause from the pain of the past.
- **H** Elena and the speaker are being watched and their conversation is being recorded.
- **J** It is nearly dusk, when people take a break from their daily activities.

______ **3.** When was the last time Elena saw her husband?

- **A** Three months ago
- **B** Three years ago
- **C** Five years ago
- **D** Thirty years ago

______ **4.** What images are juxtaposed in the third stanza?

- **F** Bones and trees
- **G** Horses and flowers
- **H** Food and body parts
- **J** Bells and gravestones

______ **5.** In the third stanza the poet pairs these particular images in order to —

- **A** show how the past and present merge
- **B** suggest that the present is better than the past
- **C** imply that food has great power to soothe people
- **D** show that everything is part of nature

_____ **6.** The poet uses alliteration in the phrase, "This is the ring / of a rifle report on the stones" to suggest —

F the importance of resistance
G the sound of violence
H the newspaper stories of the murder
J Elena's lasting sorrow

_____ **7.** The speaker's tone is *best de*scribed as —

A calm and resigned
B terrified
C fierce and bitter
D impatient

_____ **8.** Carolyn Forché wrote this poem in order to —

F describe the impact of a historical event
G persuade Elena to leave her homeland
H warn people to stay away from foreign countries
J raise money to help people injured in wars

_____ **9.** Unlike Forché's poem, Bill Moyer's interview —

A includes vivid figures of speech
B presents shocking images of the scene
C passes judgment on the people involved
D summarizes the story of Elena and her husband

_____ **10.** In Bill Moyer's interview, Forché —

F tells what Elena is doing today
G describes political oppression all over the world
H persuades people to fight dictatorships
J explains her reason for writing "The Memory of Elena"

NAME ______________________ CLASS ______________ DATE __________ SCORE __________

LITERARY FOCUS: IMAGERY *(20 points; 5 points each)*
On the line provided, write the letter of the *best* answer to each of the following items.

______ **11.** Read the following image from the first stanza: "the dark tongues of bells / that hang from ropes waiting / for the silence of an hour." To which senses does it appeal?

- **A** Touch and taste
- **B** Sight and sound
- **C** Taste and sight
- **D** Touch and smell

______ **12.** What tone does the poet achieve with the image of "the soft blue of a leg socket" in the third stanza?

- **F** Gentle and soothing
- **G** Encouraging
- **H** Grim and horrifying
- **J** Appetizing

______ **13.** The image of "the hollow / clopping of a horse" most strongly appeals to the sense of —

- **A** sound
- **B** touch
- **C** smell
- **D** sight

______ **14.** The repeated image of "bells / waiting with their tongues cut out" serves all the following rhetorical purposes *except* to —

- **F** reinforce the poem's theme
- **G** establish the poem's setting
- **H** emphasize the poem's terrifying mood
- **J** highlight the poem's topic

CONSTRUCTED RESPONSE *(20 points)*

15. Based on your reading of "The Memory of Elena," what is Carolyn Forché's view of political oppression? How is her opinion a result of a particular historical period? On a separate sheet of paper, write a paragraph explaining your answer. Use images and figures of speech from the poem to make your point.

Ars Poetica Claribel Alegría *translated by* D. J. Flakoll

COMPREHENSION *(60 points; 6 points each)*

On the line provided, write the letter of the *best* answer to each of the following items.

______ **1.** In "Ars Poetica," Claribel Alegría defines herself as —

A a ray of sunshine
B Venus de Milo
C a crow
D a poet

______ **2.** Who or what could "condemn" the poet to be a "crow"?

F Only other poets and writers
G Society or herself
H Federal judges
J Other birds

______ **3.** You can infer from the context that the Louvre must be a —

A museum
B tomb
C statue
D government

______ **4.** By using the word *reigns* to describe the Venus de Milo, the poet suggests that —

F the Venus de Milo is vastly overrated
G people should worship the Venus de Milo
H the Venus de Milo is real
J the Venus de Milo is regal in her beauty

______ **5.** Why would the Venus de Milo "die[s] of boredom"?

A She does nothing but stand.
B She would rather be a writer.
C People never go to see her.
D She is not very intelligent.

______ **6.** You can infer from Alegría's repudiation of the Venus de Milo that the poet believes that —

F museums are boring
G people should read poems rather than view art
H poets should have an active role in the world
J the Venus de Milo is not attractive

_____ **7.** Which of the following lines contain alliteration?

A "while she reigns in the Louvre / and dies of boredom . . ."

B "and amid valleys / volcanos . . ."

C "and collects dust / I discover the sun. . . ."

D "How could I count my blessings . . ."

_____ **8.** As used in this poem, what do the "valleys," "volcanoes," and "debris of war" symbolize?

F Natural disasters

G Life's low points and dramatic events

H Conflicts between humanity and nature

J The poet's personal disappointments

_____ **9.** The tone of this poem is *best* described as —

A grisly

B despairing

C hopeful

D sad

_____ **10.** A theme of this poem might be —

F persevere and you will succeed

G life is difficult

H there is only one way to write a poem

J there is more than one way to skin a cat

LITERARY FOCUS: ALLUSION *(20 points; 5 points each)*
On the line provided, write the letter of the *best* answer to each of the following items.

_____ **11.** An **allusion** is —

A a reference to a well-known place, event, person, work of art, or other work of literature

B a brief story that interests the reader and sheds light on the writer's main idea

C the repetition of initial consonant sounds in several words in a sentence or line of poetry

D the force or person in conflict with the main character in a work of literature

_____ **12.** Writers use allusions in their works for all of the following reasons *except* to —

F convey the theme

G create a rhythm or beat

H help establish the tone

J lead to new ideas and associations

_______ **13.** The mention of the Venus de Milo is an allusion to a —

A prestigious Italian town
B celebrated political leader
C famous work of art
D notable poet

_______ **14.** By making an allusion to the "promised land" at the end of the poem, Alegría —

F forges a link between poetry and death
G implies that poets promise more than they can deliver
H implies that poets have little hope of being appreciated in their lifetime
J suggests the emotional rewards of being a poet

CONSTRUCTED RESPONSE *(20 points)*

15. Claribel Alegría identifies herself as a Salvadoran, while Derek Walcott grew up in the Caribbean. How do their different cultural traditions affect their work? On a separate sheet of paper, compare and contrast Alegría's "Ars Poetica" to Walcott's "Elsewhere," showing how they are the same as well as different. In your analysis, consider such elements as theme, style, and trends.

The Latin Deli: An Ars Poetica Judith Ortiz Cofer

COMPREHENSION *(60 points; 6 points each)*

On the line provided, write the letter of the *best* answer to each of the following items.

______ **1.** The poem's setting is a —

A church

B small neighborhood store

C big supermarket

D foreign-owned department store

______ **2.** The Patroness of Exiles is the —

F fragile old man

G poet herself

H store owner

J Cuban customer

______ **3.** What does Judith Ortiz Cofer mean by the term "canned memories"?

A The goods that help customers recall their past

B False memories that mislead people

C Speaking in foreign languages

D Stale candies that recall childhood joys

______ **4.** To which senses does the following image appeal?

"She spends her days
slicing *jamón y queso* and wrapping it in wax paper
tied with string. . . ."

F sight and smell

G touch and sound

H taste and smell

J sight, touch, and taste

______ **5.** Cofer includes sensory images for all of the following reasons *except* to —

A evoke the poem's mood

B help readers imagine the setting

C make the number of lines match established form

D convey her meaning

______ **6.** Cofer links the codfish and green plantains to "votive offerings" to suggest that —

F people worship food that is difficult to obtain

G the plantains are stale and waxy

H the store is a holy place for the comfort it offers

J people pay too much money for these foods

______ **7.** *Most* of the images in "The Latin Deli" refer to —

A food and places

B money and work

C toys and gifts

D travel and leisure items

______ **8.** The poem's tone is *best* described as —

F tragic and depressing

G gentle and understanding

H ironic

J smug and scornful

______ **9.** The *central* character in this poem is —

A the ghost of the speaker's lost love

B a female shopkeeper

C a poet who writes in Spanish

D the speaker's sister

______ **10.** The poem's theme is *best* stated as —

F People often have trouble adjusting to life in a new country.

G America is the land of opportunity.

H Dreams die hard.

J Offering comfort to others is a kind of poetry.

LITERARY FOCUS: CONCRETE AND ABSTRACT LANGUAGE *(20 points; 5 points each)*
On the line provided, write the letter of the *best* answer to each of the following items.

______ **11. Concrete language** is language that —

A restricts itself to one– and two–syllable words

B uses sensory details to describe

C comes from other cultures

D is hard to understand

NAME ______ CLASS ______ DATE ______ SCORE ______

______ **12.** **Abstract language** is *best* defined as —

- **F** language that people use in business settings
- **G** words that do not have synonyms
- **H** language that deals with concepts
- **J** words that have two or more syllables

______ **13.** Which of the following lines from "The Latin Deli" is the *best* example of concrete language?

- **A** "They speak to her and each other / of their dreams. . . ."
- **B** "who spends her days selling canned memories . . ."
- **C** "how she smiles understanding . . ."
- **D** "the green plantains / hanging in stalks like votive offerings . . ."

______ **14.** Which is the *best* interpretation of the abstract language in the last three lines of "The Latin Deli"?

- **F** The woman always tries to meet the unspoken needs of her customers.
- **G** Some of the woman's customers forget what they came to buy.
- **H** People from different countries ask the woman to guess what they want.
- **J** The woman needs to stock more important goods in her store.

Constructed Response *(20 points)*

15. Claribel Alegría and Judith Ortiz Cofer both wrote a poem with "Ars Poetica" in the title. Alegría is a Salvadoran, while Cofer comes from Puerto Rico. How are the two poems similar? On a separate sheet of paper, write a paragraph that explains your answer. Support your ideas with details from the two poems.

NAME ______ CLASS ______ DATE ______ SCORE ______

SELECTION TEST **Student Edition page 1083**

Testimonial Rita Dove

COMPREHENSION *(60 points; 6 points each)*

On the line provided, write the letter of the *best* answer to each of the following items.

______ **1.** Rita Dove uses the word *testimonial* to refer to —

A a certificate

B a reference

C a recommendation

D celebration and thanks

______ **2.** According to the first stanza, "Testimonial" appears to be set —

F in heaven

G before there was any life on earth

H when dinosaurs roamed the earth

J in prehistoric days, when people lived in caves

______ **3.** In actuality the opening stanza refers to —

A right before the poet was born

B the poet's childhood

C when the poet was a young wife and mother

D when the poet was in her early thirties

______ **4.** What does the phrase "rank and file" in line 8 mean?

F Rancid

G Complete

H Lying down

J In a neat order

______ **5.** How are the details and images arranged in this poem?

A In chronological order

B According to advantages and disadvantages

C From least to most important

D From most to least important

______ **6.** What does the poet mean when she says, "Each glance ignited to a gaze. / I caught my breath and called that life"?

F People stare at her because she is attractive.

G She comes to life when she becomes a poet.

H She falls in love easily, over and over.

J She is fascinated and excited by everything.

______ **7.** Someone could be "pirouette and flourish" if she —

A flaunted her talent and alienated people

B danced and prospered

C were enthusiastic and exuberant

D wrote with a large, showy scrawl

______ **8.** What mental picture does the image "filigree and flame" create?

F Harsh and metallic

G Delicate and brilliant

H Fragile but violent

J Slender and easily angered

______ **9.** Overall, how does the poet feel about her life?

A She is thrilled at the opportunities she has accepted.

B She understands that she wasted too much time.

C She feels she has been cheated in life.

D She regrets letting her luck escape.

______ **10.** What advice does Dove give to her readers?

F Seize life's opportunities.

G Get started early in life.

H Don't promise more than you can deliver.

J Never let strangers follow you.

LITERARY FOCUS: SOUND EFFECTS *(20 points; 5 points each)*

On the line provided, write the letter of the *best* answer to each of the following items.

______ **11. Sound effects** in poetry include all of the following elements *except* —

A rhyme

B stanzas

C onomatopoeia

D alliteration

______ **12.** Which of the following lines from the poem does *not* contain alliteration?

F "when all the poplars quivered"

G "melted summer into autumn"

H "I was filigree and flame"

J "How could I count my blessings"

______ **13.** Which pair of words rhyme?

A life/lemon

B flourish/flame

C blessings/names

D flame/names

______ **14.** Dove used assonance in which of the following phrases?

F "I gave my promise to the world"

G "when all the poplars quivered"

H "the world called, and I answered"

J "swooned between spoonfuls of lemon sorbet"

CONSTRUCTED RESPONSE *(20 points)*

15. Based on your reading of "Testimonial," what comment do you think Rita Dove is making about life? How does she use imagery and sounds to evoke your emotions and convey her theme? On a separate sheet of paper, write a paragraph that explains your answer. Support your ideas with details from the poem.

Coastal Mark Doty

COMPREHENSION *(60 points; 6 points each)*

On the line provided, write the letter of the *best* answer to each of the following items.

______ **1.** When and where does the poem take place?

- **A** During the winter at the Center for Coastal Studies
- **B** On a cold April day in town near the water
- **C** In February at a seashore resort
- **D** In the late afternoon by a park

______ **2.** The plumber's daughter rescues a —

- **F** bouquet of crushed tulips
- **G** sick bird
- **H** crazy person
- **J** small child

______ **3.** The poet indicates dialogue by —

- **A** using quotation marks
- **B** using italics
- **C** indenting the lines
- **D** using boldface type

______ **4.** The poet uses a metaphor in comparing the sick loon to a —

- **F** plumber's daughter
- **G** harbor
- **H** pink parka
- **J** tulip

______ **5.** At first, what is the speaker's attitude toward the girl's rescue of the loon?

- **A** Admiration for her bravery
- **B** Fear that she will be injured
- **C** Regret for her foolishness
- **D** Scorn for her ignorance

______ **6.** By calling the bird "this emissary of air," the poet suggests that it is —

- **F** a holy object
- **G** stronger than it looks
- **H** a messenger of the intangible
- **J** more human than it appears

______ **7.** What does the girl intend to do with the bird?

A Keep it as a pet
B Call the Center for Coastal Studies to rescue it
C Give it to the speaker for his children to raise
D Bring it to class

______ **8.** The girl rescues the bird because she —

F wants an unusual pet
G is compassionate
H is playing a joke on the speaker
J wants to study it

______ **9.** The image of the girl's coat as "petal-bright" suggests —

A death
B winter's chill
C the bird's blood
D her innocence

______ **10.** The title "Coastal" can be interpreted literally and symbolically as —

F the seacoast and the line between life and death
G the shore and the poet's interest in marine life
H the beach and life
J birds and death

LITERARY FOCUS: TONE *(20 points; 5 points each)*

On the line provided, write the letter of the *best* answer to each of the following items.

______ **11.** A writer's attitude toward a subject or an audience is called —

A sound
B tone
C pitch
D irony

______ **12.** Which of the following words *cannot* be used to describe tone?

F Joyful
G Melancholy
H Unrhymed
J Fiery

______ **13.** What is the speaker's tone in the last line, "Stubborn girl"?

A Sorrowful

B Pitying

C Scornful

D Admiring

______ **14.** The poet uses a shift in tone to —

F reinforce the poem's theme

G emphasize vivid visual images

H create a rhythmic pattern

J establish the setting

CONSTRUCTED RESPONSE *(20 points)*

15. Poems often evoke strong emotions in readers. Identify the feeling Mark Doty evokes in "Coastal." Then, on a separate sheet of paper, write a paragraph explaining how he creates this feeling through tone, imagery, and figures of speech. Use specific details and examples from the poem to support your analysis.

Visions and Interpretations Li-Young Lee

COMPREHENSION *(60 points; 6 points each)*

On the line provided, write the letter of the *best* answer to each of the following items.

______ **1.** From what point of view is the poem narrated?

A All-knowing

B Omniscient

C Third person

D First person

______ **2.** The poem opens with a dream. Where does the dream take place?

F Under a tree in the speaker's yard

G At the funeral of the speaker's father

H In a graveyard

J In the speaker's house

______ **3.** What does the phrase "my father came down to me" suggest about the speaker's opinion of his father?

A The speaker feels that his father was a good, virtuous man.

B The speaker thinks his father was distant and aloof.

C The speaker knows that his father was not capable of loving anyone.

D The speaker dislikes his father.

______ **4.** The phrase "never mentioned his grave, / erect like a door behind him" is an example of —

F onomatopoeia

G alliteration

H personification

J a simile

______ **5.** According to lines 18–20, how often has the speaker seen his father since he died?

A A few times

B Never

C Often

D Every week

______ **6.** What do you think the speaker means when he refers to the blossoms as "often heavy as sodden newspaper"?

F The newspaper gets wet from the water in the flowers' stems.

G He would rather be home reading his newspaper.

H He approaches his father's grave with a heavy heart.

J The flowers looks gray and unappealing.

_____ **7.** The speaker repeats the word *between* in lines 31–32 to —

A show that he is caught between two worlds
B suggest that he will die shortly and join his father
C imply that everyone is trapped between love and hate
D allude to his father's death

_____ **8.** Based on the setting and context, what do the yellow and white chrysanthemums in lines 32–33 most likely symbolize?

F Life
G Death
H Love
J Separation

_____ **9.** The speaker keeps telling the same story from different vantage points in order to —

A suggest the suffering his father endured before his death
B help himself come to terms with his father's death
C show how everyone looks at life and death from different viewpoints
D help people deal with the losses in their own life

_____ **10.** You can infer from the line "and all of my visions and interpretations / depend on what I see" that the speaker —

F believes there is only one way to understand reality
G realizes that people tend to see things in the same way
H often has hallucinations of past events
J feels that events are open to individual interpretations

LITERARY FOCUS: THEME *(20 points; 5 points each)*

On the line provided, write the letter of the *best* answer to each of the following items.

_____ **11.** A poem's **theme** —

A is the same as its topic or subject
B can be stated in one word
C is an insight about life
D is rarely linked to the poem's title

______ **12.** In general, poets often —

- **F** provide clues to the poem's theme
- **G** state their theme directly in the first or last stanza
- **H** reveal something new in their themes
- **J** deliberately make their themes difficult to figure out

______ **13.** The **subject** of "Visions and Interpretations" is —

- **A** how the poet deals with his father's death
- **B** the speaker's own death as well as his child's death
- **C** explaining death to a child
- **D** showing respect for a parent

______ **14.** The poem's **theme** can best be stated as —

- **F** everything that lives must die.
- **G** it is important to show respect for the dead.
- **H** time helps us cope with loss and deep sorrow.
- **J** it is difficult to deal with the loss of a loved one.

CONSTRUCTED RESPONSE *(20 points)*

15. Based on your reading of "Visions and Interpretations," what is the poem's message about life, loss, and love? How did Li-Young Lee convey the message through imagery, personification, figures of speech, and sounds? State the theme, and discuss at least two poetic techniques Lee uses to convey it. Support your ideas with specific details from the poem.

Medusa Agha Shahid Ali

COMPREHENSION *(60 points; 6 points each)*
On the line provided, write the letter of the *best* answer to each of the following items.

______ **1.** Who is the speaker in this poem?
- **A** Medusa
- **B** The poet
- **C** Perseus
- **D** Medusa's sisters

______ **2.** Why are men speechless when they see Medusa?
- **F** She is so beautiful that they are awe-struck.
- **G** She turns them to stone.
- **H** They do not believe that she is real.
- **J** They are too busy trying to kill her.

______ **3.** Which of the following lines from the poem contains alliteration?
- **A** "I have populated the countryside / with animals of stone. . . ."
- **B** "and sunning our ruffled snakes . . ."
- **C** "I too was human, I who now live here / at the end of the world. . . ."
- **D** "I am waiting for the Mediterranean / to see me. . . ."

______ **4.** Medusa was transformed from a —
- **F** mean person to a kind one
- **G** god to a mortal
- **H** monster to a woman
- **J** woman to a monster

______ **5.** Medusa's attitude about her life and appearance can *best* be described as —
- **A** depressed and resigned
- **B** gratified and brave
- **C** sorrowful but defiant
- **D** indifferent and apathetic

______ **6.** Medusa plans to turn into stone all the following subjects *except* —
- **F** the Mediterranean Sea
- **G** a cargo of slaves
- **H** her sisters
- **J** the sky

_____ **7.** Medusa wants to turn people and objects into stone because she —

A is angry at being denied love

B knows it will make her famous

C wants more stone statues to decorate her cave

D is bored and has nothing else to do

_____ **8.** The "sun-crimsoned shield / blinds her [Medusa] into nightmare." The shield does this by —

F turning her back into a human

G killing her

H robbing her of her sight

J dissolving her

_____ **9.** The poet creates suspense by —

A not allowing Perseus to present his side of the story

B withholding Medusa's fate until the end of the poem

C foreshadowing Medusa's fate in the opening lines

D making Medusa into an evil monster

_____ **10.** To what senses does the following image appeal?

"Restless in her sleep, she,
for the last time, brushes back
the hissing curls from her forehead."

F Sight and smell

G Touch and hearing

H Sight

J Sight, touch, hearing

LITERARY FOCUS: ARCHETYPES *(20 points; 5 points each)*
On the line provided, write the letter of the *best* answer to each of the following items.

_____ **11.** An **archetype** is —

A the repetition of initial consonant sounds

B an original pattern that is repeated through the ages

C a reference to a well-known place, event, person, or work of art

D a story of ideas instead of action

______ **12.** Which of the following items is *not* an archetype in literature and culture?

F Superman

G Cinderella

H Computers

J Lions and lambs

______ **13.** Medusa is an archetype because —

A she is an evil monster

B she is a female character

C she comes from ancient Greek myths

D her story has been retold many times

______ **14.** By using the archetype of Medusa, Agha Shahid Ali —

F links his poem to a long literary tradition

G makes his poem rhythmical

H does not have to use images or figures of speech

J reveals the poem's ending from the start

CONSTRUCTED RESPONSE *(20 points)*

15. "Medusa" concerns a famous metamorphosis, or transformation. Select another famous archetypal metamorphosis that is similar to the story of Medusa. On a separate sheet of paper, discuss how the metamorphoses are the same as well as different. Support your ideas with details from the poem and with your knowledge.

NAME ______ CLASS ______ DATE ______ SCORE ______

SELECTION TEST **Student Edition page 1098** LITERARY RESPONSE AND ANALYSIS

Man Listening to Disc Billy Collins

COMPREHENSION *(60 points; 6 points each)*

On the line provided, write the letter of the *best* answer to each of the following items.

______ **1.** You can infer from context clues that Sonny Rollins is —

A the speaker's pet bird
B a friend of the speaker's
C an actor
D a musician

______ **2.** In line 2, the poet used the word *ambling* to help readers —

F understand that the speaker is in a hurry
G visualize the relaxed way the speaker is walking
H imagine the speaker scowling at his fellow pedestrians
J feel the poem's beat

______ **3.** Which of the following phrases contains alliteration?

A "the pavement sparkling with sunlight"
B "pigeons fluttering off the curb"
C "nodding over a profusion of bread crumbs"
D "my delight at being suffused"

______ **4.** The poet breaks a sentence between the third and fourth stanzas in order to —

F show that his disc player is breaking down
G indicate that he has started humming along with the music
H suggest that he prefers one performer to another
J show the break in music from one performer to another

______ **5.** What effect does the poet create when he says, "the esteemed Arthur Taylor / who is somehow managing to navigate / this crowd with his cumbersome drums"?

A Bitterness
B Sarcasm
C Humor
D Envy

______ **6.** In the sixth stanza the poet says he feels more like the "center of the universe" than usual because —

F he is all alone on the street, having chased everyone else away
G Thelonious Monk is a personal friend of his
H the music is loud and isolates him from others
J he is the only one on the street to have a disc player

______ **7.** Why does the speaker want to tell the other pedestrians to "watch your step"?

A The musicians are pushing and shoving to get next to the speaker.

B He wants them to listen to good music, not trash.

C He imagines all the musicians are crossing the street with him.

D The pedestrians are standing too close to the speaker.

______ **8.** How many people are walking with the speaker?

F None

G One

H Two

J Five

______ **9.** The topic of this poem is —

A the poet's taste in music

B different types of music

C the importance of having friends

D the power of music and imagination

______ **10.** The tone of this poem is *best* characterized as —

F cynical and mocking

G light and humorous

H serious and thoughtful

J bitter and resentful

LITERARY FOCUS: STYLE *(20 points; 5 points each)*
On the line provided, write the letter of the *best* answer to each of the following items.

______ **11.** In literature, **style** includes all of the following elements *except* —

A genre

B word choice

C figures of speech

D sentence length and variety

______ **12.** A writer's **style** can be described in all of the following ways *except* —

F elevated

G informal

H elegant

J thematic

______ **13.** What stylistic effect does the speaker create with the following simile?

"with phrases from his saxophone—"
some like honey, some like vinegar—"

A He indicates the type of music he likes.
B He identifies the musicians in the passage.
C He mimics the sound of the music.
D He imitates the motion of the people on the street.

______ **14.** Billy Collins crafted the particular style he used in "Man Listening to Disc" to —

F distract his readers
G reinforce his topic and theme
H imitate other poets
J intensify the poem's grim mood

CONSTRUCTED RESPONSE *(20 points)*

15. In "Man Listening to Disc," Billy Collins uses language to achieve a specific aesthetic purpose. On a separate sheet of paper, identify at least two stylistic devices—irony, tone, mood, and sound devices, for example—he uses to achieve his purpose. Back up your ideas with details from the poem.

COLLECTION 6 SUMMATIVE TEST

Contemporary Literature: 1939 to Present

This test asks you to use the skills and strategies you have learned in this collection. Read the following passage from *Bone* and then answer the questions that follow it.

FROM Bone
by Fae Myenne Ng

Everything had an alert quality. Brisk wind, white light. I turned down Sacramento and walked down the hill at a snap-quick pace toward Mah's Baby Store.

Mason was the one who started calling it the Baby Store, and the name just stuck. The old sign with the characters for "Herb Shop" still hangs precariously above the door. I've offered to take it down for Mah, but she's said No every time. Mason thinks she wants to hide.

An old carousel pony with a gouged eye and chipped tail stands in front of the store like a guard looking out onto Grant Avenue. I tapped it as I walked past, my quick good-luck stroke. A string of bells jingled as I pushed through the double doors.

A bitter ginseng odor and honeysuckle balminess greeted me. Younger, more Americanized mothers complain that the baby clothes have absorbed these old world odors. They must complain about how old the place looks, too, with custom-made drawers that line the wall from floor to ceiling, the factory lighting. Leon wanted to tear down the wall of mahogany drawers and build a new storage unit. But Mah doesn't want him touching anything in her store, and I was glad, too, because I love the tuck-perfect fit of the drawers, and the *tock!* sound the brass handles make against the hard wood.

Mah was showing off her newest stock of jackets to a woman and her child. I gave a quick nod and went straight to the back, where the boxes were stacked two-high. The fluorescent lights glowed, commercial bright.

The woman tried to bargain the price down but Mah wouldn't budge; she changed the subject. "Your girl is very pretty. How about I don't charge tax?"

Hearing that gave me courage. Mah was in a generous, no-tax mood, and that gave me high hopes for some kind of big discount, too. I knew I'd be tongue-tied soon, so I tried to press my worry down by telling myself what Grandpa Leong used to tell me, that the best way to conquer fear is to act.

Open the mouth and tell.

As soon as the woman and her child walked out the door, I went up to Mah and started out in Chinese, "I want to tell you something."

Mah looked up, wide-eyed, expectant.

I switched to English. "Time was right, so Mason and I just went to City Hall. We got married there."

Mah's expression didn't change.

"In New York," I said.

No answer.

"You know I never liked banquets, all that noise and trouble. And such a waste of so much money."

She still didn't say anything. Suddenly I realized how quiet it was, and that we were completely alone in the store. I heard the hum of the lights.

"Mah?" I said. "Say something."

She didn't even look at me, she just walked away. She went to the back of the store and ripped open a box. I followed her and watched her bend the flaps back and pull out armfuls of baby clothes. I waited. She started stacking little mounds. She smoothed out sleeves on top of sleeves, zipped zippers, and cupped the colored hoods, one into another. All around our feet were tangles of white hangers.

"Nina was my witness." My voice was whispery, strange.

Mah grunted, a huumph sound that came out like a curse. My translation was: Disgust, anger. There's power behind her sounds. Over the years I've listened and rendered her Chinese grunts into English words.

She threw the empty box on the floor and gave it a quick kick.

"Just like that.
Did it and didn't tell.
Mother Who Raised You.
Years of work, years of worry.
Didn't! Even! Tell!

What could I say? Using Chinese was my undoing. She had a world of words that were beyond me.

Mah reached down and picked up a tangle of hangers. She poked them into the baby down coats, baby overalls, baby sleepers. Her wrists whipped back and forth in a way that reminded me of how she used to butcher birds on Salmon Alley. Chickens, pheasants, and pigeons, once a frog. The time with the frog was terrible. Mah skinned it and then stopped. She held the twitching muscle out toward us; she wanted us to see its pink heart. Her voice was spooky, breathless: "Look how the heart keeps beating!" Then the frog sprang out of her hand, still vigorous.

Now I said in English, "It was no big deal."

"It is!"

Mah was using her sewing-factory voice, and I remembered her impatience whenever I tried to talk to her while she was sewing on a deadline.

She rapped a hanger on the counter. "Marriage is for a lifetime, and it should be celebrated! Why sneak around, why act like a thief in the dark?"

I wanted to say: I didn't marry in shame. I didn't marry like you. Your marriages are not my fault. Don't blame me.

Just then the bells jingled and I looked up and saw two sewing ladies coming through the door. I recognized the round hair, the hawk eyes.

"What?" I was too upset to stop. "What?" I demanded again. "You don't like Mason, is that it?"

"Mason," Mah spoke his name soft, "I love."

For love, she used a Chinese word: to embrace, to hug.

I stepped around the boxes, opened my arms and hugged Mah. I held her and took a deep breath and smelled the dried honeysuckle stems, the bitter ginseng root. Above us, the lights beamed bright.

I heard the bells jingle, the latch click, and looked up to see the broad backs of the ladies going out the door toward Grant Avenue. They were going to Portsmouth Square, and I knew they were talking up everything they heard, not stopping when they passed their husbands by the chess tables, not stopping until they found their sewing-lady friends on the benches of the lower level. And that's when they'd tell, tell their long-stitched version of the story, from beginning to end.

And let them make it up, I thought, Let them talk.

VOCABULARY SKILLS *(25 points; 5 points each)*
Each of the underlined words below has also been underlined in the selection. Re-read those passages in which the underlined words appear, and then use context clues and your prior knowledge to select an answer. On the line provided, write the letter of the word or words that best completes the sentence.

_____ **1.** A plate that is placed precariously on a table —
- **A** looks elegant and stylish
- **B** is in danger of falling
- **C** does not draw attention
- **D** cost a great deal of money

_____ **2.** A gouged piece of wood probably has —
- **F** bumper stickers
- **G** new decorations
- **H** knotholes
- **J** grooves or holes

_____ **3.** A scent that gives off balminess is —
- **A** soothing
- **B** unfamiliar
- **C** addictive
- **D** foul

_____ **4.** Mahogany is a type of —
- **F** wood
- **G** paper
- **H** pasteboard
- **J** personality

_____ **5.** Words that have been rendered have been —
- **A** confronted
- **B** mocked
- **C** translated
- **D** lost

NAME ______ CLASS ______ DATE ______ SCORE ______

COMPREHENSION *(25 points; 5 points each)*

On the line provided, write the letter of the *best* answer to each of the following items.

______ **6.** When the narrator comes into the store —

F two women come in behind her

G her mother is doing business with a customer

H she immediately begins talking to her mother

J she learns that her mother has sold the business

______ **7.** In the excerpt we learn all of the following things about Mah *except* that she —

A eloped when she was her daughter's age

B used to butcher birds for food

C normally does not bargain with customers

D has been married more than once

______ **8.** Mother and daughter seem to reconcile when the —

F mother says she loves Mason

G daughter reminds her mother of her past problems

H daughter helps her mother fold baby clothes

J mother gives her daughter advice

______ **9.** How does the narrator's mood at the end of the selection differ from her mood at its beginning?

A She is more preoccupied.

B She is more relaxed.

C She seems depressed.

D She regrets her actions.

______ **10.** What are the ladies leaving the store going to do?

F Sew with their friends

G Meet their husbands

H Shop in another store

J Gossip about the narrator and her mother

Reading Skills and Strategies: Constructed Response *(30 points; 15 points each)*

Analyzing Conflict

11. What is the *most* significant external conflict in this story? On a separate sheet of paper, write the letter of the answer you choose, and briefly defend your choice. Use at least one example from the excerpt to support your idea.

A The narrator deciding whether or not to say that Mah married in shame

B The narrator trying to talk to her mother about having gotten married without her mother's knowledge

C The customer bargaining with the narrator's mother

D The narrator confronting the customers about gossiping

Analyzing Theme

12. What is the theme of this excerpt? What comment about life does the writer explore? On a separate sheet of paper, write a paragraph to explain the theme, supporting your conclusions with examples from the passage.

LITERARY FOCUS: CONSTRUCTED RESPONSE *(20 points)*

Evaluating Style

13. Authors include specific stylistic elements to achieve their purposes. Complete the following chart to explore Fae Myenne Ng's unique use of language.

Stylistic Element	Example	Purpose
Unusual use of capital letters		
Dialect		
Dialogue		
Italics		
Point of view		
Sensory details		

NAME CLASS DATE

End-of-Year Test

Reading and Literary Analysis

DIRECTIONS Read the following excerpt. Then answer questions 1 through 12.

from *Hunger of Memory*
by Richard Rodriguez

In fourth grade I embarked upon a grandiose reading program. "Give me the names of important books," I would say to startled teachers. They soon found out that I had in mind "adult books." I ignored their suggestions of anything I suspected was written for children. (Not until I was in college, as a result, did I read *Huckleberry Finn* or *Alice's Adventures in Wonderland*.) Instead, I read *The Scarlet Letter* and Franklin's *Autobiography*. And whatever I read I read for extra credit. Each time I finished a book, I reported the achievement to a teacher and basked in the praise my effort earned. Despite my best efforts, however, there seemed to be more and more books I needed to read. At the library I would literally tremble as I came upon whole shelves of books I hadn't read. So I read and I read and I read: *Great Expectations*; all the short stories of Kipling; *The Babe Ruth Story*; the entire first volume of the *Encyclopaedia Britannica* (A–ANSTEY); the *Iliad*; *Moby Dick*; *Gone with the Wind*; *The Good Earth*; *Ramona*; *Forever Amber*; *The Lives of the Saints*; *Crime and Punishment*; *The Pearl*. . . . Librarians who initially frowned when I checked out the maximum ten books at a time started saving books they thought I might like. Teachers would say to the rest of the class, "I only wish the rest of you took reading as seriously as Richard obviously does."

But at home I would hear my mother wondering, "What do you see in your books?" (Was reading a hobby like her knitting? Was so much reading even healthy for a boy? Was it a sign of "brains"? Or was it just a convenient excuse for not helping around the house on Saturday mornings?) Always, "What do you see . . . ?"

. . . I entered high school having read hundreds of books. My habit of reading made me a confident speaker and writer of English. Reading also enabled me to sense something of the shape, the major concerns, of Western thought. (I was able to say something about Dante and Descartes and Engels and James Baldwin[1] in my high school term papers.) In these

1 **Dante . . . Baldwin:** Dante Alighieri, Italian poet (1265–1321), author of *The Divine Comedy*; René Descartes, French philosopher and mathematician (1596–1650); Friedrich Engels, German writer and socialist leader (1820–1895); James Baldwin, American writer (1924–1987), author of fiction, essays, and plays

GO ON

various ways, books brought me academic success as I hoped that they would. But I was not a good reader. Merely bookish, I lacked a point of view when I read. Rather, I read in order to acquire a point of view. I vacuumed books for epigrams, scraps of information, ideas, themes—anything to fill the hollow within me and make me feel educated. When one of my teachers suggested to his drowsy tenth-grade English class that a person could not have a "complicated idea" until he had read at least two thousand books, I heard the remark without detecting either its irony or its very complicated truth. I merely determined to compile a list of all the books I had ever read. Harsh with myself, I included only once a title I might have read several times. (How, after all, could one read a book more than once?) And I included only those books over a hundred pages in length. (Could anything shorter be a book?)

There was yet another high school list I compiled. One day I came across a newspaper article about the retirement of an English professor at a nearby state college. The article was accompanied by a list of the "hundred most important books of Western Civilization." "More than anything else in my life," the professor told the reporter with finality, "these books have made me all that I am." That was the kind of remark I couldn't ignore. I clipped out the list and kept it for the several months it took me to read all the titles. Most books, of course, I barely understood. While reading Plato's *Republic*, for instance, I needed to keep looking at the book jacket comments to remind myself what the text was about. Nevertheless, with the special patience and superstition of a scholarship boy, I looked at every word of the text. And by the time I reached the last word, relieved, I convinced myself that I had read *The Republic*. In a ceremony of great pride, I solemnly crossed Plato off my list.

1 Based on this excerpt, you can conclude that *Hunger of Memory* is probably—

- **A** an editorial comment
- **B** an autobiographical essay
- **C** a personal journal
- **D** a persuasive essay

2 Which phrase BEST describes the tone of this passage?

- **A** reflective
- **B** satirical
- **C** whimsical
- **D** instructive

GO ON

3 **The passage is organized MAINLY by—**

A order of importance

B comparison and contrast

C chronological order

D citation of problems and their solutions

4 **Why did the author avoid reading children's books in elementary school?**

A He wanted to impress his peers.

B Teachers discouraged him from reading them.

C He had read all the important children's books.

D He thought they were not sophisticated enough for him.

5 **The author's selection of books during his elementary-school years can BEST be described as—**

A discriminating

B random

C varied

D simplistic

6 **The effect of his early reading on the author's high school experience—**

A brought him academic success

B brought him fame and recognition

C made him socially successful

D caused him to avoid athletics

7 **What does the author mean when he says, "But I was not a good reader"?**

A He could not pronounce hard words.

B He did not fully understand what he read.

C He did not know the history of most of the books.

D He could not remember things he had read.

8 **With which of the following statements would the author have agreed in his early years?**

A One never finds satisfying answers in books.

B Reading creates more problems than it solves.

C It is pointless to read something that you don't understand.

D An educated person is someone who has read a lot of books.

9 **Rodriguez describes his personal thirst for knowledge as—**

A the special patience

B merely bookish

C a complicated idea

D the hollow within him

10 **What important lesson did the author learn about himself?**

A He really did not like to read.

B He had been reading the wrong books.

C He had been reading for the wrong reasons.

D He had been reading too quickly.

END-OF-YEAR TEST

GO ON

11 Which sentence BEST explains what the author means in the following statement?

"...I lacked a point of view when I read. Rather, I read in order to acquire a point of view."

A He did not understand the point of view of most authors.

B He wanted to form opinions about the skill of various authors.

C He was trying to absorb information, not reflect on its meaning.

D He was trying to understand the literary concept of point of view.

12 Which question is a careful reader most likely to ask after reading this portion of Rodriguez's essay?

A Which book would he identify as the most important?

B Does he continue to read only lengthy books?

C What has he decided is the best reason for reading a book?

D Which books did he find particularly difficult to comprehend?

END-OF-YEAR TEST

GO ON

Reading and Literary Analysis *(continued)*

DIRECTIONS Read this passage about a fight for freedom of the press. Then answer questions 13 through 23.

First Fight for Freedom of the Press

William Cosby, governor of New York in the 1730s, thought he had put an end to the editorials that criticized him when he jailed John Peter Zenger, a newspaper publisher. But the governor had discounted the tenacity of Zenger's wife. While caring for her family, Anna Zenger went on publishing the paper every week for the more than eight months her husband was in jail.

Cosby, who was related by marriage to English royalty, had arrived in the colony of New York in 1731 to assume the job of governor. Few historians since the 1700s have said a good word about Governor Cosby. He often tried to use the courts to enforce his will. When courts sometimes ruled against him, Cosby arranged for trials with *no* juries or handpicked the judges himself. He simply replaced judges who stood in his way. He controlled the newspaper and made sure that it always praised him. Cosby's critics encouraged the Zengers to start another newspaper—the *New York Weekly Journal*—to expose Cosby's misdeeds. Such a man was easily ridiculed.

The *New York Weekly Journal* began to publish satirical criticisms of Cosby in editorials and advertisements. Although Zenger did not personally write the criticisms, they expressed his viewpoint, and he was willing to shield the people who wrote them. Cosby became very upset and had charges brought against Zenger for "seditious libel," harmful statements that promote revolt against the government.

Cosby saw to it that bail was set so high that neither Zenger nor his cohorts could pay it. While in jail, Zenger began to write letters criticizing Cosby. Refusing to be intimidated, his wife published the letters in their newspaper, where they reached a sympathetic audience.

In 1735, Zenger's trial began. Andrew Hamilton, a famous lawyer from Philadelphia, defended him. Cosby tried unsuccessfully to stack the jury with his supporters. Ironically, English law decreed that the greater the truth published in criticizing someone, the greater the libel. However, Zenger's lawyer convinced the jury to ignore the English law and to agree

END-OF-YEAR TEST

GO ON

that if what one publishes about a public servant is true, it is *not* libel. Zenger was acquitted by the jury and went home to resume publishing the *Journal*.

The verdict did not change British law or the English definition of libel. From that point on, however, only a foolhardy political leader would charge critics with libel. Satire of leaders became much more common. Journalists buzzed like angry bees around corrupt officials, stinging them with impunity. Thus, although the verdict had little immediate legal effect, the Zengers' brave actions helped lay the groundwork for freedom of the press in the United States.

13 What does the word tenacity mean in the following sentence?

> But the governor had discounted the tenacity of John Peter's wife.

A hostility

B persistence

C spitefulness

D intelligence

14 In early America, libel was considered "seditious" if it—

A was based on untruths

B questioned the existing government officials

C promoted revolt against the government

D offended public sentiment

15 The writer maintains reader interest by telling the account—

A as if it is happening before a judge

B in a logical, sequential way

C with the historical consequences in the first paragraph

D without revealing the result

16 What would add impact to this passage?

A quoting the legal definition of *libel*

B giving more details about how upset Cosby became

C making Andrew Hamilton the primary focus

D including examples of how Cosby was satirized in the *Journal*

17 What quotation from the passage BEST helps to reveal John Peter Zenger's character?

A Critics encouraged the Zengers to start another newspaper.

B He was willing to shield the people who wrote them.

C Zenger was acquitted by the jury and went home.

D Satire of leaders became much more common.

18 This passage makes it clear that satire is a way to—

A win the favor of the public

B disguise one's intended meaning

C defend oneself from libel

D expose the flaws of one's opponents

END-OF-YEAR TEST

GO ON

19 **Which phrase BEST describes the tone of this passage?**

- **A** completely objective
- **B** biased in favor of the Zengers
- **C** biased in favor of Governor Cosby
- **D** biased in favor of the legal system

20 **This passage suggests that in 1735, the people of New York were—**

- **A** willing to challenge their corrupt leaders
- **B** completely intimidated by the English throne
- **C** blindly loyal to their governor
- **D** making plans to revolt

21 **An editorial in a newspaper MOST often expresses—**

- **A** the will of the government
- **B** the need for conformity
- **C** untruths about officials
- **D** opinions on public issues

22 **In the final paragraph, the writer states that journalists "buzzed like angry bees." This is an example of—**

- **A** symbolism
- **B** metaphor
- **C** hyperbole
- **D** simile

23 **Why is freedom of the press important in a democracy?**

- **A** It helps newspapers sell more papers.
- **B** It gives political leaders greater control.
- **C** It helps the people gain access to information.
- **D** It helps prisoners gain their freedom.

END-OF-YEAR TEST

GO ON

Reading and Literary Analysis *(continued)*

DIRECTIONS Read the Bill of Rights, the first ten amendments to the United States Constitution. Then answer questions 24 through 30.

The Bill of Rights

The First 10 Amendments to the Constitution as Ratified by the States

Amendment I

Congress shall make no law respecting an establishment of religion, or prohibiting the free exercise thereof; or abridging the freedom of speech, or of the press; or the right of the people peaceably to assemble, and to petition the government for a redress of grievances.

Amendment II

A well-regulated militia, being necessary to the security of a free state, the right of the people to keep and bear arms shall not be infringed.

Amendment III

No soldier shall, in time of peace, be quartered in any house, without the consent of the owner; nor in time of war, but in a manner to be prescribed by law.

Amendment IV

The right of the people to be secure in their persons, houses, papers, and effects, against unreasonable searches and seizures, shall not be violated; and no warrants shall issue but upon probable cause, supported by oath or affirmation, and particularly describing the place to be searched, and the persons or things to be seized.

Amendment V

No person shall be held to answer for a capital, or otherwise infamous crime, unless on a presentment or indictment of a grand jury, except in cases arising in the land or naval forces, or in the militia, when in actual service in time of war or public danger; nor shall any person be subject for the same offence to be twice put in jeopardy of life or limb; nor shall be compelled in any criminal case to be a witness against himself; nor be deprived of life, liberty, or property, without due process of law; nor shall private property be taken for public use without just compensation.

Amendment VI

In all criminal prosecutions, the accused shall enjoy the right to a speedy and public trial, by an impartial jury of the state and district wherein the crime shall have been committed, which district shall have been previously ascertained by law, and to be informed of the nature and cause of the accusation; to be confronted with the witnesses against him; to have compulsory process for obtaining witnesses in his favor, and to have the assistance of counsel for his defense.

Amendment VII

In suits at common law, where the value in controversy shall exceed twenty dollars, the right of trial by jury shall be preserved, and no fact tried by a jury shall be otherwise re-examined in any court of the United States, than according to the rules of the common law.

Amendment VIII

Excessive bail shall not be required, nor excessive fines imposed, nor cruel and unusual punishments inflicted.

Amendment IX

The enumeration in the Constitution, of certain rights, shall not be construed to deny or disparage others retained by the people.

Amendment X

The powers not delegated to the United States by the Constitution, nor prohibited by it to the states, are reserved to the states respectively, or to the people.

24 The purpose of Amendments I through X is to—

- **A** distinguish between federal and state laws
- **B** prevent crimes and other violations
- **C** protect the rights of individual citizens
- **D** guarantee that all people are treated equally

25 For which amendment did John Peter and Anna Zenger help lay the groundwork?

- **A** Amendment I
- **B** Amendment III
- **C** Amendment IV
- **D** Amendment VI

GO ON

26 **If an individual chooses not to testify at a trial in which he or she is the defendant, which amendment protects that right?**

A Amendment II

B Amendment III

C Amendment IV

D Amendment V

27 **Because of Amendment IV, the police cannot search your home without—**

A an oath

B advance warning

C your permission

D a warrant

28 **Amendment VII ensures that if you are accused of violating the law and appear in court, you have the right to a—**

A speedy trial

B trial by jury

C court-appointed lawyer

D fair judge

29 **Which of the following would most likely violate Amendment VIII?**

A Only certain religious groups are allowed to set up holiday displays at city hall.

B Bail is set at one thousand dollars for someone accused of speeding.

C The trial for a person accused of shoplifting is delayed for one year.

D A teenager is tried twice for the same offense.

30 **The Bill of Rights was especially important to our Founders because they—**

A trusted the federal government to protect them in times of war

B wanted to be the first country to protect the rights of all citizens

C had experienced violations of human rights in some of their original countries

D thought the courts should be more powerful than any other government branch

END-OF-YEAR TEST

GO ON

NAME CLASS DATE

End-of-Year Test

Vocabulary

DIRECTIONS Choose the word that means the same, or about the same, as the underlined word. Then mark the answer you have chosen.

SAMPLE A

Something that is temporal is—

A invisible
B temporary
C fragrant
D disorderly

31 Something that is intimated is—

A hinted
B announced
C requested
D provided

32 Precarious means—

A attentive
B uniform
C uncertain
D essential

33 An encumbrance is a—

A compliment
B decoration
C rebellion
D burden

34 Someone who is lucid is—

A immoral
B drowsy
C inefficient
D clearheaded

35 Avarice is another word for—

A greed
B deceit
C modesty
D determination

36 Something that is ludicrous is—

A implied
B absurd
C impatient
D sorrowful

GO ON

DIRECTIONS Choose the word that means the same, or about the same, as the underlined word. Then mark the answer you have chosen.

SAMPLE B

I could not tell whether her actions were ingenuous or purposefully hurtful. Ingenuous means—

A dishonorable
B innocent
C imaginary
D brief

37 **The stern instructor put us through a rigorous six-month course of academic and physical training. Rigorous means—**

A severe
B calming
C wasteful
D dangerous

38 **From a distance, we heard the plaintive cry of a lonely wolf pup. Plaintive means—**

A old-fashioned
B irritating
C restrained
D sad

39 **He had the temerity to ask the overbearing foreman for a job. Temerity means—**

A boldness
B pleasure
C honesty
D curiosity

40 **We agreed to meet later and chose the train station as our rendezvous point. Rendezvous means—**

A exploratory
B favorable
C meeting
D secret

NAME ______ CLASS ______ DATE ______ SCORE ______

ENTRY-LEVEL TEST

Answer Sheet

Reading and Literary Analysis

1	Ⓐ	Ⓑ	Ⓒ	Ⓓ
2	Ⓐ	Ⓑ	Ⓒ	Ⓓ
3	Ⓐ	Ⓑ	Ⓒ	Ⓓ
4	Ⓐ	Ⓑ	Ⓒ	Ⓓ
5	Ⓐ	Ⓑ	Ⓒ	Ⓓ
6	Ⓐ	Ⓑ	Ⓒ	Ⓓ
7	Ⓐ	Ⓑ	Ⓒ	Ⓓ
8	Ⓐ	Ⓑ	Ⓒ	Ⓓ
9	Ⓐ	Ⓑ	Ⓒ	Ⓓ
10	Ⓐ	Ⓑ	Ⓒ	Ⓓ
11	Ⓐ	Ⓑ	Ⓒ	Ⓓ
12	Ⓐ	Ⓑ	Ⓒ	Ⓓ
13	Ⓐ	Ⓑ	Ⓒ	Ⓓ
14	Ⓐ	Ⓑ	Ⓒ	Ⓓ
15	Ⓐ	Ⓑ	Ⓒ	Ⓓ
16	Ⓐ	Ⓑ	Ⓒ	Ⓓ
17	Ⓐ	Ⓑ	Ⓒ	Ⓓ
18	Ⓐ	Ⓑ	Ⓒ	Ⓓ
19	Ⓐ	Ⓑ	Ⓒ	Ⓓ
20	Ⓐ	Ⓑ	Ⓒ	Ⓓ
21	Ⓐ	Ⓑ	Ⓒ	Ⓓ
22	Ⓐ	Ⓑ	Ⓒ	Ⓓ
23	Ⓐ	Ⓑ	Ⓒ	Ⓓ
24	Ⓐ	Ⓑ	Ⓒ	Ⓓ
25	Ⓐ	Ⓑ	Ⓒ	Ⓓ
26	Ⓐ	Ⓑ	Ⓒ	Ⓓ
27	Ⓐ	Ⓑ	Ⓒ	Ⓓ
28	Ⓐ	Ⓑ	Ⓒ	Ⓓ
29	Ⓐ	Ⓑ	Ⓒ	Ⓓ
30	Ⓐ	Ⓑ	Ⓒ	Ⓓ

Vocabulary

Sample A

	Ⓐ	Ⓑ	Ⓒ	Ⓓ
31	Ⓐ	Ⓑ	Ⓒ	Ⓓ
32	Ⓐ	Ⓑ	Ⓒ	Ⓓ
33	Ⓐ	Ⓑ	Ⓒ	Ⓓ
34	Ⓐ	Ⓑ	Ⓒ	Ⓓ
35	Ⓐ	Ⓑ	Ⓒ	Ⓓ
36	Ⓐ	Ⓑ	Ⓒ	Ⓓ

Sample B

	Ⓐ	Ⓑ	Ⓒ	Ⓓ
37	Ⓐ	Ⓑ	Ⓒ	Ⓓ
38	Ⓐ	Ⓑ	Ⓒ	Ⓓ
39	Ⓐ	Ⓑ	Ⓒ	Ⓓ
40	Ⓐ	Ⓑ	Ⓒ	Ⓓ

NAME _______________ CLASS _______________ DATE _______________ SCORE _______________

END-OF-YEAR TEST

Answer Sheet

Reading and Literary Analysis

1 Ⓐ Ⓑ Ⓒ Ⓓ
2 Ⓐ Ⓑ Ⓒ Ⓓ
3 Ⓐ Ⓑ Ⓒ Ⓓ
4 Ⓐ Ⓑ Ⓒ Ⓓ
5 Ⓐ Ⓑ Ⓒ Ⓓ
6 Ⓐ Ⓑ Ⓒ Ⓓ
7 Ⓐ Ⓑ Ⓒ Ⓓ
8 Ⓐ Ⓑ Ⓒ Ⓓ
9 Ⓐ Ⓑ Ⓒ Ⓓ
10 Ⓐ Ⓑ Ⓒ Ⓓ
11 Ⓐ Ⓑ Ⓒ Ⓓ
12 Ⓐ Ⓑ Ⓒ Ⓓ
13 Ⓐ Ⓑ Ⓒ Ⓓ
14 Ⓐ Ⓑ Ⓒ Ⓓ
15 Ⓐ Ⓑ Ⓒ Ⓓ
16 Ⓐ Ⓑ Ⓒ Ⓓ
17 Ⓐ Ⓑ Ⓒ Ⓓ
18 Ⓐ Ⓑ Ⓒ Ⓓ
19 Ⓐ Ⓑ Ⓒ Ⓓ
20 Ⓐ Ⓑ Ⓒ Ⓓ
21 Ⓐ Ⓑ Ⓒ Ⓓ
22 Ⓐ Ⓑ Ⓒ Ⓓ
23 Ⓐ Ⓑ Ⓒ Ⓓ
24 Ⓐ Ⓑ Ⓒ Ⓓ
25 Ⓐ Ⓑ Ⓒ Ⓓ
26 Ⓐ Ⓑ Ⓒ Ⓓ
27 Ⓐ Ⓑ Ⓒ Ⓓ
28 Ⓐ Ⓑ Ⓒ Ⓓ
29 Ⓐ Ⓑ Ⓒ Ⓓ
30 Ⓐ Ⓑ Ⓒ Ⓓ

Vocabulary

Sample A

Ⓐ Ⓑ Ⓒ Ⓓ

31 Ⓐ Ⓑ Ⓒ Ⓓ
32 Ⓐ Ⓑ Ⓒ Ⓓ
33 Ⓐ Ⓑ Ⓒ Ⓓ
34 Ⓐ Ⓑ Ⓒ Ⓓ
35 Ⓐ Ⓑ Ⓒ Ⓓ
36 Ⓐ Ⓑ Ⓒ Ⓓ

Sample B

Ⓐ Ⓑ Ⓒ Ⓓ

37 Ⓐ Ⓑ Ⓒ Ⓓ
38 Ⓐ Ⓑ Ⓒ Ⓓ
39 Ⓐ Ⓑ Ⓒ Ⓓ
40 Ⓐ Ⓑ Ⓒ Ⓓ

Answer Key

Answer Key

Entry-Level Test, *page 1*

Reading and Literary Analysis

1. D
2. A
3. B
4. B
5. C
6. A
7. B
8. D
9. D
10. C
11. D
12. A
13. A
14. B
15. D
16. C
17. B
18. C
19. A
20. C
21. B
22. B
23. B
24. A
25. B
26. C
27. D
28. C
29. D
30. B

Vocabulary

Sample A C
31. B
32. A
33. D
34. C
35. D
36. A
Sample B C
37. A
38. D
39. A
40. B

Collection 1

Collection 1 Diagnostic Test
Literature, Informational Text, Vocabulary, ***page 12***

1. B
2. H
3. D
4. F
5. B
6. J
7. C
8. J
9. C
10. G

Literary Period Introduction Test, *page 14*

Comprehension

1. A
2. F
3. C
4. G
5. C
6. G
7. D
8. F
9. D
10. H

The Sun Still Rises in the Same Sky: Native American Literature
by Joseph Bruchac

The Sky Tree
retold by Joseph Bruchac

The Earth Only
composed by Used-as-a-Shield

Coyote Finishes His Work
retold by Barry Lopez

Selection Test, *page 16*

Comprehension

1. B
2. H
3. B
4. G
5. A
6. G
7. A
8. G
9. B
10. F

Reading Skills

11. C
12. F
13. A
14. G
15. C
16. G

Literary Focus

17. B
18. H
19. D
20. H

Constructed Response

21. Students' answers will vary. A sample response follows:

Bruchac tells us that for the Native American, life is an endless circle, not a straight line. Instead of change, there is continuity. Although we pass from one day to the next day, the "sun still rises in the same sky." In other words, no matter how much things change, they stay the same. This worldview is very different from the Western or European worldview in which change is at the heart of literature. Every day, the sky is different. Every day, we move further along a progressive straight line.

Just as Bruchac indicates that Western literary tradition is rooted in oral history, citing examples like *Beowulf* and the works of Homer, so Indian literature has similar roots. It's only natural that many of the same archetypes arise—the bold warrior, the wise elder, the magic forest—in both literatures. Just as in Norse mythology there is a tree of life, so in many Indian traditions there is a tree of life or peace that symbolizes the world and the way it is organized. Like the sun and sky, some things are shared by both European and Native American literary traditions.

Here Follow Some Verses upon the Burning of Our House, July 10, 1666
by Anne Bradstreet

Selection Test, *page 20*

Comprehension

1. D
2. H
3. B
4. G
5. B
6. H
7. D
8. H
9. A
10. H

Reading Skills

11. B
12. J

Literary Focus

13. B
14. G
15. A

Constructed Response

16. Students' answers will vary. A sample response follows:

Bradstreet first makes it clear that readers should realize that material possessions are unimportant—not because we don't value them but because our spiritual life is eternal and cannot be destroyed. Second, we shouldn't worry too much about what happens to us because our fates are in the hands of God, and we must do his will. She establishes this point by talking about God as one "that gave and took." Third, she reminds the reader that God has prepared "an house on high erect" that will be our final dwelling, no matter what befalls us on earth.

World, in hounding me . . .
by Sor Juana Inés de la Cruz

Selection Test, *page 23*

Comprehension

1. C
2. F
3. A
4. G
5. C

Literary Focus

6. J
7. D
8. F
9. A

Constructed Response

10. Students' answers will vary. A sample response follows:

Both works have a profoundly spiritual tone and address spiritual issues. "The Earth Only," however, suggests that it is the physical world that endures ("the earth / only / endures), while de la Cruz's poem suggests that the world is vanity and it is only the unseen, spiritual realm that has true value. This treasure is invisible and, thus, "cheats even the practiced eye."

Answer Key

from A Narrative of the Captivity . . . by Mary Rowlandson

Selection Test, *page 25*

Comprehension

1. B	**6.** G
2. F	**7.** C
3. D	**8.** F
4. F	**9.** A
5. C	**10.** G

Reading Skills

11. C

12. H

Literary Focus

13. D

14. G

15. D

16. H

Vocabulary Development

17. b	**20.** c
18. d	**21.** e
19. a	

Constructed Response

22. Students' answers will vary. A sample response follows:

When Rowlandson's daughter dies, she sees a link to the story of Job in the Bible. Job was given many troubles by God to test his faith. To Rowlandson, she and others in her situation are like Job in this way. She also sees a connection between Jehu, a fierce military commander who pursues people in the Bible, and the English Army. Additionally, she likens her separation from her children to Jacob's separation from his children.

from Sinners in the Hands of an Angry God by Jonathan Edwards

Selection Test, *page 29*

Comprehension

1. C	**6.** F
2. F	**7.** C
3. B	**8.** G
4. J	**9.** A
5. C	**10.** H

Literary Focus

11. D	**14.** G
12. G	**15.** C
13. A	**16.** G

Vocabulary Development

17. c

18. a

19. e

20. b

21. d

Constructed Response

22. Students' answers will vary. A sample response follows:

a. No, leading a decent life is not enough; one must accept Christ or risk damnation.

b. No, one must accept Christ as well as believing in God. Edward points out that much of his audience believes in God but have not yet accepted Christ as their savior.

c. Having a good physical constitution tricks people into thinking their souls are in good condition. Edwards points out that this assumption isn't true; they must be saved spiritually, not physically.

d. In order to avoid damnation, you have to confess your sin and accept Christ.

from The Interesting Narrative of the Life of Olaudah Equiano
by Olaudah Equiano

from To the Right Honorable William, Earl of Dartmouth . . .
by Phillis Wheatley

Honoring African Heritage
by Halimah Abdullah

Selection Test, *page 33*

Comprehension

1. C
2. H
3. C
4. F
5. A
6. F
7. B
8. H
9. A
10. G

Reading Skills

11. A
12. G

Literary Focus

13. B
14. J

Vocabulary Development

15. e
16. d
17. a
18. b
19. c

Constructed Response

20. Students' answers will vary. A sample response follows:

Occasionally, Equiano is treated roughly as a slave in Africa; however, when he is taken by the widow's family, he is given respect and treated like a family member. Once on the slave ship, he is treated like an animal rather than a human being. The conditions are filthy and his captors regularly flog and maltreat the shipboard slaves. Life was better for Equiano as a slave in Africa, because he was treated as a person, at least part of the time.

from The Autobiography
by Benjamin Franklin

from All I Really Need to Know I Learned in Kindergarten
by Robert Fulghum

from Poor Richard's Almanack
by Benjamin Franklin

Selection Test, *page 37*

Comprehension

1. B
2. F
3. C
4. G
5. C
6. H
7. A
8. J
9. B
10. G

Reading Skills

11. C
12. J
13. B

Literary Focus

14. F

Vocabulary Development

15. b
16. d
17. a
18. e
19. c

Constructed Response

20. Students' answers will vary. A sample response follows:

Franklin lists silence as a virtue. By silence, he means speaking only when necessary or only when it would benefit others. It seems likely that Ben Franklin would be the kind of person who likes to give advice and express his opinion whenever possible—the whole selection is an example of this tendency, particularly the section on how to better oneself. Also, he is very industrious and probably had a hard time standing still! That trait would make tranquillity, or the ability not to be disturbed by minor events, hard, too.

Speech to the Virginia Convention
by Patrick Henry

Selection Test, *page 41*

Comprehension

1. A	**6.** J
2. J	**7.** A
3. C	**8.** G
4. H	**9.** B
5. D	**10.** G

Reading Skills

11. B

12. J

Literary Focus

13. A

14. F

Vocabulary Development

15. a

16. e

17. b

18. d

19. c

Constructed Response

20. Students' answers will vary. A sample response follows:

At the Virginia Convention today, New Hampshire delegate Mr. Patrick Henry delivered a searing speech calling upon all present to give up argument with the Crown of England and resort to arms, suggesting that all other recourse has been exhausted and, effectively, the war has already begun: troops are in the field, and the English army is here.

Delegates greeted his remarks with thunderous applause. The few advocates of compromise, however, continue to express caution.

from The Crisis, No. 1
by Thomas Paine

Selection Test, *page 45*

Comprehension

1. C	**6.** H
2. H	**7.** A
3. D	**8.** F
4. H	**9.** B
5. D	**10.** G

Reading Skills

11. D

12. H

Literary Focus

13. A

14. G

Vocabulary Development

15. b

16. d

17. c

18. a

19. e

Constructed Response

20. Students' answers will vary. A sample response follows:

The object Paine refers to is revolution and throwing out the British. When he says "lay your shoulders to the wheel" and "up and help us," he is asking the colonists to rise up and join in the fight, which is the main theme of his speech. His use of language is effective, since it stirs emotions. It arouses the colonists to action by making them feel they are joining a large number of people to achieve a great end.

from The Autobiography: The Declaration of Independence
by Thomas Jefferson

Selection Test, *page 49*

Comprehension

1. D	**6.** G
2. F	**7.** C
3. C	**8.** G
4. G	**9.** A
5. A	**10.** G

Reading Skills

11. B

12. H

Literary Focus

13. B

14. J

Vocabulary Development

15. a

16. b

17. e

18. c

19. d

Constructed Response

20. Students' answers will vary. A sample response follows:

Jefferson's style is eloquent because he tells exactly what the differences are between Americans and the British. He then gives specific examples that prove those differences are both real and unresolvable except by revolution. It is the things he is describing that seem noble then, not the high style of the language or classical allusions that make his points seem more important. He lets the situation speak for itself, which makes for good, plain writing. It's also a good example of the honest, straightforward character of Americans and the best of American writing.

from The Iroquois Constitution
by Dekanawida

Letter to John Adams
by Abigail Adams

from Declaration of Sentiments
by Elizabeth Cady Stanton

Selection Test, *page 53*

Comprehension

1. C	**6.** F
2. J	**7.** C
3. A	**8.** G
4. G	**9.** A
5. C	**10.** J

Literary Focus

11. C

12. H

13. A

14. H

15. A

Constructed Response

16. Students' answers will vary. A sample response follows:

Many of the problems Stanton cites have been resolved: Women can vote, they are legally equal in most ways to men, and the divorce laws Stanton found unfair have been changed. However, there is still evidence that women are not economically equal to men, because there is still some imbalance in the pay women get for doing the same work. Also, there are not as many women in positions of political and economic power as there are men.

Collection 1 Summative Test, *page 56*

Vocabulary Skills

1. A	**4.** H
2. H	**5.** A
3. B	

Comprehension

6. G
7. C
8. J
9. B
10. G

Reading Skills and Strategies

Understanding Cultural Characteristics

11. A

Making Inferences About Main Ideas

12. F

Students' answers will vary. A sample response follows:

Crèvecoeur criticizes the inequality of the European social structure. He mentions that in America "the rich and the poor are not so far removed from each other as they are in Europe." He cites the "pleasing uniformity" of the housing and the lack of "titles" in North America. Finally, he says that this equality will be lasting.

Analyzing Tone

13. Although Crèvecoeur does cite objective facts, the only supportable answer is that the tone is subjective, for even objective facts are couched in subjective terms filled with rich connotations that may be positive or negative. Examples of phrases and their explanations will vary. Sample responses follow:

- "It is not composed, as in Europe, of great lords who possess everything and of a herd of people who have nothing."
The word *herd* indicates a negative attitude toward this separation of wealth.
- ". . . he views not the hostile castle and the haughty mansion . . ."
Both *hostile* and *haughty* create an image of a negative and unpleasant landscape.
- "all clad in neat homespun"
The word *neat* produces a positive image of the farmers and wives that may not be literally accurate.

Literary Focus: Constructed Response

Analyzing Style: Emotional Appeal and Parallelism

14. Students' answers will vary. Sample responses follow:

Parallelism: "We have no princes for whom we toil, starve, and bleed; we are the most perfect society now existing in the world."

"Here are no aristocratical families, no courts, no kings, no bishops, no ecclesiastical dominion, no invisible power giving to a few a very visible one, no great manufacturers employing thousands, no great refinements of luxury."

Emotional Appeal: "What a train of pleasing ideas this fair spectacle must suggest!"

"For no European foot has as yet traveled half the extent of this mighty continent!"

"I wish I could be acquainted with the feelings and thoughts which must agitate the heart and present themselves to the mind of an enlightened Englishman when he first lands on this continent."

Collection 2

Collection 2 Diagnostic Test

Literature, Informational Text, Vocabulary, ***page 61***

1. A
2. G
3. C
4. J
5. B
6. G
7. B
8. H
9. D
10. F

Literary Period Introduction Test, *page 63*

Comprehension

1. A
2. G
3. D
4. F
5. D
6. G
7. C
8. F
9. B
10. H

The Devil and Tom Walker
by Washington Irving

Selection Test, *page 65*

Comprehension

1. C
2. J
3. D
4. F
5. A
6. H
7. B
8. G
9. C
10. J

Literary Focus

11. A
12. F
13. C

Reading Skills

14. F

Vocabulary Development

15. c
16. e
17. d
18. b
19. a

Constructed Response

20. Students' responses will vary. A sample response follows:

The mood of "The Devil and Tom Walker" is dark and scary. But, as anybody who has seen horror movies knows, humor often works alongside of terror. Tom Walker's situation at the beginning of the story is so hopeless that he is ready for anything. When Old Scratch appears, Tom is not very impressed. After the devil introduces himself with elaborate self-praise, Tom's response might be paraphrased as, "Oh yeah. I thought that was who you were." When Tom's wife disappears, he worries about her until he discovers that she carried off all their valuables. Then, he is more concerned about the valuables. After Tom gets religious, he is more interested in the piety of others than in his own. Irving gives us a character who is naturally mean, and Tom seems to accept the supernatural and grim happenings as a matter of course. Readers see these happenings as strange and horrible, and the contrast between this dark mood and Tom's resigned acceptance of it is funny.

Thanatopsis
by William Cullen Bryant

Selection Test, *page 69*

Comprehension

1. D
2. H
3. C
4. F
5. A
6. H
7. D
8. H
9. A
10. H

Literary Focus

11. C
12. G
13. B

Reading Skills

14. J

Constructed Response

15. Students' responses will vary. A sample response follows:

In "Thanatopsis," Bryant suggests that everyone experiences both happiness and sadness. The poem's speaker refers to both "gayer hours" and "darker musings." The speaker also emphasizes the fleeting quality of human lives. The speaker states, "each one as before will chase / His favorite phantom" in life, stressing the futility and impermanence of worldly pursuits.

Answer Key

The Tide Rises, the Tide Falls
by Henry Wadsworth Longfellow

The Cross of Snow
by Henry Wadsworth Longfellow

Selection Test, *page 72*

Comprehension

1. A
2. H
3. B
4. F
5. D
6. H
7. C
8. G
9. A
10. J

Literary Focus

11. A
12. F
13. D
14. F

Constructed Response

15. Students' responses will vary. A sample response follows:

C Longfellow's imagery in "The Tide Rises, the Tide Falls" and "The Cross of Snow" serves to call attention to the inevitable sadness of life. In "The Tide Rises, the Tide Falls," morbid imagery creates a sense of despair. The line "Darkness settles on roofs and walls" creates a visual image of creeping death and despair. In "The Cross of Snow" the painful visual imagery of "martyrdom of fire" captures the speaker's sorrow in the face of life's brutal turns. In this case, it is his wife's tragic death in a fire. The image of the snowy cross also implies, if not a healing, a constant icy consolation for that burning pain.

from Nature
by Ralph Waldo Emerson

Selection Test, *page 76*

Comprehension

1. D
2. G
3. A
4. H
5. B
6. J
7. D
8. G
9. C
10. H

Literary Focus

11. A
12. F
13. C

Reading Skills

14. J

Vocabulary Development

15. integrate
16. blithe
17. admonishing
18. perennial
19. occult

Constructed Response

20. Students' responses will vary. A sample response follows:

Emerson uses imagery in *Nature* to explain that in nature, people become aware of their spiritual unity with all other creatures—a realization that seemingly cannot fail to pacify and unite society. For example, Emerson creates the following visual image to show how nature links us spiritually: "The stars awaken a certain reverence, because though always present, they are always inaccessible." The same relationship is shown in this image: "Standing on the bare ground—my head bathed by the blithe air, and uplifted into infinite space—all mean egotism vanishes."

from Self-Reliance
by Ralph Waldo Emerson

Selection Test, *page 80*

Comprehension

1. A
2. G
3. C
4. J
5. D
6. F
7. C
8. H
9. B
10. J

Answer Key

Literary Focus

11. D

12. J

Reading Skills

13. B

14. H

Vocabulary Development

Students' responses will vary. Sample responses follow:

15. belief

16. concealed

17. plain; clear

18. inferior, substandard

19. sound moral principles; honesty

Constructed Response

20. Students' responses will vary. A sample response follows:

In "Self-Reliance," Emerson conveys the theme that individuals should trust themselves and nurture their special gifts. He argues that people should not concern themselves with society's insistence on conformity and consistency. Emerson reinforces his point with many figures of speech. For example, Emerson uses the following metaphor to show that we must believe in our own talents: "Trust thyself: Every heart vibrates to that iron string." He also uses metaphors to show that people must work hard to achieve their potential. For instance, "No kernel of nourishing corn can come to him but through his toil bestowed on that plot of ground which is given to him to till." These figures of speech and others make Emerson's abstract ideas concrete and memorable to readers.

from Walden, or Life in the Woods

Henry David Thoreau

Selection Test, *page 84*

Comprehension

1. D

2. H

3. B

4. G

5. D

6. F

7. A

8. H

9. C

10. G

Literary Focus

11. C

12. G

13. D

Reading Skills

14. H

Vocabulary Development

15. impervious

16. temporal

17. superfluous

18. encumbrance

19. pertinent

Constructed Response

20. Students' responses will vary. A sample response follows:

Thoreau believes that people should live their lives deliberately, consciously making the best choices for themselves. People should not be pressured to conform to society; on the contrary, they should make every effort to remain true to their inner star. Thoreau expresses his philosophy in many metaphors. For example, he says that a person should "step to the music which he hears, however measured or far away." In this metaphor, music stands for our dreams and goals. Thoreau also believes that people should take their time finding their path in life. As he says in this metaphor: "It is not important that he should mature as soon as an apple tree or an oak." Unlike the growth of trees, the spiritual maturation of people cannot be measured on a timetable.

from Resistance to Civil Government
by Henry David Thoreau

Selection Test, *page 88*

Comprehension

1. A	**6.** H
2. J	**7.** D
3. B	**8.** G
4. H	**9.** A
5. C	**10.** H

Literary Focus

11. A

12. G

13. C

14. J

Vocabulary Development

15. a	**18.** b
16. e	**19.** c
17. d	

Constructed Response

20. Students' responses will vary. Sample responses follow:

Thoreau is not correct when he says, "That government is best which governs not at all." On the contrary, most people cannot govern themselves and need a firm hand to avoid disaster. For example, since people cannot control themselves, the police must be called in to quell riots and looting. The government must collect taxes to pay for essential services such as water, roads, and garbage removal. Finally, government must enforce laws that are best for the majority but which individuals often find burdensome, such as maximum speed limits on highways.

Thoreau is right when he says, "That government is best which governs not at all." Thoreau envisions a society which would govern itself, free from the corruptible and slow machinery of political systems. He also feels that taxes are often the vehicle for corruption. For instance, the poll taxes that Thoreau so rightly protested have since been condemned. Taxes for essential services are now falling away in moves toward privatization. Speed limits may even go the way of the German autobahn. Perhaps a society free of corruption would not need unruly protests and would engage in civilized discussions.

from On Nonviolent Resistance
by Mohandas K. Gandhi

from Letter from Birmingham City Jail
by Martin Luther King, Jr.

Selection Test, *page 92*

Comprehension

1. D	**6.** J
2. G	**7.** A
3. B	**8.** G
4. F	**9.** D
5. C	**10.** F

Dr. Heidegger's Experiment
by Nathaniel Hawthorne

Selection Test, *page 94*

Comprehension

1. D	**6.** G
2. J	**7.** D
3. B	**8.** F
4. H	**9.** A
5. A	**10.** J

Literary Focus

11. C	**13.** A
12. G	

Answer Key

Reading Skills

14. H

Vocabulary Development

15. infamous

16. ponderous

17. effervescent

18. venerable

19. veracious

Constructed Response

20. Students' responses will vary. A sample response follows:

"Dr. Heidegger's Experiment" is an allegory because it is a literary work in which characters, setting, and events stand for abstract ideas and moral qualities. Each of the characters is a two-dimensional representation of a vice. For example, the Widow Wycherly stands for vanity, Colonel Killigrew symbolizes a libertine, and Mr. Gascoigne represents a crooked politician. The experiment stands for a second chance at life, which the characters waste.

The Minister's Black Veil
by Nathaniel Hawthorne

Selection Test, *page 98*

Comprehension

1. B

2. J

3. A

4. H

5. D

6. F

7. A

8. G

9. D

10. H

Literary Focus

11. D

12. F

13. B

Reading Skills

14. F

Vocabulary Development

Students' responses will vary. A sample response follows:

15. appearance

16. goodness

17. foolish

18. signify

19. obviousness

Constructed Response

20. Students' responses will vary. A sample response follows:

Hawthorne's choice to make the main character of "The Minster's Black Veil" a man of the cloth was deliberate, as it helped Hawthorne further his parable. First, a minister is often the person rarely suspected of feeling sinful and guilty. Indeed, people often expect ministers to be blameless and innocent. Second, as a spiritual leader, a minister's actions carry more authority than those of many other people in the community. As a result, Mr. Hooper knows that his action in adopting the veil will have serious repercussions in the community. Thus, choosing a minister as his main character helps Hawthorne strengthen the moral of his parable.

The Pit and the Pendulum
by Edgar Allan Poe

Selection Test, *page 102*

Comprehension

1. D

2. G

3. A

4. H

5. B

6. F

7. C

8. J

9. B

10. H

Literary Focus

11. A

12. H

13. B

14. J

Answer Key

Vocabulary Development

15. lucid

16. imperceptible

17. potent

18. tumultuous

19. averted

Constructed Response

20. Students' responses will vary. A sample response follows:

Based on "The Pit and the Pendulum," Poe can be considered a Dark Romantic because he uses symbolism and explores madness and derangement in the human psyche. "The Pit and the Pendulum" can be read as a symbolic story of a man who comes very close to losing his soul in the pit of hell but is saved at the last moment by God. As he travels through the darkness of his soul, the narrator comes close to losing his mind. The narrator realizes that he is going mad when he says, "By long suffering, my nerves had been unstrung, until I trembled at the sound of my own voice and had become in every respect a fitting subject for the species of torture which awaited me."

The Raven
by Edgar Allan Poe

Selection Test, *page 105*

Comprehension

1. C	**6.** G
2. H	**7.** C
3. B	**8.** H
4. J	**9.** D
5. A	**10.** J

Literary Focus

11. A

12. F

13. C

14. J

Constructed Response

15. Students' responses will vary. A sample response follows:

"The Raven" has a melancholy mood, as the speaker laments his lost love. The poem's sad mood is created by descriptions of the "dying ember," "bleak December," and the bird's "grave and stern" behavior. The poem's theme concerns the sorrow of lost love. The sorrowful mood reinforces the poem's theme as it traces the speaker's growing agitation over his conviction that the Raven is somehow connected to his dead lover, Lenore. The speaker begs the bird to reveal if he will ever be released from his sorrow. The speaker cries to the bird: "On this home by Horror haunted—tell me truly, I implore— / Is there—is there balm in Gilead?" The contrast between the speaker's anxious question and the bird's calm reply accentuates the loss expressed by a theme that is concentrated into one word: "Nevermore."

Eldorado
by Edgar Allan Poe

Selection Test, *page 108*

Comprehension

1. B	**6.** F
2. G	**7.** C
3. C	**8.** H
4. J	**9.** B
5. D	**10.** G

Literary Focus

11. A	**13.** C
12. G	**14.** J

Constructed Response

15. Students' responses will vary. A sample response follows:

In Washington Irving's "The Devil and Tom Walker," Tom Walker sets off on an archetypal quest to outsmart the devil. Tom makes a deal with the devil to lend money at very high interest rates. For many years Tom's quest is successful, as he makes a great fortune from cheating his neighbors. At the end, however, Tom is outsmarted by the devil. When Tom lies and says, "The Devil take me if I have made a farthing," the devil obliges and whisks him off to his death. All of Tom's great wealth turns to cinders and ashes. Tom's quest is an archetype because it is based on an original, imaginative pattern that appears across cultures and is repeated through the ages. For example, characters such as Marlowe's Faust and Goethe's Dr. Faustus have tried to cheat the devil but have always lost—just like Tom.

Collection 2 Summative Test, *page 111*

Vocabulary Skills

1. D
2. H
3. A
4. J
5. C

Comprehension

6. H
7. B
8. G
9. D
10. J

Reading Skills and Strategies: Constructed Response

Monitoring Your Reading

11. Students' responses will vary. A sample response follows:

Original Passages
"Stranger, if thou hast learned a truth which needs / No school of long experience, that the world / Is full of guilt and misery, and hast seen / Enough of all its sorrows, crimes, and cares / To tire thee of it, enter this wild wood / And view the haunts of Nature."

"Thou wilt find nothing here / Of all that pained thee in the haunts of men, / And made thee loathe thy life."

"Hence, these shades / Are still the abodes of gladness; the thick roof / Of green and stirring branches is alive / And musical with birds . . ."

Paraphrases
Reader, if you have realized that the world is filled with sadness and torment and you are sick of the pain you see all around, refresh your soul in nature.

There is nothing upsetting in nature, nothing that made you hate your life.

The forest is a happy place, filled with beauty and the glorious singing of birds.

Understanding Figures of Speech

12. Students' definitions of the figures of speech will vary, but their identification will not.

A sample response follows:

Personification—Example: "the sweet breeze / That makes the green leaves dance . . . "
Definition: giving human traits to non-human things

Metaphor—Example: Society is a joint stock company in which the members agree upon the distribution of bread to each shareholder.

Definition: a comparison of two unlike things, without using a comparison word such as "like" or "as"
Simile—Example: The life in us is like the water in the river.
Definition: a comparison of two unlike things, using a comparison word such as "like" or "as"

Personification—Example: "The rivulet / Sends forth glad sounds . . ."
Definition: giving human traits to non-human things

Answer Key

Drawing Inferences

13. The only supportable answer is D. Students' responses will vary, but students should use at least one example from the selection to support their ideas. A sample response follows:

The speaker begins by inviting the "Stranger" to escape the "sorrows, crimes, and cares" of the world by entering the woods. He describes the soothing effect of the forest with such words as "calm," "balm," "contentment," "tranquillity," and "love."

Literary Focus: Constructed Response

14. Students' responses will vary. A sample response follows:

a. *Characteristic:* Values feeling and intuition over reason
Example/Explanation: The woods represent feeling, which the poet values over thinking about the world's suffering.

b. *Characteristic:* Celebrates unspoiled nature
Example/Explanation: The primal curse / Fell, it is true, upon the unsinning earth, / But not in vengeance. God hath yoked to guilt / Her pale tormentor, misery. Hence, these shades / Are still the abodes of gladness . . ."

c. *Characteristic:* Contemplates nature's beauty as a path to spiritual and moral development
Example/Explanation: "enter this wild wood / And view the haunts of Nature. The calm shade / Shall bring a kindred calm . . ."

d. *Characteristic:* Prefers youthful, naive innocence to educated sophistication
Example / Explanation: "Stranger, if thou hast learned a truth which needs / No school of long experience, that the world / Is full of guilt and misery, and hast seen / Enough of all its sorrows, crimes, and cares / To tire thee of it . . ."

Collection 3

Collection 3 Diagnostic Test

Literature, *page 117*

1. B
2. F
3. D
4. G
5. C
6. J
7. A
8. F
9. D
10. J

Literary Period Introduction Test, *page 119*

1. A
2. G
3. D
4. F
5. C
6. G
7. D
8. H
9. B
10. J

I Hear America Singing

by Walt Whitman

Selection Test, *page 121*

Comprehension

1. A
2. G
3. C
4. J
5. C
6. H
7. C
8. H
9. A
10. J

Literary Focus

11. B
12. F
13. C
14. J

Constructed Response

15. Students' responses will vary. A sample response follows:

Whitman uses a catalog in "I Hear America Singing" to list the broad base of workers who help build the United States.

By picturing the workers and their tasks, Whitman demonstrates their energy and diversity. The catalog technique also shows the number and variety of people it takes to build our businesses, grow our food, and keep our homes and families running. By virtue of its size, the list vividly describes the strong, idealistic, diverse, and optimistic "song" of the average American worker.

from Song of Myself, Numbers 10 and 33
by Walt Whitman

Selection Test, *page 124*

Comprehension

1. A
2. G
3. D
4. F
5. B
6. H
7. A
8. G
9. C
10. J

Literary Focus

11. A
12. G
13. C
14. J

Constructed Response

15. Students' responses will vary. A sample response follows:

In *Song of Myself,* Whitman uses a number of stylistic devices to encourage readers to participate in the experiences and images he describes. For example, in number 10, Whitman addresses his readers directly, implying that the poet and reader know each other well. This familiarity encourages readers to accept the poet's vision and feel what he is feeling. In number 33, Whitman uses vivid imagery such as "twinges," "sting," and "cover'd with sweat" to describe the runaway slave. Sensory words like these allow readers to enter into the writer's consciousness and experience the world through his eyes.

Song of Myself, Number 52
by Walt Whitman

Selection Test, *page 127*

Comprehension

1. C
2. J
3. D
4. F
5. C
6. H
7. D
8. G
9. C
10. J

Reading Skills

11. A
12. J
13. C
14. G

Constructed Response

15. Students' responses will vary. A sample response follows:

Whitman lived during a time of hope and optimism in the United States. The Louisiana Purchase had more than doubled the country's size, and waves of pioneers trekked west with hopes of building a better life. After the Civil War the United States was unified and began to assume an identity as a world leader. The Industrial Revolution promised wondrous new timesaving devices and a better quality of life. Whitman's themes of self-reliance, individualism, and closeness to nature mirrored the optimism and enthusiasm of a country that was expanding in size, technology, and power.

Answer Key

A Sight in Camp in the Daybreak Gray and Dim
by Walt Whitman

from Specimen Days
by Walt Whitman

from Hospital Sketches
by Louisa May Alcott

Selection Test, *page 130*

Comprehension

1. B
2. J
3. D
4. H
5. B
6. H
7. A
8. F
9. C
10. J

Literary Focus

11. C
12. F
13. B
14. J

Constructed Response

15. Students' responses will vary. A sample response follows:

Whitman concentrates on describing the soldiers rather than commenting on the philosophical underpinnings of the war because he agreed—as did most Americans of his day—that civil war was inevitable. Americans realized that the country had reached a watershed in its history; that the nation was being pulled apart by conflicting values and agendas. While few people anticipated that the war would be as long, bloody, and painful as it was, it was clear that without a war the United States would not survive intact. Although the war would resolve these weighty issues, it would do so by the actions of individuals. Consequently, Whitman focuses on personal sacrifice, made universal by the three age groups of the soldiers.

Full Powers
by Pablo Neruda

Selection Test, *page 133*

Comprehension

1. C
2. H
3. A
4. G
5. B
6. J
7. D
8. F
9. C
10. H

Literary Focus

11. A
12. H
13. B
14. G

Constructed Response

15. Students' responses will vary. A sample response follows:

The poetry of Whitman and Neruda qualify as classics of world literature because their poetry expresses themes that transcend time and culture. In their works both poets explore the enduring themes of life and death, nature and art. In addition, both poets embrace individuality and creative self-expression, as shown through their use of song as metaphor. As Neruda proclaims: "I sing because I sing and because I sing." Finally, Whitman and Neruda both explore the poet's ability to express eternal truths through their art.

In Whitman this truth is expressed as an internalization of the external world—Whitman becomes what he sees. Neruda, however, seems to project his own internal processes on the physical world—the action of the waves becomes his own internal struggle. Thus, each poet expresses one of the two classic psychological relationships of the individual and the external world.

Answer Key

The Soul selects her own Society
by Emily Dickinson

If you were coming in the Fall
by Emily Dickinson

Selection Test, *page 136*

Comprehension

1. C
2. F
3. D
4. G
5. B
6. J
7. A
8. J
9. C
10. H

Literary Focus

11. B
12. F
13. A
14. G

Constructed Response

15. Students' responses will vary. A sample response follows:

Emily Dickinson uses similes and hyperbole in "If you were coming in the Fall" to help readers feel compassion for the speaker, who is despondent because her lover is away. The simile "I'd brush the Summer by / With half a smile, and half a spurn, / As Housewives do, a Fly" is a humorous way of showing that she misses her beloved. The hyperbole "If only Centuries, delayed, / I'd count them on my Hand, / Subtracting, till my fingers dropped / Into Van Dieman's Land" shows her growing anguish and frustration at her lover's continued absence.

Tell all the Truth but tell it slant
by Emily Dickinson

Apparently with no surprise
by Emily Dickinson

Success is counted sweetest
by Emily Dickinson

Selection Test, *page 139*

Comprehension

1. D
2. F
3. C
4. G
5. A
6. J
7. B
8. J
9. A
10. F

Literary Focus

11. B
12. G
13. D
14. J

Constructed Response

15. Students' responses will vary. A sample response follows:

In "Apparently with no surprise," the poet describes a world in which terrible things happen with God's approval. The poet uses vivid imagery to describe a heartless world in which "any happy Flower" is suddenly beheaded by the frost. The poet personifies the frost—the beheader of flowers—as a "blonde Assassin" to make her vision of the world more chillingly evil. The poet uses a pun on the word *unmoved* to show that even the sun is unaffected by the flower's death. The image of God in the final line reinforces the poet's vision of a cruel world, a world ruled not by a merely dispassionate God but one "Approving" of cruelty.

Answer Key

Because I could not stop for Death
by Emily Dickinson

I heard a Fly buzz—when I died
by Emily Dickinson

Much Madness is divinest Sense
by Emily Dickinson

Selection Test, *page 142*

Comprehension

1. C
2. H
3. D
4. J
5. C
6. G
7. A
8. F
9. C
10. J

Literary Focus

11. B
12. H
13. A

Reading Skills

14. H

Constructed Response

15. Students' responses will vary. A sample response follows:

Emily Dickinson uses irony and tone to demystify death in "Because I could not stop for Death." The poem is ironic because she depicts Death not as a terrifying skeleton with a scythe, but as a kindly gentleman. The speaker in the carriage with Death takes a leisurely journey to her grave past the school, the fields, and the setting sun. This calm, peaceful tone makes death seem comforting rather than frightening. Moreover, the horses merely pause, and the speaker, it must be noted, still speaks—"Centuries" since the events of the poem, evidently safe and secure in "Eternity."

Collection 3 Summative Test, *page 145*

Vocabulary Skills

1. C
2. F
3. D
4. J
5. C

Comprehension

6. H
7. A
8. J
9. D
10. G

Reading Skills and Strategies: Constructed Response

Summarizing a Text

11. Students' responses will vary. The only supportable answers are **B** and **D**.
A sample response follows:

B "Signor" could refer to any superior figure or deity. "Obedience" may refer to speaker's obedience to a higher being thereby indicating the speaker's desire to become closer to God.

Comparing Themes Across Texts

12. Students' responses will vary. A sample response follows:

Both "Aboard at a Ship's Helm" and "The Moon is distant from the Sea" deal with finding one's direction in life, but while Whitman envisions this direction as coming from within an individual, Dickinson sees it as coming from an outside source. Whitman talks about the "ship aboard the ship" and "Ship of the body . . . soul"—both of which imply that direction comes from within. Dickinson writes of a

"Signor" who gives direction. This "Signor" is a source outside of the body or distant from it, just as the moon is distant from the sea. Dickinson's speaker makes the point that this outside source of power can be exacting even though it is wielded from a distance.

Literary Focus: Constructed Response

Literary Elements: Free Verse

13. Students' responses will vary. A sample response follows:

a. *Element*—imagery; *Example*—"the freighted ship tacking speeds away under her gray sails"

b. *Element*—alliteration; *Example*—"O you give good notice indeed, you bell by the sea-reefs ringing"

c. *Element*—figure of speech; *Example*—metaphor: "Ship of the body"

Collection 4

Collection 4 Diagnostic Test
Literature, Informational Text, Vocabulary, *page 149*

1. B
2. H
3. A
4. J
5. D
6. G
7. C
8. F
9. B
10. F

Literary Period Introduction Test, *page 151*

Comprehension

1. A
2. G
3. D
4. F
5. D
6. G
7. C
8. F
9. B
10. H

from Narrative of the Life of Frederick Douglass
by Frederick Douglass

Selection Test, *page 153*

Comprehension

1. A
2. J
3. B
4. H
5. D
6. F
7. C
8. G
9. A
10. J

Literary Focus

11. B
12. J
13. C

Reading Skills

14. H

Vocabulary Development

15. c
16. e
17. d
18. b
19. a

Constructed Response

20. Students' responses will vary. A sample response follows:

In this excerpt from *Narrative of the Life of Frederick Douglass,* Douglass uses figures of speech to make his experiences vivid for his readers. For instance, when describing his escape through the woods, Douglass says that he looked "like a man who had escaped a den of wild beasts, and barely escaped them." The simile helps readers visualize how much he suffered. When Douglass says that Covey used him "like a brute for six months," the simile evokes the horror of slavery. The selection ends on a hopeful note, as the final, extended metaphor of embers, a tomb, and heaven represents rebirth and resurrection.

Answer Key

from Incidents in the Life of a Slave Girl
by Harriet A. Jacobs
Selection Test, *page 156*

Comprehension

1. D
2. G
3. A
4. J
5. C
6. F
7. B
8. G
9. A
10. H

Literary Focus

11. A
12. G
13. C
14. H

Vocabulary Development

15. kindness; benevolence
16. passionately; intensely
17. incitement; goad
18. calmed; quieted
19. urge; instinct

Constructed Response

20. Students' responses will vary. Any of the three influences can be defended. A sample response follows:

The institution of slavery was the strongest force in Jacobs's life because it ruled every aspect of it. Slavery defined her identity and controlled her existence. She was not free to live her life as she chose because she was enslaved. Since her life was not her own, Jacobs could not raise her children, live with her family members, travel freely, work at an occupation she enjoyed, or even resist the unwanted advances of her master. The institution of slavery was the overriding influence on her religious beliefs and ethical standards.

from My Bondage and My Freedom
by Frederick Douglass

Go Down, Moses

Follow the Drinking Gourd

Swing Low, Sweet Chariot

The Most Remarkable Woman of This Age
from Commonwealth *and* Freeman's Record
Selection Test, *page 159*

Comprehension

1. A
2. J
3. C
4. G
5. A
6. F
7. D
8. H
9. B
10. F

Literary Focus

11. C
12. G
13. C
14. F

Constructed Response

15. Students' responses will vary. A sample response follows:

Frederick Douglass's political message is clearer today than it was in the 1800s because time has put events in perspective. For more than one hundred years, Douglass's message has been studied and interpreted by political and historical thinkers. The description of his experience defines the "dehumanizing character of slavery" and is the foundation upon which much modern thought about civil rights and freedom are based. Douglass shows us that, regardless of race or creed, all people deserve human rights and basic freedoms. In this selection, he makes this point by comparing the "wailing notes" of the enslaved South with songs of the Irish famine of 1845–1846.

An Occurrence at Owl Creek Bridge
by Ambrose Bierce

Selection Test, *page 162*

Comprehension

1. B	**6.** F
2. H	**7.** D
3. A	**8.** F
4. J	**9.** C
5. B	**10.** J

Literary Focus

11. D

12. G

13. B

Reading Skills

14. H

Vocabulary Development

15. perilous

16. deference

17. encompassed

18. pivotal

19. sentinel

Constructed Response

20. Students' responses will vary. A sample response follows:

In "An Occurrence at Owl Creek Bridge," Bierce's purpose is to distort reality to show that Farquhar's escape is a fantasy. Bierce uses stylistic elements such as imagery, mood, and irony to rearrange time and weave fantasy into real events. For example, when Farquhar comes to the surface of the stream after he falls through the bridge, his physical senses are unnaturally keen and alert. As a result, he sees things that he could not possibly see, such as images of golden stars in strange constellations that seem to have a secret and evil significance. It is highly ironic that Farquhar believes that he has reached his wife just before he dies. In this imaginary world, events are shown as if the reader were seeing them through a kaleidoscope. All these stylistic elements help Bierce show that Farquhar dies almost instantaneously by hanging.

A Mystery of Heroism
by Stephen Crane

War Is Kind
by Stephen Crane

Selection Test, *page 165*

Comprehension

1. D	**6.** F
2. F	**7.** B
3. A	**8.** H
4. J	**9.** D
5. C	**10.** F

Literary Focus

11. A

12. H

13. D

14. J

Vocabulary Development

15. ominous

16. gesticulating

17. provisional

18. conflagration

19. stolidity

Constructed Response

20. Students' responses will vary. A sample response follows:

Collins acts both foolishly and heroically. He acts foolishly when he decides to get the water only after he is goaded by his comrades. The well and the buildings close to it are being heavily shelled in the assault and the meadow in front of the well is also under attack. However, Collins also acts heroically when he returns to the dying lieutenant and tries to give him some water. Collins fully understands that he is likely to be killed in the attempt, but he nonetheless persists. Crane uses Collins's actions to achieve his purpose: to show that people often act in contradictory ways when they are under extreme pressure. Collins's actions are ironic because they differ from what readers expect, just as real life is often highly ironic.

Letter to His Son
by Robert E. Lee

Letter to Sarah Ballou
by Maj. Sullivan Ballou

The Gettysburg Address
by Abraham Lincoln

from A Diary from Dixie
by Mary Chesnut

from Men at War: An Interview with Shelby Foote
by Ken Burns

Selection Test, *page 169*

Comprehension

1. A
2. H
3. D
4. F
5. C
6. G
7. B
8. J
9. A
10. H

Literary Focus

11. D
12. J
13. B
14. J

Constructed Response

15. Students' responses will vary. A sample response follows:

In these selections, Lee writes before battle whereas Lincoln writes after. Both Lee and Lincoln do not want the country to break in two. Lee states, "But I can anticipate no greater calamity for the country than a dissolution of the Union." Lincoln puts it another way: "Now we are engaged in a great civil war, testing whether that nation, or any nation so conceived and so dedicated, can long endure." However, Lee also states, "The South, in my opinion, has been aggrieved by the acts of the North, as you say." Although he does not want a civil war, Lee says that he will draw his sword in defense of the South. In dedication to those fallen from the sword, Lincoln is determined "that these dead shall not have died in vain—that this nation, under God, shall have a new birth of freedom—and that government of the people, by the people, for the people, shall not perish from the earth."

"I Will Fight No More Forever"
by Chief Joseph

Selection Test, *page 172*

Comprehension

1. A
2. H
3. D
4. J
5. C
6. F

Literary Focus

7. B
8. G
9. D
10. J

Answer Key

Constructed Response

11. Students' responses will vary. A sample response follows:

Chief Joseph's speech continues to affect us today because it seems to be a cry of despair from the heart. Chief Joseph speaks with dignity of the suffering his people have endured. He uses repetition of words such as *tired* and *dead* to hammer home his people's predicament. He reinforces this message with a simple parallel structure: "Looking Glass is dead. Toohoolhoolzote is dead. The old men are all dead." He ends eloquently by linking himself to the natural and spiritual world by saying, "From where the sun now stands I will fight no more forever." Even in defeat, he maintains his dignity and stature.

The Celebrated Jumping Frog of Calaveras County

by Mark Twain

Selection Test, *page 174*

Comprehension

1. A	**6.** F
2. H	**7.** C
3. C	**8.** G
4. J	**9.** A
5. D	**10.** J

Literary Focus

11. B

12. J

13. C

Reading Skills

14. F

Vocabulary Development

Students' responses will vary. A sample response follows:

15. taciturn; quiet; silent

16. famous; honorable

17. shabby; falling apart

18. brief

19. guess

Constructed Response

20. Students' responses will vary. A sample response follows:

Mark Twain creates humor in "The Celebrated Jumping Frog of Calaveras County" through exaggeration, dialect, and irony. First, Twain works within the tradition of the tall tale to wildly exaggerate characters and their actions. Jim Smiley bets on just about anything—dog races, horse races, and frog races, as well as betting on such taboo issues as the death of the Parson's wife. Second, Twain uses dialect to make his story funny. It's funny when Jim Smiley accuses the stranger of being an "amateur" when it comes to racing frogs. It's also funny when the stranger says in dialect: "Well, *I* don't see no p'ints about that frog that's any better'n any other frog." Tall tales from the nineteenth century often contain humorous dialect. Finally, Twain creates humor through irony. It's ironic that Jim Smiley never learns to give up gambling, even in the face of defeat.

The Lowest Animal

by Mark Twain

Selection Test, *page 178*

Comprehension

1. A	**6.** F
2. H	**7.** B
3. D	**8.** G
4. J	**9.** D
5. C	**10.** H

Literary Focus

11. A

12. G

13. D

Reading Skills

14. H

Vocabulary Development

15. avaricious

16. appease

17. sordid

18. allegiance

19. atrocious

Constructed Response

20. Students' responses will vary. A sample response follows:

Twain's points about cruelty and religious intolerance are his most effective arguments because he supports them with the most vivid details. His example about the earl and his companions slaughtering seventy-two buffalo but eating only part of one shows how cruel people can be. Twain contrasts this example to the snake's desire to kill only what it can consume. Twain also provides many examples of religious bigotry to make his point that we are the "lowest animals." Twain explains how religious zealots in the Middle Ages tortured people of different faiths by skinning them and burning them alive. Unfortunately, as current events in the Middle East tragically demonstrate, cruelty and religious intolerance are just as intense today as they were in Twain's day.

To Build a Fire
by Jack London

from Left for Dead
by Beck Weathers

Selection Test, *page 182*

Comprehension

1. D

2. H

3. A

4. G

5. B

6. F

7. A

8. J

9. C

10. G

Literary Focus

11. A

12. H

13. D

Reading Skills

14. F

Vocabulary Development

15. c

16. e

17. d

18. b

19. a

Constructed Response

20. Students' responses will vary. A sample response to B follows:

The statement "the man's survival depends on factors over which he has no control" best reflects naturalist theory because the statement shows that people are at the mercy of forces they can neither control nor understand. The man has no control over his environment: the extreme cold, the hidden springs, the snuffed fire. Further, he has no control over his decision to act foolishly because it is determined by his heredity and lack of experience. Imagination might help him, but, again by birth, he lacks imagination, so he cannot understand the danger he faces. Therefore, he is adrift in an indifferent universe, buffeted by his heredity and environment.

What Do You Feel Underground?
by Gabriela Mistral

Selection Test, *page 185*

Comprehension

1. A

2. H

3. B

4. G

5. C

6. F

7. B

8. G

9. C

10. H

Literary Focus

11. B

12. G

13. A

14. H

Constructed Response

15. Students' responses will vary. A sample response follows:

"What Do You Feel Underground" evokes regret and sorrow. The poet elicits these emotions through imagery and figures of speech. The images in the last stanza show the speaker's regret that her lover is dead: "But you are underground— / your tongue silenced by dust; / there is no way that you can sing with me / the sweet and fiery songs of this spring." The images in this stanza, which appeal to sight, touch, and hearing, help readers feel the speaker's grief and sorrow at her lover's death. The metaphor "the sweet liquor of veins" (line 11) compares blood to sap. The speaker is sorry that her lover cannot taste the sweetness of life.

A Pair of Silk Stockings
by Kate Chopin

Now and Then, America
by Pat Mora

Selection Test, *page 188*

Comprehension

1. D

2. H

3. A

4. J

5. C

6. F

7. B

8. G

9. D

10. J

Literary Focus

11. A

12. H

13. B

Reading Skills

14. F

Vocabulary Development

15. rash; unwise

16. measurable

17. genuine

18. dull; muddled

19. cautious; wise

Constructed Response

20. Students' responses will vary. A sample response follows:

Social and personal forces influence Mrs. Sommers to spend the fifteen dollars the way she does rather than the way she had planned. She wants to escape, if only for a few hours, from her everyday existence of scrimping and self-sacrifice. Dependent drudgery was the common role for many lower- and middle-class women in the late nineteenth century, as it is now. Once again, Mrs. Sommers wants to enjoy the pleasures of her past, if only briefly. Therefore, she indulges in pleasures she once enjoyed, including dining in a nice restaurant, buying magazines, and going to the theater.

A Wagner Matinée
by Willa Cather

Selection Test, *page 191*

Comprehension

1. B

2. G

3. D

4. H

5. A

6. F

7. B

8. G

9. A

10. H

Literary Focus

11. C

12. G

13. D

14. F

Vocabulary Development

15. B

16. E

17. D

18. C

19. A

Constructed Response

20. Students' responses will vary. A sample response follows:

As a woman living in the mid-1800s, Georgiana had been raised to sacrifice herself for others. She had been pressured by society to get married, keep a home, and have children. When she reached the age of thirty, she was considered long past her prime. Therefore, she was anxious to get married, even if the choice was unsuitable. She gave up her life of culture and comfort in Boston to follow Howard to settle on a homestead on the Nebraska frontier.

Richard Cory
by Edwin Arlington Robinson

Miniver Cheevy
by Edwin Arlington Robinson

Selection Test, *page 194*

Comprehension

1. D

2. J

3. A

4. H

5. B

6. F

7. C

8. G

9. A

10. H

Literary Focus

11. D

12. F

13. B

14. J

Vocabulary Development

15. c

16. e

17. d

18. b

19. a

Constructed Response

20. Students' responses will vary. A sample response follows:

Both poems have the same theme: appearance versus reality. The townspeople in "Richard Cory" believe that Richard Cory is very contented with his life and that they would be equally happy if they were in Cory's place. Ironically, Richard Cory is so wretchedly unhappy that he kills himself. The poem's ironic ending underscores the townspeople's total misunderstanding of Richard Cory's life. Miniver Cheevy thinks the past was much more glorious than the present. As a result, he yearns to live in the past, in places such as King Arthur's court. The poem's ironic ending shows that Miniver Cheevy escapes into drink rather than trying to build a life in the present.

Collection 4 Summative Test, *page 197*

Vocabulary Skills

1. A

2. H

3. D

4. J

5. C

Comprehension

6. G

7. A

8. F

9. D

10. H

Reading Skills and Strategies

Analyzing Sequence of Events

11. Students' responses will vary. A sample response follows:

(1) Pap gets drunk. (2) He tries to bully Judge Thatcher into giving him money. (3) After the court action, Pap threatens to whip Huck if he doesn't give him some money. (4) Pap takes the three dollars from Huck, gets drunk, and carries on till midnight. (5) Pap goes to jail. (6) Pap goes to court, then returns to jail.

Answer Key

Analyzing Text Structures: Cause and Effect

12. Student's responses will vary. A sample response follows:

Cause—Pap hears that Huck has money. *Effect—He tries to bully Huck into giving him all his money.*

Cause—Pap takes a dollar from Huck. *Effect—Pap gets drunk.*

Cause—Pap gets drunk. *Effect—Pap tries to bully Judge Thatcher into giving him Huck's money.*

Recognizing the Vernacular

13. B

Literary Focus: Constructed Response

Analyzing Comic Devices

14. Students' responses will vary. A sample response follows:

In "Pap Starts a New Life" Twain uses understatement and irony to create humor. Huck engages in understatement when he explains the judge's reaction to Pap's fall off the wagon: "The judge felt kind of sore." This understatement highlights the comic irony of the judge having believed that he could reform Pap.

Analyzing Figures of Speech

15. Students' responses will vary. A sample response follows:

Imagery—"a little blue and yaller picture of some cows and a boy"; *Emotion*—peace; compassion for Huck

Imagery—"*Ain't* you a sweet-scented dandy, though?" *Emotion*—pity; sympathy

Metaphor—"a tree-toad white, a fish-belly white"; *Emotion*—disgust

Metaphor—"and was just old pie to him" *Emotion*—humor

Simile—"you could see his eyes shining through like he was behind vines." *Emotion*—fear, loathing, hatred

Simile—"an old black slouch with the top caved in, like a lid"; *Emotion*—pity, dread

Sounds—"when my breath sort of hitched"; *Emotion*—fear

Sounds—"and went a-blowing around and cussing and whooping and carrying on . . . with a tin pan"; *Emotion*—humor

Analyzing Point of View

16. Students' responses will vary. A sample response to each choice follows:

F Huck talks about a potentially painful subject—his father's getting drunk—but describes it in such hilarious terms that it is amusing rather than sad.

G Huck's initial reaction to Pap and Huck's vivid description of Pap's appearance automatically align the reader with Huck's point of view.

H Some of the events Huck recounts—Pap's verbal abuse of Huck, constant demands for money, and drunkenness—would be too difficult for some readers to accept if they were related in a straightforward manner.

J Twain is known for his humor. For instance, Huck's account of the judge's dinner with Pap is much funnier than an objective account would be.

Collection 5

Collection 5 Diagnostic Test

Literature, Vocabulary, *page 204*

1. D	**6.** H
2. J	**7.** D
3. C	**8** G
4. H	**9.** C
5. A	**10.** J

Literary Period Introduction Test, *page 206*

1. A	**6.** H
2. G	**7.** D
3. C	**8** G
4. H	**9.** D
5. D	**10.** G

The River-Merchant's Wife: A Letter
by Ezra Pound

The Garden
by Ezra Pound

A Few Don'ts by an Imagiste
by Ezra Pound

Selection Test, *page 208*

Comprehension

1. A
2. H
3. B
4. F
5. D
6. G
7. C
8. F
9. D
10. F

Literary Focus

11. B
12. H
13. C
14. F

Constructed Response

15. Students' responses will vary. A sample response follows:

The mood of Ezra Pound's"The River-Merchant's Wife: A Letter" is a deep, autumnal sadness, a melancholy that has much beauty to it, just as the leaves falling in autumn have a great beauty. The images in the poem tend to be taken from nature, and in many cases they are images showing nature in a state of decay. This orientation is especially clear in the final stanza, in which, in contrast to the earlier stanzas, the wife is describing her life in the present. The leaves are falling early this autumn, she observes in line 22, implying that she has been overtaken by a premature sadness. In the next line the image of the paired butterflies turning yellow connects the idea of autumnal decline with the idea of a married pair—she and her husband represented by the butterflies. Another image in that stanza deals with absence rather than decline: In lines 20–21 the mosses by the gate have grown too thick to be cleared away, because the the husband's footsteps have not worn them away for five months.

The Love Song of J. Alfred Prufrock
by T. S. Eliot

Selection Test, *page 211*

Comprehension

1. B
2. H
3. A
4. H
5. C
6. F
7. A
8. J
9. B
10. G

Literary Focus

11. D
12. F
13. D

Reading Skills

14. G

Constructed Response

15. Students' responses will vary. A sample response follows:

The figure of speech I most admire in this poem is "I have measured out my life with coffee spoons." I wish I'd been the first to say that! It's a perfect metaphor to express the repetitive, dull quality of daily life. People don't literally measure out their lives with spoons, but the image rings so true that I can almost see myself doling out my life day by day with each morning's coffee. And the comparison between a life and a measure of coffee makes one's existence seem changeless, ordinary, dry—one day seeming as much like another, just as one coffee spoon resembles another. The prospect of an endless line of coffee-spoon days is a despairing one.

The nonfigurative image I like best is the one of the women in the room, walking to and fro as they discuss Michelangelo. It might at first seem as though they're doing something glamorous, but, in fact, they are probably bored. In turn, Prufrock is bored by them, and so they become boring to the reader. They are talking about great art, but only in order to relieve their boredom. The repetition of this line and others is an aspect of style that adds greatly to the feeling of tedium and despair that surrounds Prufrock. Repetition is sameness, lack of change; it's a signal that tomorrow will be exactly like today and yesterday. That's despair!

The Red Wheelbarrow
by William Carlos Williams

The Great Figure
by William Carlos Williams

This Is Just to Say
by William Carlos Williams

Selection Test, *page 214*

Comprehension

1. A
2. G
3. C
4. G
5. C
6. F
7. A
8. H
9. D
10. J

Literary Focus

11. D
12. F
13. C
14. G

Constructed Response

15. Students' responses will vary. A sample response follows:

In "The Red Wheelbarrow," William Carlos Williams creates a sense of curiosity or expectation in the first two lines: "so much depends / upon." The reader can't help but ask, "So much depends upon what? And what depends upon it?" The shortness of the lines and the simplicity of the language add to this sense of curiosity by causing the reader to wonder whether the rest of the poem is going to sound as simple as that or there's going to be a stylistic change. Then surprise comes in the form of the image of the red wheelbarrow. Is the wheelbarrow the answer to one of our questions? Is it what "so much depends / upon"? If so, that only increases our curiosity, leading to more questions.

In "The Great Figure" the title arouses curiosity: To what figure is the poet referring? A few lines later, we come upon the answer: a figure 5 in gold. This image, too, raises new questions: What is the meaning or importance of the figure 5? So, in both poems, Williams arouses our expectations and answers our questions with a simple, surprising image that opens up new avenues of curiosity rather than closing the case.

Poetry
by Marianne Moore

Ars Poetica
by Archibald MacLeish

Selection Test, *page 217*

Comprehension

1. D
2. H
3. B
4. J
5. B
6. H
7. C
8. J
9. C
10. G

Literary Focus

11. D
12. F
13. D
14. H

Constructed Response

15. Students' responses will vary. The supportable options are **B, C,** and **D.** A sample response to each choice follows:

A (*This is not a supportable response.*)

B The speaker argues that some poems focus on material that is "raw and genuine," and that other poems are trivial, derivative, or pretentious. She uses imagery of eyes dilating, hands grasping, and hair standing on end to suggest the emotional power of good poetry.

C In lines 22 and 24 the speaker refers to the importance of poetry. The last stanza emphasizes that poetry should combine the imaginary and the real. The famous image, "imaginary gardens with real toads in them," exemplifies this view of poetry.

D (*Accept any response that is supported by the selection.*)

what if a much of a which of a wind
by E. E. Cummings

"Miracles are to come"
by E. E. Cummings

somewhere i have never travelled,gladly beyond
by E. E. Cummings

Selection Test, *page 221*

Comprehension

1. B

2. H

3. A

4. H

5. C

6. J

7. A

8. G

9. D

10. F

Literary Focus

11. B

12. F

13. C

14. J

Constructed Response

15. Students' responses will vary. A sample response follows:

You can almost tell from the titles alone that the two poems are by the same author. The titles "what if a much of a which of a wind" and "somewhere i have never travelled,gladly beyond" show E. E. Cummings's inclination to cast aside traditional mechanics, such as capitalization, and to combine words in unusual, unexpected ways. The titles and the poems they represent also show Cummings's sense of playfulness. For example, "what if a much of a which of a wind" is a poem about the destruction of the universe, but the title is probably as lighthearted a way of describing that event as anyone could imagine. The other poem's title shows whimsy in juxtaposing "never travelled" with "gladly beyond."

Even so, the two poems have very different moods, despite the fact that they both involve, or at least imply, love and make reference to destruction. On the one hand, "what if a much of a which of a wind" is a whimsical poem about the end of everything, on the other hand, "somewhere i have never travelled,gladly beyond" is a rather bristly poem about tenderness. The speaker is clearly someone whose soul is as easily "closed" as it is "opened" and who is drawn to yet intimidated by his beloved's tenderness and fragility. In "what if a much . . . the images of catastrophe seem too breezy to be convincing. In "somewhere i have never travelled . . ." a deep love is conveyed with forbidding images such as "the snow carefully everywhere descending," "i cannot touch because they are too near," and "rendering death and forever with each breathing."

Answer Key

Soldier's Home
by Ernest Hemingway

Nobel Prize Acceptance Speech, 1954
by Ernest Hemingway

Selection Test, *page 225*

Comprehension

1. C	**6.** H
2. H	**7.** A
3. B	**8.** G
4. J	**9.** D
5. A	**10.** F

Literary Focus

11. B

12. J

13. D

Reading Skills

14. H

Vocabulary Development

15. d

16. c

17. b

18. a

19. e

Constructed Response

20. Students' responses will vary. A sample response follows:

If he hadn't fought in World War I, Krebs might have ended up with a life like those of his boyhood friends or that of his father, a Midwestern small-town businessman and family man. Even if Krebs had been drafted rather than enlisting, he might have better adjusted when he returned home after the war. But history changed Krebs's life. The fact that he returned too late to be welcomed as a hero—when, in fact, he had more battle experience than his friends—is a detail that shows the extent of Krebs's alienation from his former society. The story is filled with details of ordinary middle-class life that Krebs might have once enjoyed but that now leave him cold, including meals with his family, prayer, driving the family car, and dating. Details that show how American society changed during and after World War I, such as women's fashions and hairstyles, only increase Krebs's sense of detachment. Although he is a product of this very specific society and historical moment, he doesn't feel completely at home in it.

Winter Dreams
by F. Scott Fitzgerald

A Letter to His Daughter
by F. Scott Fitzgerald

Selection Test, *page 228*

Comprehension

1. A	**6.** J
2. G	**7.** D
3. B	**8.** G
4. J	**9.** B
5. C	**10.** H

Literary Focus

11. B	**13.** A
12. H	

Reading Skills

14. F

Vocabulary Development

15. B	**18.** F
16. J	**19.** B
17. A	

Constructed Response

Students' responses will vary. A sample response follows:

I think F. Scott Fitzgerald had two conflicting views of life: the view of a humane artist who recognized the importance of integrity, and the view of a snob who mistook money and social class for quality. In other words, I think he was part Dexter Green. The better part of Fitzgerald, though, was the part that sometimes succeeded in not being Dexter. The virtues and values that Fitzgerald lists for his daughter in the letter are ethically more admirable than Dexter's desire for wealth. Fitzgerald tells his daughter not to worry about popularity and success, things that obsessed Dexter and Judy. Yet, at the same time, Fitzgerald's snobbery shows in his advice to care about horsemanship. Dexter's equivalent was to care about golf. The fact that Fitzgerald wrote so knowingly about shallow people like Dexter and Judy, combined with elements of his biography, suggests that at times he shared their Jazz Age values and illusions: acquisitiveness and hedonism, a belief in the triumph of U.S. business, and social irresponsibility. Maybe Fitzgerald was trying to rid himself of his shallow side through the character of Dexter.

A Rose for Emily
by William Faulkner

Nobel Prize Acceptance Speech, 1950
by William Faulkner

Selection Test, *page 232*

Comprehension

1. B	**6.** F
2. J	**7.** D
3. D	**8.** J
4. F	**9.** D
5. B	**10.** F

Literary Focus

11. A

12. J

13. A

Reading Skills

14. J

Vocabulary Development

15. acrid

16. pauper

17. perverse

18. archaic

19. tranquil

Constructed Response

20. Students' responses will vary. A sample response follows:

Emily has been brought up to think of herself as an aristocrat, in the tradition of her family, who are the inheritors of the values of the old South. As an upper-class Southern white woman, she is protected from the outside world yet given a privileged place in that world. Colonel Sartoris protects her from having to pay taxes in town, and she willingly believes the fairy tale that justifies the exemption. She is accustomed to manipulating people through a combination of physical dependency and emotional steeliness; she treats the druggist and the Board of Aldermen this way. Through her aristocratic demeanor she bluffs people, keeps them at a distance, and even denies reality—as when she denies that her father has died. Her sense of inherited superiority, her emotional and sexual repression, and the complicity of a class-conscious society entitle her to get away with murder and necrophilia.

The Feather Pillow
by Horacio Quiroga

Selection Test, *page 236*

Comprehension

1. A	**6.** F
2. H	**7.** C
3. D	**8.** H
4. G	**9.** B
5. B	**10.** G

Literary Focus

11. D
12. F
13. D

Reading Skills

14. J

Vocabulary Development

15. d
16. a
17. b
18. e
19. c

Constructed Response

20. Students' responses will vary. A sample response follows:

The effect Quiroga wishes to achieve is one of chilling suspense that culminates in dread or horror. His main stylistic device is to record precise details in a detached, almost scientific tone, as if he were relating a medical history. Even the experience of Alicia's honeymoon is described this way in the first sentence of the story: It gives her hot and cold shivers. The specific details, as well as the way they are given, contribute to the overall effect. The whiteness, coldness, and emptiness of the house, and Jordan's reverberating footsteps are especially effective. I think that the story is successful stylistically, even though the effect of horror at the end probably isn't as great for audiences today as it was almost a century ago. Even so, the parasite hidden in the feather pillow still makes a creepy impression. This lasting effect is due not only to the power of the conception but also to the author's skill at describing horror in an understated fashion.

The Leader of the People
by John Steinbeck

Selection Test, *page 239*

Comprehension

1. C
2. G
3. A
4. J
5. A
6. H
7. D
8. F
9. A
10. G

Literary Focus

11. B
12. H
13. C
14. J

Vocabulary Development

15. c
16. g
17. a
18. f
19. d

Constructed Response

20. Students' responses will vary. A sample response follows:

An archetypal conflict in "The Leader of the People" can be found in the one between Carl and Grandfather. The archetype involved is that of the larger-than-life Western hero with his superior physical prowess versus the ordinary modern man. Or expressing the archetype in terms of ideas rather than characters, perhaps it is that of a heroic age when people did great deeds versus a modern age when people spend their time "hunting mice," as Grandfather puts it. In the story this clash is presented as an external conflict between Grandfather and Carl, although it is possible to conjecture that it is also an internal conflict for Carl, who is made to feel inferior to Grandfather. The conflict is partially but not entirely resolved in the story. There is still antagonism between the two men and the kinds of lives they represent. The partial resolution comes when Grandfather experiences a comedown and is made to see that the archetype he represents is not as universally admired as he thinks.

Answer Key

A Worn Path
by Eudora Welty

"Is Phoenix Jackson's Grandson Really Dead?"
by Eudora Welty

Selection Test, *page 243*

Comprehension

1. B
2. H
3. B
4. F
5. C
6. J
7. D
8. F
9. C
10. J

Literary Focus

11. D
12. H
13. D
14. G

Vocabulary Development

15. intent
16. illumined
17. solemn
18. appointed
19. intent or persistent

Constructed Response

20. Students' responses will vary. A sample response follows:

Eudora Welty sees life as a difficult journey, an ongoing process in which unforeseen problems arise at intervals, are solved by the human spirit, and strengthened by faith, determination, and what Welty calls the habit of love. Phoenix Jackson undertakes a journey that, at her age, could be harmful or even fatal. But she does it willingly for the sake of her grandson. Her loving determination takes on a life of its own, one that is separate from the pragmatic goal of the journey, so that even if her grandson were dead, a reader could imagine that Phoenix would continue on the journey. Welty sees this resolve as heroic and regards love as the foundation of true heroism. Love and determination are what carry Phoenix through a series of humiliations at the hands of humanity and nature. Many of her pratfalls might seem comic—just as she seems comic to the other characters—if it were not for the gravity of her purpose, which ennobles her actions and words. Although Phoenix belongs to a specific time, culture, and caste, Welty uses her as an archetype for the human spirit. Welty's choice of a representative for humanity shows her own humanity, and although the characters may slight Phoenix, Welty herself treats the old woman with a respect bordering on admiration.

The Jilting of Granny Weatherall
by Katherine Anne Porter

Selection Test, *page 247*

Comprehension

1. A
2. F
3. B
4. H
5. D
6. H
7. B
8. J
9. C
10. G

Literary Focus

11. D
12. G
13. A

Reading Skills

14. G

Vocabulary Development

15. c
16. a
17. e
18. d
19. b

Constructed Response

20. Students' responses will vary. A sample response follows:

The concluding two paragraphs of "The Jilting of Granny Weatherall" use the stream-of-consciousness technique to show that Granny is confusing her death with the jilting she experienced sixty years earlier. A key passage in the final paragraph is "For the second time there was no sign. Again no bridegroom and the priest in the house." If her dying is the second time without a sign, then the jilting was the first time. On both occasions there is a priest in the house—the first time, to officiate at a wedding; the second, to administer last rites. "Oh, no, there's nothing more cruel than this—I'll never forgive it," Granny thinks. She imagines she is in the past, experiencing her jilting for the first time, but actually she is dying in the present. The two experiences become one to her, for again she is being jilted, this time by God. In the last sentence, when she stretches and blows out the light, it is her life that is figuratively being extinguished. She may also be remembering the evening of the jilting, when she went to bed alone rather than with her new bridegroom. Now, too, at her death, she is without her beloved—God—to give her a sign of reassurance.

The Secret Life of Walter Mitty
by James Thurber

The New Yorker's Farewell
by E. B. White

Selection Test, *page 250*

Comprehension

1. C
2. J
3. B
4. F
5. B
6. F
7. C
8. G
9. C
10. J

Literary Focus

11. B
12. F
13. C

Reading Skills

14. H

Vocabulary Development

15. a
16. j
17. b
18. h
19. d

Constructed Response

20. Students' responses will vary. A sample response follows:

Thurber uses fantasy to reflect on the triteness of Mitty's life. Mitty's heroism in imagined crises is repeatedly contrasted with his meek attitude during much less challenging, real encounters with his wife, a salesclerk, and others. Initially, a parody of an adventure story about a dashing pilot is used to show that Mitty is a remarkably passive driver. The mention of Mitty's failing health leads to a fantasized medical drama about being a great surgeon. In this parody, Mitty's manual clumsiness is contrasted with his imagined brilliant, improvised repair of an anesthetizer machine. A scene of Mitty's wife interrogating him about grocery purchases leads to a parodic courtroom drama in which he is the witness who gets the better of the district attorney. Later in the story, parodies of a war story and a crime drama again show the contrast between Mitty's everyday personality and what he wishes he could be.

Common Diction
by Robert Frost

Design
by Robert Frost

Selection Test, *page 254*

Comprehension

1. C	**6.** G
2. J	**7.** A
3. D	**8.** G
4. F	**9.** C
5. B	**10.** H

Literary Focus

11. A

12. G

13. D

14. H

Constructed Response

15. Students' responses will vary. A sample response follows:

"Design" presents a view of existence in which exterior beauty masks inward horror or evil. The speaker sees the small-scale vignettes of a spider and its prey on a flower and is at first attracted to the beautiful delicacy of the spider, the moth, and the white heal-all flower that serves as the stage for the two creatures. However, unpleasant associations arise quickly: The vignette and its ingredients seem to belong to a witches' brew. In this poem, whiteness is used as a symbol of purity or goodness and darkness as a symbol of evil. In those terms the speaker wonders what the connection is between the creatures' natural whiteness and their actual nature. What have these creatures been designed for? He concludes that if there is a designer, the purpose of the design is "to appall." In other words, the apparent loveliness of such things is a snare that lures us in only to be shocked by deeper truths. The one alternative the speaker considers is that nature, at least on the scale of individual organisms, is not a product of design at all—this is the importance of the sonnet's last line. So the view of the poem is that the universe is either malignant or indifferent, not beneficent.

Nothing Gold Can Stay
by Robert Frost

Trying to Name What Doesn't Change
by Naomi Shihab Nye

Selection Test, *page 257*

Comprehension

1. D	**6.** H
2. G	**7.** C
3. A	**8.** H
4. F	**9.** B
5. B	**10.** J

Literary Focus

11. A	**13.** C
12. J	**14.** G

Constructed Response

15. Students' responses will vary. A sample response follows:

I think that in "Nothing Gold Can Stay," Frost is trying to evoke a feeling of wistful melancholy—an appreciation of beauty plus the sad awareness that beauty is fleeting. Even the poem's lines with only three accented syllables, are fleeting. The words the poet chooses are mostly short and simple; the fact that Frost doesn't give the reader much to hold onto is, in itself, a perfect expression of the poem's mood and themes. It's as if the whole poem is a quick lifting of the speaker's hands, as he tells us, "That's all there is, folks." The poem's quiet, somber tone fits in with the message of fading beauty. The repeated *g, l, h, f,* and *s* sounds create an effect of quiet but insistent alliteration, perhaps like a bell tolling. These sounds raise the reader's awareness of the poet's skill, but then they, too, are gone.

Answer Key

Birches
by Robert Frost
Selection Test, *page 260*

Comprehension

1. B	**6.** F
2. F	**7.** D
3. C	**8.** G
4. J	**9.** A
5. B	**10.** J

Literary Focus

11. D

12. J

13. B

14. H

Constructed Response

15. Students' responses will vary. A sample response follows:

Among the many emotions expressed in or implied by "Birches" are nostalgia for boyhood, a love of nature, a distaste for adult social life, a yearning for escape, religious striving, and a wish for love. All of these emotions can be gleaned here and there, with nostalgia for youth and regrets of adulthood, perhaps, being the most prominent. The overall pattern, though, conforms to the rambling musings of the speaker's thoughts and feelings. He sees a grove of trees, and it launches him into thoughts about young birch swingers; then he catches himself and returns to reality and memory. The fantasy of birch swinging keeps breaking in, however, and leads to an imagined encounter with fate, in which the speaker's wishes are judged. Both love of earthly life and hatred of it can be glimpsed in the poem. But in each case, the flow of the poet's self-correcting, self-annotating thoughts is abetted by the conversational style of the blank verse—long lines, a lack of the obvious, jangling sound play, and a quiet tone. The simplicity of the vocabulary contributes to this quiet, musing flow of verse and thought, as can be seen in lines 52–53: "Earth's the right place for love: / I don't know where it's likely to go better."

Mending Wall
by Robert Frost

Mending Test
by Penelope Bryant Turk

To the Editor
by Jeffrey Meyers
Selection Test, *page 263*

Comprehension

1. A	**6.** G
2. J	**7.** A
3. C	**8.** H
4. J	**9.** D
5. C	**10.** J

Literary Focus

11. B	**13.** A
12. H	**14.** G

Constructed Response

15. Students' responses will vary. A sample response follows:

Ambiguity adds to the intellectual richness of "Mending Wall" and to the pleasure of reading it again and again. The primary ambiguity may be the question of which side the author is on: Does Frost, like his speaker, dislike barriers between people, or does he agree when the neighbor says, "Good fences make good neighbors"? Although the speaker holds the more humane view and has the advantage of being the "I" character, one has a sneaking suspicion that Frost appreciates the value of a solid barrier against human intrusions. Of course, the poet, having created both sides, can be assumed to empathize with both. Another ambiguity lies in the question, "Is the wall in the poem a good wall or a bad wall?" Since it topples every winter, it is bad in the physical sense. And the neighbor probably doesn't think of it as a good wall, because it needs annual repair. But mending the wall strengthens the relationship between the neighbors, so in that sense the broken wall is a good one. In fact, if mending walls strengthen friendships, then bad fences make good neighbors.

The Death of the Hired Man
by Robert Frost

"I must have the pulse beat of rhythm . . ."
by Robert Frost

Selection Test, *page 266*

Comprehension

1. C
2. J
3. B
4. F
5. D
6. H
7. B
8. G
9. C
10. F

Literary Focus

11. C
12. F
13. B

Reading Skills

14. J

Constructed Response

15. Students' responses will vary. A sample response follows:

The idea of home is central to "The Death of the Hired Man." Silas comes home to die, even though he is not related to Mary and Warren. Mary tells Warren that home is "the place where, when you have to go there, / They have to take you in." Warren calls it "Something you somehow haven't to deserve." Underlining both definitions is the idea that home is a place where people will accept you for what you are, a place where you will not be forced to lose your self-respect. Mary and Warren's home fits all these definitions. Mary, of course, seems the more generous, willing to take in Silas without question. However, even though they seem to quarrel about Silas, Warren, beneath his gruff behavior, seems to feel sympathy and is not quick to turn out Silas. His actions when he returns to Mary's side after finding Silas dead reflect this concern: He "Slipped to her side, caught up her hand and waited." Silas may not have deserved their home, but it was the place to which he could come home to die.

Tableau
by Countee Cullen

Incident
by Countee Cullen

Selection Test, *page 269*

Comprehension

1. D
2. G
3. B
4. H
5. A

Literary Focus

6. G
7. D
8. H
9. C

Constructed Response

10. Students' responses will vary. A sample response follows:

Both poems are rhymed and metered compositions of twelve lines. The form and figures of speech in "Tableau" create a proud tone that elevate the poem's theme and helps accomplish its purpose. "Incident" uses a word that has tremendous shock value and that markedly contrasts with the initial tone of pride and joy in the poem. "Tableau" celebrates friendship between races. With metaphors of lightning and thunder as well as words such as *splendor*, Cullen elevates childhood innocence to grandeur, suggesting that friendship between the races will triumph. This is contrasted in the relationship between the two boys in "Incident." In this poem, Cullen focuses on the power of a single word to wound and suggests the importance of this word by indicating how it inflicts pain that will be remembered over time.

The Weary Blues
by Langston Hughes

Harlem
by Langston Hughes

Heyday in Harlem
by Langston Hughes

Selection Test, *page 271*

Comprehension

1. A
2. H
3. B
4. F
5. C
6. J
7. B
8. J
9. D
10. G

Literary Focus

11. A
12. G
13. D
14. G

Constructed Response

15. Students' responses will vary. A sample response follows:

Both poems have serious, unhappy moods, but the mood of "The Weary Blues" is musically melancholy, while that of "Harlem" is political and angry. Because it is set in a blues club and offers the rhythms and sounds of blues lyrics, "The Weary Blues" shares in the ability of the blues to heal, to make one feel better about one's sufferings. The poem's lyrics and the speaker's repetitions are upbeat, even though their contents speak of weariness. Rhyming sounds, such as *croon/tune* and *stool/fool,* have a musical, soothing sweetness that matches the feeling of the blues. Although the final line, "He slept like a rock or a man that's dead," makes a stark, chilling statement, it is such a beautiful figure of speech that it thrills at the same time. In contrast, in "Harlem," the voice is more clipped though still colloquial. This speaker hasn't the inclination to sweeten life with pretty sounds and figures of speech. The rhythms are those of flat speech rather than song, and the realities are stated in stark economic terms. This poem sounds less pretty—and appropriately so.

The Negro Speaks of Rivers
by Langston Hughes

the mississippi river empties into the gulf
by Lucille Clifton

Selection Test, *page 274*

Comprehension

1. B
2. F
3. C
4. G
5. C
6. J
7. A
8. J
9. A
10. F

Literary Focus

11. D
12. H
13. D
14. G

Constructed Response

15. Students' responses will vary. A sample response follows:

In "The Negro Speaks of Rivers" Hughes may have been trying to evoke feelings of solemn pride. There is an almost oratorical rhythm to much of the poem, especially the lines beginning, "I've known." The claim of knowledge is, in itself, a statement of pride. The repetition invites belief and assent on the part of the reader. This part of the poem sounds like a call to collective consciousness. The stately, often slow rhythms of the lines, which feel like the movement of slow rivers, foster emotions of satisfaction and calm, as do words like *lulled, golden, bosom,* and *dusky*. The images are ones of age and wisdom—"ancient as the world and older than the flow / of human blood in human veins." The final three lines, which are repetitions of earlier lines, are virtual invitations to the reader to nod in agreement at the poet's wisdom.

from Dust Tracks on a Road
by Zora Neale Hurston

Selection Test, *page 277*

Comprehension

1. B
2. F
3. C
4. G
5. C
6. J
7. A
8. J
9. A
10. F

Literary Focus

11. B
12. G
13. A
14. H

Vocabulary Development

15. e
16. c
17. b
18. a
19. d

Constructed Response

20. Students' responses will vary. A sample response follows:

Subjective details in the selection show that from an early age Hurston was independent and willing to take risks. For example, her affectionate disdain for her grandmother's warnings, as well as the girl's adventurous initiatives with strangers, show her strong will. Intent on doing what she wants, she is also eager to show off for rewards, another characteristic that would serve her well as a writer. Her response to the attention of the visitors is geared to make the most of the situation; she isn't deterred by negative comments from peers. Her subjective comments throughout the selection, on topics such as Mrs. Calhoun's switch and on the visitors' hands, show a brightness and wit that suit a budding writer. Her tendency to be thrilled by literature also shows a writerly bent. One subjective detail that doesn't fit is her dislike for writing lessons at school, but, obviously, her love of books enables her to get over this distaste.

Collection 5 Summative Test
page 280

Vocabulary Skills

1. C
2. F
3. B
4. J
5. A

Comprehension

6. G
7. D
8. J
9. A
10. G

Reading Skills and Strategies: Constructed Response

Identifying Main Ideas and Supporting Ideas

11. Responses will vary, but students should use at least one example from the selection to support their ideas. The only supportable answers are **A** and **D**. Sample responses follow:

A Some makings of the sun are designated as "waste and welter" and the "ripe shrub." The shrub is a thing of the natural world; "waste and welter" could describe the chaotic nature of the natural world. The poet's poems have a "character" of the "planet" to which they belong. This character is, or could be, in the poet's imagination.

D The poem does not have to last but does have to have the "lineament" or "character" of the "planet" of which it is a part. This planet is "on the table," which could mean "on the page," and, therefore, it is a reflection of the poet's mind.

Literary Focus: Constructed Response

Recognizing Theme

12. F

Identifying and Analyzing Theme

13. Students' responses will vary. A sample answer follows:

Image: swamp mist, clay after rain, hands touching one another

Sense: sight, smell, touch

Interpretation: These images create a sense of earthiness, beauty, and wonder. They present the idea of daybreak in Alabama as a renewal of life. They bring an uplifting mood and a sincere tone to the poem, and suggest that beauty and wonder can be found even in difficult circumstances such as poverty and oppression.

Comparing and Contrasting Poems

14. Students' responses will vary. A sample answer follows:

Langston Hughes—Free verse connected to sounds of jazz and blues; Use of dialect; Concern with social issues

Wallace Stevens—Formal, elevated style; Aesthetic intent

Both Poets—Experimentation; Exploration of new ideas

15. Students' responses will vary. A sample response follows:

Poetry and nature are shown to be two parallel kinds of creation in "The Planet on the Table." The title of the poem implies this correlation immediately: A poem on a table is equivalent to a planet. The metaphorical "ripe shrub writhed" is contrasted with poems, because although both are "makings of the sun," poems are more shapely. Poetry is not necessarily a more long-lived type of creation than nature ("It was not important that they survive"), but it is a successful kind because of its shapeliness, which bears "some lineament or character" of its origin, its "planet." Ironically, words are not the most important things in poems; more important is what is glimpsed behind the words—ideas and emotions. This attitude is especially ironic, because Stevens's words are evidently chosen with the greatest care, skill, and intelligence. Without using obvious sound devices, Stevens unifies the poem through subtle alliteration, assonance, and a flexible three-stress rhythm—demonstrating the worth of poetry by practicing it.

Collection 6

Collection 6 Diagnostic Test

Literature, Informational Text, Vocabulary, *page 285*

1. C
2. F
3. A
4. J
5. B
6. G
7. B
8. F
9. B
10. H
11. D
12. G
13. D
14. J
15. A
16. H
17. C
18. G
19. D
20. J

Answer Key

Literary Period Introduction Test, *page 289*

Comprehension

1. B
2. H
3. C
4. J
5. A
6. G
7. B
8. A
9. A
10. F

The Death of the Ball Turret Gunner
by Randall Jarrell
Selection Test, *page 291*

Comprehension

1. B
2. H
3. D
4. J
5. A
6. G
7. C
8. F
9. D
10. H

Literary Focus

11. A
12. G
13. C
14. F

Constructed Response

15. Students' responses will vary. A sample response follows:

Randall Jarrell chose to write about a ball turret gunner to convey the horror of war. The poem's fierce imagery and implied metaphor—the ball turret gunner's fetal position and his gruesome death—graphically express the devastating effects of war. The gunner's youth, in an implied comparison to an unborn animal, further draws out readers' feelings of sympathy and horror. The vaguely impersonal tone of the poem is underscored by the setting. By placing the young soldier in an aircraft—far from any face-to-face encounter with the enemy and removed from the results of the aircraft's fire—Jarrell underscores war's impersonality. The last line, "they washed me out of the turret with a hose," underscores the waste of war. It is this waste that seems to most appall Jarrell and, no doubt, leaves him to cast a critical eye on cavalier military solutions to political problems.

from Night
by Elie Wiesel
Selection Test, *page 294*

Comprehension

1. A
2. H
3. B
4. J
5. C
6. F
7. D
8. H
9. A
10. J

Literary Focus

11. C
12. J
13. D
14. H

Vocabulary Development

15. c
16. d
17. b
18. e
19. a

Constructed Response

20. Students' responses will vary. A sample response follows:

Wiesel includes specific incidents to show the brutal effects of the Holocaust on the human spirit. He notes how the prisoners forget to say the Kaddish for Akiba. If they had not been in the concentration camp, the prisoners would have remembered to say the prayers because they are solemn and important obligations of the Jewish faith. Wiesel's description illustrates the fact that at the limits of human endurance, survival subsumes spirituality. To make and extend this point, Wiesel describes how a desperate son runs ahead of his father, a rabbi. Not only does spirituality fade, but even family love fades.

Perhaps, though, by merging family and spirituality, Wiesel is implying that they are the same. Yet, Wiesel asserts that it is faith and faith alone that sustains those who survive; those who lose faith die.

A Noiseless Flash *from* Hiroshima
by John Hersey

Selection Test, *page 297*

1. C
2. J
3. B
4. H
5. D
6. F
7. C
8. J
9. A
10. G

Literary Focus

11. C
12. H
13. B

Reading Skills

14. J

Vocabulary Development

15. incendiary
16. notorious
17. convivial
18. debris
19. obsessed

Constructed Response

20. Students' responses will vary. A sample response follows:

John Hersey blended fiction and nonfiction in *Hiroshima.* The book contains vivid characters and builds suspense, both characteristics of fiction. However, the book also contains many characteristics of nonfiction. For example, it is also based on facts and filled with statistics and details of the lives of six people. In addition, Hersey maintains objectivity, allowing readers to draw their own conclusions. Hersey combines genres to convey his horror about the atomic attack on Hiroshima and its cost in human lives and suffering, despite its necessity to end the war with Japan.

"The Arrogance and Cruelty of Power"
from Speech at the Nuremberg Trials, November 21, 1945
by Robert H. Jackson

Selection Test, *page 300*

Comprehension

1. D
2. J
3. C
4. F
5. B
6. H
7. D
8. G
9. A
10. G

Literary Focus

11. C
12. F
13. B
14. J

Vocabulary Development

15. magnitude
16. arrogance
17. vengeance
18. malignant
19. vindicate

Constructed Response

20. Students' responses will vary somewhat. A sample response follows:

(1) purpose of inquest

(2) need for trial

(3) description of defendants and what they represent

(4) what prosecutor will show about defendants

(5) conspiracy of defendants

(6) what prosecutor will not emphasize

(7) what case presented by the United States will be concerned with

Answer Key

from The Diary of a Young Girl
by Anne Frank

"The Biggest Battle of All History"
by John Whitehead
from The Greatest Generation Speaks
by Tom Brokaw

from April in Germany
by Margaret Bourke-White

Selection Test, *page 304*

Comprehension

1. D
2. G
3. A
4. F
5. C
6. J
7. B
8. F
9. D
10. J

Speaking of Courage
by Tim O'Brien

Selection Test, *page 306*

Comprehension

1. D
2. J
3. A
4. H
5. C
6. F
7. D
8. G
9. B
10. F

Literary Focus

11. A
12. G
13. C

Reading Skills

14. J

Vocabulary Development

15. mesmerizing
16. drone
17. tepid
18. recede
19. affluent

Constructed Response

20. Students' responses will vary. A sample response follows:

Nixon apparently hoped for a victorious end to the war, while Paul Berlin is trying to resolve his inner conflicts and find a more personal peace. Paul's needs for peace include the courage to face not only himself but also the uncaring world to which he has returned. Paul seems better able to cope with the outside world when he stops at the drive-in restaurant and opens his window to order food. At the end of the story, he even gets out of the car to watch the fireworks, which he is able to enjoy somewhat. These actions show that he is trying to rejoin civilian society and find a peace he can live with.

Game
by Donald Barthelme

Selection Test, *page 310*

Comprehension

1. D
2. F
3. C
4. H
5. C
6. J
7. A
8. F
9. A
10. H

Literary Focus

11. C
12. J
13. A
14. H

Vocabulary Development

15. c
16. a
17. e
18. d
19. b

Constructed Response

20. Students' responses will vary. A sample response follows:

In "Game" the stressful confinement of the men responsible for operating the control panel during a nuclear war leads to their increasingly paranoid behavior. They become more and more childish, playing with jacks and rocking each other to sleep at night. Barthleme's story exposes the absurdity and fear of life in the nuclear age. He specifically criticizes the madness of stockpiling nuclear weapons and the terrifying atmosphere it has created.

Everything Stuck to Him
by Raymond Carver

A Still, Small Voice
Jay McInerney

Selection Test, *page 313*

Comprehension

1. D
2. F
3. A
4. J
5. C
6. H
7. D
8. G
9. B
10. J

Literary Focus

11. A
12. F
13. C

Reading Skills

14. H

Vocabulary Development

15. coincide
16. striking
17. coincide
18. fitfully
19. striking

Constructed Response

20. Students' responses will vary. A sample response follows:

In "Everything Stuck to Him," Carver suggests that life changes, even when we do not want it to. The young woman requesting to hear a story about when she was a child suggests that the man telling the story is her father. It is also likely that the young couple (the "boy and girl") in the story the man tells are her parents. Since the daughter is visiting her father in Milan and her mother's presence isn't mentioned, the couple in the story are likely divorced. The title "Everything Stuck to Him" may refer to how the man remembers the good and bad parts of his entire life but cannot get the good parts—his love for his ex-wife—to last. Or the title may refer to a time in the past (as the past tense in the title implies) when the man was able to draw people to him (a mixed experience of pleasure and chagrin, as the spilled plate of pancakes implies), although now he is alone.

Daughter of Invention
by Julia Alvarez

Selection Test, *page 317*

Comprehension

1. D
2. J
3. A
4. H
5. B
6. F
7. C
8. G
9. A
10. F

Literary Focus

11. D
12. G
13. A

Reading Skills

14. J

Vocabulary Development

15. reconcile
16. ultimatum
17. florid
18. eulogy
19. noncommittal

Constructed Response

20. Students' responses will vary. A sample response follows:

The narrator and her mother conflict in part because the narrator is embracing American values while her mother retains the values of her homeland. The narrator believes in self-expression and individuality while the mother favors children being part of a family and knowing their place. The narrator and her mother also clash because the narrator resents the time her mother spends with her inventions.

The Handsomest Drowned Man in the World
by Gabriel García Márquez

Selection Test, *page 321*

Comprehension

1. D
2. H
3. B
4. J
5. B
6. F
7. D
8. G
9. A
10. H

Literary Focus

11. B
12. J
13. C
14. H

Vocabulary Development

15. virile
16. frivolity
17. haggard
18. bountiful
19. destitute

Constructed Response

20. Students' responses will vary. A sample response follows:

This story can be read as a transformation myth. As the story progresses, Esteban changes from a nameless corpse into a superhero. When his body first washes up on shore, Esteban is "dark and slinky," a filth-encrusted anonymous creature. As the women scrape off the mud and scales, however, they realize that he is tall, strong, virile, and handsome. He is so heroic that he makes all the men in the village seem weak and useless. The men first view him as a useless object, a "piece of cold Wednesday meat." Yet, they are taken by his size and perfect shape and soon come to admire him. In fact, they want to be worthy of him, to be like him in the way that they imagine him to be. So, they undertake many positive changes in the village and in their attitudes. By the end of the story, Esteban, through the imaginations of the villagers, has been transformed into a galvanizing force for positive change in the village.

Rules of the Game *from* The Joy Luck Club
by Amy Tan

Selection Test, *page 324*

Comprehension

1. D
2. G
3. A
4. J
5. A
6. H
7. C
8. G
9. B
10. F

Literary Focus

11. B
12. H
13. D
14. J

Vocabulary Development

15. c
16. d
17. a
18. e
19. b

Constructed Response

20. Students' responses will vary. A sample response follows:

Mrs. Jong's ambition drives much of the plot. Mrs. Jong wants Waverly to fit into American culture and move up the social ladder. To further her goal, Mrs. Jong encourages Waverly to practice her chess strategies and participate in tournaments. She relieves Waverly from family responsibilities, which causes her brothers to resent her. The plot reaches its climax when Mrs. Jong proudly shows off Waverly to her friends during a Saturday shopping trip. She likes to brag about how far her daughter has risen in society due to her success at playing chess. Waverly tells her mother how embarrassed she feels at being shown off and then runs away. Later that night, she returns home but the family shuns her. Waverly retreats to her room to plot her next move.

When Mr. Pirzada Came to Dine
by Jhumpa Lahiri
Selection Test, *page 327*

Comprehension

1. A
2. G
3. C
4. F
5. B
6. H
7. C
8. J
9. A
10. H

Literary Focus

11. B
12. G
13. C
14. J

Vocabulary Development

15. autonomy
16. austere
17. impeccably
18. deplored
19. placid

Constructed Response

20. Students' responses will vary. A sample response follows:

In "When Mr. Pirzada Came to Dine," Lahiri shows the central role of compassion in life. Through Mr. Pirzada's anxiety and Lilia's parents' care for him, Lilia learns that other people have value and that their feelings may be deep and well hidden. At first, Mr. Pirzada's primary role for the girl is gift-giver. Then, slowly, the author reveals Mr. Pirzada's terror at losing his family in small ways: his panic at Lilia going trick-or-treating, his sudden jerk with the knife when he sees on television that war has been declared in Pakistan. Even though Lilia's parents and Mr. Pirzada are separated by religion—Mr. Pirzada is a Muslim—they set aside their differences for the sake of friendship. Lilia's parents offer Mr. Pirzada support, warmth, and companionship to help him get through the panic of not knowing if his wife and seven daughters have been massacred by the enemy or have made it to safety. As the reality of the war and Mr. Pirzada's family's danger dawns on Lilia, she begins to pray, something she has never done before. Her prayer for his family represents the birth of compassion in her young soul and the beginning of her true humanity. Through this story, Lahiri shows that it is compassion that can bridge the gulf between people and prevent war.

The Book of the Dead
by Edwidge Danticat
Selection Test, *page 330*

Comprehension

1. B
2. G
3. A
4. H
5. C
6. J
7. B
8. F
9. D
10. H

Answer Key

Literary Focus

11. A

12. F

13. C

14. J

Vocabulary Development

Students' responses will vary. A sample response follows:

15. garish

16. spellbound

17. indestructible

18. created

19. plain

Constructed Response

20. Students' responses will vary. A sample response follows:

"The Book of the Dead" is ironic on several levels. Most clearly, readers expect Annie's father to be a good and heroic person, but he was actually a vicious prison guard. Annie had long believed that her father was beaten while serving a year in jail after he fought with a soldier. However, in actuality, her father was in jail as a guard and beat other prisoners. As he confesses to Annie, he was the hunter, not the prey. The irony of reality and deception between the father and daughter are mirrored in another father and daughter—Gabrielle and her father. It is ironic that Gabrielle should choose a sculpture of the hands of a prison guard to remind her father of home, and, further, that they should entertain a prison guard.

from Black Boy
by Richard Wright

Selection Test, *page 333*

Comprehension

1. B

2. H

3. C

4. J

5. A

6. F

7. D

8. G

9. B

10. J

Literary Focus

11. A

12. F

13. D

14. H

Vocabulary Development

15. b

16. e

17. d

18. a

19. c

Constructed Response

20. Students' responses will vary. A sample response follows:

In this excerpt, Richard Wright describes a series of difficult situations that he faced as a child. From these descriptions young Richard emerges as a sensitive and resourceful child with a healthy pride. For example, he is hurt and frightened when he realizes that his mother will not let him into the house until he defends himself against the neighborhood gang, but he fights the boys and wins. Richard displays his pride when he refuses to ask his father for money even though he is very hungry.

The Girl Who Wouldn't Talk *from* The Woman Warrior
by Maxine Hong Kingston

Selection Test, *page 336*

Comprehension

1. C

2. J

3. B

4. H

5. A

6. F

7. C

8. J

9. B

10. G

Literary Focus

11. D

12. H

13. B

Answer Key

Reading Skills

14. J

Vocabulary Development

15. sarcastic

16. temples

17. loitered

18. habitually

19. nape

Constructed Response

20. Students' responses will vary. A sample response follows:

The narrator tries to force the quiet girl to speak because the narrator cannot stand what she sees as her own shortcomings reflected in the quiet girl. Both girls refrain from hitting the ball while playing baseball and are chosen last for team sports. The narrator, feeling an internal conflict, hates the quiet girl's fragility and strikes out at her for what she perceives as a weakness that can easily be overcome. The narrator pinches the quiet girl, pulls her hair, and taunts her. The narrator's efforts are unsuccessful, and her continual badgering manifests itself as an illness that lasts a year and a half in the quiet girl.

from The Way to Rainy Mountain
by N. Scott Momaday

Selection Test, *page 339*

Comprehension

1. D
2. J
3. A
4. J
5. C
6. F
7. B
8. G
9. B
10. F

Literary Focus

11. A

12. G

13. C

Reading Skills

14. J

Vocabulary Development

15. infirm

16. opaque

17. tenuous

18. indulge

19. wariness

Constructed Response

20. Students' responses will vary. A sample response follows:

The Kiowas move from Yellowstone to the Black Hills to the plains of Oklahoma. Momaday wanted to trace the journey that the Kiowas took when they moved from western Montana to Oklahoma. His purpose was to see the places his grandmother had known about but had not visited herself. By analyzing the journey of his ancestors, Momaday came to feel how small his life is.

from In Search of Our Mothers' Gardens
by Alice Walker

Selection Test, *page 343*

Comprehension

1. B
2. H
3. C
4. F
5. A
6. G
7. D
8. H
9. C
10. J

Literary Focus

11. D
12. H
13. A

Reading Skills

14. J

Vocabulary Development

15. medium

16. profusely

17. ingenuous

18. conception

19. vibrant

Constructed Response

20. Students' responses will vary. A sample response follows:

Walker searches for her mother's garden because she views it as the source of her own creative spark. She discovers that her mother, like herself, was a storyteller. In the process, Walker discovers that art is not just a product of high culture but is also the creation of people who are not typically considered artists. Thes include people like her mother, who created beautiful flower gardens, and the anonymous woman who sewed the quilt of the Crucifixion.

Autobiographical Notes
by James Baldwin

from On James Baldwin
by Toni Morrison

Selection Test, *page 346*

Comprehension

1. D
2. F
3. A
4. J
5. B
6. H
7. D
8. G
9. A
10. J

Literary Focus

11. A
12. F
13. C

Reading Skills

14. H

Vocabulary Development

15. B
16. D
17. A
18. E
19. C

Constructed Response

20. Students' responses will vary. A sample response follows:

Baldwin uses a reflective, personal tone to explain his ideas. The opening is light and humorous in a non-threatening way, as is evident when he remarks that concerning his early efforts at poetry, "the less said, the better." Baldwin is also self-deprecating when he describes his first two books, which he calls "unsalable." His use of the first-person point of view also contributes to this thoughtful, intimate tone because it makes readers feel as though he is personally addressing them.

Straw into Gold
by Sandra Cisneros

Selection Test, *page 349*

Comprehension

1. D
2. J
3. A
4. H
5. B
6. F
7. C
8. G
9. A
10. F

Literary Focus

11. D
12. G
13. A

Reading Skills

14. J

Vocabulary Development

15. taboo
16. intuitively
17. ventured
18. flourished
19. prestigious

Constructed Response

20. Students' responses will vary. A sample response follows:

In "Straw into Gold," Cisneros mentions many things drawn upon as subjects for her writing. These include her family, her Mexican American heritage, and the neighborhood during her teen years. All of these details are similar because they have influenced her writing in important ways. Cisneros chose these over others because these personal experiences gave her a unique voice. They enable her to convey a perspective that is hers alone. For example, the very anecdote that begins this essay draws on her Mexican ancestry, and the book that she mentions, *The House on Mango Street*, reflects her reliance on the memories of her neighborhood.

Night Journey
by Theodore Roethke

Selection Test, *page 352*

Comprehension

1. B
2. H
3. D
4. J
5. A
6. H
7. C
8. F
9. D
10. H

Literary Focus

11. A
12. G
13. C
14. F

Constructed Response

15. Students' responses will vary. A sample response follows:

"Night Journey" makes me feel excited because I feel as though I am on the train with the speaker, seeing the countryside unfold in front of me. I feel happy that I am racing across America seeing beautiful "bridges of iron lace" and "a lap of mountain mist." Roethke uses sound devices to help him create these feelings. For example, the sound of the repeated *r* in the line "we rush into the rain" makes me feel as though I am running into the rain, too. The line "wheels shake the roadbed stone" echoes the rattle of the train racing over the stones.

The Beautiful Changes
by Richard Wilbur

Selection Test, *page 355*

Comprehension

1. C
2. F
3. A
4. J
5. B
6. G
7. D
8. F
9. C
10. H

Literary Focus

11. A
12. G
13. C
14. H

Constructed Response

15. Students' responses will vary. A sample response follows:

The title of Richard Wilbur's poem, "The Beautiful Changes," is ambiguous because it has more than one meaning. If "Beautiful" is read as an adjective and "Changes" is read as a noun, the title emphasizes the beauty inherent in change itself. However, if "Beautiful" is read as an noun and "Changes" is read as a verb, the title has an entirely different meaning. In this case it suggests that beauty changes. I think the poem supports the former reading because the images show the beauty that results from change, as in the charm of a chameleon's changing skin (line 8) and the splendor of a mantis on a leaf (lines 9–12).

The Fish
by Elizabeth Bishop

One Art
by Elizabeth Bishop

Selection Test, *page 358*

Comprehension

1. D
2. F
3. C
4. G

5. A
6. J
7. B
8. G
9. D
10. F

Literary Focus

11. A
12. J
13. B
14. H

Constructed Response

15. Students' responses will vary. A sample response follows:

By using images and figures of speech to portray the fish in "The Fish" as a heroic old warrior, Elizabeth Bishop helps readers feel admiration for it. The image of the fish trailing hooks and lines "like medals with their ribbons / frayed and wavering" makes the fish seem like a much-decorated war veteran. The image of the hooks as "a five-haired beard of wisdom" add to our respect for the fish. These images help readers see the fish as a soldier who fought bravely to survive. The simile comparing the fish's swim-bladder to "a big peony" and the metaphor comparing the fish's eyes to "tarnished tinfoil / seen through the lenses / of old scratched isinglass" also adds to readers' admiration for the fish. These figures of speech show the fish's ability to survive adversity.

Mirror
by Sylvia Plath

Mushrooms
by Sylvia Plath

Selection Test, *page 361*

Comprehension

1. C
2. F
3. A
4. J
5. B
6. H
7. C
8. F
9. D
10. G

Literary Focus

11. B
12. G
13. A
14. J

Constructed Response

15. Students' responses will vary. A sample response follows:

Sylvia Plath choice of speakers in "Mirror" and "Mushrooms" helps her achieve her purpose. Plath's purpose in "Mirror" is to explore how some people want desperately to stay young. Plath chooses an inanimate object—the mirror—as the speaker to help her achieve a neutral and detached tone ("I am not cruel, only truthful"). If the speaker had been the woman in the mirror, the tone would have been more emotional. Plath's purpose in "Mushrooms" is to suggest how the meek will inherit the earth. She once again chooses an object—this time, mushrooms—to be the speaker to create a playful, light tone ("We / Diet"). Plath combined this speaker with brief sentences, vivid images, and personification to suggest the power of quiet determination to triumph.

The Bells
by Anne Sexton

Young
by Anne Sexton

Selection Test, *page 364*

Comprehension

1. C
2. G
3. A
4. H
5. B
6. G
7. D
8. F
9. C
10. J

Literary Focus

11. B
12. F
13. D
14. H

Constructed Response

15. Students' responses will vary. A sample response follows:

"The Bells" and "Young" evoke strong feelings in readers. "The Bells" elicits feelings of nostalgia and happiness, while "Young" calls forth feelings of loneliness and isolation. The cheerful images of "the wild parade" and "the flying man breast out / across the boarded sky" in "The Bells" help readers share the speaker's happiness at the memory of attending the circus with her father. The comforting sounds of "the distant thump of the good elephants" and "the voice of the ancient lions" evoke a safe feeling. In contrast the images and sounds in "Young" create a sad mood. Images of "the boards of the house" being "smooth and white as wax" suggest the speaker is cut off from other people, that she is isolated in her own loneliness. This emotion is reinforced by the sound of the alliteration in "white" and "wax" and the depiction of her parents as far away—her mother in her room and her father, by implication, half sleeping.

The Bean Eaters
by Gwendolyn Brooks

In Honor of David Anderson Brooks, My Father
by Gwendolyn Brooks

Selection Test, *page 367*

Comprehension

1. D
2. F
3. A
4. G
5. B
6. J
7. C
8. H
9. B
10. F

Literary Focus

11. A
12. J
13. C
14. G

Constructed Response

15. Students' responses will vary. A sample response follows:

In the poem, "In Honor of David Anderson Brooks, My Father," Gwendolyn Brooks pays homage to her father. She conveys this theme in several ways, especially through sound devices. The exact end rhymes "tended/ended" (the first stanza) and "revives/strives" (the third stanza) create a stately, elegant tone. These sounds suggest that the poet's father was a noble man. The alliteration in "light and lease" (line 4), "cramping chamber's chill" (line 7), and "strikes and strives" (line 12) echo this majestic tone. The sounds also suggest that Mr. Brooks led a virtuous life, filled with harmony.

Elsewhere
by Derek Walcott

Selection Test, *page 370*

Comprehension

1. B
2. G
3. A
4. J
5. C
6. G
7. D
8. F
9. B
10. J

Literary Focus

11. B
12. H
13. D

Reading Skills

14. G

Constructed Response

15. Students' responses will vary. A sample response follows:

In his poem, "Elsewhere," Derek Walcott vividly describes terrorism around the world. His purpose is to spark our conscience and move us to take action against injustice. Walcott uses a number of devices to achieve his aim. For example, the image of "a small harvest / of bodies in the truck" ironically suggests the much larger body count. This implication reinforces the poem's meaning and grim mood. By personifying a writer's work as a person whose "throat [is] slit by the paper knife of the state," Walcott again shows the violence around the world and the harsh mood it creates. The simile of the faces of prisoners, "like the faceless numbers / that bewilder you in your telephone / diary" reinforces the poet's philosophical argument that we must not let ourselves become complacent about terrorism. Instead, we must follow our conscience and fight injustice and evil around the world.

Yet, this fight cannot be waged through writing alone. When Walcott says, "Through these black bars," he means the lines "of these stanzas." Behind his words are real people and real suffering. Art imprisons them, covers them up, and turns them into mere artistic "signs" and "wonders." "The darker crime" is to deal with that suffering through art alone, "to make a career of conscience." "To feel through our own nerves the silent scream" is to pretend we understand. And that is a crime, for the dead are no poetic "winter branches." In attempting to transfer the attention away from the all too real horrors of terrorism, Walcott uses startling images as "signs" and "wonders" like rhyme.

The Memory of Elena
by Carolyn Forché

Bearing Witness: An Interview with Carolyn Forché
by Bill Moyers

Selection Test, *page 373*

Comprehension

1. D
2. G
3. B
4. H
5. A
6. G
7. C
8. F
9. D
10. J

Literary Focus

11. B
12. H
13. A
14. G

Constructed Response

15. Students' responses will vary. A sample response follows:

In "The Memory of Elena," Carolyn Forché strongly condemns Argentina's cruel dictatorship. As someone raised in a country and era that prizes freedom and liberty, Forché is appalled by the political oppression she finds in Buenos Aries. The violent images of "the soft blue of a leg socket" and the "bells / waiting with their tongues cut out" show her horrified reaction to the murder of Elena's husband and Elena's disfigurement after she was attacked by the police. The alliteration of "the ring / of a rifle report on the stones" reinforces the horror.

Answer Key

Ars Poetica
by Claribel Alegría
Selection Test, *page 376*

Comprehension

1. D
2. G
3. A
4. J
5. A
6. H
7. B
8. G
9. C
10. F

Literary Focus

11. A
12. G
13. C
14. J

Constructed Response

15. Students' responses will vary. A sample response follows:

A writer's cultural traditions affect his or her work. For example, Claribel Alegría's "Ars Poetica" and Derek Walcott's "Elsewhere" show the effect of each poet's heritage. Stylistically Alegría's poem is compact and hopeful, while Walcott's is long and very despairing. However, both poems have vivid images, such as Alegría's "valleys" and "volcanoes" and Walcott's "blue letter, / its throat slit by the paper knife of the state."

Even though Alegría and Walcott come from different backgrounds, they both believe in the redemptive power of literature. This belief is shown in the themes of "Ars Poetica" and "Elsewhere." Alegría wrote "Ars Poetica" during a terrible war in her homeland. Nonetheless, the poem expresses hope that poets can help humanity, shown symbolically when Alegría says that through poetry she can "discover the sun" and "catch sight of the promised land." Walcott brings the problems of oppression to the attention of his readers so they will listen to their conscience and take action against terrorism.

The Latin Deli: An Ars Poetica
by Judith Ortiz Cofer
Selection Test, *page 379*

Comprehension

1. B
2. H
3. A
4. J
5. C
6. H
7. A
8. G
9. B
10. J

Literary Focus

11. B
12. H
13. D
14. F

Constructed Response

15. Students' responses will vary. A sample response follows:

Claribel Alegría and Judith Ortiz Cofer each wrote a poem with "Ars Poetica" in the title. Despite the poets' different cultural backgrounds—Alegría is Salvadoran; Cofer is Puerto Rican—their poems are very similar. Both poems address poetry directly; both contain vivid images and sensory language, such as Alegría's image of "the promised land" and Cofer's image of "dried codfish, the green plantains." Both poems have similar themes, as well, as they discuss the art of poetry. Alegría explores the joy of being a poet, shown in the line "I discover the sun." Cofer believes that a kind of beautiful poetry exists from Spanish words found on grocery lists spoken fondly by the deli customers.

Testimonial
by Rita Dove
Selection Test, *page 382*

Comprehension

1. D
2. G
3. B
4. J
5. A
6. J

7. C
8. G
9. A
10. F

Literary Focus

11. B

12. F

13. D

14. J

Constructed Response

15. Students' responses will vary. A sample response follows:

In "Testimonial" Rita Dove expresses her gratitude for the opportunities she has been given and has accepted. Through the poem's images and sound devices, Dove suggests that people should seize life's opportunities. The images of the poet as "pirouette and flourish" and "filigree and flame" evokes her passion for living. The alliteration in the phrases "each glance ignited to a gaze" and "swooned between spoonfuls of lemon sorbet" create an excited feeling, as the readers are joined in Dove's excitement and passion for life.

Coastal
by Mark Doty
Selection Test, *page 385*

Comprehension

1. B
2. G
3. B
4. J
5. C
6. H
7. B
8. G
9. D
10. F

Literary Focus

11. B

12. H

13. D

14. F

Constructed Response

15. Students' responses will vary. A sample response follows:

"Coastal" evokes two different feelings in me: scorn and admiration. In the beginning of the poem, I felt the plumber's daughter was silly to try to save the bird. The overblown metaphor of the loon as an "the emissary of air" and the absurd image of it being cradled in the "pink parka" created this tone. By the end of the poem, however, I admired the girl for her compassion. The image of the girl wanting to "swaddle the bird / in her petal-bright coat" made me feel respect for her. The word *swaddle* creates a metaphor that compares the bird to a baby. This association made me feel tender toward the girl.

Visions and Interpretations
by Li-Young Lee
Selection Test, *page 388*

Comprehension

1. D
2. H
3. A
4. J
5. B
6. H
7. A
8. G
9. B
10. J

Literary Focus

11. C
12. F
13. A
14. J

Constructed Response

15. Students' responses will vary. A sample response follows:

"Visions and Interpretations" by Li-Young Lee concerns life, loss, and love. Lee's theme explores the difficulty of dealing with the loss of a loved one. The image of flowers that are "not always bright, torch-like, / but often heavy as sodden newspaper" shows how his grief blankets him like a wet newspaper. This simile reinforces the sad mood. Personifying rain as "migrant" adds to the speaker's sorrowful mood, as the rain trails him as he become an exile from the world of happiness. The repetition of "between" and "chrysanthemums" symbolizes his grief and loss, too. Li-Young Lee's theme helps readers understand how hard it can be to cope with the death of a cherished person.

Medusa
by Agha Shahid Ali
Selection Test, *page 391*

Comprehension

1. A
2. G
3. B
4. J
5. C
6. H
7. A
8. G
9. B
10. J

Literary Focus

11. B
12. H
13. D
14. F

Constructed Response

15. Students' responses will vary. A sample response follows:

The characters Medusa and the Incredible Hulk each go through a well-known metamorphosis. Medusa is turned from a human into a violent and dangerous monster who changes people into stone. Her head is covered in "hissing curls," and she and her sisters spend their time "massaging poisons" into their scalps. As described in Ali's poem, Medusa is vindictive. She wants to harm people because her life has been destroyed. "Then why let anything remain / when whatever we loved / turned instantly to stone?" she asks. Like Medusa, the Incredible Hulk was turned into a monster. However, the Hulk became a monster when he was exposed to a gamma bomb. Also unlike Medusa, he looks normal most of the time. He even has an everyday identity, Dr. Robert Bruce Banner, but when he gets stressed, he turns into a green monster with superhuman strength. However, the Hulk uses his powers to help humanity. Medusa only destroys people.

Man Listening to Disc
by Billy Collins
Selection Test, *page 394*

Comprehension

1. D
2. G
3. A
4. J
5. C
6. H
7. C
8. F
9. D
10. G

Literary Focus

11. A
12. J
13. C
14. G

Constructed Response

15. Students' responses will vary. A sample response follows:

In "Man Listening to Disc," Billy Collins used language to create a light and amusing tone. For example, the poem starts off humorously with the line: "This is not bad—/ ambling along 44th Street." The verb "ambling" sets the relaxed tone and mood. Collins adds irony when he warns the other pedestrians to get out of the way because he and the five musicians are crossing the street. This image is ironic because the speaker is all alone. Collins also uses sound devices to achieve the casual, relaxed rhythm of the poem, as is shown in the alliteration of "south side of the street," and "this crowd with his cumbersome drums."

Collection 6 Summative Test
page 397

Vocabulary Skills

1. B
2. J
3. A

4. F

5. C

Comprehension

6. G

7. A

8. F

9. B

10. J

Reading Skills and Strategies: Constructed Response

Analyzing Conflict

11. The only supportable answer is **B**. Choice **A** is an internal conflict; choice **C** is not significant because it does not concern the two main characters; choice **D** is not a conflict in this story. Students' responses will vary. A sample response follows:

The most significant external conflict in this story concerns the narrator trying to talk to her mother about having gotten married without her mother's knowledge. This conflict is the one most significant because the narrator risks being misunderstood by Mah and thus being rejected by her. The tension the narrator feels as she tells Mah about her marriage is revealed when she fears being tongue-tied and remembers how Grandpa Leong encouraged her to conquer her fears by taking action.

Analyzing Theme

12. This passage explores the importance of bridging differences in opinion through dialogue. The narrator had assumed that her mother was against her marriage to Mason because she thought the older woman did not like him. On the contrary, Mah loves Mason, which she states by using the Chinese words that mean "to embrace, to hug." This revelation helps the narrator and her mother become closer.

Literary Focus: Constructed Response

Evaluating Style

13. Possible response:

Stylistic Element—Unusual use of capital letters; *Example*—"Mother Who Raised You." *Purpose*—To indicate emphasis and anger

Stylistic Element—Dialect; *Example*—Mah; *Purpose*—To help readers understand the characters' heritage

Stylistic Element—Dialogue; *Example*—"'Mah?' I said. 'Say something.'" *Purpose*—To move the narrative along; to make the story interesting

Stylistic Element—Italics; *Example*—"*Open the mouth and tell*"; *Purpose*—To show dialogue from the past; to link present and past

Stylistic Element—Point of view; *Example*—first-person "I"; *Purpose*—To give the story a personal and immediate power

Stylistic Element—Sensory details; *Example*—"A bitter ginseng odor and honeysuckle balminess greeted me; *Purpose*—To enable readers to visualize the setting more vividly

End-of-Year Test, *page 403*

Reading and Literary Analysis

1. B

2. A

3. C

4. D

5. A

6. A

7. B

8. D

9. D

10. C

11. C

12. C

13. B

14. C

15. B

16. D

17. B

18. D

19. B

20. A

21. D

22. D

23. C

24. C

25. A

26. D

27. D

28. B

29. B

30. C

Answer Key

Vocabulary

Sample A B

31. A

32. C

33. D

34. D

35. A

36. B

Sample B B

37. A

38. D

39. A

40. C

Skills Profile

NAME _______________ CLASS _______________

Skills Profile

Student's Name _______________ **Grade** _______________

Teacher's Name _______________ **Date** _______________

For each skill, write the date the observation is made and any comments that explain the student's development toward skills mastery.

SKILL	NOT OBSERVED	EMERGING	PROFICIENT
Literature			
Analyze characteristics of subgenres of novels, short stories, poetry, plays, and other basic genres.			
Analyze the way the theme of a selection represents a comment on life.			
Analyze the way an author's style achieves specific rhetorical or aesthetic purposes.			
Analyze ways poets use imagery, figures of speech, and sounds.			
Analyze works of American literature: a. Trace the development of American literature from the Colonial period forward. b. Contrast the major periods and works by members of different cultures in each period. c. Evaluate the political, social, and philosophical influences of the historical period that shaped characters, plots, and settings.			
Analyze archetypes drawn from myth and tradition.			
Analyze works of world literature from a variety of authors: a. Compare literary works of different historical periods.			

NAME ______________________ CLASS ______________

SKILL	NOT OBSERVED	EMERGING	PROFICIENT
b. Relate literary works and authors to the major themes and issues of their eras. c. Evaluate the philosophical, political, religious, ethical, and social influences of the historical period.			
Analyze political points of view in a selection of literary works on a topic.			
Analyze the philosophical arguments in literary works and their impact on the quality of each work.			
Informational Text			
Analyze the way authors use the features and rhetorical devices of public documents.			
Analyze the way patterns of organization, repetition of main ideas, and word choice affect the meaning of a text.			
Verify and clarify facts in expository text by using consumer, workplace, and public documents.			
Make reasonable assertions about an author's arguments by using elements of the text to defend interpretations.			
Analyze an author's philosophical assumptions and beliefs about a subject.			
Critique the validity, appeal, and truthfulness of arguments in public documents.			

SKILL	NOT OBSERVED	EMERGING	PROFICIENT
Vocabulary			
Trace the etymology of historical and political terms.			
Use knowledge of Greek, Latin, and Anglo-Saxon roots and affixes to determine the meaning of scientific and mathematical terms.			
Within analogies, analyze specific comparisons as well as relationships and inferences.			